3/02

The NEW ENCYCLOPEDIA *of* SOUTHERN CULTURE

VOLUME 4 : MYTH, MANNERS, AND MEMORY

Volumes to appear in
The New Encyclopedia of Southern Culture
are:

Agriculture and Industry	Law and Politics
Architecture	Literature
Art	Media
Education	Music
Environment	Myth, Manners, and Memory
Ethnicity	Race
Folklife	Recreation
Foodways	Religion
Gender	Science and Medicine
Geography	Social Class
History	Urbanization
Language	Violence

The NEW

ENCYCLOPEDIA *of* SOUTHERN CULTURE

CHARLES REAGAN WILSON General Editor

JAMES G. THOMAS JR. Managing Editor

ANN J. ABADIE Associate Editor

VOLUME 4

Myth, Manners, and Memory

CHARLES REAGAN WILSON Volume Editor

Sponsored by

THE CENTER FOR THE STUDY OF SOUTHERN CULTURE

at the University of Mississippi

THE UNIVERSITY OF NORTH CAROLINA PRESS

Chapel Hill

© 2006 The University of North Carolina Press

All rights reserved

This book was published with the assistance of the Anniversary
Endowment Fund of the University of North Carolina Press.

Designed by Richard Hendel

Set in Minion types by Tseng Information Systems, Inc.

Manufactured in the United States of America

The paper in this book meets the guidelines for permanence and
durability of the Committee on Production Guidelines for Book
Longevity of the Council on Library Resources.

Library of Congress Cataloging-in-Publication Data

The new encyclopedia of Southern culture / Charles Reagan
Wilson, general editor ; James G. Thomas Jr., managing editor ;
Ann J. Abadie, associate editor.

p. cm.

Rev. ed. of: Encyclopedia of Southern culture. 1991.

"Sponsored by The Center for the Study of Southern Culture
at the University of Mississippi."

Includes bibliographical references and index.

Contents: — v. 4. Myth, Manners, and Memory.

ISBN-13: 978-0-8078-3029-1 (cloth : v. 4 : alk. paper)

ISBN-10: 0-8078-3029-1 (cloth : v. 4 : alk. paper)

ISBN-13: 978-0-8078-5692-5 (pbk. : v. 4 : alk. paper)

ISBN-10: 0-8087-5692-4 (pbk. : v. 4 : alk. paper)

1. Southern States—Civilization—Encyclopedias. 2. Southern
States—Encyclopedias. I. Wilson, Charles Reagan. II. Thomas,
James G. III. Abadie, Ann J. IV. University of Mississippi.
Center for the Study of Southern Culture.
V. Encyclopedia of Southern culture.

F209.N47 2006

975.003—dc22

2005024807

The *Encyclopedia of Southern Culture*, sponsored by the Center for
the Study of Southern Culture at the University of Mississippi, was
published by the University of North Carolina Press in 1989.

cloth   10 09 08 07 06   5 4 3 2 1

paper   10 09 08 07 06   5 4 3 2 1

Tell about the South. What it's like there.

What do they do there. Why do they live there.

Why do they live at all.

WILLIAM FAULKNER

Absalom, Absalom!

CONTENTS

In 1989 years of planning and hard work came to fruition when the University of North Carolina Press joined the Center for the Study of Southern Culture at the University of Mississippi to publish the *Encyclopedia of Southern Culture*. While all those involved in writing, reviewing, editing, and producing the volume believed it would be received as a vital contribution to our understanding of the American South, no one could have anticipated fully the widespread acclaim it would receive from reviewers and other commentators. But the *Encyclopedia* was indeed celebrated, not only by scholars but also by popular audiences with a deep, abiding interest in the region. At a time when some people talked of the "vanishing South," the book helped remind a national audience that the region was alive and well, and it has continued to shape national perceptions of the South through the work of its many users—journalists, scholars, teachers, students, and general readers.

As the introduction to the *Encyclopedia* noted, its conceptualization and organization reflected a cultural approach to the South. It highlighted such issues as the core zones and margins of southern culture, the boundaries where "the South" overlapped with other cultures, the role of history in contemporary culture, and the centrality of regional consciousness, symbolism, and mythology. By 1989 scholars had moved beyond the idea of cultures as real, tangible entities, viewing them instead as abstractions. The *Encyclopedia*'s editors and contributors thus included a full range of social indicators, trait groupings, literary concepts, and historical evidence typically used in regional studies, carefully working to address the distinctive and characteristic traits that made the American South a particular place. The introduction to the *Encyclopedia* concluded that the fundamental uniqueness of southern culture was reflected in the volume's composite portrait of the South. We asked contributors to consider aspects that were unique to the region but also those that suggested its internal diversity. The volume was not a reference book of southern history, which explained something of the design of entries. There were fewer essays on colonial and antebellum history than on the postbellum and modern periods, befitting our conception of the volume as one trying not only to chart the cultural landscape of the South but also to illuminate the contemporary era.

When C. Vann Woodward reviewed the *Encyclopedia* in the *New York Review of Books*, he concluded his review by noting "the continued liveliness of interest in the South and its seeming inexhaustibility as a field of study." Research on the South, he wrote, furnishes "proof of the value of the *Encyclopedia* as a scholarly undertaking as well as suggesting future needs for revision or supplement to keep up with ongoing scholarship." The decade and a half since the publication of the *Encyclopedia of Southern Culture* have certainly suggested that Woodward was correct. The American South has undergone significant changes that make for a different context for the study of the region. The South has undergone social, economic, political, intellectual, and literary transformations, creating the need for a new edition of the *Encyclopedia* that will remain relevant to a changing region. Globalization has become a major issue, seen in the South through the appearance of Japanese automobile factories, Hispanic workers who have immigrated from Latin America or Cuba, and a new prominence for Asian and Middle Eastern religions that were hardly present in the 1980s South. The African American return migration to the South, which started in the 1970s, dramatically increased in the 1990s, as countless books simultaneously appeared asserting powerfully the claims of African Americans as formative influences on southern culture. Politically, southerners from both parties have played crucial leadership roles in national politics, and the Republican Party has dominated a near-solid South in national elections. Meanwhile, new forms of music, like hip-hop, have emerged with distinct southern expressions, and the term "dirty South" has taken on new musical meanings not thought of in 1989. New genres of writing by creative southerners, such as gay and lesbian literature and "white trash" writing, extend the southern literary tradition.

Meanwhile, as Woodward foresaw, scholars have continued their engagement with the history and culture of the South since the publication of the *Encyclopedia*, raising new scholarly issues and opening new areas of study. Historians have moved beyond their earlier preoccupation with social history to write new cultural history as well. They have used the categories of race, social class, and gender to illuminate the diversity of the South, rather than a unified "mind of the South." Previously underexplored areas within the field of southern historical studies, such as the colonial era, are now seen as formative periods of the region's character, with the South's positioning within a larger Atlantic world a productive new area of study. Cultural memory has become a major topic in the exploration of how the social construction of "the South" benefited some social groups and exploited others. Scholars in many disciplines have made the southern identity a major topic, and they have used a variety of methodologies to suggest what that identity has meant to different social groups. Literary critics have adapted cultural theories to the South and have raised the issue of postsouthern literature to a major category of concern as well as exploring the links between the literature of the American South and that of the Caribbean. Anthropologists have used different theoretical formulations from literary critics, providing models for their fieldwork in southern communities. In the past 30 years anthropologists have set increasing numbers of their ethnographic studies in the South, with many of them now exploring topics specifically linked to southern cultural issues. Scholars now place the Native American story, from prehistory to the contemporary era, as a central part of southern history. Comparative and interdisciplinary approaches to the South have encouraged scholars to look at such issues as the borders and boundaries of the South, specific places and spaces with distinct identities within the American South, and the global and transnational Souths, linking the American South with many formerly colonial societies around the world.

The first edition of the *Encyclopedia of Southern Culture* anticipated many of these approaches and indeed stimulated the growth of Southern Studies as a distinct interdisciplinary field. The Center for the Study of Southern Culture has worked for more than a quarter century to encourage research and teaching about the American South. Its academic programs have produced graduates who have gone on to write interdisciplinary studies of the South, while others have staffed the cultural institutions of the region and in turn encouraged those institutions to document and present the South's culture to broad public audiences. The center's conferences and publications have continued its long tradition of promoting understanding of the history, literature, and music of the South, with new initiatives focused on southern foodways, the future of the South, and the global Souths, expressing the center's mission to bring the best current scholarship to broad public audiences. Its documentary studies projects build oral and visual archives, and the New Directions in Southern Studies book series, published by the University of North Carolina Press, offers an important venue for innovative scholarship.

Since the *Encyclopedia of Southern Culture* appeared, the field of Southern Studies has dramatically developed, with an extensive network now of academic and research institutions whose projects focus specifically on the interdisciplinary study of the South. The Center for the Study of the American South at the University of North Carolina at Chapel Hill, led by Director Harry Watson and Associate Director and *Encyclopedia* coeditor William Ferris, publishes the lively journal *Southern Cultures* and is now at the organizational center of many other Southern Studies projects. The Institute for Southern Studies at the University of South Carolina, the Southern Intellectual History Circle, the Society for the Study of Southern Literature, the Southern Studies Forum of the

European American Studies Association, Emory University's SouthernSpaces .org, and the South Atlantic Humanities Center (at the Virginia Foundation for the Humanities, the University of Virginia, and Virginia Polytechnic Institute and State University) express the recent expansion of interest in regional study.

Observers of the American South have had much to absorb, given the rapid pace of recent change. The institutional framework for studying the South is broader and deeper than ever, yet the relationship between the older verities of regional study and new realities remains unclear. Given the extent of changes in the American South and in Southern Studies since the publication of the *Encyclopedia of Southern Culture*, the need for a new edition of that work is clear. Therefore, the Center for the Study of Southern Culture has once again joined the University of North Carolina Press to produce *The New Encyclopedia of Southern Culture*. As readers of the original edition will quickly see, *The New Encyclopedia* follows many of the scholarly principles and editorial conventions established in the original, but with one key difference; rather than being published in a single hardback volume, *The New Encyclopedia* is presented in a series of shorter individual volumes that build on the 24 original subject categories used in the *Encyclopedia* and adapt them to new scholarly developments. Some earlier *Encyclopedia* categories have been reconceptualized in light of new academic interests. For example, the subject section originally titled "Women's Life" is reconceived as a new volume, *Gender*, and the original "Black Life" section is more broadly interpreted as a volume on race. These changes reflect new analytical concerns that place the study of women and blacks in broader cultural systems, reflecting the emergence of, among other topics, the study of male culture and of whiteness. Both volumes draw as well from the rich recent scholarship on women's life and black life. In addition, topics with some thematic coherence are combined in a volume, such as *Law and Politics* and *Agriculture and Industry*. One new topic, *Foodways*, is the basis of a separate volume, reflecting its new prominence in the interdisciplinary study of southern culture.

Numerous individual topical volumes together make up *The New Encyclopedia of Southern Culture* and extend the reach of the reference work to wider audiences. This approach should enhance the use of the *Encyclopedia* in academic courses and is intended to be convenient for readers with more focused interests within the larger context of southern culture. Readers will have handy access to one-volume, authoritative, and comprehensive scholarly treatments of the major areas of southern culture.

We have been fortunate that, in nearly all cases, subject consultants who offered crucial direction in shaping the topical sections for the original edition have agreed to join us in this new endeavor as volume editors. When new volume editors have been added, we have again looked for respected figures who can provide not only their own expertise but also strong networks of scholars to help develop relevant lists of topics and to serve as contributors in their areas. The reputations of all our volume editors as leading scholars in their areas encouraged the contributions of other scholars and added to *The New Encyclopedia*'s authority as a reference work.

The New Encyclopedia of Southern Culture builds on the strengths of articles in the original edition in several ways. For many existing articles, original authors agreed to update their contributions with new interpretations and theoretical perspectives, current statistics, new bibliographies, or simple factual developments that needed to be included. If the original contributor was unable to update an article, the editorial staff added new material or sent it to another scholar for assessment. In some cases, the general editor and volume editors selected a new contributor if an article seemed particularly dated and new work indicated the need for a fresh perspective. And importantly, where new developments have warranted treatment of topics not addressed in the original edition, volume editors have commissioned entirely new essays and articles that are published here for the first time.

The American South embodies a powerful historical and mythical presence, both a complex environmental and geographic landscape and a place of the imagination. Changes in the region's contemporary socioeconomic realities and new developments in scholarship have been incorporated in the conceptualization and approach of *The New Encyclopedia of Southern Culture*. Anthropologist Clifford Geertz has spoken of culture as context, and this encyclopedia looks at the American South as a complex place that has served as the context for cultural expression. This volume provides information and perspective on the diversity of cultures in a geographic and imaginative place with a long history and distinctive character.

The *Encyclopedia of Southern Culture* was produced through major grants from the Program for Research Tools and Reference Works of the National Endowment for the Humanities, the Ford Foundation, the Atlantic-Richfield Foundation, and the Mary Doyle Trust. We are grateful as well to the individual donors to the Center for the Study of Southern Culture who have directly or indirectly supported work on *The New Encyclopedia of Southern Culture*. We thank the volume editors for their ideas in reimagining their subjects and the contributors of articles for their work in extending the usefulness of the book in new ways. We acknowledge the support and contributions of the faculty and staff at the Center for the Study of Southern Culture. Finally, we want especially to honor the work of William Ferris and Mary Hart on the *Encyclopedia of Southern Culture*. Bill, the founding director of the Center for the Study of Southern Culture, was coeditor, and his good work recruiting authors, editing text, selecting images, and publicizing the volume among a wide network of people was, of course, invaluable. Despite the many changes in the new encyclopedia, Bill's influence remains. Mary "Sue" Hart was also an invaluable member of the original encyclopedia team, bringing the careful and precise eye of the librarian, and an iconoclastic spirit, to our work.

The South occupies a central place in the American imagination. The *Myth, Manners, and Memory* volume of *The New Encyclopedia of Southern Culture* examines how representations of the region and its people, their patterns of etiquette and social interaction, and their remembrance of the past have helped make it a region that resonates with people who see its many creative expressions. Historians have been studying the mythic South for decades, and the section on that topic in the *Encyclopedia of Southern Culture* helped focus attention on its breadth and depth as a topic for study. More recently, literary critics and cultural studies scholars have examined representations of the region, with several drawing on theoretical formulations and calling for recognition of overlooked typologies from southern history. Meanwhile, the term "myth" continues to be used by scholars who recognize the role that "the mind of the South" has long played in making the South a distinctive region.

The editors have added entries that reflect new scholarship, such as work on the body, clocks and time, and the myth of black Confederates. The family has become such a key topic in southern cultural studies that we commissioned a new article on that topic. We have added articles on memory and on Civil War reenactments to show how the South continues to construct historical memory as a part of its ongoing cultural identity. We have strengthened the discussion of manners through articles on ladies and gentlemen and on visiting, a once-crucial social practice in the South. Theoretical perspectives are everywhere included, but a new entry on postmodernism is especially important in indicating new directions in the study of southern culture. Many entries have been expanded because of the impact of theoretical and methodological developments. The author of the cult of beauty entry has reworked it to emphasize viewpoints from feminist scholars and from religious studies. The community article reflects an increased awareness of the diversity of southern society and ways that a concern for community can, and cannot, foster unity. Few topics have changed as dramatically in the last decade as that of sexuality, and a revised entry reflects new insights from the work of historians, literary critics, and sociologists. That entry ends with a brief discussion of the contemporary South, where the growing public role of gays and the rise of the conservative Religious Right have made sexuality a focal point for public policy discussions. The sexuality entry is a good indicator of how much culture has changed in the

South since the *Encyclopedia of Southern Culture* appeared in 1989 and yet how tensions between change and tradition persist.

Matters related to myth, manners, and memory will recur in other volumes of *The New Encyclopedia of Southern Culture*. These are central concerns that relate to many other topics, and the editors are exploring the overlap of topics among volumes as a way to overcome sometimes-rigid disciplinary boundaries. This volume features as well entries that might seem offbeat—such as those on "See Rock City" and black collectibles—but which will bring a nod of recognition to anyone familiar with the American South.

The NEW ENCYCLOPEDIA *of* SOUTHERN CULTURE

VOLUME 4 : MYTH, MANNERS, AND MEMORY

MYTH, MANNERS, AND MEMORY

Few topics are more important than mythology in understanding the origin and development of the American South as a distinctive place. Mythology was at the center of regional consciousness, as socioeconomic characteristics of the region became reified into cultural imagery that came to represent the region's values and worldviews, nurturing a sense of difference between the South and other American places. Elites used the mythology of Cavaliers and moonlight-and-magnolias plantations to construct a romantic region that obscured differences across the South's regions and among its social groupings. Mythology could also function to provide dignity and self-respect to the disinherited. Southern mythology was never static, though, and it evolved as the South modernized.

Mythology and Southern Identity. Mythology provided the images that promoted the emergence of a southern regional identity. Early European advocates of colonization portrayed the southeastern parts of North America as a Garden of Eden, a lush land suggesting ease of living. If the environment lay at the core of this consciousness of place, an alternate image soon developed as well. Early settlers in Jamestown and later colonists in Lowcountry South Carolina faced high mortality rates from the deadly climate that nurtured diseases that killed European and African settlers and brought Europeans to think of the South as a death trap. Such tensions would encourage complex images of the South: it was the harmonious plantation and the benighted slave breeding ground. The bright glow of such heroic images as the Cavalier was matched by the dark underside of a gothic South. The Civil War stands at the center of southern history, and the mythology of it became part of the origin myth of a distinctive people. Southern whites were divided by the war, but afterward politicians, ministers, writers, and other cultural leaders used the memory of the Lost Cause to construct an elaborate cult of the dead, dedicated to romantic nationalism, or in this case the regional remnants of a failed nationalism. White supremacy became another mythic foundation for the regional identity that had dominated the South's public culture until recently.

The South's people lived mostly in rural areas and small towns until the mid-20th century, and they worked predominantly in agricultural pursuits. Perhaps

A 1906 postcard depicting the cotton boll, a symbol of the South (Ann Rayburn Paper Americana Collection, Archives and Special Collections, University of Mississippi Library, Oxford)

it was inevitable that agrarianism would form another anchor for mythic representations of the region. From Thomas Jefferson's farmers as God's chosen people to the defense of agrarianism by the writers of *I'll Take My Stand* (1930), agrarian images have often evoked the South itself in literature and popular culture. A late 20th-century U.S. president, Jimmy Carter, made much of his being a peanut farmer; he was also a nuclear engineer, but that image did not resonate with southerners or other Americans quite so well. One rural image, the hillbilly, has not generally been a positive one, but it survives well on television and in the movies. The term itself becomes an in-group term of pride, but for those not in the group to use it courts trouble. Dolly Parton has shown how a entrepreneurial southerner can profit from employing the hillbilly image in national popular culture.

The South is the Bible Belt, an appropriate image to suggest that religion has created its own mythology. The camp meeting, the summer revival, the fire-and-brimstone preacher, the river baptism — all suggest powerful images of religion's role in the South. These images are re-created in modern ways. The Bill Gaither Homecomings are huge entertainment productions that evoke the religious meeting at the brush arbor and offer updated old-time sacred music. The black church was the mythic center of the black community, but Atlanta minister Creflo Dollar has created a megachurch fitting suburban lifestyles that earlier African American southerners would hardly recognize as "church."

Much of southern mythology has seemed to privilege traditionalism. When the railroads became southern icons after the Civil War, they were immortalized in song and story, but the corporations that ran them often chose figures from the past, Confederate generals, as the symbolic figures to represent these modernizing businesses. Eventually, business figures and industrialists would become southern icons themselves. The flamboyant Ted Turner made Atlanta a world media center, even if he idealized *Gone with the Wind*. Sam Walton was the shrewdest of businessmen but nurtured a down-home image by driving his pickup truck. And the ironies of Colonel Sanders as an icon of worldwide marketing are obvious.

Style is essential to southern mythology. Historian C. Vann Woodward once wondered whether the southern identity would one day become like an old sweater that one could comfortably put on and take off. In fact, southerners have always "put on" a southern identity. Wearing khaki pants or overalls was a revealing fashion statement but also a prime image of social class in the rural South. Today, wearing a seersucker suit evokes a South of small-town courthouse lawyers on sweltering summer days. "Stylin'," in the African American culture that has so influenced southern culture, involves not just clothes but also body movement, gestures, language, all presenting a self that performs cultural identity. Fashion can be related to role-playing for other southerners as well. You must dress the part but also know your lines. Tallulah Bankhead became a caricature, yet she knew innately how to perform one version of a southern identity that brought her international notoriety. Her films, in turn, made her a role model for any woman wanting to play the part.

Study of Southern Mythology. George Tindall labeled mythology a new frontier of southern history more than four decades ago, but scholars since then have analyzed it from a variety of perspectives. Literary critics have produced a large body of work about the use of regional mythology by southern writers, while intellectual and cultural historians have studied political, economic, religious, military, and journalistic aspects of various myths. Sociologists look at social typologies, and the work of scholars on African American culture bears on the region's mythology. Interdisciplinary cultural studies authors talk of representations. Tara McPherson has recently argued that "the South is figured via a stock set of recurring icons, characters inhabiting stage sets of an imagined gentility and charm that makes other mobilizations and other emotional scripts difficult to imagine." McPherson focused on overlooked figures of southern culture, consciously striving to reimagine southern iconography. Such scholars as McPherson show more subjectivity and self-reflexivity than most historians would in discussing southern representations. Stress on the social construction of the South has blurred lines between the categories of "history" and "mythology."

Scholarly work on the South's visual culture is especially revealing of developments in the study of southern mythology. Postcard images in public exhibitions dramatize the horrors of lynching victims; black-and-white photographs from the Farm Security Administration provide a familiar visual model for understanding southern life; television news footage documents civil rights protests and connects the mental imagination to a compelling era; and the World Wide Web presents a new "virtual South" with eclectic images of the region. Studies of films about the South have shown how long-standing mythological images are given a new life through media portrayals that reach large audiences. An increased recognition of the diversity of the South itself led the editor of a recent book of southern images to suggest the volume could have been titled "Images of Some Souths, or Constructions of a Few Regional Subcultures."

Mythology is related to cultural identity, and historian Fitzhugh Brundage has noted that the southern identity "will endure as long as people imagine themselves within a southern historical narrative." Documentary films have been especially significant in keeping alive central southern narratives, as the region has undergone social, economic, and political changes that have led some commentators to talk of a vanishing South. *Eyes on the Prize* and Ken Burns's *The Civil War* were landmark public broadcasting productions that presented evocative images and sounds to connect viewers emotionally with the experiences of the civil rights movement and the Civil War. Both series were about American experiences, but their southern settings and the cast of characters that emphasized the centrality of southern leaders highlighted specifically regional meanings.

Manners. Manners have been intimately linked to mythology in southern culture. The representations that make up a regional mythology underlay the imagined southern community, and manners long provided a way to perform the regional identity. Despite the complex diversity of southern society, a culturally sanctioned body of etiquette instructed many southerners on how to enact regional social typologies. Proper performance of racial etiquette in the Jim Crow South could be a life-or-death situation for black southerners. Scott Romine has noted that manners never derived from a common view of reality in the South, but "manners might be said to produce a commonly held view of reality." A distinctive view of community was central to traditional regional understandings of the southern identity, and Romine has recently offered a reimagined definition of the southern community as cohering "by means of norms, codes, and manners that produce a simulated, or at least symbolically constituted, social reality." As John Shelton Reed has shown, southern social typologies were not isolated tropes but parts of a structured system.

Memory. The topic of collective memory provides a new approach to the South's mythic representations. The establishment of collective memory in a society involves negotiations among competing memories, with conflict an inherent part of the discussions about the past. Collective memory focuses on issues of identity, cultural authority, cultural norms, and social interaction. Decoding collective memory can reveal whose interests are served when one group's memories are enshrined as the official mythology of the society. Southern elites have sometimes claimed that the cultural symbols enshrined on courthouses, in town squares, on flags, and elsewhere were immutable representations of the one and only South, but, as Eudora Welty wrote, "memory is a living thing— it too is in transit."

The study of memory can show not only how specific symbolic and ritual representations of the South took root but also how they evolved. Changes in the political and social position of groups in the South affected the region's collective memory. Who had power and access to it has determined, for example, whether the Civil War narratives of blacks or whites became the version taught in schools and praised by political and educational leaders. Blacks were conspicuously absent from the culturally dominant Lost Cause mythology for a century after the Civil War, coinciding with Jim Crow segregation and political disfranchisement. While whites retain a dominant role in the region's mythical self-representation, one can measure changes in the South's collective memory by the presence of a statue of an African American, Arthur Ashe, on Richmond's Lost Cause thoroughfare, Monument Avenue. January once was best known in the South as the month of Robert E. Lee's birthday, but far more community energy now goes into honoring the birthday that month of Martin Luther King Jr. The contemporary South's passionately fought battles over Lost Cause symbolism suggest the continuing hold it has on some of the region's people and the commitment of others to change that symbolism as inappropriate to a desegregated southern public culture.

It is useful to remember that differing collective memories in different parts of the South contribute to the region's overall mythology. South Louisiana enshrines the story of Acadian exile that gave rise to today's Cajun population. The Mississippi Delta narrative includes Jews, Lebanese, Italians, and Chinese, more so than in many areas of the South. Music, specifically the blues, is central to images of the Delta as a mysterious place of the Crossroads, where musicians sell their souls to the devil for musical gifts. Birmingham now looks back on Italians as hardworking progenitors of its steel mills, the economic foundation for the city's early development. Today, in the changing South, Hispanics march in processions to Confederate monuments, but they carry images of Our Lady of Guadalupe to honor her as a new icon of an evolving regional society.

The Recent South. Tourism in the contemporary South has found earlier mythology a profitable resource. Pilgrimage tours showcase older southern houses, often with hoopskirted tour guides evoking the lost past. The French Quarter in New Orleans and Beale Street in Memphis market images of southern music that once expressed the countercultural urges of many of the South's people but now represent entertainment opportunities. Emeril Lagasse moved from New England to New Orleans and soon became identified as a classic New Orleans chef, suggesting an ease of identification with southern imagery. Meanwhile, subdivisions throughout the South put columns on middle-class houses to suggest a regional past. Many have the traditional front porch, which once symbolized family and community conversations but which now too often remain silent.

Recent history has produced new social types and institutions that reflect evolving southern mythology. The southern yuppie, for example, came out of the prosperous decade of the 1990s, a variant of an upper-middle-class character that has become a part of national popular culture. The southern yuppie might buy the same SUV or BMW as other yuppies across the nation, but the southerner is more likely to eat catfish pâté or black-eyed pea salsa and enjoy listening to the blues or jazz he heard at his fraternity or she danced to at her sorority. *Southern Living* magazine is a highly self-conscious promoter of middle-class southern ways, with which southern yuppies are familiar. It is unclear whether the arrival of a wave of Hispanic immigration is producing distinctive regional types yet, but Tish Hinajosa is a Mexican American country-folk singer whose song "Taos to Tennessee" suggests a cultural movement across space. Dat Nguyen, the son of Vietnamese refugees in the 1970s, has grown up to embrace southern culture by becoming a successful linebacker first at Texas A&M University and then with the Dallas Cowboys.

In the last decade or so, the South has produced two United States presidents, and each embodied aspects of southern mythology. Bill Clinton became known as "Bubba," a social type of recent origin but drawing from older working-class, good old boy stereotypes. Clinton hated the term, and his detractors used it more than his defenders, suggesting a politicization of southern mythology. A regional magazine called *Bubba* featured Clinton as the cover story in its first issue. Clinton's successor, George W. Bush, has relentlessly identified with Texas mythology, helping him bond red-state political success, through his identification with such regional symbols as support for guns, evangelical religion, family values, and the military tradition, and even through his use of language.

The term "Sunbelt" continues as a significant descriptor of southern economic development, linking the region's booming economy with those of the Southwest and West Coast. It is less useful, though, than it was in the 1970s and 1980s as a general political and cultural term. Tying the South together with southern California, as speaking of the Sunbelt does, makes less sense in a nation now more often characterized as red state/blue state.

CHARLES REAGAN WILSON
University of Mississippi

W. Fitzhugh Brundage, ed., *Where These Memories Grow: History, Memory, and Southern Identity* (2000); Bruce Chadwick, *The Reel Civil War* (2001); Allison Graham, *Fram-*

ing the South: Hollywood, Television, and Race during the Civil Rights Struggle (2001); Anthony Harkins, *Hillbilly: A Cultural History of an American Icon* (2004); Karl G. Heider, ed., *Images of the South: Constructing a Regional Culture on Film and Video* (1993); Tara McPherson, *Reconstructing Dixie: Race, Gender, and Nostalgia in the Imagined South* (2003); John Shelton Reed, *Southern Folk, Plain and Fancy: Native White Southern Types* (1986); Scott Romine, *The Narrative Forms of Southern Community* (1999); J. W. Williamson, *Hillbillyland: What the Movies Did to the Mountains and What the Mountains Did to the Movies* (1995).

African Influences

In 1935 Melville J. Herskovits asked in the pages of the *New Republic*, "What has Africa given America?" In his answer, a radical response for the time, he briefly mentioned the influence of blacks on American music, language, manners, and foodways. He found most of his examples in the South. Several decades later the answer to this question could be longer, perhaps less radical, but still surprising to many. Much of what people of African descent have brought to the United States since 1619 has become so familiar to the general population, particularly in the South, that the black origins of specific customs and forms of expression have become blurred or forgotten altogether.

Consider, for example, the banjo. Not only is the instrument itself of African origin, but so is its name. Although the banjo is encountered today chiefly in bluegrass ensembles where it is considered an instrument of the Appalachians, it was first played by slaves on Tidewater plantations in the 17th and 18th centuries. It was taken up into the Piedmont and mountains only during the 19th century, by blacks working on railroad gangs. Although the contemporary banjo is physically quite different from its African American folk antecedent, it retains nonetheless the unique sounds of its ringing high drone string and its drum head. These are the acoustic reminders of the instrument's African origins.

Linguists have noted that southern speech carries a remarkable load of African vocabulary. This assertion is all the more remarkable when one recalls that white southerners often claimed to have little interaction with blacks. Some regional words have murky origins, but there is no controversy for such terms as "boogie," "gumbo," "tote," "benne," "goober," "cooter," "okra," "jazz," "mumbo-jumbo," "hoodoo," "mojo," "cush," and the affirmative and negative expressions "uh-huh" and "unh-uh." All are traceable to African languages and usages. The term "guinea" is used as an adjective for a number of plants and animals that were imported long ago from Africa. Guinea hens, guinea worms, guinea grass, and guinea corn, now found throughout the South, are rarely thought of as exceptional, even though their names directly indicate their exotic African origins.

Beyond basic words, blacks have created works of oral literature that have become favorite elements of southern folklore. Looking at the whole cycle of folktales with animal tricksters—those put into written form by Joel Chandler Harris and others—some may have European analogies, but most appear to have entered the United States from Africa and the West Indies. The warnings they provide concerning the need for clever judgment and social solidarity are lessons taken to heart by both whites and blacks. The legacy of artful language in African American culture is manifested further in other types of performance such as the sermon, the toast, and contests of ritual insult. For people who are denied social and economic power, verbal power provides important compensation. This is why men of words in the black community—the good talkers—are highly esteemed. The southern oratorical style has generally been noted as distinctive because of its pacing and imagery and the demeanor of the speaker. Some of these traits heard in speeches and sermons are owed to black men of words who of necessity refined much of what is today accepted as standard southern "speechifying" into a very dramatic practice.

In the area of material culture blacks have generally been assumed to have made few contributions to southern life, but such an assessment is certainly in error. There have, over the last four centuries, existed distinctive traditions for African American basketry, pottery, quilting, blacksmithing, boatbuilding, woodcarving, carpentry, and graveyard decoration. These achievements have gone unrecognized and unacknowledged. Take, for example, the shotgun house. Several million of these structures can be found all across the South, and some are now lived in by whites, although shotgun houses are generally associated with black neighborhoods. The first of these distinctive houses, with their narrow shapes and gable entrances, were built in New Orleans at the beginning of the 19th century by free people of color who were escaping the political revolution in Haiti. In the Caribbean such houses are used both in towns and in the countryside; they were once used as slave quarters. Given its history, the design of the shotgun house should be understood as somewhat determined by African architectural concepts as well as Caribbean Indian and French colonial influences. Contemporary southern shotgun houses represent the last phase of an architectural evolution initiated in Africa, modified in the West Indies, and now in many southern locales dominating the cultural landscape.

The cultural expressions of the southern black population are integral to the regional experience. Although the South could still exist without banjos, Brer Rabbit, goobers, and shotgun houses, it would certainly be less interesting. The black elements of southern culture make the region more distinctive.

JOHN MICHAEL VLACH
The George Washington University

J. L. Dillard, *Black English* (1972); Dena J. Epstein, *Ethnomusicology* (September 1975); Leland Ferguson, *Uncommon Ground: Archeology and Early African America, 1650–1800* (1992); Melville J. Herskovits, *New Republic* (4 September 1935); Joseph E. Holloway, ed., *Africanness in American Culture* (1990); Robert Farris Thompson, *Flash of the Spirit: African and Afro-American Art and Philosophy* (1983); John

Michael Vlach, *The Afro-American Tradition in Decorative Arts* (1978), *Back of the Big House: The Architecture of Plantation Slavery* (1993), *Pioneer America* (January 1976).

Automobile

"Nobody with a good car needs to be justified," said Hazel Motes in Flannery O'Connor's *Wise Blood*. She was satirizing the idea, but the suggestion that the automobile can be the source of salvation was not far off for many southerners in the 20th century. The automobile had a profound impact in changing the region. It affected class relationships, economic development, geographical mobility, and physical and psychological landscapes. "Such names as Ford, Chrysler, Olds, Willis, Nash, Shakespeare, Reo, Studebaker, and Dodge had more long-range economic meaning for the South than all the Civil War generals combined," writes historian Thomas D. Clark. "The established way of life in the South was shaken to its very foundation by this new Yankee machine."

The South was the scene of occasional early automotive activity. In 1906, for example, at a mile run at Ormond Beach, Fla., a Stanley Steamer averaged the unheard-of speed of 127.66 miles per hour. Long-distance road races stressing speed were started in the late 1890s, and many were held over closed routes on southern public highways. The American Automotive Association sponsored the Vanderbilt Cup races in Georgia and Florida; the nationwide Glidden tours came into the South for the first time in 1910 and 1911; and the National Association of Automobile Manufacturers held the first official showing of 1910 model cars in Atlanta, the first time the show had been held outside of New York or Chicago. All this promoted a new attitude toward the South in the industry.

Despite such activity, motor vehicles at first made less impact in the South than elsewhere. The region's poverty made the automobile a luxury for most, and its dispersed rural population meant no concentrated urban market. In 1910 statistics on the ratio of automobiles registered to persons aged 18 or over showed the highest-ranking southern state to be Louisiana, but it ranked only 33d. All the southern states were well below the national average. In the geographic distribution of registered automobiles by state, Texas was the highest ranking of the former Confederate states in 1900 at 12th, with only 180 cars. But change was coming. "Southerners have finally awakened to the importance of the automobile," said a writer in *Motor* magazine in 1909. The South is now home to the Birthplace of Speed Museum in Ormond Beach, Fla., which tells the story of early automobile racing.

The key decade of the automobile's introduction into the region was the

Young people and the automobile, Florida, 1930s (Marion Post Wolcott, photographer, Library of Congress [LC-USF-34-54195-E], Washington D.C.)

1920s. Historian Blaine A. Brownell has argued that the southern attitude toward the automobile in that decade was one of "ambiguity and uncertainty" that "cut across class and racial lines." People in the region bought cars and adopted the car culture, but this involved dramatic changes, which were part of the general rural-urban conflict of the times. Newspapers promoted the automobile through special advertising and travel sections. Annual automobile shows promoted awareness of the car, and roads improved dramatically. In 1921 a writer in *Motor* praised "the tendency of the automobile to bring into intimate and helpful contact sections of our population which normally would never meet." Automobile outings and vacations became national institutions in the 1920s, as the car became a middle-class possession, and it fostered a new mobility of the labor force as well. Buses soon crisscrossed the region, facilitating the movement of people and freight. A few motor vehicle assembly plants were brought to such southern states as Georgia, and raw materials needed for automobile manufacturing were processed in the South. The development of wholesale and retail businesses related to some aspect of the car was especially significant in the regional economy. In a typical case, car dealerships represented 14.4 percent of Birmingham's 1929 retail trade, and businesses listed in the U.S. census as automobile related accounted for 20.5 percent of retail trade that year in Nashville and 16.5 percent in Atlanta.

Although southerners adopted the automobile, some of them criticized its effect on living patterns. Jonathan Daniels referred to the salesmen of Chevrolets as the "most profoundly disturbing agitators" in the region. Ministers blamed the automobile for leading to a decline in sexual morality by loosening courtship habits, and they said it nurtured crime, desecrated the Sabbath, hurt family bonds, and reinforced materialistic instincts. One of the most frequent complaints was of traffic congestion. As Faulkner noted in his 1927 novel *Mosquitoes*, traffic in New Orleans "inched forward, stopped, inched forward again." The lack of parking space was a continual concern of businesses seeking customers downtown. The rising number of deaths and injuries from automobile accidents also was a concern. The country music song "Wreck on the Highway," with its graphic images of shattered glass, screams, and whiskey and blood running together, conveyed the negative side of the automobile's impact in the region.

The automobile led to the reshaping of the southern land through road building. Organized southern efforts toward good roads began in the 1890s. By the second decade of the 20th century, writes historian Thomas D. Clark, "surfaced roads were still so much a novelty that pictures of them appeared in southern elementary textbooks as modern wonders." By this time, though, "the southern campaign for good roads had almost achieved the fervor of a religious revival." By 1920 all the southern states had established state highway commissions, which acquired tremendous amounts of money and power. In 1918 North Carolina voters, for example, approved a $50 million bond issue to build improved road systems, and in 1956 they took on $76 million in debt for 1,771 miles of new roads. Governors and county officials found this a major source of patronage.

The automobile helped to revolutionize the southern relationship to the federal government. The passage of the Federal Highway Act of 1921 led to a massive involvement of the federal government in the southern states. It pumped billions of dollars into the region for road building, and the Federal Bureau of

Highways standardized requirements for bridges, roadbeds, and road markings and employed inspectors to administer the guidelines. Despite recurrent talk of states' rights by southern congressmen, they did not oppose federal support for interstate highways.

Southerners are supposedly not attuned to technology, but this has not been so with automobiles. In Faulkner's *The Reivers*, a character has a vision of the nation's future "in which the basic unit of its economy and prosperity would be a small mass-produced cubicle containing four wheels and an engine." Despite this fear, the image of the mechanic as a rather romantic working-class hero has been common, "the romance of the backyard mechanic with grease up to his elbows," says Sylvia Wilkinson. The good old boy image is closely tied to the automobile. Like the cowboy and his horse, the good old boy needs his car. A good man knows cars and takes care of them.

The current image of the automobile man in the South is the clean professionalism of a stock car driver and crew. To be sure, the driver may have wild tales to tell of his youth. Robert Mitchum symbolized this as a moonshine runner in the film *Thunder Road*, and Burt Reynolds's series of *Smokey and the Bandit* movies has taken it to its extremes. It is a male world in its imagery; women are not allowed in the pits and are considered to be bad luck. It is a sometimes violent world, where violence is direct and graphic. Junior Johnson recalled that in his early days driving on dirt tracks in the South the drivers "liked to fight about as good as race." He remembered arming himself with a cola bottle for a fight with a competitor on the infield. The "rambling man" is another romantic southern figure associated with the automobile. He is a common figure in country music as far back as Jimmie Rodgers. Merle Haggard's 1977 song "Rambling Fever" expressed this theme, as did Kris Kristofferson's "Me and Bobby McGee." Even the automobile factory worker has made it into regional folklore. A Johnny Cash song tells of an assembly-line automobile worker who sneaks car parts out of the factory, one piece at a time, until he has a new automobile at home. The plight of southerners working in northern automobile plants is poignantly explored in "Detroit City." A great number of blues and rock-and-roll songs—such as "Mabelline"—celebrate the automobile.

The automobile has affected modern southern recreation. Hank Williams wrote that "a hot-rod Ford and a two dollar bill" were all that were required in the 1950s for a southern good time, while Lefty Frizzel in "If You've Got the Money, I've Got the Time" sang of good times in Cadillacs. In stock car racing, the South produces the majority of the tracks, races, and participants, as well as a massive turnout of spectators. Dirt-track racing is an important participant form of southern sport in local communities throughout the region. Recreational vehicles are pressed into service on weekends for camping, promoting the traditional southern pastimes of fishing and hunting.

The National Association of Stock Car Auto Racing (NASCAR) has reflected the organization and commercialization of the South's love of automobiles. The guiding spirit behind its growth was William Henry Getty "Big Bill" France. He moved to Daytona Beach, Fla., in 1935, operating a service station there and sometimes driving in local races. After World War II he realized the possibilities of organizing the boisterous races that were occurring across the South. He joined with three dozen other men in 1947 to organize NASCAR. Races with all stock cars — which were ordinary automobiles modified for speed and power — became part of the Grand National competition. Racers were predominately male, but such women as Sara Christian and Louise Smith were competitive, as was African American racer Wendell Scott. By the mid-1970s, NASCAR sanctioned 1,600 races in 34 states and Europe, having moved well beyond its southern origins.

One should not forget the recreational significance of the drive-in movie, a good example of a new recreational institution based on the automobile. The first drive-in opened on 6 June 1933 in Camden, N.J. It helped to structure recreation for a generation of Americans. The drive-in was at its peak in the 1950s, serving as a source of family entertainment and a central locale for teenage courtship. The number of drive-ins was greatest in 1958, when 4,000 were in operation. The "passion pits" have continued that role, although the number is on the decline, with 3,178 drive-ins operating nationwide by September of 1982, and only 419 open in 2005. While New York led the nation in drive-ins in 2005 with 32, numbers in the South ranged from none in Louisiana to 3 in Arkansas, 10 in Florida, 15 in Tennessee, and 18 in Texas. Most now are located in suburban areas, on the edge of cities, or in rural areas and small towns. Drive-in movies were surely not uniquely southern, yet the southern climate and the pervasiveness of small towns and rural communities have given them special recreational significance in the region. They are open later in the year than elsewhere and are a larger component of entertainment in small towns and rural communities.

The automobile had a particularly important effect on the southern poor. Mobility liberated impoverished sharecroppers from their chains to the land. In their automobiles they found "both dignity and independence," says historian Thomas D. Clark. Rich and poor, black and white, all rode in the same kind of vehicle, which proved to be a leveling device. W. J. Cash pointed out that the mill worker as well gained status from the car.

Mobility and speed were the keys to understanding the special appeal of the automobile to a southern populace suffering geographic and social stagnation. In Flannery O'Connor's short story "The Life You Save May Be Your Own," Mr. Shiflet notes that "the body, lady, is like a house: it don't go anywhere: but the spirit, lady, is like a automobile: always on the move, always." "Sugar-Boy couldn't talk," said Jack Burden while riding with Willie Stark's driver in Robert Penn Warren's *All the King's Men*, "but he could express himself when he got his foot on the accelerator." The automobile meant escape from the farm or the mill village. It was a way out of poverty. It represented an escape from the negative side of the strong southern sense of place, the static rootedness. Thanks to the car, says the hitchhiker in Warren's novel, "a man could just get up and git, if'n a notion came on him."

Some scholars argue that southerners have shaped the very character of the nation's car culture. Landscape historian John Brinckerhoff Jackson has written that "the rest of the United States sees the highway and the car culture as essentially a southern phenomenon." He outlines the southern roots of the contemporary car culture:

> Our interstate highways are extensions of the Southern landscape: truck stops as far west as Utah or Colorado provide Southern breakfasts and Southern music on the jukeboxes, Southern banter with the waitresses. Small (and I must say) uninviting roadside nightclubs advertise the music of young Southerners with names like Clyde and Jessie and Leroy and Floyd. The Southern accent is widely adopted by used car salesmen all over America.

Other scholars, however, would see some of his examples as more national than regional.

The contemporary era has seen the increasing impact of motor vehicles on southern cities, furthering suburban growth, close rural-urban ties, and inter-regional connections. The problems of the automobile have been recognized in the South, as in the nation. The sheer number of cars is a key concern, especially because of air pollution. Heavy traffic leads to congestion equal to that of the California freeways on streets sometimes not even built for automobiles. The lack of planning and zoning has created a cluttered jungle of businesses serving the automobile and its inhabitants. Moreover, automobiles are violent killers in the South. As historian Clark wrote, "They take an annual toll of life that approaches that of the old regional diseases." The poverty of the South's people has made the accident and death problems worse, because poor tires and poorly maintained cars hamper safety. Finally, the South has become a new center of American automobile production, with BMWs, Toyotas, Nissans,

Saturns, and other automobiles produced in a southern belt stretching across the Carolinas and Tennessee into Alabama and Mississippi.

CHARLES REAGAN WILSON
University of Mississippi

Blaine A. Brownell, *American Quarterly* (March 1972); Thomas D. Clark, *The Emerging South* (1961); Pete Daniel, *Lost Revolutions: The South in the 1950s* (2000); Cynthia G. Dettlebach, *In the Driver's Seat: The Automobile in American Literature and Popular Culture* (1976); William E. Geist, *New York Times* (7 June 1983); John Brinckerhoff Jackson, *The Southern Landscape Tradition in Texas* (1980); Howard L. Preston, *Automobile Age Atlanta: The Making of a Southern Metropolis, 1900–1935* (1979), *Dirt Roads to Dixie: Accessibility and Modernism in the South, 1885–1935* (1991); Sylvia Wilkinson, in *The American South: Portrait of a Culture*, ed. Louis D. Rubin Jr. (1980).

Beauty, Cult of

"The modern Southern belle has, of course, long been the Pageant ideal," writes Frank Deford of the Miss America contest, "so that—even in those years when a Southerner does not win—the likely winner is still probably patterned after that type." The "fundamental Southern-belle personality" that has become the nation's beauty ideal is "vivacious, sparkle-eyed, full of fun, capable of laughing at herself, and incapable of speaking either (a) briefly, or (b) without using the hands to illustrate all points." She has poise and personality beneath the outward physical attractiveness.

Beauty pageants such as the Miss America competition suggest the influence of southern ideas in shaping national ideals of beauty. Within the specifically southern context, beauty pageants are part of a cult of beauty, with certain definite ideas on what beauty is and why it is significant to be beautiful. The South's cult of beauty reflects southern attitudes on race, social class, and especially gender and sexuality, and these attitudes have changed significantly over time.

Beauty has long been related in the South to color. English colonists in North America brought European concepts of beauty, which became a factor justifying the enslavement of black Africans. Historian Winthrop D. Jordan has noted that "the English discovery of black Africa came at a time when the accepted standard of ideal beauty was a fair complexion of rose and white. Negroes not only failed to fit this ideal but seemed the very picture of perverse negation." Judged on this standard, blacks were seen as "pronouncedly less beautiful than whites." In his age, Thomas Jefferson asked whether skin color is not "the foun-

Florida bathing beauties, 1970
(Florida Photographic Collection, State Archives of Florida, Tallahassee)

dation of a greater or less share of beauty in the two races?" He insisted that "the fine mixtures of red and white" were "preferable to that eternal monotony" of black skin. Jefferson's concept of beauty included "flowing hair" and an "elegant symmetry of form," both of which he attributed to whites more than to other races. "The circumstance of superior beauty," he wrote, "is thought worthy of attention in the propagation of our horses, dogs, and other domestic animals; why not in that of man?" The idea of beauty was tied in for southern whites with ideas of sexuality and morality. Southern whites used the dark skin color of slaves as an outward indicator of the immorality of blacks, attributing to them impurities, lasciviousness, and evil.

The myth of the Old South included a prominent role for the beautiful white lady. Indeed, as W. J. Cash noted in *The Mind of the South* (1941), she became identified "with the very notion of the South itself." Physical beauty was a part of the definition of southern womanhood. The 19th-century conception of woman's appearance emphasized her fragility, purity, and spirituality, rather than her physical nature. The southern lady, according to Anne Firor Scott, was to be "timid and modest, beautiful and graceful." Anne Goodwyn Jones has pointed out that white women in the Old South "became not only the perfect embodiments of beauty" but also "the appropriate vehicles for the expression of beauty in language." Beauty itself, like the lovely woman who best represented that quality, "was fragile and ethereal, or sensuous and pleasurable, but it was finally irrelevant to the serious business of life." Beauty was a culturally admired trait, but it was also a limiting one for women.

The identification of whiteness and women with beauty survived into the 20th century. Cash wrote that the southern woman was "the South's Palladium," "the shield-bearing Athena gleaming whitely in the clouds," "the lily-pure maid of Astolat." Carl Carmer wrote in *Stars Fell on Alabama* (1934) of the University of Alabama fraternity dance that included a toast: "To Woman, lovely woman of the Southland, as pure and chaste as this sparkling water, as cold as this gleaming ice, we lift this cup, and we pledge our hearts and our lives to the protection of her virtue and chastity."

The southern ideal of the beautiful woman has evolved, though. The Scarlett O'Hara type, who is associated with the Old South, is beautiful but somewhat artificial. Sexuality is much more openly associated with beautiful women in the modern South. Victoria O'Donnell's typology of images of southern women in film points out that one dominant type is the "Sexual Woman": "She is beautiful, voluptuous, only partially clothed, and openly erotic. She is able to give sexual fulfillment, but she does so in order to impart strength to her man." Sometimes the beautiful southern woman becomes the "Rich, Spoiled Woman," who has "beauty, money, men, and friends" but is "spoiled and wild." Another film image of the modern southern woman portrays her as "earthier, gaudier" than women of the past, embodying open "carnal qualities, for she has lost her purity and chastity and is glad of it." The "Unfulfilled Sexual Woman" wants to be sexually appealing, but she is frustrated because "she has little to offer in terms of physical beauty." For all of these social types in the southern imagination, beauty remains an important ingredient of culturally determined happiness, which now includes sexual satisfaction.

Changing attitudes toward the sun have affected the southern ideal of beauty. In Western civilization white, pallid skin was traditionally a sign of upper-class status, and such makeup as face powder and rouge highlighted whiteness. With industrialization, upper-class Europeans and white Americans, including eventually southerners, developed an interest in outdoor life. The laboring class now worked indoors, so the upper class sought suntans and outdoor recreation as indicators of social-class status. "The lithe, sun-tanned, tennis-playing, outdoor woman," writes Marvin Harris, "became a respectable alternative to the cloistered, snow-and-alabaster ideal of the old regimes." Soon the middle class adopted this ideal of a physically healthy, athletic, sun-tanned woman.

This cultural change had special significance in the South, where the sun is intensely felt and "whiteness" has its most deeply rooted racial-cultural meaning. The sun has long helped determine southern social status — rednecks were laborers, and their women were said to be less beautiful because they were less pallidly white than the plantation wife. By the 1920s the South, according to historians Francis Butler Simkins and Charles Roland, had "learned to regard its very hot and very bright sun as a beneficent friend instead of as a cruel tyrant." Sunbonnets and long, tight-fitting clothes were abandoned for lighter garments, and the sun was soon regarded as a source of health. Sunbathing gradually became common, and "the acme of Southern comeliness became blue eyes, blond hair, and brown skin."

Black attitudes toward beauty have gone through their own changes. Illustrations of African Americans up to the 1880s show a predominance of natural hair and little cosmetic beautification of the face. By the start of the 20th century, though, black males were beginning to use hot combs to straighten their hair, while black women used oils and pomades. Evidence suggests that many blacks internalized white ideals of beauty. They used cosmetics to lighten the skin color and hair straighteners to "conk" the hair in attempting to approach the white ideal. This probably reached a peak during the 1940s. Beauty parlors became important institutions of the black community, and cosmetics manufacturers were among the wealthiest of black Americans.

Skin color has been a symbol of social class status within the black community. John Dollard noted in *Caste and Class in a Southern Town*, his 1937 study of Indianola, Miss., that "consciousness of color and accurate discrimination between shades is a well-developed caste mark in Southerntown; whites, of course, are not nearly so skilful [*sic*] in distinguishing and naming various shades." Toni Morrison's *The Bluest Eye* (1970) portrays the tragic results of a black family's self-hatred because of a "white skin" ideal of beauty. Lawrence

Levine cautions, however, against overemphasizing the effect of a cultural ideal of white beauty on blacks. For many blacks a light skin did not suggest social status within the black community, but rather a corruption of the race. If some black people have admired white skin, others have viewed black skin as natural, and many cosmetics have existed not to cloak that color but to highlight it. Moreover, when color preference has been seen in black cultural expressions such as blues lyrics, it has most often been brown, rather than either black or white-yellow. Paul Oliver's study of blues lyrics, *Blues Fell This Morning: The Meaning of the Blues* (1960), found that rural folk expressed an ideal of beauty somewhat different from the urban black and white ideal of "the streamlined woman." Bluesmen admired the "big, fat woman with the meat shaking on her bone." They also celebrated certain physical features, such as teeth that "shine like pearls" as a natural and attractive contrast with dark skin.

The civil rights movement of the 1950s and 1960s surely strengthened pride in a black ideal of beauty. "Black Is Beautiful" reflected a new appreciation of dark skin specifically as well as a more general pride in black culture. Magazines such as *Beauty Trade* and *Essence* are now published by blacks outside of the South, but their ideas influence the southern beauty industry and black ideals of beauty. Beauty pageants have become a fixture on black campuses and in black communities across the South.

The beauty pageant is the ritual event that best displays modern national and regional attitudes about beauty. Predecessors of American beauty pageants were European festivals that crowned queens. European May Day activities have included selection of beautiful women as symbols of fertility. In the colonial era this custom took root in the South more than among the Puritans. Schools for young southern white women throughout the 19th century included contests for selection of attractive, popular queens. Southern romanticism expressed itself in antebellum tournaments, recreating medieval pageants, and these festive occasions included queens selected for their beauty. Postbellum festivals also included selection of beauties. Mardi Gras chose its first queen in 1871, despite the protest of some moralists who objected to any public display of women. These May Day, tournament, and festival queens were upper-class figures, and these contests reinforced, as historian Lois Banner has written, "the centrality of physical beauty in women's lives and made of beauty a matter of competition and elitism and not of democratic cooperation among women."

Commercial beauty pageants appeared first in the late 19th century. P. T. Barnum sponsored a female beauty pageant in 1854, but it involved only the display of daguerreotypes of women, with observers voting on winners. Carnivals in the South, often attached to agricultural fairs, helped pave the way for beauty contests displaying beautiful women in native costumes from around the world. The Atlanta International Cotton Exposition of 1895 had a beauty show on its midway, and this part of the exposition was described as "the Mecca of the show." By 1900 chambers of commerce and fraternal groups in the South sponsored carnival beauty shows at fairs, but it was still not considered appropriate for middle-class women to be on display in competitive contests. The first true competitive beauty contest was the Miss United States contest held at Rehoboth Beach, Del., in 1880, but the South's beach resorts did not follow suit generally until after the turn of the century.

The Miss America pageant began in 1921, but the judges did not select a southerner until Texan Jo-Carrol Dennison was chosen in 1942. With the Americanization of the South — and the southernization of the United States — in recent decades, southerners have become identified with love of beauty pageants. *Newsweek* magazine (17 September 1984) estimated that 750,000 beauty contests are held each year in the United States, ranging from pageants for school homecoming queens, county- and state-fair queens, and festival representatives to the Miss America contest. "The phenomenon is strongly regional," said *Newsweek*. "The 'Pageant belt' stretches from Texas (where there are men who will date only titleholders) throughout the South, overlapping the Bible belt with odd precision."

Beauty pageants in the South are part of a regional cult of beauty. Young southern white ladies have long been encouraged in the feminine arts, and aspects of beauty have been taught in female academies, charm schools, and modern modeling salons. Cosmetologists, beauticians, and hairdressers are well-known figures in small and large southern towns, where concern for "looks" is endemic. Eudora Welty reproduced the ambience and conversational sound of the southern beauty parlor in her short story "Petrified Man."

Cosmetics were slow to take root in the poor rural South of the early 20th century. Even today, some Pentecostal-Holiness groups stress an ascetic ideal of outward plainness and inner beauty. Nevertheless, most women in small southern towns and cities have long accepted national views on cosmetics. Mary Kay Ash, founder of the successful Mary Kay Cosmetics, is from Texas; a key figure in the black cosmetics industry in this century, Madame C. J. Walker, came from Louisiana. Changes in contemporary southern religion's attitude toward beauty are evinced by Tammy Faye Bakker, the television celebrity formerly on the Pentecostal-oriented show, the *PTL Club*. Bakker flaunted her makeup by using a great deal of it. She even launched her own line of cosmetics.

Beauty pageants are central to small-town, middle-class life in the South and the nation. In 1970, for example, only 8 of 50 contestants in the Miss America pageant were from the nation's 25 largest cities. Few large urban areas sponsor contests, and even statewide beauty pageants tend to take place in smaller cities and towns. James Rucker, a former executive director of the Miss Mississippi contest, notes that whereas big-city northern girls enter the contest for the scholarship money or a chance at show-business success, "in Mississippi, it's tradition for the best girls to come out for the Pageant. In Mississippi, the best girls just want to be Miss America."

Beauty contests are community events in towns and small cities. The Universal/Southern Charm children's beauty pageant illustrates the pageant appeal. Arkansan Darlene Burgess founded Southern Charm in 1980 to provide an honest and professionally run pageant structure, holding contests in small towns throughout the region. Susan Orlean studies the pageants sponsored by Southern Charm and noted the appeal for participants. "They were ordinary people," she writes, "dazzled by glamour, and they believed truly and uncynically in beauty and staked their faith on its power to lift you and carry you away." For a child to win a beauty crown "might be the chance for your beautiful baby to get a start on a different life, so that someday she might get ahead and get away."

Beauty contest winners are contemporary regional celebrities—the female equivalents of football stars. Beauty queens, whether Miss America or Miss Gum Spirits (representing the southern timber industry), make personal appearances, travel extensively, earn scholarship money, and have their photos on calendars. Meridian, Miss., rewarded Susan Akin, Miss America in 1985, with an enthusiastic hometown parade. She rode through town before a cheering crowd that included young girls who had won their own honors as Deep South Beauty Queen, Cameo Girl, Mini Queen, and Miss Cinderella Queen. This ritual event showed an intense American middle-class patriotism. The band played "This Is My Country" and "God Bless America." State representative Sonny Meredith was there to praise her, and Meridian's mayor named the day in her honor. Religion was a central feature. The pastor of the First Baptist Church gave an invocation, thanking God for "letting us live in a country where a neighborhood girl could be selected Miss America." The Baptist kindergarten students had penned portraits of the queen. A friend from childhood told the crowd that Susan Akin was "the one of us who earned immortality."

The culture of the modern South includes important religious anchorings, and evangelical attitudes toward beauty rooted in the middle and working classes are important ones in understanding its significance. The evangelical ideal of woman traditionally centered on her special moral and spiritual nature. She was an idealized symbol of region but at the same time a specific symbol of home and family. She represented the restraint, zealous morality, refinement, and self-discipline valued by evangelical culture. Samuel Hill has written of this idealized role model as the ideal of sainthood in the South, and "'she' is not likely to be perceived in corporeal terms."

Modern southern evangelicals have redefined their culture, though, so that now beauty queen seems a quite acceptable role for a moral southern woman. One can see the process through the example of Cheryl Prewitt, Miss America of 1980. Prewitt grew up in Choctaw County, Miss., the daughter of pious evangelicals. She attended church whenever the doors were open and sang gospel music with her performing family, the Prewitts. She was severely injured at age eleven in an automobile accident, which left one leg two inches shorter than the other. Overcoming the physical injury became the focus of Prewitt's testimony to God's power. At a revival she realized the need to be born again and to "discover for what reason God had put me into the world." She realized she would never be alone because she "would always have Jesus as my very real friend and guide." A Pentecostal preacher soon healed her through the laying on of hands at a prayer meeting. She was transported "to some faraway bright-shining place — a private place inhabited only by myself and Jesus." Afterward, her crippled left leg extended by two inches, until her heels met, "like two perfectly matched bookends."

The healing miracle set the stage for the transformation of the evangelical woman into the beauty queen, which represented the final stage of the miracle. Against her father's wishes, she enrolled in the Miss Choctaw County beauty contest in hopes of winning scholarship money for college. The economic meaning of beauty pageants to modern southern plain folk families is of paramount importance, even overcoming stern fathers' anxieties. Prewitt went on to win the Miss America pageant. Her father relented his opposition and attended the pageant, telling her afterward, "I believe it's God's will that you won tonight. . . . Now you just be sure you live up to the big job He's given you, hear?" The beauty queen can thus witness for the faith.

Participants in the Miss America pageant and those who have studied it believe that southerners who compete have an advantage. After Tennessee's Kellye Cash won in 1986, another contestant claimed that Cash had won because judges desired a "sweet kind of non-aggressive Southern belle." Cash revealed her regional consciousness, when she said she was "basically a conservative Southern gal." The contestant representing Mississippi that year insisted southerners had no special advantage, except that "they just work harder." Eight of the 10 finalists, in any event, were from former Confederate states. Miss Montana, Kamala Compton, gave no evidence of knowing about John C. Calhoun's concept of the concurrent majority, which proposed presidents from the North and the South, but she suggested a variation of it. Southerners were "just a lot more prepared than us Western girls who try once for a title," she told a reporter. "I mean, they should have a Southern Miss America and a Western Miss America."

Southerners clearly devote considerable time and resources to doing well in the Miss America pageant. University of Southern Mississippi sociologists Don Smith, Jim Trent, and Gary Hansen have theorized in unpublished research reported in the Jackson, Miss., *Clarion-Ledger* (15 October 1986) that southern contestants are likely do better in the national contest because of three factors: (1) pageant officials, judges, and contestants assume, based on past experience, that southerners will do well; (2) the southern states encourage beauty contestants; and (3) southern states have strong pageant systems. Twenty-five states have never won the contest, whereas Arkansas has won twice (1964, 1982), Texas has won three times (1942, 1971, 1975), as has Alabama (1951, 1995, 2005), and Mississippi has won four times. In the 2005 Miss America pageant, four of the top five finalists were from the South.

Texas spends on contestants' clothes more than twice as much as Vermont spends for its entire pageant. Vermont has never placed a contestant in the top 10 at Miss America, but Texas obviously values its success. From 1945 to 1970 California led the nation in scholarship prize money ($47,300) awarded to contestants. Mississippi was second ($43,000), but Mississippi's commitment was much greater, given that the state had a tenth of California's population. Four of the top seven states in awarding scholarship money up to 1970 were Arkansas, Alabama, South Carolina, and Mississippi.

African Americans were barred from participating in the Miss America pageant until the late 1960s. The first African American to win a state contest did so in 1970, in Iowa, and the first black Miss American was Vanessa Williams in 1983. In 1994, Kimberly Aiken became the first black Miss America from a former Confederate state (South Carolina). Since 1990, African American contestants have won the pageant five times (1990, 1991, 1994, 2003, 2004).

The Miss America contest and beauty pageants in general earn the condemnation of many men and women. "The whole gimmick is one commercial shell game to sell the sponsors' products," said critic Robin Morgan in 1968. "Where else could one find such a perfect combination of American values? Racism, militarism, and capitalism—all packaged in one 'ideal' symbol: a woman." Spokesmen for the Miss America pageant defend it, noting it is the largest provider of scholarships for women in the United States. Women themselves are, of course, actively involved as participants and, behind the scenes, as trainers and managers, but men run the Miss America contest and other beauty contests. In September 1986, for example, no women served on the 12-member commission that represented the state pageants. The Jaycees are sponsors of most local Miss America contests, and men's service clubs are involved in other beauty contests. Pageants are hobbies for many men, a time for having fun and for theatrical displays. The head of the Miss Arkansas contest wears a hog suit and cheers for his choice each year; the state chairman in Mississippi dresses in a tuxedo made from Confederate flags. Beauty pageants, like other rituals of the South's culture of beauty, such as sorority rush, have often been rituals for the performance of what Elizabeth Boyd calls a "fairly specific, regional understanding of gender." Through speech, gestures, and adornment, "as well as codes of conduct and choreography, a regional, racialized definition of gender gets performed, again and again." The changes in the contemporary South show an evolution of such performances. The India Association of Mississippi staged its first Miss India-Mississippi beauty pageant, for example, in 2004. Contestants competed in the chapel at Millsaps College, performing Indian dance, music, martial arts, and theater for the talent segment. Contestants dressed in Punjabi costumes — golden turbans and embroidered vests — and some adapted rap dance moves to songs from India's Bollywood movies. India Association president Hitesh Desai reminded the audience of the association's many activities but noted that the "pageant is a step for us and it's big y'all."

CHARLES REAGAN WILSON
University of Mississippi

Lois Banner, *American Beauty* (1983); Julie Kirk Blackwelder, *Styling Jim Crow: African American Beauty Training during Segregation* (2003); Elizabeth Bronwyn Boyd, "Southern Beauty: Performing Femininity in an American Region" (Ph.D. dissertation, University of Texas, 2000), *Southern Cultures* (Fall 1999); Frank Deford, *There She Is: The Life and Times of Miss America* (1971); Lisa DePaulo, *TV Guide* (6 September 1986); *Ebony* (May 1983); Marvin Harris, *Natural History* (August–September 1973); Shelby Hearon, *Texas Monthly* (October 1974); Anne Goodwyn Jones, *Tomorrow Is Another Day: The Woman Writer in the South, 1859–1936* (1981); Winthrop D. Jordan, *White over Black: American Attitudes toward the Negro, 1550–1812* (1968); Robin T. Lakoff and Raquel L. Scherr, *Face Value: The Politics of Beauty* (1984); Lawrence W. Levine, *Black Culture and Black Consciousness: Afro-American Folk Thought from Slavery to Freedom* (1977); Tara McPherson, *Reconstructing Dixie: Race, Gender, and Nostalgia in the Imagined South* (2003); Mobile, Ala. *Register*, 10 June 2004; Victoria O'Donnell, in *The South and Film*, ed. Warren French (1981); Susan Orlean, *New Yorker* (August 4, 1997); Dawn Perlmutter, in *Beauty Matters*, ed.

Peg Zelin Brand (2000); Kathrin Perutz, *Beyond the Looking Glass: America's Beauty Culture* (1970); Cheryl Prewitt, *A Bright-Shining Place* (1981); Julia Reed, *Queen of the Turtle Derby and Other Southern Phenomena* (2004); Anne Firor Scott, *The Southern Lady: From Pedestal to Politics, 1830–1930* (1970); Francis Butler Simkins and Charles P. Roland, *A History of the South* (1972); Elwood Watson and Darcy Martin, eds., *"There She Is, Miss America": The Politics of Sex, Beauty, and Race in America's Most Famous Pageant* (2004).

Benighted South

If the 19th-century South was viewed by romantics, North as well as South, as the primal garden, Eden before the Fall, the 20th-century South—at least to many image makers—was often something quite different. To be sure, the Benighted or Savage South had its origins in the 19th century: William Lloyd Garrison had referred to the region as the "great Sodom" and Frederick Law Olmsted, Harriet Beecher Stowe, and other northern writers had written harshly of it. But in the early 20th century—more particularly in the decade of the 1920s—the idea that the South was savage or barbarian took hold even more strongly than before. The new image of the Benighted South was a result partly of actual events in the South during the 1920s and partly of the writings of social critics and novelists who focused attention on the dark side of the contemporary South. The writers did not, as traditional southerners often charged, invent the negative southern image: the events did that. The Scopes evolution trial in Dayton, Tenn., in July 1925; the anti-Catholicism shown during Al Smith's presidential campaign in 1928; textile strikes and violence in Gastonia and Marion, N.C., and in Elizabethton, Tenn., in 1929; the rise of the modern Ku Klux Klan and numerous lynchings, outbreaks of nightriding, and other manifestations of racial injustice—these events drew the attention of national journalists such as H. L. Mencken and Oswald Garrison Villard; of prominent magazines such as the *Nation*, the *New Republic*, and the *Century*; and of social scientists such as Frank Tannenbaum of Columbia University, who wrote the aptly entitled *Darker Phases of the South* (1924). The Yankee crusade against the romantic southern image was carried out on several fronts, Tannenbaum concentrating on social ills, Villard and W. E. B. Du Bois, the black editor of the *Crisis*, focusing on racial matters, and Mencken in general command, attacking intellectual and cultural sterility. Mencken's essay "The Sahara of the Bozart" (1920) was the most trenchant—and readable—indictment of the South, contributing more than any other work to the popular image of the Benighted South.

But the outsiders were hardly alone in portraying the South of the early 20th century as uncivilized, unsanitary, and violent. A native group of journalists and literary figures was perhaps even more effective in this role, presumably because they, as southerners, knew whereof they spoke. North Carolina newspapermen Gerald W. Johnson and W. J. Cash sent essay after essay to their mentor, Mencken, at the *American Mercury*, and the subjects of their essays were southern racism, religious barbarism, and intellectual sterility. Southern editors took their stands against racism and religious bigotry, and won Pulitzers for their courage. As George B. Tindall has written, a "fifth column of native Menckens and Tannenbaums" found "an almost ridiculously simple formula for fame": they revealed "the grotesqueries of the benighted South."

Southern novelists were perhaps even bolder, or at least more graphic. Beginning in the early 1920s, writers such as T. S. Stribling of Tennessee and Clement Wood of Alabama, and slightly later Erskine Caldwell of Georgia, portrayed Dixie as a land of poverty, sloth, ignorance, and racial injustice. Stribling's Tennessee hillbillies and corrupt folk of northern Alabama were depicted in *Birthright* (1922), *Teeftallow* (1926), *Bright Metal* (1928), and his late trilogy: *The Forge* (1931), the Pulitzer Prize–winning *The Store* (1932), and *The Unfinished Cathedral* (1934). Caldwell became famous for his pictures of depraved poor whites in *Tobacco Road* (1932) and *God's Little Acre* (1933). And on their heels came greater, less exclusively regional writers, whose portrait of the South, for all its artistry, was judged by reviewers to be no more flattering. In *Look Homeward, Angel* (1929) Thomas Wolfe—in the words of one reviewer—"spat upon" the South. Wolfe's fictional town of Altamont—based closely on his hometown of Asheville, N.C.—he described as a "barren spiritual wilderness," which maintained a "hostile and murderous intrenchment against all new life." If Wolfe's South was intellectually barren and culturally sterile, that of William Faulkner was downright frightening. Between 1929 and 1936 the young Mississippian burst forth with a series of novels portraying a South of decaying gentry, idiocy, religious fanaticism, murder, rape, and suicide. *The Sound and the Fury* (1929) depicted the decline and fall of the Compson family, antebellum aristocrats who could not cope with the new order. *As I Lay Dying* (1930), Faulkner's tragicomic story of the attempt of a dirt-poor Mississippi family to bury their wife and mother, seemed to reinforce the worst images of southern degradation brought out by the journalists of the 1920s. *Sanctuary* (1931) was even more depraved—and, because it was sold to Hollywood, even more influential in creating the image of a savage South. *Light in August* (1932) presented a gallery of southern grotesques and eccentrics. *Absalom, Absalom!* (1936), perhaps Faulkner's greatest novel, pictured a dark and violent antebellum South. And

Faulkner's conniving poor whites, the Snopeses, were yet to come in *The Hamlet* (1940), *The Town* (1957), and *The Mansion* (1959).

By the mid-1930s the depiction of the South in contemporary fiction had become so sordid that even that earlier iconoclast, Gerald W. Johnson, was moved to call this latest Dixie-in-print "The Horrible South." Faulkner, Stribling, Caldwell, and Wolfe, he wrote, were "real equerries of Raw-Head-and-Bloody-Bones . . . the merchants of death, hell, and the grave . . . the horror-mongers-in-chief." *Sanctuary*, Johnson insisted, "put me under the weather for thirty-six hours." Yet, as he maintained, the new picture of the South was a necessary corrective to the romantic picture of the Old South, an antidote to Thomas Nelson Page. The South of 1930 was not so bad as its writers suggested — but the South of 1830 had never been so good.

The image of the Benighted South remained firmly entrenched in the national mythology throughout the 1930s. The Scottsboro case early in the decade and President Roosevelt's pronouncement in 1938 that the South was "the Nation's No. 1 economic problem" insured that. Events of the next two decades did little to modify the image, and those of the 1960s brought the South the same widespread negative attention it had attracted in the 1920s and 1930s. Now Oxford and Selma and Birmingham were in the news, not Dayton and Gastonia and Scottsboro, but the result was the same: outside reporters again flocked South and reported that Dixie remained benighted, savage, somehow out of touch with modern civilization.

Only with the end of the civil rights movement — and the rise of the Sunbelt of the 1970s — did the image of the Benighted South begin to fade. In truth, perhaps the coming of interstate highways and widespread air-conditioning had as much to do with the new positive image of Dixie as the departure of lynching and the decline of racial segregation. In any case, as the South entered the last two decades of the 20th century, it was bolder and more confident than before, possessing shining new cities, a new base of wealth dependent on oil, aerospace industries, real estate, and leisure, and a working knowledge of the power of public relations. The image of the Benighted South it had consigned, in large part, to its past, although the resurgence of fundamentalist religion, the persistence of rural poverty, and the trials of accused killers of civil rights workers can still evoke the image.

FRED HOBSON
University of North Carolina at Chapel Hill

Kees Gispen, *What Made the South Different?* (1990); Fred Hobson, *Tell about the South: The Southern Rage to Explain* (1983), *Virginia Quarterly Review* (Summer

1985); Gerald W. Johnson, *Virginia Quarterly Review* (January 1935); H. L. Mencken, *Prejudices, Second Series* (1920); George B. Tindall, *The Benighted South* (1964), *Virginia Quarterly Review* (Spring 1964), C. Vann Woodward, *The Burden of Southern History* (revised ed., 1982).

Body

From the sectional debates of the antebellum years to the Sunbelt period of the 1970s and 1980s, political and scholarly discussions of southern identity and regional distinctiveness have typically been organized around *ideas*. The plantation ideal; the influence of frontier ideology on southern culture and character; the much-ballyhooed "sense of place" and "the land"; the Agrarian vision; the emphasis on memory and history; the tension between regional loyalty and regional alienation in the careers of southern artists and intellectuals; the oral tradition; the interplay between honor and violence; the legacy of slavery and the Civil War; the imagery and thematics of white supremacy and the related question of the "southernness" of African American identity, experience, and expression; the seductive but monolithic image of the community—these broad themes have shaped the definition and study of the South for generations, with undeniably fruitful results. But the thematic approach has also worked to divert critical attention from the body work that has always served as the South's material ground. For if the southern way of life has been built upon ideas, it has in an even more fundamental sense been built upon, and by, southern bodies.

Our understanding of the South, then, has been overintellectualized, overidealized; it needs to be rematerialized, grounded in the activity and sentient experiences of southern bodies, and in the cultural values assigned to them. After all, southern bodies are where southern ideas, including ideas of southernness itself, ultimately *happen*. It is one thing, for instance, to see "the plantation" as a concept, as the foundation and expression of a hierarchically organized, classically inspired civilization, as George Fitzhugh and his fellow antebellum apologists did. It is quite another thing, however, to see a southern plantation as what the sociologist Erving Goffman would call a total institution, mobilizing the disciplinary force of law, architecture, religion, science, clothing, literature, and other discourses to coordinate bodies in space and time—naming, feeding, clothing, training, punishing, directing, and differentiating them, harnessing their energy, orchestrating their interaction and even their intercourse, all in order to produce material wealth and to reproduce relations of power. A similar point could be made about "segregation" as a system of material practices regulating the activity and movement of southern bodies in social space: as Grace Elizabeth Hale and Jay Watson have recently argued, following the earlier analyses of Lillian Smith and others, the ideology of segregation actively produced the racialized bodies and identities it purported to discriminate between.

Scholars working in the field of gender studies have taken the lead in rematerializing the study of the South through close attention to the way ideas about identity, difference, and power work themselves out in, on, and through southern bodies. As Anne Goodwyn Jones and Susan Donaldson have written, such bodies "bear . . . inscriptions of age-old stories of masculinity and femininity" that are always already entangled with other inscriptions of racial, class, sexual, sectional, and even national identities. As such, southern bodies become the relay points along a complex circuit of meaning, where the "interlocking logics of dichotomy . . . that have characterized the dominant public written discourse of the South" can be concretely focused, organized, and contained — or critically interrogated, challenged, and resisted. If it is thus true that southern bodies are "haunted by society," it is equally true that they haunt society in turn, with a recalcitrance, instability, and excess that "echo with the possibilities of alternative and opposite meanings." This haunting strangeness is at the heart of Patricia Yaeger's analysis of the southern grotesque, a representational strategy that enlists images of distorted, fragmented, or hyperbolic bodies as a form of somatic testimony, countering dominant fictions of southern identity and society with the hard facts of southern embodiment. For Yaeger, grotesque bodies record the pressure and strain of conforming to the supposedly benign, supposedly legitimate hierarchies of the southern social order — the strain, that is, of incarnating southern ideas.

Moreover, theorist Judith Butler's influential definition of gender identity as performative rather than essential, as "the repeated stylization of the body," offers a useful model for the study of southern identity generally. Consider, for example, how speech, gesture, dress, posture, physical size, eating and drinking habits, medical symptoms, injuries, and other bodily signifiers interact in various ways to fashion individuals as southern, in what amounts to a physiology of regional character; or how a whole gallery of quintessentially/stereotypically southern figures — the planter gentleman, the mountaineer, the steel magnolia, the black preacher, the honky tonk angel, the mammy, the belle, the redneck, the fugitive slave, the poor-white jezebel, and so on — are defined in performative terms, through the adornment, modification, dysfunction, control, and overall choreography of the body. Historian Kenneth Greenberg, for instance, sees the antebellum phenomenon of southern honor in these terms: as the leading public edge of elite white male identity in the Old South, the body was indeed where southern honor happened, where it was performed, which explains at once the calculated nonchalance with which antebellum duelists placed their bodies in harm's way, the fury with which gentlemen reacted to bodily affronts such as nose-pullings, and the culturally overcoded distinctions between their bodies and the bodies of slaves.

Or consider the role played by dialect writing in ascribing a material, bodily dimension to the language performances of distinct social groups in the South. As it emerged in the 1830s and 1840s to explore the political and social implications of enfranchising poor whites (southwestern humor) and reemerged in the 1870s and 1880s in a similar response to the black franchise (Joel Chandler Harris, Thomas Nelson Page), southern dialect writing typically functioned as an attempt by conservative southern whites to marginalize the emergent voices of their class or racial others by materializing those voices, drawing on nonstandard spelling, orthography, and punctuation to pull the spoken language of poor whites and African Americans "down" from the realm of mind, thought, and spirit into the "lower," less privileged realm of the body—all the while reserving the luxury of literacy for their middle- and upper-class characters, who speak the grammatically correct, orthographically unmarked, socially proper language of intellect uncorrupted by body. By this means, the genre illustrates the relationship between embodiment and political power described by theorist Elaine Scarry: whereas the powerless must bear the burdens of embodiment, disembodiment remains the privilege and refuge of the powerful. It would fall largely to Mark Twain (in *Huckleberry Finn*) and Charles W. Chesnutt (in his conjure tales) to overturn this logic by fully embracing the materiality of the southern dialect voice as a source of vitality, poetry, and authority.

Yet southern bodies have never functioned solely as sites for the application of power or as vehicles for disciplinary control but have also been sites and sources of resistance to regional ideology. From the emergence of "mulatto" as a U.S. Census category in 1850, for instance, the ambiguous bodies of mixed-race southerners have offered irrefutable, transgressive evidence of sexual intimacy between blacks and whites and provided the occasion for countless literary and historical acts of racial "passing." In both ways, the mulatto body has worked to thwart reigning fictions of the color line. With their strategies of civil disobedience, the civil rights demonstrators of the 1960s made their bodies into even more overt sources of resistance, in carefully orchestrated acts of guerrilla theater directed against the social, spatial, and racial logic of southern jails. By filling up these jails with the peaceable, orderly, clean, well-dressed, singing bodies of ordinary black and white citizens, rather than the unruly bodies of social outcasts and deviants, activists *dramatized* a new, utopian image of southern society from the margins of public space, as if to challenge their un-incarcerated counterparts and captors with the question Thoreau once asked Emerson: "What are you doing out *there*?" Their subversive performance exposed the absurdity, violence, and blindness of a southern regime unable to imagine an integrated world as other than out of bounds. More recently, anthropologist Kathleen Stewart's work among the natives of West Virginia's coal camps documents their efforts to create room to maneuver in their dealings with an unsympathetic state apparatus by exploiting the fictions of bodily difference and disability routinely imposed on them by judges, clerks, and other public functionaries.

A more body-conscious study of the South is developing on other fronts as well. Medical historians have called attention to the role played by diseases such as malaria, yellow fever, hookworm, and pellagra in shaping distinctive patterns of life and thought in the region—and distinctive stereotypes about it, such as the popular 19th-century image of the "lazy" southerner. Contemporary historians are also becoming more aware of the constitutive role played by migration in the history of the South: from European colonization, Indian removal, and the Middle Passage to the Great Migration and the more recent phenomenon of the Sunbelt, the large-scale displacement and redistribution of bodies and populations have had a dramatic impact on the economy, politics, society, and culture of the region (and indeed the nation). In these ways and others, the body is emerging as an important methodological tool in the analysis of southern culture.

JAY WATSON
University of Mississippi

Judith Butler, *Gender Trouble: Feminism and the Subversion of Identity* (1990); George Fitzhugh, *Cannibals All! or, Slaves without Masters* (1857); Erving Goffman, *Asylums: Essays on the Social Situation of Mental Patients and Other Inmates* (1961); Kenneth S. Greenberg, *Honor and Slavery* (1996); Grace Elizabeth Hale, *Making Whiteness: The Culture of Segregation in the South, 1890–1940* (1998); Anne Goodwyn Jones and Susan Donaldson in *Haunted Bodies: Gender and Southern Texts*, ed. Jones and Donaldson (1997); Todd L. Savitt and James Harvey Young, eds., *Disease and Distinctiveness in the American South* (1988); Elaine Scarry, *The Body in Pain: The Making and Unmaking of the World* (1985); Lillian Smith, *Killers of the Dream* (1949; 1961); Kathleen Stewart, *A Space on the Side of the Road: Cultural Poetics in an "Other" America* (1996); Jay Watson, *American Quarterly* (September 1997); Patricia Yaeger, *Dirt and Desire: Reconstructing Southern Women's Writing, 1930–1990* (2000).

Clocks and Time

The belief that southerners have always embraced a natural conception of time, one dependent more on the putatively gentle rhythms of sun and season than on the clipped, relentless, and precise ticking of clock or watch, is among the most tenacious myths surrounding southern culture. That the belief exists and has proven so enduring is understandable. After all, historians have traditionally attributed the decline of a task-oriented, natural time consciousness and the emergence of a clock-dependent time awareness to large-scale industrialization, urbanization, and free wage labor, forces largely alien to the antebellum American South. Therefore, so the thinking goes, slavery and the predominantly rural and agricultural way of life it engendered also rendered the region and its people hostage to a naturally defined temporal sensibility, which, in turn, tends to reaffirm widely held assumptions concerning antebellum southern slowness and a preoccupation with leisure and rest.

Such reasoning is theoretically and empirically suspect. First, clock time and natural time are not mutually exclusive. Times rooted in and guided by nature can be rigorous, pushing work to be done within a naturally defined timeframe. Second, the empirical evidence shows clearly that, with one important exception, southern conceptions and uses of time were very similar to northern and to Western European temporal sensibilities and applications.

These similarities were apparent in the colonial period. Southern merchants, for example, displayed the same preoccupation with time thrift and the same secular concern with improving time articulated by those in northern colonies; southern and northern colonial towns were regulated by both visual and aural time, most commonly in the form of church clocks and bells, which regulated civic and religious affairs; and colonials generally, regardless of region, shared a sophisticated understanding of calendar time.

If there was a peculiarly southern dimension to time consciousness, it is found in the antebellum period because slavery shaped the ways that bondpeople and slave owners understood and applied time. While in many respects echoing the northern industrial application of the clock, the exigencies of southern slaveholding society, its preoccupation with both profit and discipline, meant that masters and slaves used clock time differently. As northerners gradually replaced slave labor with free workers and industrialism became more important to the northern economy and northern society, managers and workers began to supplement their reliance on natural and task-oriented time with a sense of time dependent on the clock and watch. Free wage labor required a mechanical time discipline because the clock increasingly measured and regulated labor in northern factories. Managers rang factory bells at particular times in an effort to regulate work and instill discipline in laborers. For their part, antebellum northern workers embraced mechanical time, arguing less about the legitimacy of clocks and watches as arbiters of labor but more about the amount of clock-measured time to be worked. In this way, the working class in the North came—as it had in most industrializing, wage labor 19th-century societies—to accept the legitimacy of clock-defined work.

The forces promoting clock consciousness in 19th-century industrial capitalist societies were also at work in the Old South, principally after the 1830s. Urban preoccupations with clock time and punctuality percolated into the southern countryside and then into the minds of planters and farmers courtesy of the market and transport revolutions. Postal schedules, train times, and market times became increasingly clock dependent, and southern agriculturalists scheduled daily work regimens accordingly. In addition, the push for a more scientific, efficient southern agriculture became pronounced in and after the 1830s. Planters soon parroted Benjamin Franklin's advice that "time is money" and echoed the Yankee who "has no time" for trifling because "with him life is too short to lose a moment; every hour has its business." Slaveholders were urged: "Let us imitate them in all their good and valuable qualities." The logic was extended to the plantation, where slaveholders insinuated clock time and time thrift within the natural rhythms of the agricultural year to increase efficiency and order labor. Agricultural journals advised planters to regulate slave labor by the clock. In 1843 the *Southern Planter* counseled slaveholders, "Let regularity mark every action, and the consequence will be, that every thing will be in its right place and at its right time." As a result, southern planters became as much "lovers of system" as northern (and southern) factory managers and demonstrated a preoccupation with making the most of clock-defined time in their own letters and diaries. Little wonder, then, that levels and rates of clock and watch ownership were high and roughly the same north and south for much of the 19th century. About 70 percent of rural white southerners and rural northerners owned a clock or watch by the end of the antebellum period.

The difference between southern planters and northern industrialists with regard to the use and understanding of time is best measured in degrees, not absolutes. Both classes wanted a workforce regulated and disciplined by the clock. But unlike northern factory workers, whose clock consciousness was inspired in part by their purchase and use of watches, most slaves were denied access to mechanical timepieces. Because they were chattel for life, masters reasoned, slaves had no business owning the symbol and arbiter of time. As a result, few slaves were taught to tell time, and fewer still had legitimate access to watches, lest, slaveholders feared, they begin to debate whose time was true time. Masters tried to inculcate in slaves not a time discipline but, rather, an obedience to a clock time regulated by the slaveholder. The key tools in planters' arsenal were the sound of time, punched into the ears of slaves through plantation bells or horn, and the whip. The sound of plantation time was perfectly acceptable to southern planters because it was at once pastoral and industrial, ancient and modern. Former slaves were less enamored. William Byrd of Texas recalled: "Master, he had great iron piece hanging just outside his door and he hit that every morning at 3:30. The Negroes they come tumbling out of their beds. If they didn't master he come round in about thirty minutes with that cat-o-nine tails and begins to let Negro have that and when he got through they knew what that bell was the next morning." The sound of time, coupled with punishment for slave tardiness, enabled masters to pursue an "alternate route to modernity."

Although much research remains to be done on southern temporal sensibilities in the 20th century—especially on the relationship between segregation, integration, and temporal authorities and strategies as well as on southern responses to the implementation of Daylight Saving Time—we do know that the Civil War and emancipation ushered in important changes in how black southerners viewed and used time. Put simply, freedpeople could now own watches and were in a position to debate the worth of their time and labor power. Postbellum southern planters still attempted to regulate labor by the clock and, like antebellum northern industrialists, often indexed work and wage to clock time. But now freedpeople had access to clock time, which they tried to use to guard against exploitation. In this sense, freedpeople, some differences notwithstanding, had become very much like every other time-disciplined, clock-consciousness working class in the modern 19th-century world. The postbellum South, then, joined the world of clock consciousness principally because antebellum southern slave society had always been in and of it.

MARK M. SMITH
University of South Carolina

Martin Bruegel, *Journal of Social History* (Spring 1995); Paul B. Hensley, *New England Quarterly* (December 1992); Michael O'Malley, *Keeping Watch: A History of American Time* (1990); Mark M. Smith, *American Historical Review* (December 1996), *Mastered by the Clock: Time, Slavery, and Freedom in the American South* (1997), *Past and Present* (February 1996), *William and Mary Quarterly* (October 1998); E. P. Thompson, *Past and Present* (December 1967).

Community

For contemporary southerners the small-town community assumes mythic qualities. Images of community in southern history include plantations in the countryside, a separate black sense of community embodied in the slave quarters, mill villages in the Carolina Piedmont, brush arbor camp meetings, crossroads country stores, the courthouse square, and neighborhoods in cities. The term "community" evokes feelings of warmth and sociability, yet it also summons memories of the violent compulsion of orthodoxy—the lynch mob was a symbol of the white community's consensus on racial mores in the age of segregation.

Pioneering anthropologists and sociologists used the "community approach" in studying small-town southern life in the 1930s. The Institute for Research in Social Science at the University of North Carolina at Chapel Hill, founded by Howard W. Odum in 1924, supported research on southern communities for the next two decades. Most southern community studies in the 1930s and 1940s were concerned with the internal structures and dynamics of community. While studies were done of mill towns, the classic community research of the 1930s dealt with race and class. John Dollard's *Caste and Class in a Southern Town* (1937) was an attempt to understand "the emotional structure" of Indianola, Miss. Dollard set out to study the personality of southern blacks through their life histories and saw a need to study the community in order to understand individuals living there. He called Indianola "Southerntown," suggesting the influence of Robert S. Lynd and Helen M. Lynd's *Middletown* (1929). Other community studies in the South at this time include Allison Davis, Burleigh Gardner, and Mary Gardner's *Deep South: A Social Anthropological Study of Caste and Class* (1941), Hortense Powdermaker's *After Freedom: A Cultural Study in the Deep South* (1939), and Allison Davis and John Dollard's *Children of Bondage: The Personality of Negro Youth in the Urban South* (1940). These studies analyzed social classes and racial groups and argued that southern towns and cities formed not one community but several.

Southern community studies of the 1940s and 1950s continued to be strongly influenced by social science. John Gillin (of the University of North Carolina at Chapel Hill) and his students analyzed five representative communities, publishing three of the studies (Morton Rubin, *Plantation County*, 1951; Hylan Lewis, *Blackways of Kent*, 1955; and John Kenneth Morland, *Millways of Kent*, 1958). Researchers used observation, questionnaires, interviews, statistical information, and even Rorschach tests to describe the way of life in each community and to place it in a broader theoretical framework designed by Gillin.

Solon T. Kimball and Marion Pearsall's *The Talladega Story: A Study of Community Process* (1954) employed "event analysis," a new technique of southern community research, which explored how the people of Talladega, Ala., carried out a local study of health needs. Pearsall's *Little Smoky Ridge: The Natural History of a Southern Appalachian Neighborhood* (1959) related a small mountain community to its physical setting, internal dynamics, and surrounding countryside. John Kenneth Morland's 1967 essay "Anthropology and the Study of Culture, Society, and Community in the South" suggested the need for community research dealing with southern values, sociocultural transmission, and educational development, none of which had been the central concerns of earlier studies.

Recent studies view southern communities as historical processes rather than static institutions. To understand any community, one must observe and analyze its development over time. Although historians have produced numerous studies of colonial New England communities, surprisingly few studies exist of southern colonial communities. Darrett B. Rutman and Anita H. Rutman's *A Place in Time: Middlesex County, Virginia, 1650–1750* (1984) is a model work. Orville Vernon Burton's *In My House Are Many Mansions: Family and Community in Edgefield, South Carolina* (1985) and Randolph B. Campbell's *A Southern Community in Crisis: Harrison County, Texas, 1850–1880* (1983) bridge the antebellum and postbellum eras. Gail W. O'Brien's *The Legal Fraternity and the Making of a New South Community, 1848–1882* (1986) is a careful case study of how an elite group imposed its values on one southern community. Historians have not been alone in studying southern communities over time. Sociologist Elizabeth R. Bethel, in *Promiseland: A Century of Life in a Negro Community* (1981), and folklorist William Lynwood Montell, in *The Saga of Coe Ridge: A Study in Oral History* (1970), study black communities over time. The "community studies" approach today uses interdisciplinary methods and theories to explore southern culture from the grass roots in a way pioneered by the French *Annales* historians.

Modern southern literature preserves the image of small-town community life. Literary critics have linked the declining sense of community to the 20th-century Southern Literary Renaissance. Louis D. Rubin Jr. wrote that the southern community of the late 19th and early 20th centuries "had been self-sufficient, an entity in itself, with a mostly homogenous population, relatively orderly and fixed in its daily patterns." Southern writers at that time were a part of their communities. They lived spiritually satisfying lives but did not produce great art. White writers of the post–World War I South, members of the generation that witnessed the breakup of cohesive community life, were unable to find "spiritual sustenance and order within community life itself" and became literal or symbolic exiles. Their great art was anchored in the creation of community images—Faulkner's Yoknapatawpha County, Miss.; Wolfe's Altamont, N.C.; and Welty's Morgana, Miss.

Recent literary studies view community as socially constructed, with writers playing a crucial role in formulating ideas of what Scott Romine calls the "paternalistic or hegemonic community" that provided ideological coherence in traditional southern culture. Romine concludes that community in the South was achieved through "avoidance, deferral, and evasion," necessary to achieve a "simulated consensus" by means of which "the South could establish the essentially cohesive nature of its social order."

The southern sense of community has expressed itself in three important institutions. The courthouse square is perhaps the most potent, distinctive symbol of southern community. It is a center of business, political, and economic life drawing together people from both the small town and surrounding rural areas. The courthouse building and a tall Confederate monument (likely dating from between 1890 and 1920 and facing north) towered over the typical square. Around the square, government offices, jails, and banks were symbols of power. There were also lawyers' offices, physicians' offices, hardware stores, department stores, furniture stores, drug stores, hotels, cafes, and, by the 20th century, perhaps a funeral home and a dentist office. The blacksmith was a fixture, succeeded in the 20th century by the gas station. There was often a farmers' market near the courthouse, with fresh vegetables and fruits displayed. John Dollard noted in the 1930s that the movie theater was a major community gathering spot.

Some community institutions around the courthouse square appealed primarily to women, others to men. The beauty parlor was a gathering place for women rich and poor. Eudora Welty's "Petrified Man" captures the conversations of the small-town beauty shop as women exchanged news and gossip. Here, young girls were initiated into the roles expected of women.

The barber shop and the pool hall were equivalent male institutions. The pace in the barber shop, as in the beauty parlor, was typically slow, and the shop filled not only with those getting their hair cut but with others simply talking or listening. The pool hall was a rougher place, with aggressive talk. In it adolescents exchanged opinions on sex, drinking, and gambling, and sometimes the exchange became violent. Playwright Mart Crowley grew up listening to such stories in his father's pool hall, Crowley's Smoke House, in Vicksburg, Miss. In *Intruder in the Dust* Faulkner portrayed the barber shop and the pool hall as community institutions where one found expression of consensus and orthodoxy. The lynch mob might plot its action and gather up the young men hanging out in those places.

Another typically southern part of community life was the county, an important political and administrative institution. Amateur and professional historians have long used county history to define local history, and the modern "new social history" uses census, tax, court, and voting records to reconstruct life at the county level and relate it to broader regional patterns. As historian Robert C. McMath Jr. notes, southerners thought of the government and the county as the same. "The seat of the county court also became a center of trade and, to a lesser extent, of organized social life."

Counties are made up of smaller communities or rural neighborhoods, which are often groups of extended kin living within territorial boundaries centered around a country store or church. These small hamlets include a tavern, a church, a store, a mill, a few houses, and, before the days of consolidation, perhaps a school. Post–Civil War sharecroppers and tenants often moved within the bounds of these subcommunities within counties. While county government brought all citizens together for social, economic, and political reasons, pronounced differences existed between townspeople and those living in the nearby rural countryside. Townspeople saw themselves as more sophisticated than country people — often looked down on them, in fact — but depended on them economically.

The church was a third focus for the southern community. Colonial Anglican churches aspired to achieve community but had failed to do so by the mid-1700s. The rise of the evangelical sects in the 1700s established dissenting communities emphasizing personal religious experience, the symbolic ritual of baptism, and church discipline, and separating the chosen from the larger society. Southern evangelical Protestantism is a religion of individual experience, but conversion is the entrance to communal church life. Dominant evangelical churches in the South were intensely involved in caring for members of their religious communities. Historian Donald Mathews describes the southern church of the early 19th century as "a redemptive community."

The church building itself does not tower over the southern landscape the way the courthouse has, but the pervasiveness of small churches suggests that religious communities are organized by sect, race, and social class. Neighborhoods were commonly located around church buildings, representing what historian Orville Vernon Burton calls "communities within the larger community." Churches established community values and a rigorous moral code in frontierlike rural areas. The church was also a major focus for women's community concerns. Limited in their public roles in other areas of southern life, women were active in church groups, and those involvements often led to larger community involvement.

Blacks developed their own community in the South. The slave quarters, the Black Belt, the Delta plantation, the Carolina Lowcountry, and Tuskegee represent images of distinctly black southern communities. Even for migrants out of the region, the South and its local black communities remain "down home." As Robert B. Stepto notes, these places represent "the exhilarating prospect of community, protection, progress, learning, and a religious life while often birthing and even nurturing (usually unintentionally) a sense of enclosure that may reach claustrophobic proportions." Black folk culture has been a prime means for preservation of a distinctive sense of black community. In blues music and in tales of black folk heroes, individual characters symbolize the black community. "What the black southern writer inherits as a natural right is a sense of *community*," writes Alice Walker in stressing that experience as a literary resource.

The relationship of blacks to the overall southern community remains unclear. Blacks had their own communities, but there was also a larger community that had to be dealt with. Until very recently, this community was clearly dominated by whites. Whites controlled the power, set the agenda, and created the myths. James McBride Dabbs noted that blacks "were never a true part of this community," yet "the community was there, in some ways they belonged to it, household servants rather intimately." The South's elaborate rules of interracial etiquette, manners, and customs were designed to facilitate the functioning of communities inhabited by two races. The folk culture of blacks and whites, especially in small towns and rural areas, was a major expression of a shared sense of southern community, beyond ideology. Folktales, folksongs, and folk art all represented the preservation and transmission of a regionally distinct culture.

The civil rights movement was an effort to integrate the southern community. The movement integrated specific public schools and restaurants and developed a broader definition of the community of people who called themselves southerners. A central idea for Martin Luther King Jr. was the "beloved community," and the title of his last book, *Where Do We Go from Here? Chaos or Community?*, indicated his concern for achieving a sense of community in both the region and the nation.

The civil rights movement occurred in the South in the context of specific communities—Montgomery, Selma, Albany, Birmingham, Memphis, and countless others. Scholars who have begun to explore the origin and development of the movement within specific communities include William H. Chafe in *Civilities and Civil Rights: Greensboro, North Carolina, and the Black Struggle for Freedom* (1980), Aldon D. Morris in *The Origins of the Civil Rights Movement: Black Communities Organizing for Change* (1984), and Robert J. Norrell in *Reaping the Whirlwind: The Civil Rights Movement in Tuskegee* (1985).

A final symbol of community in the contemporary South is the city neighborhood. The 1950s and 1960s were years of urban renewal, which often destroyed older structures and displaced people from their homes. Wealthy white suburbs grew on the edges of southern cities until the 1970s and 1980s, when a new trend developed. The energy crisis of the early 1970s, federal government Community Development Block Grants, and interest in historical preservation led affluent white southerners to look again to urban neighborhoods as residential areas. Ansley Park and Inman Park in Atlanta, Oakwood in Raleigh, Trinity Park in Durham, and the Oakleigh District in Mobile are but a few of the older urban neighborhoods that have been revived as places to live. Sometimes these areas become havens for southern yuppies at the expense of working-class people traditionally living there, but not always. In explaining the trend, Philip Morris of *Southern Living* stressed "the sense of place and community that most residents of reviving districts comment upon. They like the diversity of ages, of interests, of architecture, of viewpoint, that come together as an urban place." This interest in urban neighborhoods represents an attempt by southerners to preserve the regional ideal of community, a small-town southern ideal surviving in the context of big-city living.

The dramatic social, economic, and cultural changes in the recent South are changing the context for ideas of community. The arrival of new immigrants from Latin America, the Caribbean, and Asia, as well as Americans from other parts of the nation, creates ethnic neighborhoods and retirement communities with distinctive social norms. Gated communities symbolize the growing economic gap among social classes.

CHARLES REAGAN WILSON
University of Mississippi

Orville Vernon Burton and Robert C. McMath Jr., eds., *Toward a New South?: Studies in Post–Civil War Southern Communities* (1982); James McBride Dabbs, *The Southern Heritage* (1958); Jean E. Friedman, *The Enclosed Garden: Women and Community in the Evangelical South, 1830–1900* (1985); Rhys Isaac, *The Transformation of Virginia, 1740–1790* (1982); Norman K. Johnson, *Southern Living* (January 1980); John Brinckerhoff Jackson, *The Southern Landscape Tradition in Texas* (1980); Lawrence W. Levine, *Black Culture and Black Consciousness: Afro-American Folk Thought from Slavery to Freedom* (1977); Donald Mathews, *The Religion of the Old South*

(1977); John Kenneth Morland, in *Perspectives on the American South: Agenda for Research*, ed. Edgar T. Thompson (1967); Philip Morris, *Southern Living* (November 1976); Scott Romine, *The Narrative Forms of Southern Community* (1999); Louis D. Rubin Jr., *Writers of the Modern South: The Faraway Country* (1967); Stephen A. Smith, *Myth, Media, and the Southern Mind* (1985); Robert B. Stepto, *From Behind the Veil: A Study of Afro-American Narrative* (1979); Julius E. Thompson, *Black Life in Mississippi: Essays on Political, Social, and Cultural Studies in a Deep South State* (2001); Alice Walker, *In Search of Our Mothers' Gardens* (1983).

Confederate Monuments

Confederate monuments are among the most ubiquitous and characteristic features of the civic landscape of the South. A recent tally has identified well over 700 freestanding Confederate monuments in the states that sanctioned slavery in 1860, not including monuments in military parks or at gravesites of individuals. These tributes range in scale from the obelisks and soldier statues found in cemeteries and courthouse squares throughout the South to such elaborate constructions as the colossal relief of Robert E. Lee, Stonewall Jackson, and Jefferson Davis carved into Stone Mountain, outside Atlanta, and the statues of Lee, Jackson, Davis, J. E. B. Stuart, and Matthew Fontaine Maury that line Monument Avenue in Richmond. The grounds of many southern state capitols showcase multiple Confederate monuments, as do the dramatic landscapes of memory at Magnolia Cemetery in Charleston, Metairie Cemetery in New Orleans, and Hollywood Cemetery in Richmond.

Confederate monuments enjoy a dominance in southern commemoration that far exceeds the breadth of support the Confederacy achieved during its tumultuous existence. Very few monuments recall the white and black southerners who opposed the Confederacy. Kentucky, which supplied the Confederacy with only half as many white soldiers as it contributed to the Union and only about one-third as many total soldiers, dedicated 41 monuments to Confederate soldiers, three monuments to Union soldiers, and one monument to the soldiers of both sides between 1865 and 1920; another five monuments in national cemeteries typify the regional representation of Unionism as an alien force occupying scattered beachheads. Other border states and the secessionist states similarly present remarkable displays of Confederate solidarity. Even West Virginia, formed in resistance to the Confederacy, has more Confederate monuments than Union monuments.

Although they are important emblems of regional identity, Confederate monuments share enough of the values of their more numerous northern coun-

Lloyd Tilghman monument, Vicksburg, Miss., battlefield
(Walker Evans, photographer, Library of Congress [LC-USF-342-8083-A] Washington, D.C.)

terparts to have played an important part in fostering a culture of sectional reconciliation during the late 19th and early 20th centuries. Tacitly accepting the preservation of the United States, southern monuments rarely represent the Confederacy as a political movement that climaxed in disunion. William Lowndes Yancey, Robert Barnwell Rhett, Edmund Ruffin, and other prophets of secession did not receive the tributes that commemoration of the American Revolution awarded to Patrick Henry and Samuel Adams. Confederate monuments instead tell a story that begins in 1861. As in Union monuments, that story focuses overwhelmingly on soldiers, whom Confederate monuments usually salute for martial virtues, patriotic love of home, and devotion to perceived duty—qualities admired in the postwar North as well as the South. The monuments that describe Confederate ideology in more detail, usually in such terms as "constitutional liberty" or "states' rights," do not often maintain that reunion precluded the achievement of those ideals. To the contrary, many Confederate monument campaigns looked back not merely at the war but also at the end of Reconstruction and declared victory for "self-government." The white supremacism embodied by these monuments also drew the approval of northern majorities retreating from the wartime promise of black freedom and citizenship. The culture of sectional reconciliation was cemented at such events as the 1895 dedication of a Chicago monument to Confederate prisoners who died in the city, the 1914 dedication of the Confederate monument in Arlington National Cemetery, and the appearance of President Franklin D. Roosevelt at the 1936 dedication of the Lee Memorial in Dallas.

The strong resemblance between Confederate and Union monuments reflects this cultural overlap. As might be expected from the relative postwar wealth of the sections and their different patterns of art patronage, southern monuments tended to be less expensive and grand than northern monuments, but monument sponsors in both sections followed similar design principles. The most common design for soldiers monuments across North and South in the immediate aftermath of the war was an obelisk, later superseded by variations on the single-figure soldier statue that first appeared in the North during the 1860s. Monuments in larger communities such as Raleigh (1894) and Dallas (1897) featured soldier statues at the base of a shaft surmounted by a figure, which in the South was usually another soldier but in some places, such as Montgomery (1898), was the sort of allegorical figure more common in the North. In both sections, the soldiers in most statues stood in a rest position, though active stances became increasingly common after 1890.

Confederate monuments have in some other respects differed significantly from Union remembrances of the Civil War. Most obviously, southern monuments honor the side that lost the war. Historians of Confederate commemoration have disagreed about the extent to which Lost Cause ideology during the heyday of monument construction from 1865 to 1920 shared the emphasis on the regional experience of failure that William Faulkner, Allen Tate, Robert Penn Warren, C. Vann Woodward, and other writers would develop during and after the Southern Literary Renaissance. Public monuments tilt toward one side of this debate, for the military monument was less readily adaptable than such cultural forms as the religious sermon to appreciation of Confederate defeat as an illustration of human limitations. Some monuments did address these themes. The 90-foot-tall granite pyramid placed over the Confederate dead at Hollywood Cemetery, in Richmond, in 1869 was perhaps the most striking attempt to identify the Confederate defeat with the unchanging, mysterious human condition. William Henry Trescot's oft-quoted inscription for the monument in Columbia, S.C., (1879) was similarly solemn in its praise for the soldiers "who have glorified a fallen cause by the simple manhood of their lives, the patient endurance of suffering, and the heroism of death . . . and who, in the dark hours of imprisonment, in the hopelessness of the hospital, in the short, sharp agony of the field, found support and consolation in the belief that at home they would not be forgotten."

The more numerous later monuments less frequently identified failure as central to the Confederate legacy. Defeat echoed through these monuments primarily in the shrillness with which they celebrated the unmatched prowess, unsullied virtue, and holy cause of the Confederate soldier. For these works, the outcome of the war was incidental and even misleading. One popular inscription declared: "It is not in the power of mortals to command success / The Confederate Soldier did more—he deserved it." Though they emphasized triumph rather than tragedy, the Lost Cause monuments installed throughout the region could not help but remind thoughtful white southerners of a history at odds with American narratives of success.

Consistent with the disproportionate suffering of the soldiers they honored, Confederate monuments lingered longer than Union monuments on the theme of death. In the North, new monuments dedicated to all soldiers who had served in the Civil War began during the 1880s to outnumber new monuments dedicated to the dead. In the South, the same transition did not take place until the first decade of the 20th century. A similar pattern might be observed in monument designs. The single-figure soldier statue replaced the funereal obelisk as the most common Civil War monument design in the North during the 1880s but not in the South until the 1890s. The location of monuments provided the starkest regional contrast in mourning practices. Communities in the Northeast placed the majority of Civil War monuments at noncemetery sites from an early stage. In the South, about three-quarters of all monuments dedicated before 1890 were placed in cemeteries. When the region turned to installation of monuments on town sites, however, it did so emphatically. About seven-eighths of Confederate monuments dedicated from 1900 to 1919 were located outside cemeteries.

Beyond these differences within the sets of Confederate and Union monuments, the full sets expanded at separate paces. Union monuments began to appear during the war and proliferated steadily afterward. In contrast, more than two-thirds of Confederate monuments in place by 1920 were unveiled in the 20th century. The distance of these initiatives from the war years serves as a reminder that Confederate monuments, like other forms of collective memory, were not a simple, immediate response to the events they commemorated but an instrument through which white southerners negotiated the tensions of their age. Veneration of Confederate heroes provided legitimation for the consolidation of Democratic hegemony and the Jim Crow regime and a cultural anchor amid the changes associated with the acceleration of industrialization and urbanization.

The gender dynamics in the construction of Confederate monuments were particularly distinctive. White southern women assumed commemorative leadership earlier and exercised it more fully than northern women. Ladies Memorial Associations, often formed by members of wartime soldiers' aid societies, directed the reburial of the Confederate dead in special sections of southern cemeteries and raised funds for monuments they commissioned. Women's leadership in commemoration also ranged beyond cemeteries to the centers of towns, including many of the major cities of the South. Unlike northern women, who rarely initiated large-scale Civil War monuments, white southern women sponsored the principal memorials in such places as Augusta (1878), Columbia (1879), Jackson (1891), and Louisville (1895), as well as figuring prominently in the making of the Lee Monument in Richmond (1890). The coordination of these activities moved beyond the local level in 1894 with the formation of the United Daughters of the Confederacy (UDC), through which the postwar generation of white southern women organized the major phase of monument construction. In addition to UDC chapters' sponsorship of local monuments across the South, the UDC conducted regionwide campaigns for the Jefferson Davis Monument in Richmond (1907), the Confederate Monument at Arlington National Cemetery (1914), and the monument to Confederate soldiers at Shiloh (1917). Beginning in the 1890s white southern women also became the subjects of their own Confederate monuments. Although an effort to place a tribute to Confederate women on the grounds of every southern statehouse splintered, most former Confederate capitols did put up a monument, as did other communities. Very few northern monuments parallel this celebration of women of the Civil War.

Dedications of Confederate monuments were for several decades among the most important rituals of southern memory. The unveiling of the Jefferson Davis Monument in Richmond drew a crowd estimated to be as large as 200,000 people. The carefully choreographed exercises at such ceremonies envisioned a model of the southern social order. After dedication, monuments framed stages on which everyday life took place against the backdrop of the Confederate legacy. A variety of literary works dramatize the resonance that Confederate monuments thereby added to southern communities. In William Faulkner's

The Sound and the Fury (1929), for example, the lead character, Benjy, depends on the soldier statue in the central square of Jefferson to maintain his precarious sense of orientation and composure while traveling in town.

Construction of Confederate monuments outside battlefield parks dwindled with the broader decline of public monuments in the 1920s. Although major Civil War monuments continued to be erected in the South later than in the North, Confederate commemoration increasingly shifted to new forms such as highways named for Jefferson Davis and Robert E. Lee, movies such as *Birth of a Nation* (1915) and *Gone with the Wind* (1939), and, more recently, the re-enactment of encampments and battles. But the Confederate monument remains conspicuous in the symbolic landscape of the South. That prominence has been challenged by several attempts to remove or recontextualize Confederate monuments, most notably the 1996 addition to Monument Avenue of a statue honoring tennis champion Arthur Ashe, a black Richmond native who had protested racism. Although civic monuments have less often been the focus of the debate over Confederate commemoration than the names of public institutions and state displays of the Confederate battle flag, it remains to be seen whether all of the bronze and stone soldiers of the Confederacy have fought their last battle.

THOMAS BROWN
University of South Carolina

David W. Blight, *Race and Reunion: The Civil War in American Memory* (2001); Thomas J. Brown, *The Public Art of Civil War Commemoration: A Brief History with Documents* (2004); Gaines M. Foster, *Ghosts of the Confederacy: Defeat, the Lost Cause, and the Emergence of the New South* (1987); Kirk Savage, *Standing Soldiers, Kneeling Slaves: Race, War, and Monument in Nineteenth-Century America* (1997); Charles Reagan Wilson, *Baptized in Blood: The Religion of the Lost Cause, 1865–1920* (1980).

Debutantes

The social institution known as the debutante season is certainly not a peculiarly southern (or even American) phenomenon, but in the face of the turbulent 1960s and 1970s, it exhibited more tenacity and vitality in Dixie than elsewhere in the United States or in Great Britain, where the custom began. A number of factors help explain the custom's popularity: the South's pride in its womanhood, a tendency to keep women on a pedestal, a conservative clinging to venerable institutions, the persistence of social distinctions by status, and a belief in a Cavalier heritage.

Although many societies, both primitive and advanced, have had their own rituals to signal the coming of age of men and women, England's Queen Elizabeth I supposedly began the custom of formal presentations of eligible young women at court. However, nearly three centuries later, Great Britain's young Queen Victoria, shortly after she married Prince Albert, gave the ritual much of its present form, when the daughters of the rising haute bourgeoisie of the Industrial Revolution began to be included in court presentations, along with those of the nobility and gentry. A century later, yet another British queen, Elizabeth II, ended such events after the last presentations in March of 1958.

The custom of debutante presentations spread across the Atlantic when America began to prosper during the late 19th-century Gilded Age. In New York, according to social historian Cleveland Amory, public presentations began in 1870 at Delmonico's. Dixon Wecter wrote 50 years ago how the costly rituals of debutante presentations symbolized the wealth of fathers. On the other hand, in the impoverished postwar South the custom displayed another dimension—emphasizing who had been well born before all was "gone with the wind." The criterion was necessarily not one of wealth but of the family's antebellum status and lineage.

At the beginning of the 20th century the most exclusive of the southern debutante seasons was held in Charleston. The St. Cecilia Society began in 1737 as America's first concert society but abandoned that function by 1822 and became a purely social organization. This elite all-male society began to sponsor what has been termed "the ultimate debutante presentation in the South, if not the whole United States." It is so proper and exclusive that any local publicity about either the society or its ball is taboo.

In Montgomery, Ala., Lila Matthews was presented to society with a dance and collation at her parents' house in 1884. The 1900 *Social Directory of Montgomery, Alabama* listed 33 debutantes, and the Montgomery Debutante Club began in the depths of the Depression in 1931. Today, young women of Montgomery society are presented at junior, senior, and debutante assemblies and at mystic society balls. Most notable of these are the New Year's Eve Ball given by the men of the Mystic Order of Revelry, the Mardi Gras Ball of the male Krewe of the Phantom Host, and the ball of the female Mystic Order of Minerva, where debutantes are presented in pastel Victorian court dress with plumes, trains, 18-button gloves, and fan bouquets. There are also presentations of military officers' daughters at nearby Maxwell Air Force Base, and since 1970 Montgomery's black debutantes have been sponsored by the local chapter of the national black teachers' sorority Phi Delta Kappa, founded in 1923.

In Mobile, where mystic societies in America began, the season's leading debutante is queen of Mardi Gras, and she and King Felix III salute merrymakers from the Athelstan Club. Each season's debutantes are presented first at the Camellia Ball at Thanksgiving time. In New Orleans, which is synonymous with Mardi Gras, debutantes reign over the predominantly all-male Krewe festivities and are presented at the Debutante Club and Les Débuts des Jeunes Filles de la Nouvelle Orléans and many private debut parties.

Space permits only a limited listing of the debutante balls in other southern cities. Baltimore has its Bachelors' Cotillion; Washington, D.C., has its Debutante Cotillion and Thanksgiving Ball; Richmond has the Bal du Bois in June at the Country Club of Virginia; and the all-male Norfolk German Society selects those who will come out in that city. Raleigh's Terpsichorean Club stages the North Carolina Debutante Cotillion; Savannah features the Cotillion and Parents' Debutante Ball; Atlanta has its Halloween Ball at the Piedmont Driving Club; and Jacksonville has its Presentation Ball at the Florida Yacht Club.

In Birmingham the Redstone Club Christmas Ball is at the Birmingham Country Club and the Beaux Arts Ball at the Mountain Brook Country Club. The Mississippi Debutante Ball is in Jackson, while the Delta Debutante Ball is at the Greenville Country Club. In Memphis the Queen of Cotton Carnival reigns, and there is a ball at the Hunt and Polo Club. Texarkana has the Cotillion Club Ball, San Antonio the German Club Ball, and Austin the Bachelors Cotillion. Dallas has its Idlewild Ball, where debutantes bow to the floor in all white at the beginning of the season and its Terpsichorean Ball, where they make their final bow in pastels.

CAMERON FREEMAN NAPIER
Montgomery, Alabama

D. Susan Barron, *Sunday New York Times Magazine* (15 January 1984); Stephen Birmingham, *The Right People: A Portrait of the American Social Establishment* (1968); Lisa Birnbach, ed., *The Official Preppy Handbook* (1980); Bethany Bultman, *Town and Country* (November 1977); Michaele Thurgood Haynes, *Dressing Up Debutantes: Pageantry and Glitz in Texas* (1998); Karal Ann Marling, *Debutante: Rites and Rituals of American Debdom* (2004); *Montgomery Advertiser* (6 February 1884, 4 November 1931, 15 April 1984); Cameron Freedman Napier, *Social Register Observer* (Summer 1998); Mary Ann Neeley, *Alabama Review* (April 1979); *New York Times* (19 March 1958, 21 March 1958); Dixon Wecter, *The Saga of American Society: A Record of Social Aspiration, 1607–1937* (1937).

Etiquette of Race Relations in the Jim Crow South

In "The Ethics of Living Jim Crow," black novelist and autobiographer Richard Wright described the "ingenuity" required of black southerners who wanted "to keep out of trouble" with whites. "It is a southern custom that all men must take off their hats when they enter an elevator," Wright explained. "And especially did this apply to us blacks with rigid force." Unable to remove his hat in an elevator one day because his arms were full of packages, Wright faced two white men who stared at him "coldly." Finally, one of the men took off Wright's hat and placed it on top of his packages. "Now the most accepted response for a Negro to make under such circumstances is to look at the white man out of the corner of his eye and grin," Wright wrote. "To have said: 'Thank you!' would have made the white man *think* that you *thought* you were receiving from him a personal service. For such an act I have seen Negroes take a blow in the mouth. Finding the first alternative distasteful, and the second dangerous, I hit upon an acceptable course of action which fell safely between these two poles. I immediately—no sooner than my hat was lifted—pretended that my packages were about to spill, and appeared deeply distressed with keeping them in my arms. In this fashion I evaded having to acknowledge his service, and, in spite of adverse circumstances, salvaged a slender shred of personal pride."

Many autobiographers, historians, and other observers have commented on the customs that guided day-to-day encounters between blacks and whites in the Jim Crow South. Like Wright, they have noted that the definition of good manners depended on one's race, that there were "accepted responses" for blacks in interacting with whites and vice versa, and that rules of appropriate behavior applied to blacks with especially rigid force. Increasingly, this "etiquette of race relations" has attracted the attention of scholars interested in its purpose and effects, as well as its significance to historical interpretations of the Jim Crow era.

Among the first and most influential of these scholars was sociologist Bertram Wilbur Doyle, author of an often-cited 1937 book titled *The Etiquette of Race Relations in the South: A Study in Social Control*. Doyle outlined customary forms of deference and paternalism between slaves and masters in the Old South, and then offered myriad examples of how these practices continued, with some alteration, up to his own day. He also emphasized, and indeed encouraged, blacks' "adjustment" to unjust social relations to a degree that seems difficult to comprehend given that he was himself a black southerner. However, Doyle was also a student of pioneering sociologist Robert E. Park at the University of Chicago and, according to Gary D. Jaworski, believed in a "race relations cycle" delineated by Park and his colleague Ernest W. Burgess, in which accommodation was a step toward inevitable, if gradual, assimilation, while any evidence of conflict between the races signified a lack of progress. Doyle recognized that blacks' performance of humility could be insincere, a matter of survival rather than belief. But his model provided very little room for theorizing black resistance.

Although more recent scholars have not adequately addressed the question of continuity vs. change in racial etiquette and have almost universally disagreed with Doyle's portrayal of black southerners as fully accommodated to racism, they have frequently adopted the word "etiquette" and drawn on Doyle's work (as well as that of John Dollard, Hortense Powdermaker, Allison Davis, Charles S. Johnson, and other Depression era social scientists) to detail the codes that governed interpersonal relations between blacks and whites under Jim Crow. In brief, these codes required blacks to *demonstrate* their subordination and supposedly natural inferiority, while whites demonstrated white supremacy. For example, whites denied blacks common courtesies, above all the titles "Mr.," "Mrs.," and "Miss," while insisting that blacks be polite, respectful, and even cheerful toward whites at all times. In addition to using racial epithets and calling blacks of all ages by their first names, white southerners often substituted generic names such as "George" or "Suzy," "boy" or "girl," or the somewhat more respectful (from the white point of view) "uncle" or "aunt." White men did not tip their hats to blacks, including black women, and to shake hands with a black person was a self-conscious gesture denoting unusual intimacy or noblesse oblige. Blacks, on the other hand, were expected to tip or remove their hats in whites' presence, step out of whites' way on sidewalks, and enter white homes only by the back door. In some communities, whites' demands for precedence even extended to the roadways, making it perilous for a black driver to pass a white one. Blacks could also expect to be kept waiting in stores rather than being helped on a first-come-first-served basis, and many stores that relied on black customers refused to allow them to try on hats, gloves, and other articles of clothing because to do so would make the items unfit to sell to whites.

As this prohibition illustrates, racial etiquette distinguished not only between dominant and subordinate, but also between pure and impure, embodying the principle that, as Mary Douglas explained in her classic *Purity and Danger*, dirt is "essentially disorder" or "matter out of place" and thus can be threatening to the social order itself. "The most important of all rules of purity involved sexual contact," historian J. William Harris adds, noting that "sexual contact between black men and white women was an extraordinary symbolic threat precisely because it occurred at the point where systems of race and gen-

Sign at a bus station, Rome, Ga., 1953 (Esther Bubley, photographer,
Library of Congress, [LC-USW-3-37393-E], Washington, D.C.)

der intersected in the southern cultural matrix." Within this matrix, whites
sometimes perceived little distance between the breaking of one taboo and the
breaking of another; thus, prohibitions against blacks and whites eating and
drinking together on a basis of equality were upheld with almost as much force
as prohibitions against interracial sex. (And both prohibitions were nonetheless also breached, as much recent scholarship on interracial sex in the South
indicates.)

"All told, this was a social code of forbidding complexity," historian Neil
McMillen summarizes. Not only local customs but also individual whites' expectations could vary, yet blacks had to try to anticipate what was expected of
them. Failure to do so could result in a verbal rebuke, a beating, or even ar-
rest and imprisonment or lynching. For all of its capriciousness, however, racial

etiquette was "anything but irrational." As McMillen explains, "If violence was the 'instrument in reserve' — the ultimate deterrent normally used only against the most recalcitrant — social ritual regulated day-to-day race relations." Racial etiquette "assured white control without the need for more extreme forms of coercion."

Like McMillen, other historians, including Jacquelyn Dowd Hall, David R. Goldfield, and Leon F. Litwack, have wisely emphasized the role of violence in maintaining racial etiquette as an everyday form of social control. Important essays by J. William Harris and Jane Dailey have reiterated this connection but also theorized racial etiquette at a deeper level. Arguing that "race" is "a matter of culture; it is part of a system of meanings," Harris understands racial etiquette as not merely reflective of racial power relations, but as constitutive of "race" itself. Dailey is most interested in blacks' everyday forms of resistance and the extent to which blacks' and whites' shared recognition of what civil behavior was and what it meant allowed "the discourse of civility itself" to become "a primary mode of confrontation" for blacks and whites in street-level encounters. Dailey also notes parallels between post–Civil War practices of racial etiquette and older notions of "honor" that, as Bertram Wyatt-Brown and other historians have argued, had long been dear to white southerners, especially men.

Focusing on racial etiquette can result in valuable insights about the "public transcript" of white dominance. Recognizing that racial etiquette and other "vertical" and largely face-to-face forms of domination continued to operate in white households, on farms, and in urban spaces such as stores and sidewalks that were difficult to regulate, Jennifer Ritterhouse argues that the "horizontal" system of segregation has occupied too prominent a place in historical scholarship. Although both legal and customary forms of white supremacy were important, it was largely the continued salience of racial etiquette that allowed the majority of white southerners to convince themselves that white supremacy was "natural" rather than violently and governmentally enforced. Considering the significant role that racial etiquette played in white children's racial socialization (and, in an oppositional mode, in black children's as well), Ritterhouse also sheds light on the social reproduction of the South's racial culture and on women's, especially mothers', very important contributions to patterns of domination and resistance.

Used with care, the notion of an "etiquette of race relations" can reveal a great deal about southern culture. Nevertheless, as Richard Wright's explanation of how he "salvaged a slender shred of personal pride" indicates, blacks were able to keep their emotional distance from the demands of racial etiquette and, despite the ever-present threat of violence, often refused to provide the "accepted responses" that Jim Crow customs required.

JENNIFER RITTERHOUSE
Utah State University

Jane Dailey, *Journal of Southern History* (August 1997); Allison Davis, Burleigh B. Gardner, and Mary R. Gardner, *Deep South: A Social Anthropological Study of Caste and Class* (1941); John Dollard, *Caste and Class in a Southern Town* (1937); Mary Douglas, *Purity and Danger: An Analysis of Concepts of Pollution and Taboo* (1966); Bertram Wilbur Doyle, *The Etiquette of Race Relations in the South: A Study in Social Control* (1937); David R. Goldfield, *Black, White, and Southern: Race Relations and Southern Culture, 1940 to the Present* (1990); Jacquelyn Dowd Hall, *Revolt Against Chivalry: Jessie Daniel Ames and the Women's Campaign Against Lynching* (1979; rev. ed., 1993); J. William Harris, *American Historical Review* (April 1995); Gary D. Jaworski, *Sociological Inquiry* (May 1996); Charles S. Johnson, *Patterns of Negro Segregation* (1941); Leon F. Litwack, *Trouble in Mind: Black Southerners in the Age of Jim Crow* (1998); Neil R. McMillen, *Dark Journey: Black Mississippians in the Age of Jim Crow* (1989); Hortense Powdermaker, *After Freedom: A Cultural Study in the Deep South* (1939); Jennifer Ritterhouse, *Growing Up Jim Crow: How Black and White Southern Children Learned Race* (2006); James C. Scott, *Domination and the Arts of Resistance: Hidden Transcripts* (1990); Richard Wright, *Uncle Tom's Children* (1936); Bertram Wyatt-Brown, *The Shaping of Southern Culture: Honor, Grace, and War, 1760s–1880s* (2001), *Southern Honor: Ethics and Behavior in the Old South* (1982).

Family

People in the South sometimes like to claim that an attachment to family, or even a sense of family, is an important regional trait, but their definitions of family vary so widely that it is clear the concept has far different meanings for different people. Perhaps the best generalization is that people in the South have often used the concept of the family to think and argue — and have sometimes used it to fight — about who they are and want to be. To some southerners, family means a group of people one sees at reunions or holiday dinners and honors in cemeteries or pictures on mantles; to others, family means an expectation of sharing work and resources and the goal of living up to the family name; to still others, family has to do with frustrations about wrongs handed down through the generations. To many, but far from all, people in the South, family seems a nearly permanent relationship, although the nature of that relationship has changed over southern history.

In the 1600s and 1700s, different groups of southerners faced new challenges to their understandings of family life, and many responded by adapting to dramatically new definitions of family. New mixings of people, uneven gender ratios, new household and work situations, new insecurities about but also new hopes for the possibilities of frontier life, new health conditions, and the drastic changes involved in colonial slavery all tested older definitions of family among Native Americans, Africans, and Europeans in the colonial South.

Most Native American tribes in the South practiced matrilineal kinship patterns, in which property and family name passed down through the female line. The demographic disasters of the colonial period, along with the new realities of intermingling with Europeans and, for some, the adoption of new notions of private property, all challenged those traditional kinship patterns.

English colonists from Virginia to South Carolina faced new challenges as well. Poor health conditions complicated family relationships, and many children were raised by a series of step-parents and foster parents. Wealthier English colonists hoped that economic success in America might set them up to live as English gentlemen, with land and wealth for a long line of descendants. One reason wealthy Anglo-Caribbean planters moved to South Carolina was to escape the even worse disease environment of the Caribbean that made it difficult to build up family dynasties. Many despaired of the unsettled nature of the colonial South, especially in the 1600s, but others such as William Byrd II of Virginia began to imagine his plantation as a setting in which family successfully extended to all of his dependents. Byrd wrote in 1726, "I have a large family of my own and my doors are open to every body. . . . Like one of the patriarchs, I have my flocks and my herds, my bond-men and bond-women, and every sort of trade amongst my own servants, so that I live in a kind of independence on every one, but Providence."

Ripped from their African homelands, slaves faced dramatic demographic challenges and the central reality that they could not organize their family lives as they wished. Learning new languages, confronting new health problems, and facing the threat of sale meant reinventing some aspects of family life.

Issues of race became crucial to definitions of family early in southern history, when people used parentage to identify some people as white, and deserving of certain privileges, and to call other people nonwhite, with certain clear disadvantages. Colonial legislatures passed laws in the 1660s that made the racial identity of a child dependent on the identity of the mother. This had numerous consequences, most obviously confining a number of children to slavery and creating tension over the obligations of people related to each other by biology but not by family name, affection, or sense of responsibility.

In the antebellum period some groups of southerners began to carve out distinctive regional definitions of the family. Most obviously, political and intellectual leaders, in part in response to the abolitionist movement, claimed that the South had developed a form of paternalism that made fatherly kindness and control a key to organizing a humane society. From the 1830s through the 1850s, with the rise of a British and northeastern middle class that idealized motherly affection, valued smaller families, and separated home from work, many abolitionists condemned slavery for separating slave families and allowing owners to have unchecked sexual control over slaves. Upper-class southerners responded that the antebellum South was based on paternalism, an old ideal with a newly professional and Christian face. Slave owners who wrote in their diaries about "my family, white and black" claimed that they considered all of their dependents to be part of their extended household, and that they loved them and punished them all to fit into their proper stations in life. Paternalism did not idealize motherly affection in the same way northeastern family ideals tended to do; paternalists claimed that both fathers and mothers had roles in alternating affection with discipline.

The other family image developing into a southern ideal was that of the yeoman male, who valued independence from the control of anyone as a central goal. Yeomen shared with paternalists the goal of controlling dependent laborers, but most of those dependents were wives and children. Yeoman families remained large long after middle-class family size outside the South began to decline. The issues of the Civil War era—those related to slavery in the West, local control over laborers, and wartime taxation, impressments, and the draft —all offered challenges to yeomen's notions that they controlled what took place inside their own homes.

African Americans used notions of families under pressure as part of their call for an end to slavery. In some of the most memorable early scenes of his autobiography, Frederick Douglass described living for only a short time with his mother, not knowing his father (or who his father was), and living with continuing uncertainties about what constituted a household. Other narratives such as Harriet Jacobs's Incidents in the Life of a Slave Girl demonstrated intense commitments to staying with family members, especially children, under extraordinary pressure. African Americans developed an understanding of family that was adaptable, with fictive kin, informal adoption, and special importance for the role of elders.

After the Civil War, discussions of family often centered on either creating families or preserving them. During and after the war, African Americans faced the exhilarating possibilities of creating and controlling their own households. During and shortly after the Civil War, many ranged far to find family members from whom they had been separated by slavery and war. Many African Americans built on the adaptable, multigenerational understandings of family they had developed under slavery. Sharecropping and tenancy tended to encourage large families working together, hoping to produce independence through large crops and shared thrift. But poverty and racial segregation often put heavy pressures on African American family life, and rates of divorce and abandonment were high in the late 1800s and early 1900s. Author Richard Wright gave voice to both realities, celebrating family life while detailing its difficulties. In *Black Boy*, he created an image of a troubled family, where he hardly knew his father, and his grandmother and depressed mother tried to teach him the rules of segregation. On the other hand, he celebrated the communal interest in children in his *12 Million Black Voices*: "Some people wag their heads in amusement when they see our long lines of ragged children, but we love them. . . . Like black buttercups, our children spring up on the red soil of the plantations. When a new one arrives, neighbors from miles around come and look at it, speculating upon which parent it resembles."

White evangelicals developed their own version of the Victorian family, with mothers as central figures in teaching religious morality, but with the influences of male recreation and African Americans, rather than the northern and British Victorian fear of the harsh public worlds of work and politics, as the primary counterpoints. Most of the ways evangelicals defined sin seemed a violation of home and family. Dancing seemed frivolous and too fashionable for solid church folk, while drinking alcohol, gambling, and fighting were primarily male activities that involved competition to the point of a loss of self-control that violated expectations of family harmony. Surely one of the ugliest sides of southern conceptions of family life has been the recurring idea that African Americans posed threats to the home and family lives of whites, who in the late 1800s and early 1900s used family protection as justification for segregation, prohibition laws, and lynchings. African American evangelicals developed their own versions of respectability, calling for particular emphases on dignity and self-control that rejected accusations that their families did not teach those virtues.

White southerners' discussions of family also moved toward ancestor worship, with groups like the Daughters and then the Sons of Confederate Veterans taking central roles in defining how contemporary generations should venerate their ancestors. Along with ancestor worship, southerners in the 20th century often engaged in troubled love/hate relationships with their older family members. The works of William Faulkner, Lillian Smith, W. J. Cash, Robert Penn Warren, and others show people who imagined a great past, only to discover that greed, lies, and hypocrisy made a tragedy of what scholar Richard King has called "the family romance." Some of the idealizing of southern family life came from people who witnessed or feared the decline of farm life. Country musicians and southern writers such as the Vanderbilt Agrarians sang and wrote about responsibilities that transcended lines of generation and gender, and they feared those responsibilities and certainties were on the decline. Agrarianism balanced traditions of southern family life against modern movements toward individualism and argued that upholding family traditions held the only hope for the modern world.

Definitions of family again became objects of controversy during the civil rights movement. Supporters of civil rights, especially those inspired by religious commitments, frequently called on the concept of brotherhood, sometimes called the Brotherhood of Man under the Fatherhood of God, as the most important reason to oppose racial discrimination. Family thus seemed something flexible and useful in uniting people who faced similar challenges. On the other hand, opponents of the civil rights movement criticized "brotherhood-ism" as naive and said families with clear parental authority were the key to an orderly society.

Some African Americans, after generations of defending black families against charges of fragility or the absence of effective parents, began more than ever to celebrate a tradition of family flexibility. Many were offended by the 1965 report by Daniel Patrick Moynihan called *The Negro Family: A Case for National Action*, which blamed the persistence of African American poverty on a history of troubled family life, especially the absence of fathers as economic and personal contributors to family life. In the late 1960s and increasingly in the 1970s, many African American writers and political figures began to praise black family life for its adaptability, arguing that what had long seemed a weakness was in fact a strength in the ability of the black community to take care of many people outside a nuclear family structure. The most dramatic and popular example was Alex Haley's book *Roots* and the television series based upon it, which detailed generations of African Americans respecting, negotiating, and redefining—but always valuing—family life. More recently, African American authors, such as Joyce Ladner and Clifton Taulbert and child welfare leader Marian Wright Edelman, have used traditions of adaptable family life to offer how-to books for raising children.

Opponents of the civil rights movement condemned school desegregation for its potential to encourage white children to reject the example of their parents. Some of the more vocal opponents of civil rights claimed that school desegregation was all about sexual integration and worried that it would produce more mixed-race families. The Citizens' Council hailed the conclusions of the Moynihan Report as proof that African American families were in deep trouble and, therefore, that white children should stay away from black children.

Beginning in the late 1970s, the Religious Right made stern calls for a return to schools and homes with clear parental authority. The concept of family values, as newly voiced in the decade, said certain household arrangements were families and others were not. Moral Majority leader Jerry Falwell rejected the conclusions of a 1979 White House Conference that, as he wrote in *The New American Family*, "finally decided that any persons living together constituted a family." Arguing that such a definition sanctioned homosexuality, encouraged government day care programs, and did nothing to combat abortion, Falwell sided instead with the definition of the National Pro-Family Coalition that "a family consists of persons who are related by blood, marriage, or adoption." The American Family Association, emerging in the 1980s and led by Methodist minister Donald Wildmon of Tupelo, Miss., argued that a wide array of forces, especially in the media but also in the law and public education, were challenging parental control over what children believed about God, right and wrong, and the definition of the family.

People who claim that attachment to family is a distinctively southern attribute are most likely incorrect. Family has had too many connotations for a term such as "the southern family" to have much meaning. Perhaps the safest generalization one can make about contemporary southern family life is that problems and arguments over definition continue. Southern rates of single parenthood, poverty in female-headed households, and divorce are higher than the national average, but the South also seems to lead the nation in calls for a return to traditional family life.

TED OWNBY
University of Mississippi

Nancy Bercaw, *Gendered Freedoms: Race, Rights, and the Politics of Household in the Delta, 1861–1875* (2003); Kathleen M. Brown, *Good Wives, Nasty Wenches, and Anxious Patriarchs: Gender, Race, and Power in Colonial Virginia* (1996); Jerry Falwell, *The New American Family: The Rebirth of the American Dream* (1992); Elizabeth Fox-Genovese, *Within the Plantation Household: Black and White Women of the Old South* (1988); Eugene D. Genovese, *Roll, Jordan, Roll: The World the Slaves Made* (1974); Glenda Gilmore, *Gender and Jim Crow: Women and the Politics of White Supremacy in North Carolina, 1896–1920* (1996); Alex Haley, *Roots* (1976); Jacquelyn Dowd Hall et al., *Like a Family: The Making of a Southern Cotton Mill World* (1987); Winthrop D. Jordan, *White over Black: American Attitudes toward the Negro, 1550–1812*

(1968); Richard King, *A Southern Renaissance: The Cultural Awakening of the American South, 1930–1955* (1980); Ann Patton Malone, *Sweet Chariot: Slave Family and Household Structure in Nineteenth-Century Louisiana* (1992); Bill Malone, *Don't Get Above Your Raisin': Country Music and the Southern Working Class* (2002); Stephanie McCurry, *Masters of Small Worlds: Yeoman Households, Gender Relations, and the Political Culture of the Antebellum South Carolina Low Country* (1995); Daniel Patrick Moynihan, *The Negro Family: A Case for National Action* (1965); Ted Ownby, *Subduing Satan: Religion, Recreation, and Manhood in the Rural South, 1865–1920* (1990); Brenda E. Stevenson, *Life in Black and White: Family and Community in the Slave South* (1996); Stewart Tolnay, *The Bottom Rung: African American Family Life on Southern Farms* (1999); Richard Wright, *12 Million Black Voices* (1941).

Fashion

In the South, as in the rest of the nation, fashion serves a variety of functions. People pursue fashion because they seek meaning in their existence or a sense of personal identity. They may use fashion to enhance their social status or to demonstrate their affluence. Fashion also expresses the nature of society—its ideas, values, and roles. In a rapidly changing society, fashion is a form of control, offering people a particular direction out of the myriad possibilities. Fashion can also be used by people to facilitate change, as when women adopt a style that clearly rejects a traditional female role.

During the colonial and antebellum years, fashion both reflected and helped maintain the white southern way of life with its dominant planter class and its dependence upon England. The lavish, extravagant fashions of the upper class, in contrast to the homespun apparel of slaves and the white lower classes, reinforced the stratification of society. Inventories of clothing from the period reveal costly wardrobes of silk, satins, and laces for both males and females. Clothing and materials were imported from England and followed the latest London fashions. Most of the fashions, particularly those of women, were impractical, nonfunctional, and mainly decorative—the ideal apparel of an upper class that wanted to display its wealth and secure its status. For example, the hoopskirts of upper-class women in the 18th century could reach six feet in diameter. They were both inconvenient and costly, requiring yards of material. Shoes, available in bright colors and rich materials, were also useless for work or exercise. Perhaps the greatest impracticality and frivolousness was the fashion in hairstyles. The tower or commode arrangement had the hair piled high in rigid curls and puffs on a wire frame. The whole was intertwined with various ornaments. The elaborate hairstyles required a professional hairdresser and consumed extensive amounts of time. Consequently, arrangements were often made to last for weeks or even months, an unsanitary condition to say the least.

In the years leading up to the Civil War, fashion became an even greater factor in maintaining southern society. In response to rapid change, fragmentation, and challenge, the white South clung tenaciously to what it saw as the essence of its society—the planter's Cavalier tradition with its emphasis on aristocracy, stability, gentility, and honor. Women played a central role in this tradition. The southern woman, viewed as inferior by nature and thus subject to the domination of her husband, was nonetheless idealized as the possessor of higher morals and purity. As she kept her place and her purity, she played an important stabilizing force in a threatened society. And her fashions provided guidelines for what was acceptable behavior. The restricted functions and ornamental nature of upper-class women were accentuated—waistlines became smaller as corsets became tighter, petticoats became heavier, and skirts became longer and more cumbersome. Indeed, the symbol of the Cavalier tradition and southern chivalry was the pure, white female with her ever-present parasol to protect her pale complexion from the hot sun.

The decades following the Civil War witnessed a growing democratization in southern fashion. The hardships of war, to be sure, contributed to this. One traveler noted the decline in fashions and said that South Carolina was an excellent place to live for one who was forced to wear old clothes. The war also militated against the presumed uniqueness of the southern way of life and with it the system of rigid stratification. The realities of war, the impact of industrialization, the increased availability of ready-mades, sewing machines, inexpensive patterns, and dry goods all combined to eradicate the sharp class distinctions in fashion.

From the final decades of the 19th century to the present, the South has experienced trends in fashion that have characterized the entire nation. Hemlines have risen and fallen; waistlines have shifted, disappeared, and reappeared; areas of focus in women's fashions have moved from head to bosom to leg and back again; the modal type has moved from the "Gibson girl" to the "flapper" to the "New Look" and, ultimately, the "American Look." The American Look is characterized by egalitarianism, freedom, comfort, casualness, and action. These varied fashion trends have reflected and facilitated change toward an increasingly homogenized national lifestyle.

Southern blacks have adopted a number of noteworthy fashion traditions, based in a visual style that emphasizes bright colors and sometimes bold designs. The zoot suits of the 1940s, dashikis of the 1960s, and untied, high-top sneakers of the 1990s did not originate in the South, but many southern blacks adopted and popularized these styles. Black southern women helped make such African-derived ceremonial items as capes, turbans, caftans, and braided hair into modern fashion wear. In addition, African American women, who in the past were often in domestic service and were limited to uniforms during the week, began expressing their sense of identity and freedom by dressing well for church and other special occasions. Although the fashions have changed, this tradition continues to the present.

Although the American Look reigns supreme, local and sectional variations still exist. In part, variations are a practical response to differences in climate (differences that central heating and air-conditioning have minimized though not eliminated) and professional requirements (the fashion choices of a Georgia farmer's wife are very different from those of a female lawyer in Atlanta). But a good part of the variation arises from the more conservative traditions of the South.

The 19th-century view of woman and her role lingers among some segments of southern society. Consequently, many of the more radical fashion changes, which seem to threaten the virtue and place of women, have met with resistance. Religious leaders, newspaper editors, and public officials have openly denounced radical fashions, whether the slit skirt of 1913, the miniskirt of the 1960s, or the tight jeans and tattoos of the early 2000s. Fashions of this sort have been more slowly, and sometimes less widely, adopted in the South. The conservative tradition means that styles that are perfectly acceptable in most other parts of the nation may not be acceptable in areas of the South. For example, in some small-town and rural settings neither the local minister nor his wife may, with impunity, appear publicly in shorts. Nevertheless, with the exception of some women's fashions, and with due consideration for climatic differences and local moral codes, department stores in the South, especially the urban South, offer customers the same styles available in stores throughout the nation. Fashion serves the same functions for southerners as for the rest of Americans. For that reason, southerners are as fashion conscious as other Americans, though they may be a bit more cautious and discriminating.

JEANETTE C. LAUER
ROBERT H. LAUER
Alliant International University

Michael Batterberry and Ariane Batterberry, *Mirror, Mirror: A Social History of Fashion, 1900 to the Present* (1977); Linda Baumgarten, *What Clothes Reveal: The Language of Clothing in Colonial and Federal America* (2002); Herbert Blau, *Nothing in Itself: Complexions of Fashion* (1999); Clement Eaton, *The Growth of Southern*

Civilization, 1790–1860 (1961); Jeanette C. Lauer and Robert H. Lauer, *Fashion Power: The Meaning of Fashion in American Society* (1981); Belinda Orzada, *African American Dress in the 1980s and 1990s* (1998); Naomi Sims, *All about Health and Beauty for the Black Woman* (1976); Julia Cherry Spruill, *Women's Life and Work in the Southern Colonies* (1938).

Fatherhood

Historically, sharp divisions between males and females characterized family responsibilities in the South. The man was regarded as the unchallenged patriarch, the strong, respected provider, the mainstay of southern society. The traditional image of the chivalrous southerner, as opposed to the greedy Yankee, was centered in the southern father's devotion to family, tradition, and race; all these restrained the "natural man" that supposedly emerged in the Yankee. At the same time the South has often been celebrated as a region that stressed so-called masculine traits, a region demarcated by violence, hard-nosed football, stock car racing, a proclivity toward the military, and hawkish attitudes about war and foreign affairs. Yet, in literature and sometimes in actuality, it is often a Scarlett O'Hara or her mother who ends up running the plantation and the mill.

The patriarchal nature of the southern family has been attributed to slavery. Dependent upon slaves as producers of income, the family head, the southern father, had to maintain control of the peculiar institution, and attempts by family members to assert themselves against the head were thought to threaten slavery itself. As proslavery theorists justified the institution of slavery with every branch of knowledge, from the Bible to science, the rationale for the authority of the father in the household became increasingly the received wisdom of all southerners. Family, church, and community all reinforced patriarchy. Male dominance persisted in the political, cultural, religious, and economic spheres of the South.

Cotton ruled as king, not queen, in the South. In the early 20th century, powerful U.S. senator Ben Tillman used a South Carolina law allowing him to deed his grandchildren to himself, thus thwarting their mother's claim to custody. Except for a brief period during Reconstruction, not until after World War II was divorce legalized in South Carolina. Before child labor laws, southern children commonly worked in textile mills for a family wage, which was paid directly to the father. In the South the father was the family head, and considerable legal authority fortified his power.

Bertram Wyatt-Brown has shown that southerners venerated their male ancestors. Naming patterns in the South signified the importance of patriarchy.

The tendency to name children after male family elders remains strong in the South, where phone books today still show many juniors and thirds after a name. Although individualistic impulses were in some ways influential, duty to family and one's forebears was paramount. The southerner's respect for history and tradition was reinforced by his obedience to his forefathers.

The legendary southern father was much like the southern gentleman of myth: well-educated and genteel, with a firm and commanding personality, who demanded deference from all family members and from nonaristocratic whites. Thus, the myth of southern fatherhood has a distinct class bias. Eugene D. Genovese's brilliant work showing that slaves had room for cultural autonomy and arguing the patriarchal nature of slavery suggests that the hegemony of the planter class prevented lower-class whites and slaves from being patriarchs themselves. Other scholars, disagreeing, have demonstrated that the planters' status did not prevent less affluent white or slave males from reigning in their own families. Patriarchal values pervaded all levels of southern society and culture.

Popular literature, however, has characterized the lower-class white family as a disorderly one led by an irresponsible, lazy, drunken father. Thus, ironically, in the South, which supposedly counterpoints the North's emphasis on lucre, fatherly success was associated with financial success.

The father in the black family was generally believed to be absent or nonexistent. Studies of urban areas in the North have shown that racism in the occupational structure of modern society has made it difficult for African American men to get jobs in cities. Careful scrutiny of census and other demographic records shows that this is just as true of southern cities and even small towns and villages. Whereas towns and cities offered both protection and domestic jobs for black women, black men there were excluded from jobs other than those associated with farming. Hence, when sociologists studied black families in cities, they found males absent. In the rural South, however, where most blacks lived after slavery, landowning and tenant families were almost always headed by black men. White landowners were not willing to rent to female household heads unless they had nearly grown children to help in the fields. Thus, in the sparsely settled rural areas, not the cities where interviews and records were more easily available, scholars found the black patriarch ruling his family very much as did his white counterpart.

Scholars have some records suggesting how planter-class fathers treated their children. Fathers had intense but ambivalent feelings about their children. They lavished affection on them during infancy but were torn between their love for their children and their desire to see the children — especially the males — become independent. They might be terribly affectionate with the children one day and then completely out of sight the next. One fatherly technique was to alternate providing and withdrawing intimacy in order to teach discipline and right behavior; this technique internalized guilt and shame in the children.

Parents were seen as exemplars. The children were expected to emulate their parents and other worthy relatives as much as possible, to respect adults, and to follow their basic moral precepts. Although fathers sought to teach their children independence, they also wanted the children to learn that they were not so much individuals as extensions of their parents. Their every move, therefore, was not only an indication of their own goodness, but, just as important, a reflection of parental worthiness.

One of the most important aspects of behavior that southern fathers could teach their children was aggressiveness. Even young girls were encouraged to be aggressive. But, of course, boys, and particularly the eldest boy, were the focus of this assertiveness training. Many southern fathers thought children should be given freedom to explore their surroundings, thus gaining the confidence needed to assert themselves fully. Sometimes, however, fathers went too far and merely spoiled their children. This mistake could end tragically, with the sons of prominent men often leading short and dissolute lives.

A variety of father images have appeared in southern literature and music, suggesting other dimensions to the role of the father in regional life. Sometimes fathers, like mothers, are sentimentalized, as in the Jimmie Rodgers country songs of the 1930s, "Daddy and Home" and "That Silver-Haired Daddy of Mine." This reflected the long-lasting Victorian influence in the South. More recently, Beverly Lowry's novel *Daddy's Girl* (1981) offered a humorous look at one of the most important southern family relationships—father and daughter, an excessively loving, manipulative, and demanding relationship. The nurturing father is an equally strong image and shows the father passing down folk skills and wisdom to sons and daughters.

Fathers have also been portrayed in harsh terms. Religion has contributed a powerful father image: the father as the Calvinist God's patriarch on earth, the person ruling the southern household and the plantation with an iron fist. The father, to Joe Christmas in William Faulkner's *Light in August*, is a stern figure, always judging, ready to mete out justice to wayward children. The poverty of the postbellum and modern eras and the humiliation for blacks in the racial caste system have also shaped cultural attitudes toward fatherhood. One country song says father was "a farmer but all he ever raised was us." The sharecropping father is seen as frustrated, unable to provide a good life for his family.

Richard Wright's harsh portrait of his father in *Black Boy* is an extreme version of this, but Alex Haley's *Roots* gives images of warm, loving, and strong black fathers.

The sociological study of fatherhood is relatively new, and as yet there is little reliable information on regional differences in attitudes toward fathering, the degree of involvement of fathers in child care, or parental authority patterns. In married-couple families with children present, southern fathers have already experienced marked changes in their sole responsibility as breadwinners during the last several decades because over half of their wives work outside the home. In the South, as elsewhere in the nation, the number of divorced fathers who have either sole or joint custody of their children is rising. Increasingly, fathers are emphasizing their nurturant roles, though social class differences, among others, still shape views about fathers as the authority figure in families.

Economic conditions dramatically affect the possibilities of the father's role in African American communities. By the mid-1990s, the growing economic divergence of black families became clear. About one-third were prospering, with married couples the most typical arrangement. Only 7 percent of African American families of married couples lived in poverty in 1998. But a third of the nation's African American families were the working poor and an underclass found in northern cities and in the rural South. African American families headed by females had a poverty rate of 41 percent. The sheer unavailability of African American men became a notable social problem in the 1990s. High unemployment rates and relatively high incarceration rates, as well as higher mortality rates for black men compared to black women, have contributed to a weakened role of father in underclass families.

Literary critic Richard King argues that the intellectuals and writers of the Southern Literary Renaissance in the 20th century were attempting symbolically to define their relationship with the region's "fathers." He notes the portraits of the "heroic generation" of ex-Confederates, the pictures of "stern, untroubled, and resolute" fathers that hung in southern parlors. Ironic sons and strong fathers have been predominant images in modern southern literature. Allen Tate explored this theme in his one novel, entitled *The Fathers*. Jack Burden in Robert Penn Warren's *All the King's Men* searches for an understanding of his — and through him, the region's — past by defining a complex relationship to his father, both real and figuratively (in Willie Stark). William Faulkner seemed fascinated with the father, portraying ruthless, sometimes cruel patriarchs such as Thomas Sutpen, Carothers McCaslin, and the older Sartoris. These powerful figures succeed yet eventually, through self-centered pride, are brought to earth. Sutpen's downfall, in particular, comes from his failure to acknowledge his son because the son has black blood; issues of race are tied with fatherhood, as in other areas of southern life.

ORVILLE VERNON BURTON
University of Illinois

Andrew Billingsley, *Climbing Jacob's Ladder: The Enduring Legacy of African American Families* (1992); Orville Vernon Burton, *In My Father's House Are Many Mansions: Family and Community in Edgefield, South Carolina* (1985); Jane Turner Censer, *North Carolina Planters and Their Children, 1800–1860* (1984); Richard H. King, *A Southern Renaissance: The Cultural Awakening of the American South, 1930–1955* (1980); Daniel Blake Smith, *Inside the Great House: Planter Family Life in Eighteenth-Century Chesapeake Society* (1980); Bertram Wyatt-Brown, *Southern Honor: Ethics and Behavior in the Old South* (1982).

Fighting South

Few dimensions of southern cultural distinctiveness have provoked more comment than the supposed proclivity of Dixie's citizenry toward personal and societal violence. Prior to the Civil War numerous European and northern travelers reported from the slave states that the southern people enjoyed soldiering and resolved interpersonal disputes with violence to an unusual degree. Twentieth-century scholars substantiated this impression, meticulously delineating antebellum southern enthusiasm for wars, the national military establishment, private military academies, filibustering, dueling, and a wide array of other activities indicative of a peculiarly martial/violent regional temperament. The South's martial reputation survived Civil War defeat, won endorsement in the Lost Cause legend, and gained new vitality in the 20th century. It has been a popular concept that southerners have monopolized the army's officer corps, provided disproportionate support for America's role in both world wars and in Vietnam, perpetuated martial instincts with military titles and military preparatory schools, and enshrined violence (high homicide rates, the Ku Klux Klan) within their social mores.

Some recent commentators would relegate unique southern militarism to the realm of myth. The North, it has been discovered, also fostered a plethora of antebellum military academies and volunteer militia companies. Emphasis has been placed upon violence as an American problem rather than as a regional trait. Still, the South's fighting fame persists, encouraged by a tendency of southerners themselves to claim a special military heritage.

If myth, southern militarism has nonetheless been an operative fiction with

The Alamo, a shrine of the fighting South, San Antonio, Tex.
(Library of Congress [LC-USZ62-87798], Washington, D.C.)

considerable impact upon the region's historical experience. Pre–Civil War antislavery capitalized upon perceptions of an aggressive, violent "Slave Power." A mistaken faith that southerners—by virtue of their military traditions— would prove superior to northerners on the battlefield explains much of the risk-taking intrinsic to secession. In the Civil War northern stereotypes of southern warrior propensities retarded the progress of Union army campaigns. Recent evidence of the myth's substantive impact is more elusive, but when President Jimmy Carter in 1980 attributed his commitment to strategic arms limitation to a recognition that his native region had traditionally venerated "the nobility of courage on the battlefield," thus inducing southerners to lead "the rolls of volunteers and also . . . the rolls of casualties" in America's wars, he gave testimony to a lingering influence of perceptions of southern militarism upon the nation's history.

ROBERT E. MAY
Purdue University

Michael C. C. Adams, *Our Masters the Rebels: A Speculation on Union Military Failure in the East, 1861–1865* (1978); F. N. Boney, *Midwest Quarterly* (Winter 1980);

David Goldfield, *Still Fighting the Civil War: The American South and Southern History* (2002); Robert E. May, *Historian* (February 1978).

Fraternal Groups

Fraternal organizations have long been an important part of the social life of southern communities, large and small. Beginning with the introduction of Freemasonry in the colonial era, the spirit of fraternalism grew after the Civil War to support the Sons of Temperance, Good Templars, Red Men, Woodmen of the World, Knights of Pythias, Odd Fellows, Grangers, Masons, and others. Blacks in the region had separate, distinctive fraternal groups that were nonetheless closely related to white groups in style and significance. Patriotic societies such as the United Daughters of the Confederacy, the United Confederate Veterans, and the Sons and Daughters of the American Revolution were based on race and ancestry and thrived in the tradition-oriented South. The region had fewer immigrant societies, such as the Ancient Order of Hibernians and the Sons of Italy, because of the proportionately smaller number of immigrants in the region. The Knights of Columbus was a popular organization among southern Catholics. The Ku Klux Klan represented many things, and narrowly defined secretive fraternalism was one of them. "The elaborate ceremonies and rituals, colorful costumes, and mysterious titles helped members escape the humdrum aspects of their daily lives," concluded historian John S. Ezell. In the 20th century, service organizations such as the Kiwanis, Rotary, Lions, and Service International clubs emerged as middle-class, business-oriented versions of fraternalism.

The Masonic order is the oldest and most extensive fraternal society in the Western world. Coming mainly from Britain and to a lesser degree from France, Freemasonry makes use of symbols and allegories derived from the craft guilds of the Middle Ages. It preaches the universal virtues of friendship, morality, truth, charity, and prudence. It does not permit discussions of religion and politics within its temples. Consequently it has surmounted many difficulties associated with those topics, even during the period of American fratricidal strife in the 1860s.

The Masonic order has two rites, commonly called York and Scottish, which allow for advancement in their particular teachings. The individual local lodge is governed by a Grand Lodge, which generally follows state lines and is sovereign within its jurisdiction. Although the two rites are international, they remain subordinate to their respective Grand Lodges. Masonry is secret only in certain salutations and dramatic rituals. Otherwise its membership, times and

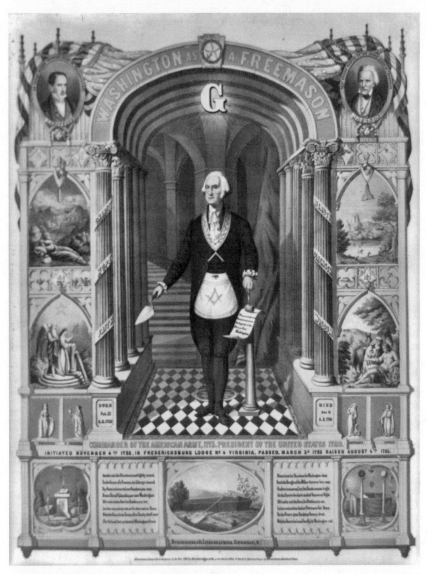

George Washington as a freemason, c. 1867
(Library of Congress, [LC-USZ62-4667], Washington, D.C.)

places of meeting, and organization are well known. As an organization, the Masonic order seldom, however, appears in public, except at the laying of the cornerstone of a building or at graveside ceremonies for its deceased members.

Attached to the lodge and its rites are bodies like the Shrine, Order of the Demolay (for boys), Order of the Rainbow (for girls), and Order of the Eastern Star (largely female). An adopted southerner, Rob Morris, originally from Massachusetts, founded the Eastern Star in the 1850s at the "Little Red Schoolhouse" — now known around the world as a sacred spot to members of the group — at Richland in Holmes County, Miss. He wrote many of the manuals and originated the rituals still in use in the group.

In most states, Masonic lodges maintain homes to provide care for orphans, the aged, and the infirm. The Shrine has hospitals that specialize in treatment of crippled children and burn victims. Knights Templar, the peak of the York Rite, offers funds for treatment of correctable eye maladies; the Scottish Rite provides funds for the treatment of aphasia and also scholarships for students of political science.

The term "lodge" is also applied to the structure where Masons meet. Often in the past such a building was owned jointly by the Masons and a church, a school, or a business firm. More recently, however, the building typically is owned and used only by the order. The architecture varies from a simple, unobtrusive frame or brick structure to a pretentious edifice adorned with columns and exotic representations. But regardless of size or ornamentation, the lodge has been a center of unity for vast segments of the southern male population, Jew and Gentile alike.

The Masonic order that came to the South during the colonial era was derived mostly from the York Rite. Operating in the three basic degrees of "Blue Lodge" Masonry, these early York Rite lodges received their charters mainly from the Grand Lodges of either England or Scotland. The other primary Masonic movement in the colonial South was the Scottish Rite, which was introduced from either France or the West Indies.

Among the first of the early colonial lodges comprising the Provincial Grand Lodge of Virginia (where Masonry was introduced as early as 1729) were the Royal Exchange Lodge 172, established at Norfolk under an English charter in 1733, and Kilwinning Port Royal Cross Lodge, formed under a Scottish Charter in 1730. Elsewhere in the colonial South, first lodges were chartered in North Carolina at Wilmington (1755), in South Carolina at Charleston (1760), and in Georgia (through Solomons Lodge, organized by the founder of Georgia, James Oglethorpe, under an English Charter in 1734 and now the oldest of the English lodges in the United States).

After the Revolutionary War, the Provincial Grand Lodges became independent from their mother lodges in England and Scotland and enunciated the doctrine of "exclusive jurisdiction" — only the Grand Lodge of any state had authority over the lodges within that state's borders. However, in the newly created states to the west of the Atlantic Seaboard, the several Grand Lodges were free to charter and establish daughter lodges. In that way, the Grand Lodges of Virginia, North Carolina, South Carolina, and Georgia were largely responsible for the spread and diffusion of Freemasonry across the South. By 1800 Kentucky, Tennessee, and French colonial Louisiana had new York Rite lodges as well as those derived from the colonial period. By 1820 additional Grand Lodges had been established in Alabama, Mississippi, and Louisiana. The next three decades added Arkansas, Texas, and Florida. In the case of Florida, Freemasonry had been introduced during the British colonial period in the form of military lodges chartered in Scotland. The story of Louisiana Freemasonry was a particularly complex one of struggle between French and Spanish colonists and their descendants, the early York and Scottish rites, and American and Spanish authorities in West Florida. In 1812, 12 Masonic lodges were chartered in Louisiana. From the five French-speaking lodges, the Grand Lodge of Louisiana was formed in 1812; 14 years later they were joined by the English-speaking York Rite lodges.

Masonry spread widely after the American Revolution and was a conspicuous feature of southern life. Virginian George Washington used a Masonic Bible during his first inauguration and a Masonic trowel in ceremonies laying the cornerstone for the Capitol building in Washington, giving the Masonic order new prominence. This prominence eventually resulted in suspicions of the secret order and a wave of anti-Masonic hysteria that affected the South, as well as the rest of the nation, in the late 1820s and 1830s. This was one of the few periods of Masonic involvement in national affairs.

Prominent southern Masons from the 19th century included U.S. Supreme Court Chief Justice John Marshall (Virginia), Senator John C. Breckinridge (Kentucky), Confederate general Albert Sidney Johnston (Texas), and Governor Robert Toombs (Georgia). Former confederate general Albert Pike from Arkansas edited and rewrote the rituals of the Scottish Rite in the late 19th century.

Masonry is typical of other fraternal groups in being far more than a strictly regional association, yet it has been an important institution for southerners and has taken on peculiar features at times in adapting to the regional context. In the 1890s, for example, a controversy appeared in Freemasonry over whether it should go beyond its traditions and become more explicitly religious, specifically acknowledging Christianity. Southerners and midwesterners, according to historian Lynn Dumenil, tended to link the health of Masonry to orthodox interpretation of the Bible. They were especially prone to "Masonic Biblicism." A few trials were even held in the South with the purpose of expelling nonbelieving Masons. At times, also, southerners showed a greater interest than other Masons in becoming involved in politics. The Southern Jurisdiction of Scottish Rite Masons, for example, enthusiastically supported political involvement in the 1920s. Leaders of Masonry in the region did, however, speak out against any Ku Klux Klan–Masonry connection in that period. Masonic magazines have supported good citizenship, public education, and "True Americanism," the latter a favorite phrase.

ALLEN CABINISS
Oxford, Mississippi

ERNEST EASTERLY III
Baton Rouge, Louisiana

Allen Cabiniss, *Freemasonry in Mississippi* (1976); George B. Clark, *From Whence Came We: Masonic Ancestry and Antecedents of the Grand Lodges of the United States* (1953); Henry W. Coil, *Freemasonry through Six Centuries*, 2 vols. (1967); Lynn Dumenil, *Freemasonry and American Culture, 1880–1930* (1984); Glen L. Greene, *Masonry in Louisiana* (1962); Ray B. Harris, *Eleven Gentlemen of Charleston: Founders of the Supreme Council, Mother Council of the World* (1959); William J. Hughan, G. P. Jones, and Ray B. Harris, *Freemasonry* (1958); H. Paul Jeffers, *Freemasons: A History and Exploration of the World's Oldest Secret Society* (2005); Christopher J. Kauffman, *Patriotism and Fraternalism in the Knights of Columbus: A History of the Fourth Degree* (2001); Nancy MacLeau, *Behind the Mask of Chivalry: The Second Making of the Ku Klux Klan* (1994); Jasper Ridley, *The Freemasons: A History of the World's Most Powerful Secret Society* (2002).

Fraternal Orders, Black

The African American fraternal orders and mutual benefit societies that proliferated throughout the South following emancipation evolved over several generations. They emerged from a rich underground of "invisible" institutions and folkways that slaves had created in their plantation communities; and insofar as they represented a folk culture, they owed their origins and style in part to Africa. They also resembled mutual benefit societies among European immigrants and often began out of purely pragmatic necessity. Melville J. Herskovits possibly exaggerated when he argued for a direct link with African cults and secret societies; and W. E. B. Du Bois probably strained the spiritual connection when he argued for a lineal descent from the West African Obeah worship. During slavery these voluntary associations were doubly clandestine, evolving out of a tradition of secret societies and the need to conceal organized behavior from the master class. As a consequence scholars know very little about the existence of orders and lodges among slaves, although Vincent Harding has

identified the Twelve Knights of Tabor as a secret network of 40,000 slaves organized in 1846 with the aim of overthrowing slavery.

Among free blacks a more conspicuous tradition accounted for the formal
or "visible" side of institutional development. As early as the 18th century, free
blacks formed "African Societies" in northern and southern urban communities, most notably the Free African Society of Philadelphia, founded in 1787. The
Free African Society is more often remembered as the parent organization of the
African Methodist Episcopal Church, but its own origins were decidedly secular, designed to provide a system of cooperative social welfare for the struggling
black community of Philadelphia. This example of the mutual benefit society
preceding the church points to the primacy of these societies and to the hazy
distinction between the spiritual and the secular in African American culture.

The program of mutual assistance among urban free blacks, especially the
African American elite of Charleston and New Orleans, often reflected biases of
class and color as well as a European orientation. Founded in 1790, Charleston's
Brown Fellowship Society, for example, limited its membership to mulattoes, a
practice that prompted darker-skinned free blacks to launch their own equally
exclusive society, the Free Dark Men of Color. In other cases, most obviously
the black Masons (1787) and the Odd Fellows (1843), separate lodges grew out of
their exclusion from the mainstream of white societies. Similar black counterpart groups, like the Elks and the Knights of Pythias, were founded after the
Civil War.

Indeed the Civil War and emancipation set off an explosion in the number
and variety of African American societies. Four million ex-slaves seeking social and economic expression valued only the family and possibly the church
above the benefit society in their hierarchy of basic institutions. In many cases
the mutual aid society, the church, the school, and rudimentary insurance and
business enterprises were linked by a common founder and a common set of
buildings. Du Bois, writing in 1906 about the social phenomenon as a whole,
concluded that "no complete account of Negro beneficial societies is possible,
so large is their number and so wide their ramification. Nor can any hard
and fast line between them and industrial insurance societies be drawn." Their
mixed function, he continued, was "partly social intercourse and partly insurance. They furnish pastime from the monotony of work, a chance for parade,
and insurance against misfortune. Next to the church they are the most popular organizations among Negroes."

However pressing the force of discrimination in the drive to establish separate black institutions, it would be a mistake to interpret these expressions of
black culture as merely a response to exclusion. Black fraternal and mutual

benefit societies took on a life and style of their own, tantamount to a southern folkway in the estimation of anthropologists Hylan Lewis and Hortense Powdermaker. In their respective studies of communities in South Carolina and Mississippi, Lewis and Powdermaker agreed that the "insurance envelope" was an omnipresent feature in humble cabins, and that "insurance" along with "church going, hunting and fishing" was a cultural staple. Doubtless, the vast array of lodges and societies provided an outlet for leadership and an avenue for status, respect, and recreation in compensation for what the larger society denied. In remembering his father as the Grand Marshall of the New Orleans Odd Fellows parade, Louis Armstrong may have caught the essence of this positive function: "I was very proud to see him in his uniform and his high hat with the beautiful streamer hanging down. . . . Yes, he was a fine figure of a man, my dad. Or at least that is the way he seemed to me as a kid when he strutted by like a peacock at the head of the Odd Fellows Parade."

Finally it should be emphasized that black women served as role models playing key parts as both members and organizers in black fraternal and benefit societies. Most conspicuous among the leaders was Maggie Lena Walker, who in 1899 assumed leadership of the Independent Order of St. Luke, a Richmond fraternal society founded in 1867 by an ex-slave, Mary Prout. Under Walker's administration, the Order of St. Luke, like its larger Richmond rival, the Grand United Order of True Reformers, embraced an ideology of self-help and racial solidarity, attempting to organize and uplift the entire black community through a broad range of institutions, including a savings bank, a newspaper (the *St. Luke Herald*), and the St. Luke Emporium. The True Reformers added a utopian vision in its retirement community and cooperative farm. Walker's organization did not survive the Great Depression, but as an illustration of its cultural legitimacy, and hence the cultural depth of black fraternal societies, black women in the early years of the 21st century continue to organize employing its principles and convictions.

WALTER B. WEARE
University of Wisconsin–Milwaukee

W. E. B. Du Bois, *Economic Cooperation among Negro Americans* (1907), *Efforts for Social Betterment among Negro Americans* (1909); Vincent Harding, in *The Making of Black America*, ed. August Meier and Elliot Rudwick (1969); Melville J. Herskovits, *The Myth of the Negro Past* (1941); Lawrence W. Levine, *Black Culture and Black Consciousness: Afro-American Folk Thought from Slavery to Freedom* (1977); Hylan Lewis, *Blackways of Kent* (1955); Gertrude Woodruff Marlowe, *Right Worthy Grand Mission: Maggie Lena Walker and the Quest for Black Economic Empowerment* (2003);

August Meier, *Negro Thought in America, 1880–1915* (1963); William J. Muraskin, *Middle Class Blacks in a White Society: Prince Hall Freemasonry in America* (1975); Hortense Powdermaker, *After Freedom: A Cultural Study in the Deep South* (1939); Walter B. Weare, *Black Business in the New South: A Social History of the North Carolina Mutual Life Insurance Company* (1973).

Garden Myth

Although it is a regional variant of the generalized image of America as "the garden of the world," the pastoral image of the South may best be understood in contrast to that of New England. This contrast originated in the attitudes of the settlers of Massachusetts and Virginia toward the archetypal pastoral dominions of Western culture: the Hebraic Garden of Eden and the Hellenic domain of Arcadia. During their long history in the Western literary imagination these concepts have been interwoven. Eden and Arcadia have been symbols of the replacement of the cosmic (the nonconscious or organic) state of human existence with the consciousness of time and history. Simultaneously they have been symbols of an illusory recovery, through pastoral vision and artifice, of the prehistoric state of harmony among God (or gods), man, and nature.

The Edenic and Arcadian images have also served as metaphors of the poetic consciousness. The poetic consciousness has conceived of itself as a garden that has been invaded by history and dispossessed, as Emerson said, of its "original relation to the universe." For the first and last time the New World settlement, in particular the English settlement along the Atlantic Seaboard, seemed to make possible the inclusion of the pastoral vision in the historical consciousness. This golden prospect of the recovery of the archetypal garden was wholly illogical, since the pastoral vision had arisen in response to the differentiation of history. But in defiance of logic the tension between the fiction of the possible recovery of the garden and the reality of history has been, at least until very recently, at the center of the American literary mind.

In the course of New England settlement, notably in Massachusetts, the prospect of a pastoral restoration was associated primarily with the biblical image of Eden. Under the terms of their covenant with God, the Puritan migrants envisioned making their new home a "pleasure garden of the Lord God of Hosts." Transformed from a "garden of the covenant," a homeland of the Puritan elect, into the homeland of a post-Revolutionary line of secular literary spirits (running from Emerson through Robert Lowell), New England remained a coherent symbol of an Edenic and/or Arcadian intervention in history. But in the South the pastoral vision developed differently. Although Edenic and Arcadian images of Virginia emerged in the writings of John Smith in the early 17th century, and these no doubt bear a relation to the vivid pastoral images in Robert Beverley's *History and Present State of Virginia* a century later, they did not constitute a continuous, closely structured vision of the South as the scene of pastoral redemption. The fundamental reason lies in the emphasis on the secular in the planting of the southern colony. In Virginia, as Perry Miller pointed out, historical expediency dictated the propagation of tobacco rather than the propagation of the faith. Increasingly tied to a chattel slave labor system by the development of a world marketplace economy, tobacco cultivation provided the model for the South's use of land and slaves in the subsequent production of sugarcane and cotton. Although owning slaves was by no means universal among southerners who owned land, slavery, becoming the South's "peculiar institution," frustrated the desire of the literary mind to project the South as a pastoral homeland.

In the mythic rendition of the plantation as a garden, the slave master might be portrayed as a man of letters with his Virgil or Horace in hand while he supervised his slaves, but in truth the gardener was his illiterate African chattel. This knowledge haunted the quest in the South for the image of the pastoral as an intervening force in history. Its disturbing influence may be seen in Thomas Jefferson's turning from his one explicit denunciation of slavery in the *Notes on the State of Virginia* (1785) to a vision of the American yeoman on his freehold as the representative American, in John Pendleton Kennedy's equivocal treatment of slavery in *Swallow Barn* (1832), and in William Gilmore Simms's account of the relationship between Porgy and his slave Tom in *Woodcraft* (1852). Unwittingly, Simms dramatized the insight of Hegel into the master-slave connection. Although the master believes he lives in the superiority of his own will, Hegel suggested, in actuality he has no will and no existence save in the consciousness of his slave. The slave, moreover, knows this. In this symbiotic situation in the South all men of letters, being connected with the figure of the slave master through their involvement in the defense of slavery, were psychically dependent on the unlettered slave.

The repressed tension between the quest for pastoral redemption and historical reality did not become overt in the southern literary expression until the distance between the South of slavery and the South of freed slaves and freed masters (a society still more complex than the antebellum southern society) allowed for the ironic insights of William Faulkner, John Crowe Ransom, Allen Tate, Robert Penn Warren, Eudora Welty, William Styron, Walker Percy, and other white southern writers. Together with a small but significant number of southern black writers — among them Charles W. Chesnutt, Jean Toomer, Richard Wright, Ralph Ellison, and Ernest Gaines — 20th-century white southern writers realized the literary possibilities of the drama of the dispossession of the pastoral ethos by the ethos of history. Making this drama their subject, they made the alienated literary imagination, the dispossessed garden, yield the rich flowering known as the Southern Renaissance.

LEWIS P. SIMPSON
Louisiana State University

David Brion Davis, *The Problem of Slavery in the Age of Revolution, 1770–1823* (1975); John Grammer, *Pastoral and Politics in the Old South* (1996); Richard Gray, *Writing the South: Ideas of an American Region* (1997); Leo Marx, *The Machine in the Garden: Technology and the Pastoral Ideal* (1964); Lewis P. Simpson, *The Brazen Face of History: Studies in the Literary Consciousness in America* (1980), *The Dispossessed Garden: Pastoral and History in Southern Literature* (1975); Henry Nash Smith, *Virgin Land: The American West as a Symbol and Myth* (1950).

Gays

Lesbian, gay, bisexual, and transgender (LGBT) people seem to encounter more difficulties in the South than in other regions. In surveys, southerners are more likely to oppose gay rights and describe homosexuality as sinful than respondents from any other section of the United States. Some of the nation's foremost antigay activist organizations have been headquartered in the South, from Anita Bryant's Save Our Children in the 1970s to Donald Wildmon's American Family Association in the 1990s. And despite repeated retractions, televangelists such as Virginia's Jerry Falwell and Pat Robertson persist in denunciations of same-sex relations, which in turn help fuel gay bashings. As one of a growing number of antiviolence projects reported, in 1995 in the state of North Carolina, two separate murders were attributed to antigay hate. Two occurred in Houston in 2002. With uneven police recordkeeping, however, such crimes are underreported and the criminals frequently unapprehended.

Sodomy statutes remained on the books longer in southern states, yielding the two most important Supreme Court rulings affecting LGBT Americans: *Bowers v. Hardwick*, from Georgia, upholding the constitutionality of sodomy laws in 1986, and *Lawrence v. Texas*, which finally overturned them in 2003 and expanded the right to privacy. In both cases, gay male couples literally had been arrested in their own bedrooms. In many states, lesbian mothers have had their children taken from their homes. Through the years, doctors have prescribed shock treatment; to this day, quacks concoct "coming-out-of-homosexuality" regimens. The South's religious, legal, and medical establishments—pastors, politicians, policemen, and physicians—often have been decidedly hostile to its LGBT citizens.

Nonetheless, LGBT southerners have demonstrated extraordinary daring and ingenuity in building networks and crafting relationships. The nominally conservative institutions of small-town and rural life—home, church, school, and workplace—have in many instances been the very sites where queer sexuality flourished. For rural southerners, these mainstream community institutions have served as the key sites for meeting friends and sex partners: at house parties and church choir practice, in school gymnasiums and on the shop floor. Though usually clandestine, same-sex relations have been enabled by the distinctive qualities of rural landscapes and social structures. Though they may publicly denounce homosexuality, many southerners practice a day-to-day, quiet accommodation of difference.

Often made to feel as if they are "the only one," rural queers have used cars and roads, letters and the internet, to overcome distances and avoid isolation. Unsurprisingly, with private homes—even bedrooms—under surveillance, they have often reappropriated public spaces such as roadside rest areas, parks, riversides, and beaches. Unlike residents of gay enclaves in major cities, they have relied on circulation more than congregation. They've set up households together or devised acceptable roles within their families of origin as spinster aunts or confirmed bachelor uncles.

Same-sex schools and colleges can facilitate homosexual interaction, and, for women in particular, they often instil feminist ideals. Other homosocial environments, such as the South's numerous military bases, likewise provide homosexual possibilities. Camps and other rural retreats have proven important in fostering the LGBT community. Laurel Falls summer camp for girls, on Old Screamer Mountain, Ga., run by partners Lillian Smith and Paula Snelling in the 1930s and 1940s, was a forerunner of Camp Sister Spirit, near Ovett, Miss., operated by Brenda and Wanda Hinson since the early 1990s. The gay men's spiritual/pagan collective Radical Faeries holds regular international gatherings and publishes its long-running magazine *RFD* on Short Mountain, Tenn.

In the more anonymous urban areas, ostensibly freed from small-town values, LGBT southerners have developed elaborate institutions and rituals. Much more than watering holes, queer bars are bedrock community centers and information clearinghouses. Whereas the sole gay bar in a small city becomes a remarkably democratic space, the large numbers in major metropolitan areas such as Atlanta or Dallas can lead to a specialization of bars, not unlike in mainstream culture, along lines of age, class, and race (black, white, Latino, Asian American), as well as gender (women, men, trans) and self-presentation or erotic proclivity (lipstick lesbian, bulldyke, s/m, leather, hustler, country/western, club kid, gym bunny, bear).

Many LGBT clubs and organizations meet in bars before or in lieu of acquiring their own buildings. Among these are sports teams, especially lesbian softball squads, gay men's choruses, reading groups, and religious organizations. In addition to local congregations of the Metropolitan Community Church, founded in Los Angeles in 1968 by southerner Troy Perry, the South is home to active affiliates of gay-supportive groups within mainline Christian denominations, including Catholic Dignity, Episcopal Integrity, Methodist Affirmation, and the More Light Presbyterians. Lesbian readers have supported cutting edge literary/political magazines such as *Feminary*, published in the 1970s, and they have constructed vibrant community hubs interconnected with lesbian-feminist bookstores such as Atlanta's Charis Books and More, one of the nation's oldest.

Annual LGBT pride parades and events are held in many localities, usually in the summer, in part to commemorate New York's Stonewall Riots of late June 1969. Vital in reaching young adults questioning their sexuality, university student groups are also alternative social institutions, and they often organize spring breaks at Daytona Beach and elsewhere. Many LGBT southerners spend Memorial Day weekend in Pensacola and Labor Day weekend in New Orleans. Inevitably, a few organizations seem predicated less upon lesbian and gay communion and more upon race and class exclusion: certain "executive networks," business associations, "A-list" events, and circuit parties. While some retail establishments, including video shops and bathhouses, live or die by the "gay dollar," some weekly newspapers, to secure advertising, overstate its power.

Indeed, employment discrimination based upon sexual orientation has left many in precarious economic circumstances and has led to the South's most visible and sustained LGBT political action. When Cracker Barrel Restaurants announced its antigay employment policy in 1991 and fired at least 16 workers, the multiracial Atlanta chapter of Queer Nation mounted protests and directed a national boycott that garnered the support of a variety of liberal organizations and leaders, including Coretta Scott King. Cracker Barrel, headquartered in Lebanon, Tenn., finally rescinded its policy and included sexual orientation in its equal opportunity statement a decade later.

Building upon mainstream folk traditions of womanless weddings and all-male beauty pageants, transgender people have engaged in intricate drag performances perceived as distinctively southern. As early as the 1940s, black drag troupes toured juke joints across the region, including among their ranks the notorious Princess Lavone, aka "Little Richard" Penniman. For over 30 years, the Miss Gay America pageant has been conducted by white Arkansan Norma Kristie. Today, performances range from the racist blackface drag of Mississippi's Shirley Q. Liquor to the inventive "Sunday services" of Georgia's biracial Gospel Girls, who sing hymns and pass the collection plate. North Carolina's Cuntry Kings are just what the name suggests: drag kings performing country music.

For transgender persons seeking sex reassignment surgery, an increasing number of hospitals offer the procedure. But with costs rarely covered by insurance, many go away—as far as Belgium—for affordable services. Perhaps more urgently than for the repeal of sodomy laws, trans activists have fought for the right to change the sex designation on their legal and medical documents, such as driver's licenses and birth certificates.

In the South, especially, race and sexuality are inextricably intertwined. Lesbians and gays of various levels of outness were among the leaders and rank-and-file participants in the African American civil rights movement. And segregationists not only red-baited but also queer-baited the activists. While some gay male organizations have expressly promoted interracial relationships—first Black and White Men Together, then Men of All Colors Together—racial fetishization remains a danger. The gay argot "dinge queen" and "dairy queen," referring to white men who mostly date nonwhites and vice versa, are sometimes as much derogatory as descriptive labels.

As it did elsewhere, AIDS transformed LGBT life in the South. As lesbians rallied around gay men hit hard by the crisis—and simultaneously established new lesbian health initiatives—many early AIDS service organizations like AID Atlanta and Birmingham AIDS Outreach faced charges of racial bias. After Senator Jesse Helms's trademark homophobic response to a plea on behalf of their sons, two North Carolina women founded MAJIC, Mothers Against Jesse in Congress. The direct action group ACT UP forced important changes in federal policy, in part by splashy demonstrations at the Centers for Disease Control in Atlanta. And generally in the 1990s, "sex-positive" groups such as Lesbian Avengers pushed a radical over reformist agenda.

Such radical sentiments may be on the wane in the South. With increased "visibility"—of an assimilationist sort—in the mainstream mass media, many gays and lesbians may have become complacent. But the backlash against lesbian and gay marriage, Clinton's backtracking on military service, and a con-

tinuing climate of violence and discrimination suggest that efforts may be re-
doubled.

JOHN HOWARD
King's College, University of London

John Howard, *Men Like That: A Southern Queer History* (1999); John Howard, ed.,
Carryin' On in the Lesbian and Gay South (1997); Suzanne Pharr, *Homophobia: A
Weapon of Sexism* (1988); Minnie Bruce Pratt, *Rebellion: Essays, 1980–1991* (1991);
Mab Segrest, *My Mama's Dead Squirrel: Lesbian Essays on Southern Culture* (1985).

Icons, Southern

Icons are generally those items perceived as images (representations) that are
important, enduring symbols. Southern icons are important symbols oriented
toward the South or symbols recognized as typically southern. Southerners
often place a great deal of pride in their icons. Symbols of the South vary from
people and places to foods consumed.

Several locations in the South are considered icons. Graceland, in Memphis,
Tenn., is one of the more well known. At the home of Elvis Presley, the wrought-
iron gates designed as musical pages are as iconic as "the King" himself. Atlanta,
Ga., in and of itself is a southern landmark, particularly with ties to the Civil
War, Coca-Cola, and *Gone with the Wind*. Several places associated with the
Civil War are icons of the South, including Stone Mountain, Ga., with its memo-
rial carving on the north face, depicting Confederate heroes Jefferson Davis,
Robert E. Lee, and Thomas J. "Stonewall" Jackson. Among the other icons of
the Civil War are the First White House of the Confederacy in Montgomery,
Ala., and the Confederate Executive Mansion in Richmond, Va., and numerous statues and battlefields scattered throughout the South. Regardless of any
Civil War connection, southern plantations are icons of the South that still capture the imagination of southerners and tourists alike. Plantation tours are a
huge part of the southern tourism industry, especially in South Carolina, Alabama, Mississippi, and Louisiana. These venues often include men and women
dressed in period costumes, particularly women in "southern belle" attire.

While the civil rights movement was not particular to the South, many of the
most well known sites associated with the movement are located in the South.
The Dexter Avenue Baptist Church in Montgomery, Ala., and the Lorraine
Motel, now the National Civil Rights Museum, in Memphis, Tenn., are icons
of the movement. The Dexter Avenue Baptist Church parsonage, once home
to Martin Luther King Jr. and now a museum, was the site of the decision to
begin the bus boycott — arguably the beginning of the civil rights struggle — and

the Lorraine Motel was where Martin Luther King Jr. was assassinated. Other places with icon status associated with the civil rights movement are Central High School in Little Rock, Ark.; Sixteenth Street Baptist Church (now the site of a civil rights museum) in Birmingham; the campus of the University of Mississippi, associated with James Meredith; and the campus of the University of Alabama, where George Wallace "stood at the schoolhouse door."

Another icon entwined with the South is the Mississippi River. Though the river begins further north, its longtime association with riverboats and gambling in the South, its literary connection with books such as *Huckleberry Finn*, and its commercial impact on places like Memphis and New Orleans have made it part of southern legacy. The lazy-flowing Suwannee River (Georgia and Florida) and the Chattahoochee River (Georgia and Alabama) join the Mississippi River as icons of the South celebrated in song and folklore.

Besides King Cotton, the South has other flora that have achieved icon status. One is Spanish moss (*Tillandsia usneoides*), which, in the United States, grows only in the Southeast, from the coastal side of Virginia all along the southeastern coastline to Texas.

The southern magnolia (*Magnolia grandiflora*) is a popular symbol of the South. Not only is it the state flower of both Mississippi and Louisiana, but it also provides the nickname of Mississippi: the Magnolia State. Typically, it ranges from eastern North Carolina, along the Atlantic Seaboard, and west through northern Florida and southern Georgia, Alabama, Mississippi, and Louisiana.

The official state vegetable of Georgia (it is also trademarked) is the Vidalia onion. The secret to this icon is that sweet Vidalia onions, which are sometimes eaten like apples, are grown in soil that can be found only in the unique region around the town of Vidalia, Ga.

The goober, or peanut (*Arachis hypogaea*), is a southern icon grown in the lower regions of the Deep South. A number of towns there have peanut festivals, and Dothan, Ala., home of the National Peanut Festival, claims the title "Peanut Capital of the World."

Joining peanuts as a boiled or fried iconic southern delicacy is okra (*Hibiscus esculentus*). Okra (or gumbo) is sometimes pickled, but in the South it is most often found on the dinner plate fried up into bite-sized nibbles or boiled in Louisiana gumbo or Kentucky burgoo.

Frying foods is typical of southern dining. On the list of foods usually associated with the South are fried chicken, fried okra, fried pickles, and fried catfish. Joining these foods on the iconic southern table are biscuits with gravy (white or red-eye), grits, collard greens, poke salad, sweet potatoes, chitlins, and rhubarb or lemon icebox pie. Washing all of this fare down are icons associated with southern thirst-quenching, such as Dr. Pepper, Coca-Cola (Coke), or the table wine of the South, iced tea.

Iconic to the southern eating experience is barbecue, revered for providing delicious fare at popular southern events such as stock car races, fishing tournaments, and college football games. Memphis holds a championship barbecue competition, but many places throughout the South have their own versions of barbecue from "dry" to "wet" varieties of pork, chicken, and other meats.

People also fit the mold of the southern icon. Former presidents Jimmy Carter and Bill Clinton are icons of the South and southern politics. Strom Thurmond joins them as well in the political arena. Ted Turner, Andrew Young, and Lewis Grizzard are Atlanta icons who are known the world over for being southern. Elvis Presley, Dixie Carter, Oprah Winfrey, Andy Griffith, and Sela Ward join the list.

Many southern icons are manifestations of centuries-old tradition or practices passed down through the generations. They become reified for their association with the South and are passed down from one generation to another as the "essence" of the region. The people who are raised up as icons generally embody what is celebrated by fellow southerners as typical of southern pride and tradition.

ERNEST J. ENCHELMAYER
Troy State University

Peter Guralnick, *Last Train to Memphis: The Rise of Elvis Presley* (1995); John Shelton Reed, *Whistling Dixie: Dispatches from the South* (1990); John Shelton Reed and Dale Volberg Reed, *1001 Things Everyone Should Know about the South* (1996); Charles Reagan Wilson, *Judgment and Grace in Dixie: Southern Faiths from Faulkner to Elvis* (1995).

Ladies and Gentlemen

Anyone with the mildest exposure to American popular culture has a firm, though probably paradoxical, image of the southern lady and the southern gentleman, both in real life and in fiction. Dinner party arguments—or barroom fights—can be ignited by trying to decide who qualifies and who does not. Melanie Hamilton, Coretta Scott King, and Rosalynn Carter easily make the ladyhood list, but does Dolly Parton? Robert E. Lee, Arthur Ashe, and Coach Bobby Bowden are surely southern gents, but is Lyndon Johnson?

Whether ladies and gentlemen are born or made is a quintessential southern philosophical debate. Scarlett O'Hara opines that you can't be a lady without money. For Caroline Compson, in Faulkner's *The Sound and the Fury*, lady-hood is an absolute: "I was taught that there is no halfway ground, that a woman is either a lady or not." As for the southern gentleman, he tends to come in two flavors, contemplative or active, Hamlet or Hotspur, or, to put it in regional terms, Quentin Compson or J. E. B. Stuart. His position is just as vexed as the southern lady's. Members of the Kappa Alpha Order, a fraternity founded in 1865 to (among other things) venerate the "parfit gentil knight" Robert E. Lee, call themselves "the last southern gentlemen." They wear Confederate uniforms and hold an annual party, Old South, to which they invite young women in hoopskirts, the tribal costume of the southern lady. Much alcohol is consumed and, not infrequently, the ideal of the "chivalrous warrior of Christ" and the "purity of southern womanhood" comes under some strain.

Sex and violence are key elements in the making of the lady and gentleman. Southern ladies are supposed to be miraculously immune to desire, and south-ern gentlemen are to retain the potential for violence in the name of honor. These class-based behavioral roles descend from British and continental Euro-pean models of the 18th century. Antebellum white women could be born ladies or have ladyhood thrust upon them through marriage or education. But if a woman transgressed sexually, she became, as Mary Chesnut says in her diary, "a thing we cannot name." Chastity for middle-class women was essential to property inheritance, but it became celebrated as a moral imperative, a mark of women's spiritual elevation.

Men were free to be as unchaste as they liked, even with (in some cases especially with) female slaves, though never to discuss their behavior in mixed company. There was a famous toast, reported in the 1930s by Carl Carmer in *Stars Fell on Alabama*, "To Woman . . . as pure and chaste as this sparkling water, as cold as this gleaming ice." In *Southern Ladies and Gentlemen* (1975), Florence King translates this as "To Woman, without whose purity and chastity we could never have justified slavery and segregation, without whose coldness we wouldn't have had the excuse we needed for messing around down in the slave cabins. . . . We pledge our hearts and our lives to the protection of her virtue and chastity because they are the best political leverage we ever did see."

Being a gentleman implied a certain amount of wealth (either in the present or in the past) and behavior according to a complex code that included gener-osity, ferocious protection of his and his family's good name, and a measure of (apparent) Victorian respectability. Birth into a prominent family accorded an automatic assumption of gentlemanliness, but the antebellum South's class sys-tem was fluid, allowing a working-class white man to rise through ownership of land and slaves. In *The Mind of the South* (1941), Cash describes an Irish immigrant who starts off a small farmer with a log cabin and ends up a Carolina planter universally described at his death as "a gentleman of the old school." In Faulkner's *Absalom, Absalom!* (1936), however, Thomas Sutpen comes up from Appalachian poverty to found (or "tear violently" according to Miss Rosa Coldfield, the novel's arbiter of gentlefolks' ways) the greatest estate in Yoknapatawpha County but is never accepted as a gentleman of any school, old or new.

Black men and women have only recently gained access to the status of lady or gentleman. Under slavery, black men could not be self-determining and black women could not assume that white men would respect the integrity of their bodies. In *Incidents in the Life of a Slave Girl* (1861), Harriet Jacobs argues for a redefinition of ladyhood taking into account the fact that black women did not always have the luxury of chastity. She exhorts white women "whose purity has been sheltered from childhood, who have been free to choose the objects of your affection, whose homes are protected by law, do not judge the poor desolate slave girl too severely!" Until the 1970s, blacks were rarely accorded courtesy titles or called "sir" and "ma'am." These days, however, a rising southern black bourgeoisie has created its own ceremonies and trappings of lady- and gentlemanhood: sororities and fraternities, Jack and Jill debutante balls, golf and tennis clubs, and charity work.

Literature by white southerners did much to codify the iconic figures of the lady and the gentleman. Plantation novels such as John Pendleton Kennedy's *Swallow Barn* (1832), William Gilmore Simms's *Guy Rivers* (1834), and Mary H. Eastman's *Aunt Phillis's Cabin* (1852), to name but a few, reiterate the "natural superiority" of the lord and lady of the Big House as a justification for slavery. Lost Cause writing represented the lady especially (the gentlemen had often died at Manassas or Gettysburg) in quasi-religious terms. In "Social Life in Old Virginia before the War," Thomas Nelson Page says breathlessly of the plantation mistress, "What she really was, was known only to God." In her 1904 memoirs, Virginia Clay likens the "brutalization" of upper-class white women during the Civil War to the trials of French aristocrats during the Reign of Terror. Still, she suffers with grace, comparing southern ladies to flowers—"the more they are bruised and oppressed the sweeter and stronger they grow!"

Even William Faulkner, who pitilessly deconstructs the moonlight and magnolias of plantation fiction, is susceptible to this white aristocratic myth. Col. John Sartoris, both Bayards, and Gavin Stevens are recognizable from literary antecedents of a century before, while Isaac McCaslin and Quentin Compson struggle to redefine what being a gentleman in the postslavery South might mean. Miss Jenny DuPre and Miss Habersham perfectly fulfill the role of Confederate lady as she was defined by the Lost Cause, while Faulkner's younger upper-class women — Temple Drake and Caddy Compson most notably — jump down from their pedestals straight into sex and "depravity," shattering the lady's statuelike perfection.

The lady and the gentleman have been under siege ever since the cocktail-drinking, bob-haired Zelda Sayre Fitzgerald (a Montgomery ex-debutante) became a more important role model than the doe-eyed Bride of the Confederacy, Varina Davis. Margaret Mitchell's *Gone with the Wind* (1936) is rightly castigated for its reactionary racial politics. But the novel is also a debate on the viability of traditional gender and class roles in the New South. Ashley Wilkes exemplifies the chivalrous southern gentleman, utterly unlike the cad of a blockade-runner Rhett Butler, of whom one society maven says, "he is not *received.*" The self-sacrificing, forgiving Melanie Hamilton is contrasted with the grasping, greedy Scarlett O'Hara, who knows — because her mother and her mammy told her — how to be a lady, but just can't help herself. Mitchell makes it clear that Ashley and Melanie belong to the ruined, outmoded Old South while Rhett and Scarlett personify the future.

The lady and the gentleman still wield cultural power in the South, where gender roles have been slower to change than in the rest of the country. Etiquette classes, cotillions, and an obsession with manners still define the middle-class South. But the old ways are under siege. Instead of suffering in saintly silence, Maybelle, who still goes to the Junior League when she can fit it in around her interior design business, is demanding a divorce from Beauregard plus half the assets and the bass boat, too. Beauregard, raised, as Quentin Compson says, never to disappoint a lady, is in therapy trying to confront his feelings about his mother and the failure of his marriage to Maybelle. The rules are different. The gentleman still believes in chivalry — even if he's on Prozac. The lady still believes in the purity of Southern womanhood — or at least its appearance. As always in the South, the negotiation between ideal and real continues.

DIANE ROBERTS
University of Alabama

Virginia Foster Durr, *Outside the Magic Circle* (1987); Richard Dyer, *White* (1992); Jacquelyn Dowd Hall, *Revolt Against Chivalry: Jessie Daniel Ames and the Women's Campaign Against Lynching* (1979); bell hooks, *Ain't I a Woman? Black Women and Feminism* (1981); Tara McPherson, *Reconstructing Dixie: Race, Gender, and Nostalgia in the Imagined South* (2003); Marlyn Schwarz, *A Southern Belle Primer* (1991); Bertram Wyatt-Brown, *Southern Honor: Ethics and Behavior in the Old South* (1982).

Lynching

Lynching is part of the American, especially southern, tradition of vigilante terrorism. Vigilantism has taken several forms, depending on purpose: white-cappers usually flogged, or made threatening night visits, to "regulate" or intimidate their enemies; the charivari was usually a semifestive ritual (such as tar-and-feathering or merely serenading with "rough music") meant to humiliate transgressors of community standards; lynch mobs killed their victims. Thus lynching is the deadliest form of vigilantism.

Colonel Charles Lynch of Virginia, whose extralegal "court" sentenced Tories to floggings during the American Revolution, apparently provided the origin of the term "lynch-law." Until the 1850s lynch-law (lynching) was commonly associated with corporal and extralegal punishment, but not killing. Then, during the last decade before the Civil War, southern vigilantes, particularly in Louisiana and Texas, routinely inflicted death on outlaws and on individuals suspected of plotting slave insurrections. That is when lynching took on its lethal connotation.

The Civil War and Reconstruction intensified southern lynching activity. Vigilantism in Texas alone during the war probably accounted for over 150 deaths. Lynching became more widespread in the Reconstruction years and was directed mostly at ex-slaves, because the free blacks, no longer valued as property, were often viewed as threatening the existence of white civilization. The specter of Haiti, and its bloody slave rebellion of the 1790s, white fear, and predictions of race war helped multiply acts of terrorism.

Not until 1882 were efforts made to gather data on lynching across the United States. During the 70 years from 1882 to the early 1950s, by which time lynching had virtually ended, a total of 4,739 persons reportedly died at the hands of lynch mobs in the United States. (Since these figures were compiled solely from lynching stories printed in leading urban newspapers of each state, it is likely the actual total was nearer 6,000.) Lynching statistics do not, of course, include those blacks or whites who died in race riots; nor would ordinary interracial homicides, where a person of one race killed someone of another race, be listed.

Reported lynchings for the entire United States averaged 150.4 per year during the last 19 years of the 19th century. The greatest number of lynchings in a single year occurred in 1892, when there were 230. During the first decade of the 20th century, lynchings nationally averaged 84.6 per year, and their number dropped further for 1911–20 (to an average of 60.6 annually). After 1920 reported lynchings continued to decline, with the decade of 1921–30 averaging 27.5 per year. For 1931–40 there were 114 total lynchings (11.4 annual average). The decade of 1941–50 averaged 3 per year. Then lynching virtually ceased.

Lynching of Gus Goodman, Bainbridge, Ga., 1905
(Georgia Department of Archives and History, Atlanta)

From 1951 to 1985 only 10 lynching deaths were reported in the United States. Approximately 82 percent of all lynchings recorded since 1882 took place in the South (defined as the 15 slave states of 1860). Western and midwestern states account for nearly all the remainder. Nationally, 72 percent of all lynch-mob victims were black; in the South, 84 percent were black. Over 95 percent of the victims, both nationally and regionally, were males. Among the states, Mississippi ranks first in number of lynchings from 1882 to the present, with 581 deaths (539 of the victims being black); Georgia is second with 530 (491 black), Texas third with 493 (352 black), and Louisiana fourth with 391 (335 black). Very few participants in lynch mobs were prosecuted in any state, and prior to World War II almost none ever served time in prison.

Lynch-law was supposed to be, in the blunt words of one advocate of the practice, "the white woman's guarantee against rape by niggers." Ridding society of "black brutes" who violated Caucasian females was indeed the most often mentioned justification for lynching. "Whenever the Constitution comes between me and the virtue of the white women of South Carolina," exclaimed Governor Cole Blease, "then I say 'to hell with the Constitution.'" Since an accused black rapist in 1910s South Carolina would almost certainly face quick legal execution, why was mob action deemed necessary? Because, according to the rationale of lynching, a ravished white woman must be spared the agony of testifying in court, while the accused presumably would enjoy and be flattered by "the pomp and ceremony of formal justice."

In fact only about one-third of all lynching victims were suspected of rape or attempted rape. Murder or attempted murder was more often the alleged crime. Others who died at the hands of lynch mobs were accused of transgressions of descending importance, such as arson, burglary, slapping a white person, stealing chickens, chronic impudence, or simply being "vagrant and lewd." Whatever the supposed crime, lynching was widely assumed by whites to be a significant deterrent to black criminality. Black males were thought to be more afraid of lynch mobs than anything else. And rape, despite its secondary place in lynch-law statistics, was of prime importance in justifying the concept of vigilante action. Whenever lynching was discussed, rape became the central theme. Whites who objected to lynching ran the risk of being accused of sympathy for black rapists.

Most lynch mobs killed swiftly. The typical victim, after being hoisted with a rope tossed over a tree limb, trestle, or utility pole, would have his death throes ended by a fusillade of bullets. But some lynchings involved prolonged torture and fire. Mississippi, Georgia, and Texas were most likely to have witnessed scenes of medieval horror during the years from 1890 to 1920. Nearly all torture-lynching victims were blacks accused of both raping and murdering whites. Most were burned at the stake, after preliminary tortures. One accused murderer in Louisiana, a white man, was slowly skinned alive.

Lynch mobs are not easily categorized. The larger throngs were probably made up of people who thought of themselves more as observers than as participants, such as the "hundreds of the best men in Atlanta" who, in 1899, boarded "excursion trains" bound for Newnan, Ga., to see accused rapist-murderer Sam Hose burn at the stake. Sometimes lynch mobs were racially integrated, as were most of the crowds who watched legal executions. Occasionally, black mobs lynched blacks accused of crimes against members of their race. There is one reported case of a white South Carolinian, in jail for molesting and murdering a black child, being handed over to an enraged black mob.

The stereotyped image of poor "redneck" whites making up the mobs who lynched blacks is only partially true. White vigilantes came from all strata of society. Middle- and upper-class participation in lynch mobs was especially common in Louisiana. True, most of the vocal opposition to lynchings came from prominent whites, notably religious leaders, lawyers, and judges. But without the tacit approval of most of the dominant elements in the white community, lynching could not have been so frequent. The South, after all, was essentially a hierarchical society.

Southern newspapers prior to 1920 usually hedged on the question of lynching and seldom condemned it if the mob victim was a black male accused of raping a white female. An outspoken defender of vigilante murder was Henry J. Hearsey (1840–1900), editor-publisher of the New Orleans *Daily States*, the official journal of that city's government. The question of actual guilt, Hearsey admitted, did not really concern him; he was sure lynching deterred black crime, and that was the important thing. Other journalists, not as bloodthirsty, sometimes became so desensitized to lynching that they reported on it with sly humor. As one example, the Port Gibson (Miss.) *Reveille* in 1892 thus described the death of John Robinson, black, who had robbed and killed a white man: "He offered to lead the mob to a railroad trestle under which the money lay buried. John and the money have now exchanged locations."

Antilynching crusaders, both nationally and within the South, began to see public opinion drift in their favor after 1920. Women such as Jessie Daniel Ames and Ida Wells-Barnett and groups such as the Association of Southern Women for the Prevention of Lynching were especially significant. Also, growing fear of legal consequences probably discouraged many would-be lynchers. The last known lynching took place in Neshoba County, Miss., when three civil rights activists were murdered in 1964.

The public presentation of lynching photographs and postcards in the past decade has focused renewed attention on lynching, and a spate of academic studies reflects a growing interest in lynching and its role in southern culture. A U.S. Senate resolution in 2005 officially apologized for the Senate's repeated failure to pass antilynching legislation.

WILLIAM I. HAIR
Georgia College

James Allen, Hilton Als, John Lewis, and Leon F. Litwack, *Without Sanctuary: Lynching Photography in America* (2003); Edward L. Ayers, *Vengeance and Justice: Crime and Punishment in the 19th-Century American South* (1984); Ray Stannard Baker, *Following the Color Line* (1908; reprint 1969); Richard Maxwell Brown, *Strain of Violence: Historical Studies of American Violence and Vigilantism* (1975); W. Fitzhugh Brundage, *Lynching in the New South: Georgia and Virginia, 1880–1930* (1993); W. Fitzhugh Brundage, ed., *Under Sentence of Death: Lynching in the New South* (1997); James H. Chadbourn, *Lynching and the Law* (1933); James E. Cutler, *Lynch-Law: An Investigation into the History of Lynching in the United States* (1905); Phillip

Dray, *At the Hands of the Unknown: Lynching of Black America* (2002); George C. Rable, *But There Was No Peace: The Role of Violence in the Politics of Reconstruction* (1984); Arthur F. Raper, *The Tragedy of Lynching* (1933); Stewart Emory Tolnay and E. M. Beck, *A Festival of Violence: An Analysis of Southern Lynchings, 1882–1930* (1995); Walter White, *Rope and Faggot* (1929); George Wright, *Racial Violence in Kentucky, 1865–1940: Lynching, Mob Rule, and "Legal Lynchings"* (1990).

Maiden Aunt

She is a favorite character of fiction and stereotype, but a person who in fact touched the lives of most southerners — the maiden aunt. The demand for marriageable women exceeded the supply during the colonial era, but by the time of the American Revolution the spinster (single women at home were often drafted to the female task of spinning, the origin of the term) was a folkloric figure in southern states. The never-wed woman in southern culture was not only dependent upon men, like her married counterpart, but was also denied the status accorded to matrons and mothers. She was forced to live out her life on the fringes of society, a perpetually lone figure in a culture of tightly knit couples and children. Within the home (usually that of a brother or sister), however, she was often a cherished and fond member of the family circle. Indeed, the maiden aunt became both influential and indispensable.

It was assumed, because of social pressures to marry, that most unmarried women had been rejected, passed over, or never given an opportunity to snare a husband. This promoted several unattractive images of old maids. One antebellum girl described them as "forlorn damsels who made the midnight air echo with their plaintive bewailings, for only bats and owls return their melancholy strains." In southern society the "old" maid ranged anywhere from age 18 to 80. A girl might feel spinsterish if younger sisters married before she did, if she was not married by age 21, or simply if all her friends had "deserted" her for husbands.

Southern women, as a rule, married very young — younger than their northern counterparts and much younger than men. Shortly after puberty, black women often selected a mate, whom they married by folk custom though not by law. Historians of the slave community have found teenaged brides common on the plantation. Studies of planters have confirmed that white women also commonly wed as schoolgirls. In the Old South the average age of marriage for white women was 20, and that of black women was slightly lower. Thus, women who remained unmarried in the South were classified as spinsters at a much earlier age than elsewhere.

The Civil War, of course, greatly reduced the supply of young men to marry. Many southern daughters during the second half of the 19th century were thus demographically deprived of husbands. Strikingly, the Reconstruction era was the first period since early colonial days when interracial sexual relations and even marriage were accepted to any notable extent. However, a large number of single white women — and especially those of the upper and middle classes — remained unattached, many becoming leaders in shaping new educational and employment opportunities for women. Gradually, career opportunities for females expanded, and the stigma associated with women who lived alone lessened.

Nevertheless, throughout most of the 19th century and well into the 20th, southern society attempted to shelter and confine single women. Those who failed to marry were more often forced by custom or circumstance to spend their time and energy with "other women's families." Spinsters clearly served surrogate roles with the family — single daughters or maiden aunts might be welcome as an extra pair of hands or as substitute mothers — but they were also social outcasts, denied the status a woman could achieve only through her role as matriarch. Few parents, even those of enormous wealth, would bequeath money to an unmarried daughter.

Only in modern times have single women in the South received any of the family resources. Traditionally, a woman was expected to inherit through her dowry. If she did not marry, she could rely only on the charity of parents or siblings. Brothers and sisters eagerly provided these spinsters with homes in exchange for valuable domestic services. Maiden aunts were teachers and nurses, confidants and disciplinarians. Indeed, their whole lives were bound up with the strenuous chores of child rearing, but, like servants, they tended children that were not their own.

"Aunt adoption" was a particularly southern phenomenon. Women often singled out a niece for special affection and in many cases quite lavish consideration. This cultivation of a favorite by aunts was traditional and certainly not limited to unmarried or childless females. It was not uncommon for a southern mother to "donate" one of her several daughters to the family of a beloved brother or sister who had no children, or even merely no female offspring. This would reduce the burden of the natural parents (costs for living expenses and dower) while maintaining family ties and offering emotional, and sometimes financial, benefits for the adopted child.

Upon occasion a pregnant mother would secure a promise from a favorite sister that if she did not survive the ordeal of childbirth, the surviving sister would look after the orphaned children; in some cases women wanted their husbands to remarry these spinsters. With the rate of death in childbirth uncommonly high in the South until the 20th century (nearly double that in the North), unmarried women sometimes literally inherited an entire family through marriage to the spouse of a dead sibling. These cases were extreme, yet they reflect the pivotal importance to southern women of the maiden aunt, despite her never-married, childless status.

The stereotypes of these women were most often unflattering exaggerations. Many fictional portraits of maiden aunts painted them as dizzy and foolish, the proverbial "Aunt Pittypat" character of *Gone with the Wind*. A more sympathetic portrayal has been developed by several southern authors who have characterized sturdy, proud females channeling their energies and talents into their nephews and nieces and leading challenging and fulfilling lives: variants on the theme established in one of Faulkner's early novels, *Sartoris*, with the spirited and understanding Miss Jenny. Many of these characters, especially those created by women novelists such as Ellen Glasgow, possess a feminist component: they chose not to enter the ranks of women trapped and trampled by husbands.

Another significant variant for the never-married woman was the portrait of a lady of questionable character. There were women in southern society and southern fiction who chose to lead lives unhampered by spouses but who refused to deny themselves sexual companionship. For some, their reckless behavior at a younger age had supposedly robbed them of their reputation for virtue, leading to a devaluation on the marriage market. Others purportedly were predisposed to this character defect—loose and immoral without hope of redemption. In either case, perpetual singlehood was their fate. This semitragic figure was most poignantly revealed in Tennessee Williams's Blanche DuBois, the fading belle of *A Streetcar Named Desire*.

The plays, films, and novels of the South depict lone women in their variety and complexity, but these myriad roles cannot match the mark such women have made in the great drama of real life. Their impact has been enormous and their contributions monumentally enriching to southern culture.

CATHERINE CLINTON
The Gilder Lehrman Center for the Study of Slavery, Resistance, and Abolition
Yale University

Josephine Carson, *Silent Voices: The Southern Negro Woman Today* (1969); Catherine Clinton, *The Plantation Mistress: Woman's World in the Old South* (1982); Laura L. Doan, ed., *Old Maids to Radical Spinsters: Unmarried Women in the Twentieth-*

Century Novel (1991); Maria Fletcher, "The Southern Heroine in the Fiction of Representative Southern Women Writers" (Ph.D. dissertation, Louisiana State University, 1963); Elizabeth Fox-Genovese, *Within the Plantation Household: Black and White Women of the Old South* (1988); Anne Goodwyn Jones, *Tomorrow Is Another Day: The Woman Writer in the South, 1859–1936* (1981); John C. Ruoff, "Southern Womanhood, 1865–1920: An Intellectual and Cultural Study" (Ph.D. dissertation, University of Illinois, 1976); Lillian Smith, *Killers of the Dream* (1949); Julia Cherry Spruill, *Women's Life and Work in the Southern Colonies* (1938); Alice Walker, *In Love and Trouble: Stories of Black Women* (1973).

Manners

Manners are a formal code of proper behavior. The South has stressed etiquette and has attributed much significance to the form of verbal expression and behavior in a group. Stark Young wrote in *I'll Take My Stand* (1930) that "manners are the mask of decency that we employ at need, the currency of fair communication," and William Alexander Percy insisted in his memoir *Lanterns on the Levee* (1941) that "manners are essential and are essentially morals." Southerners have, in fact, traditionally equated manners—the appropriate, customary, or proper way of doing things—with morals, so that unmannerly behavior has been viewed as immoral behavior. Thus, in the South, moral codes, laws, and manners have been intertwined, with the aim of curbing individual aggressiveness and maintaining social order through a combination of external community pressures and internalized individual motivation.

"He did everything correctly, but with the faintest smile, as though to say he knew what he was doing and could do it another way if necessary," wrote James McBride Dabbs in *The Southern Heritage* (1958) about his bachelor uncle who embodied the ideal of manners many southern mothers taught their children. "He was a balance of reserve and openness, of formality and informality, which the South aimed at but often failed to attain." Southerners such as Dabbs who have written about manners use terms such as "polite," "courteous," "kind," "gentle," "hospitable," "friendly yet dignified." Rigidity in following the rules is not prized as much as the flexibility and resiliency that enable the well mannered to handle any situation graciously. There are, to be sure, rules: one must respect one's parents ("Yes, sir," "No, ma'am"), honor obligations to kin, welcome neighbors, and protect the weak and helpless; a gentleman must open doors for a woman and stand when she enters a room; one must not dive into the food before grace is said and everyone served. In the colonial era, particularly, manners were of a prescriptive nature, defining for the upper classes the standards for behavior indicative of refinement, good breeding, and sophistication. Among the wealthy, manners served in general as parameters for social class relations.

The concern for manners goes far back in southern history. The ideal of the English country gentleman provided the basis for proper manners among colonial planters. European, particularly English, books on manners were commonly found in plantation libraries: Richard Brathwaite's *The English Gentleman*, Harry Peacham's *The Compleat Gentleman*, Count Baldesar Castiglione's *The Book of the Courtier*, and the most influential of all for the southern elite — *The Whole Duty of Man* (usually attributed to Richard Allestree), one of the first books printed in Virginia and a popular source for guidelines on behavior until the mid-19th century. Estates with English names, such as Drayton, Berkeley Hundred, and Exeter Lodge, became famous centers of the best formal colonial manners. William Byrd II chronicled in his diary the etiquette of the people in that society, suggesting their power, the respect they received when displaying their manners, and their aspirations to noblesse oblige. A code of honor appeared that provided strict rules for proper conduct in all situations.

The frontier was a very different force that affected the development of manners among early southerners. Observers characterized plain folk on the frontier and in settled areas as generous, hospitable, and polite. Everyone also agreed their behavior was deplorably crude. Travelers from abroad saw little refinement or sophistication among them and were sometimes dismayed at southerners' disregard for the proper rules of behavior. The formal manners of the Virginia and Carolina Tidewater, to be sure, were transferred to the southwestern frontier. Andrew Jackson was a frontiersman, but in social circles he displayed the courteous manners expected of the planter he became. On the frontier, manners could help an ambitious person create a persona with a well-bred background. Manners among the nouveau planters were, nonetheless, simpler and less formal than among the Tidewater elite. The veneer came off easily on the frontier. Disagreements were often settled with an angrily drawn pistol instead of through the honorable code duello. W. J. Cash insisted, though, that an enduring and basically admirable ideal of manners developed among the antebellum frontier plain folk, an ideal that promoted, he wrote, "a kindly courtesy, a level-eyed pride, an easy quietness, a barely perceptible flourish of bearing."

Between 1830 and 1850 the southern cult of chivalry became a major expression of southern romanticism, and the cult had significance for manners. Southern whites believed they were descended from aristocratic English noblemen, from Cavaliers, who were the ultimate embodiment of proper manners. The key was in ritual. After a trip to Richmond in 1853, Frederick Law Olmsted noted that "more ceremony and form is sustained" among southerners than "well-bred people commonly use at the North." A regional fondness for the splendid gesture, theatrical behavior, and extravagant pageantry had appeared.

Women in the antebellum era were central to the southern code of manners. The cult of chivalry taught that the mythic lady was the essence of manners. A white woman's social role was highly restricted by "proper" conduct, and the men around her had to be on their best behavior as well. The myth of the lady was not unique to the South, but, as Anne Firor Scott stresses in *The Southern Lady* (1970), southern regional culture was distinctive in the intensity and tenacity of the ideal. Southern courtship and marriage had clear expectations of correct behavior stressing male aggressiveness and female coyness. This romanticized ideal of mannerly behavior between the sexes was reinforced in the late 19th and early 20th centuries by Victorian sentimentalism and Protestant moralism. Those attitudes are no longer predominant in the 21st-century South, but the code of southern courtship manners retains vestiges from the past. Florence King's *Southern Ladies and Gentlemen* (1975) is a near-definitive account of southern sexual manners practiced by regional types such as the Self-Rejuvenating Virgin, Dear Old Thing, Good Old Boy, Bad Good Old Boy, and Gay Confederate. She explores such central southern concepts as "trashy" behavior, "passing the time of day," the "freeze" (a blood-curdling look of disapproval), the "pert plague" among women, and the "deliverance syndrome" among men.

Tara McPherson sees a continued close relationship between femininity and manners, "as gender and etiquette endlessly reinforce each other within the southern landscape." Rosemary Daniell recognizes that southern women have long used feminine manners to survive in the region's patriarchal culture, and at times this critic of traditional southern femininity longs for its comforts, seeing it as being "as addictive as magnolia blossoms or Jack Daniel's."

Southern culture has much lore on the effort to teach manners to the young. Manners have been encouraged by schools and churches and sometimes by legal systems. Folklore from the region's blacks and whites tries to link crude manners with unpleasant results. Singing while eating will bring bad luck; taking the last bit of bread on a plate means a young man will never find a wife; and eating too rapidly leads to marriage before one is ready. Such sayings are apparently intended to scare the young into respectability.

Accounts of teaching manners in the South frequently focus on meals. In *Black Boy* (1945) Richard Wright told of the preacher coming to Sunday dinner, finishing his soup early, and then eating piece after piece of fried chicken before young Wright could even finish his soup. He finally stood up and said, "that preacher's going to eat all the chicken!" His mother, he wrote, gave him "no dinner because of my bad manners." In *To Kill a Mockingbird* (1960) young Scout is reprimanded when she comments on her classmate Walter's habit of putting syrup on all his food. The young man had come to lunch, and Scout's father had made him feel at home until her breach of manners. Her father pours syrup on his own bread to put the guest back at ease — another gesture of good manners. The black housekeeper Calpurnia lectures Scout for poor behavior. All of these examples suggest the crucial role of women, black and white, in nurturing southern manners. Sometimes manners are enforced with the harsh discipline of Calvinistic patriarchs, but more commonly women teach proper behavior.

An emphasis on manners reflects the South's stress on community. As Stark Young wrote in *I'll Take My Stand*, manners are only understood in regard to "a state of society that assumes a group welfare and point of view." Southerners have valued their individualism, but their regard for manners has been the counterbalance to individualism. In the large industrial cities of the North from the 19th century on, people have moved among strangers, creating little pressure for observing the niceties of behavior in a pressurized world. In contrast, in the South's characteristic smaller communities and rural areas one conducted business and daily living among people one saw all too frequently. "Manners are to be seen," wrote James McBride Dabbs, suggesting that manners are a public matter of image among a group of people well known to each other. The upper-class elite, in particular, set the tone for etiquette in society. "The aristocrat was to reveal," observed Dabbs, "to make public, what life could, and should, be."

Southern manners were not only a community binding force, an agreed upon code for groups to aspire to; they were also divisive, separating those with manners from those without. The Tidewater planter looked down on the manners of backcountry folk. Virginians looked down on the manners of those in early North Carolina (William Byrd II referred to them as lazy, ignorant, and filthy). Southerners by the antebellum era looked down on northern manners. South Carolina congressman Preston Brooks cane-whipped Massachusetts senator Charles Sumner in 1854 over alleged poor manners, an insult to honor, contained in a Sumner speech. Such violence has often been ascribed to violations of the code of honor, and mannerly behavior has cloaked violent instincts. A southerner is courteous and friendly, goes an old saying, until he is mad enough to kill. Southerners ironically viewed manners and decorum as so vital to the maintenance of social order that defense of such codes warranted violence.

This double-edged emphasis on manners has been apparent in other ways, too. In many cases manners have been a veneer that masked social inequities while institutionalizing them. Manners have been seen as one aspect of upper-class ideology and power. The southern elite used manners to soften tendencies toward social class conflict. At public gatherings, wrote W. J. Cash of a typical plain farmer, "there would nearly always be a fine gentleman to lay a familiar hand on his shoulders, to inquire by name after the members of his family, maybe to buy him a drink." The result was to patronize the yeoman farmer, but in such a smooth way that he went home "not sullen and vindictive" at all over the planter's wealth and prestige. Manners were an aspect of a paternalistic style. The personal kindness and thoughtfulness of the landowner and later the mill owner, moreover, bound whites together. Mannerly behavior between whites of different social groups helped cement Cash's "Proto-Dorian" bond.

A deeply rooted code of etiquette is found among black families in the South. Frederick Douglass suggested black etiquette derived from similar African codes and noted, "There is not to be found, among any people, a more rigid enforcement of the law of respect to elders, than they maintain. . . . There is no better material in the world for making a gentleman, than is furnished in the African."

Melville Herskovits in *The Myth of the Negro Past* (1942) argued that "outstanding among the intangible values of Negro life in the United States is strict adherence to codes of polite behavior." Newbell Niles Puckett in *Folk Beliefs of the Southern Negro* (1926) also stressed the importance of etiquette in black life, which links "unpleasant results with uncouth manners in an attempt to frighten the young into a quicker acquisition of American good-breeding." Herskovits noted a number of practices of etiquette that have important African roots. Respect for elders among southern blacks can also be found among Africans who feel that "old folks" are "almost ghosts." An ancestral cult thus developed with the understanding that ancestors have the power to help or harm their descendants.

Herskovits also observed African etiquette in "the matter of turning the head when laughing (sometimes with the hand over the mouth), or in speaking to elders or other respected persons of averting the eyes and perhaps the face." In the *Etiquette of Race Relations* (1939) Bertram Doyle showed how such politeness was adopted in dealing with whites. Gestures of respect reserved in Africa for elders were a defense against white aggression in the South. Black writers such as Ralph Ellison have preserved this racial etiquette in their fiction. Ellison's protagonist in *Invisible Man* remembers his father's advice: to survive in the white man's world, you must "yes'em to death." Politeness is the ultimate weapon the old man bestowed on his son.

Black etiquette is thus a double-edged tradition. Its African roots, like those of white etiquette in Europe, were formed in Old World cultures to regulate relationships within families and communities. Faced with slavery and later with segregation, southern blacks adopted etiquette as a means of survival. They developed a racial etiquette as a foil to the racism of southern whites.

Racial etiquette also revealed a southern stress on personal relationships. Post–Civil War southerners developed a complex and elaborate ritual to govern interracial behavior. William Alexander Percy argued that only their good manners enabled the two different races to live together in an orderly, single way of life: "The Southern Negro has the most beautiful manners in the world, and the Southern white, learning from him, I suspect, is a close second." But, in addition to this, a distinctive caste etiquette worked to maintain racial separation. The etiquette required whites to behave in certain ways toward blacks, ways seemingly at odds with their normal code of good manners. One should use first names, not "Mr." or "Mrs.," in addressing blacks; one did not shake hands with a black person or tip a hat. Blacks should address all whites with respect, should not crowd whites on sidewalks, should enter the home of a white person through the back door, should sit at the back of a bus, and should stand or wait at the end of a line for service until all whites had been served. Segregation laws enforced some racial behavior, but "manners" were enforced by individual and collective white intimidation of blacks. "Uppity" blacks were a constant worry of southern whites. A breech of racial manners by a black man could lead to a tongue-lashing, humiliation, and sometimes violence. When black teenager Emmett Till violated ultimate sexual-racial manners in Mississippi in the 1950s by whistling at a white woman, he was lynched.

Racial manners were justified by the "best" people as a way to maintain social distance between the races and thus prevent overt aggression. Interracial etiquette did at times ease tensions between blacks and whites. Kindly manners between persons who happened to be of different races helped to soften the rigidity of segregated society. Many southern whites treated blacks with respect and were concerned not to hurt their feelings. Kindly manners did not, however, ease the injustice of southern society; instead they nurtured a ritualized, daily sense of inferiority among blacks. Outsiders were expected to follow southern racial manners, and there are legendary stories of northerners moving south and adopting them more enthusiastically than southern whites. The requirements of racial manners in the South meant that blacks lived in an atmosphere of daily intimidation and frequent anxiety. Blacks were polite because they were dealing with a life-and-death matter — an ultimate expression of southern regard for manners.

With the end of racial segregation laws in the 1960s an accompanying change in southern racial manners took place. The decline in the formal code of polite and honorable behavior that both black and white southerners have proclaimed seems to be a by-product of long-term social changes in the region. W. J. Cash saw a decline in southern manners dating back to the New South era of the late 19th century. A grafting of northern backslapping heartiness onto southern geniality, he wrote, created "the Rotary ideal," which represented "an unfortunate decline in the dignity of the southern manner." The Agrarians of *I'll Take My Stand* saw threats to the survival of formal manners in any industrial, business-oriented society. Robert B. Heilman, in an essay entitled "The Southern Temper," warned of a decline of manners in the contemporary South because southern whites had "popularized and made the object of public self-congratulation" their tradition of manners. "Promotional facsimilies" of manners, involving the exploitation of hoopskirted ladies dressed for tourists, marks, he said, a decline in the real thing.

Sociologist John Shelton Reed's studies of contemporary North-South attitudes have shown that both northerners and southerners continue to see southerners as more mannerly than persons from north of the Mason-Dixon line. Respondents to a North Carolina opinion poll in the early 1970s described southerners by using words such as "considerate," "polite," "friendly," "courteous," "hospitable," "genteel," "cordial," and "nice" — terms synonymous with the manners that southern mothers, black and white, have tried to teach their children.

Southerners have not written any widely known etiquette books despite the continued fascination of the gentry and the upwardly mobile with manners. One theory for explaining this is that southerners prefer to learn proper behavior from mothers rather than from books. Southerners are rarely mentioned in etiquette books nowadays. Judith Martin, better known as Miss Manners, has chastised southerners for wearing white shoes after Easter rather than at the proper time, after Memorial Day. The often-hot southern spring is perhaps responsible for this abiding regional faux pas, but her criticism is a reminder that northerners, not those from the South, have traditionally set national standards of manners.

The last 15 years have seen the appearance of a number of half-humorous treatments of "southern ways." *A Southern Belle Primer* (1991) offered etiquette suggestions for survival in the modern South. The title of *Being Dead Is No Excuse: The Official Southern Ladies Guide to Hosting the Perfect Funeral* (2005), by Gayden Metcalfe and Charlotte Hays, suggests the continuing familiarity of many southerners with the social rules even at the time of death.

The southern fascination with manners has been well expressed in literature.

Peter Taylor's short stories, Reynolds Price's and Hamilton Basso's novels, and all of Eudora Welty's works are among the most subtle explorations of southern manners. Three of Welty's best-known works show how the southerner's sense of ritual led to an appreciation of form: *Delta Wedding* explores a happy ceremony of marriage, *Optimist's Daughter* a sad one of death, and *Losing Battles* a joyous yet melancholy family reunion. Southern concern with family and kin, the proper clothing, food, courtesy in daily living, talking and visiting—all are expressed in the region's best writing.

The contemporary period has seen the appearance of etiquette and finishing schools for young southerners. Working parents and busy recreational lives for youth have disrupted traditional family life, including the teaching of manners. One school in Louisiana that has been around for two decades teaches students from Louisiana, Mississippi, Alabama, and Texas lessons on using the proper fork and writing thank-you notes but also addresses such topics as body piercing ("do not" is the teaching). A public school teacher in Memphis, Tenn., instructs students in manners, outside of class, free of charge. One African American mother of a 10-year-old boy spoke for some older southerners, noting that "in today's society, with the younger generations, manners have gone astray. It's a good thing for him to learn manners."

Other southern women reject the traditional centrality of etiquette to understanding southern culture. Writer Mab Segrest sees manners as a cloak for social injustices that are finessed through manners and not addressed openly. Minnie Bruce Pratt, a poet, feminist activist, and lesbian activist from Alabama, similarly indicts southern manners because they "can be used to cage us and keep us from shouting for changes." Manners make privileged status seem natural, legitimating a hierarchical society. Pratt rejects as stylized "southern manners," but claims a southern identity free of what she sees as the indirections, evasions, and deferrals of the social role that manners can demand of women in the South.

CHARLES REAGAN WILSON
University of Mississippi

W. J. Cash, *The Mind of the South* (1941); Stephen L. Carter, *Civility: Manners, Morals, and the Etiquette of Democracy* (1998); Thomas D. Clark, *Rampaging Frontier: Manners and Humors of Pioneer Days in the Southern Middle West* (1964), *Travelers in the New South*, 2 vols. (1962), *Travelers in the Old South*, 2 vols. (1959); James McBride Dabbs, *The Southern Heritage* (1958), *Who Speaks for the South?* (1964); John Dollard, *Caste and Class in a Southern Town* (1937); Bertram Doyle, *The Etiquette of Race Relations in the South* (1937); Clement Eaton, *The Mind of the*

Old South (1967); Melville Herskovits, *The Myth of the Negro Past* (1941); Florence King, *Southern Ladies and Gentlemen* (1975); Tara McPherson, *Reconstructing Dixie: Race, Gender, and Nostalgia in the Imagined South* (2003); Ellen M. Plaute, *Women at Home in Victorian America: A Social History* (1997); Minnie Bruce Pratt, *Rebellion: Essays, 1980–1991* (1991); Newbell Niles Puckett, *Folk Beliefs of the Southern Negro* (1926; reprint 1969); John Shelton Reed, *The Enduring South: Subcultural Persistence in Mass Society* (1972), *Southerners: The Social Psychology of Sectionalism* (1983); Anne Firor Scott, *The Southern Lady: From Pedestal to Politics, 1830–1930* (1970); Oliver Stanley, "Minding Manners," Memphis *Commercial Appeal* (May 8, 2005); Margaret Visser, *Rituals of Dinner: The Origin, Evolution, Eccentricities, and Meaning of Table Manners* (1991); Bertram Wyatt-Brown, *Southern Honor: Ethics and Behavior in the Old South* (1982).

Memory

The South since the Civil War, wrote William Faulkner, has been "peopled with garrulous outraged baffled ghosts" (*Absalom, Absalom!*). The ghosts of southern memory have remained strong into the 21st century, and the argument can be made that no other American region (with perhaps the exception of New England) has rooted its identity so powerfully in its own historical consciousness. The South represents what could be called a culture of remembrance, meaning not only that the public face of southern life borrows heavily from themes from the past (historical monuments, public symbols, historical tourism) but also that the values of southern life are deeply influenced by the values of commemoration and ancestral meaning. Those values themselves are constantly undergoing reinterpretation, as they are "re-remembered" by contemporary southerners.

The outcome of the Civil War accounts for much of the South's obsession with historical memory. In the colonial and Revolutionary period, the region showed no particular penchant for memorializing its past. In fact, outside of South Carolina and Virginia, much of the South had only recently been opened up to white settlement and existed primarily as frontier. Like much of the rest of the new nation, the South had no past to remember. Antebellum southern novelists, such as William Gilmore Simms, sometimes attempted to craft a past from the Revolutionary era. Their concerns did not, however, focus solely on regional identity and had a more national intent.

Defeat in the American Civil War led many white southerners to imagine and reimagine what southern life had been before the war came, a process that did much to shape a particular construction of southern identity. Most white southerners adopted an elegiac mood about the world before the war, using the conflict as mental shorthand to account for their current dissatisfactions. During Reconstruction, white southern leaders found historical memory to be a powerful ideological tool. Confederate veterans rallied around the standard of the fallen Confederacy to overthrow Reconstruction governments in southern states and reinstitute "home rule." The white unity created by the memory of the Confederacy had much to do with the political course of the South into the next century.

Memory would continue to play an important role in southern political, social, and cultural life in the 20th century. One of its most important effects became the celebration of the Lost Cause, a ritualistic commemoration of the Confederacy and of Confederate heroes. The Lost Cause movement found expression in the building of monuments, political campaigns, and the celebration of Confederate Memorial Day. Postbellum white conservatives made special use of the Lost Cause movement, investing its rituals and mystagogy with their values.

A number of factors in the 20th century helped to further shape the South into a culture of remembrance. Rural poverty created by a collapsing agricultural economy caused many white southerners to construct an antebellum golden age or to link themselves to a glorious family ancestor. White southerners sometimes used the past as a weapon against northern critics of southern peculiarities and atrocities, from segregation to the prevalence of lynching. During the freedom struggle, black southerners sometimes responded to the evocation of states' rights and the memory of the Civil War with countermemories of their own, evoking the memory of Reconstruction as a time when they had held real political power and attempted to create a tradition of progressive democracy in the postbellum South.

A final, much more commercial, reason for the continuing power of southern memory is the importance of historical tourism in the new regional economy. Northerners, historian Nina Silber has argued, have viewed the American South as a link to an older, and a simpler, America. The South has capitalized on such notions by transforming its past into a commodity. The development of the historical tourism industry and the values of the 20th-century historic preservation movement went hand in hand, as evidenced by the success of tourism in Charleston, Williamsburg, San Antonio, and New Orleans. In places like Natchez, Miss., acts of ritual piety such as the "Pilgrimage" of the United Daughters of the Confederacy openly joined with the demands of commercial tourism.

Black southerners have had a complex relationship to the public world of southern historical memory, in large part because the memory of the Confederate cause completely dominated the landscape for so long. African Americans are, however, as deeply rooted in the American South as whites and have placed a strong emphasis on sustaining their relationship to family memories and exploring genealogical links to the southern past. In recent years, as African American political power in the South has grown, efforts have been made to reassert blacks' place in the public memory of the South. These efforts have resulted in very intense public controversies, particularly over the display of the Confederate flag, the inclusion of Confederate symbols in state flags, and the propriety of other public and state-sponsored efforts to remember the Confederacy. Increasingly, black southerners are working, sometimes with limited success, to publicly assert the importance of black life in the South. Regional and county museums devoted to the southern African American experience have emerged throughout much of the region. Major efforts are currently under way to build a national monument to the slave experience as well as to create a national museum of African American history. In the urban South, African Americans hope to transform a landscape littered with monuments to the Confederate cause. In Charleston, S.C., an effort that began in the mid-1990s, so far unsuccessful, has been made to build a monument to Denmark Vesey, the leader of a failed slave conspiracy in 1822 and a cultural hero to Lowcountry South Carolina African Americans.

A number of white southerners in the modern era have criticized the southern obsession with the past, suggesting that it has created a profound cultural myopia in the region. Some entrepreneurial promoters and boosters have called on the South to disentangle itself from the power of memory, though criticism has also come from intellectuals who do not accept the promises of untrammeled progress any more than the brooding of southern revanchists. The best example of this nuanced approach comes from Robert Penn Warren. Warren, a native Kentuckian who had been part of the Nashville Agrarian movement, charged that southerners had used the memory of the Civil War as "the Great Alibi." The memory of defeat, Warren believed, had become the white South's way to avoid dealing with the present concerns of its people, black and white. Southern liberals often joined in the general condemnation of southerners' fascination with the past and apathy about the future. Upcountry South Carolina journalist Harry Ashmore wrote that southerners "ran and hid because their grandfathers once took a terrible licking." Ashmore's fellow South Carolinian Ben Robertson told a stunned audience at the College of Charleston in 1935 that they should go and plant a tree every time they thought about the Civil War since then at least some good would come from the southern obsession with memory.

Criticisms such as these notwithstanding, all indications are that the southern past will have a remarkable, though a complicated, future. Historical tourism acts as the bulwark of hundreds of local southern economies. Historical writing about the American South and graduate programs in southern history proliferate exponentially. A number of signs suggest that southern memory will develop in more sophisticated directions in the 21st century. The era of the Civil War and Reconstruction will continue to play a seminal role in the development of memory and myth. However, as C. Vann Woodward once pointed out, the iconography of the civil rights movement will itself provide fruitful ground for southern memory. This trend can already be seen in the cities such as Atlanta, Memphis, and Birmingham, where major civil rights memorials and museums remind the historical tourist of the freedom struggle. We can predict that the stone Confederate soldier, lonely on his perch in the southern courthouse square, will soon cease to be the archetypal symbol of southern memory. In the southern future to come, the southern past will change.

W. SCOTT POOLE
College of Charleston

William A. Blair, *Cities of the Dead: Contesting the Memory of the Civil War in the South, 1865–1914* (2004); David W. Blight, *Beyond the Battlefield: Race, Memory, and the American Civil War* (2002), *Race and Reunion: The Civil War in American Memory* (2000); W. Fitzhugh Brundage, ed., *Where These Memories Grow: History, Memory, and Southern Identity* (2000); Alice Fahs, ed., *The Memory of the Civil War in American Culture* (2004); John R. Neff, *Honoring the Civil War Dead: Commemoration and the Problem of Reconciliation* (2005); Ben Robertson, *Red Hills and Cotton: An Upcountry Memory* (1991); Charles Reagan Wilson, *Baptized in Blood: The Religion of the Lost Cause, 1865–1920* (1980); C. Vann Woodward, *The Burden of Southern History* (revised ed., 1982).

Modernism

Modernism is a specific international cultural and arts movement that had its greatest impact in the South starting around 1920. "Modern" is simply that which is up to the moment, and the word gained currency in the 17th and 18th centuries when intellectuals in France and England joined battle over whether contemporary thought and expression could match the classics that the European Renaissance recovered, revered, and increasingly imitated and also whether intellectual progress was indeed even possible. This was the so-called Battle of the Books or the Quarrel of the Ancients and the Moderns. The issues raised in this old quarrel surfaced, perhaps ironically, in the American South of the 20th century, where reverence for the classics and doubts about scientific and cultural progress played a role in what is called the Southern Renaissance, the term used to speak about the period in which literary modernism first manifested itself in the former slave states.

Scholars disagree as to the precise years of the international modernist movement. Southern scholar Monroe Spears, in *Dionysus and the City* (1970), a study of modernism in poetry, suggests 1870 as a rough beginning for "modernism as an epoch in the cultural history of the West." The British novelist Malcolm Bradbury and his coeditor James McFarlane entitle their wide-ranging collection of essays on the movement *Modernism 1890–1930*. Influences leading to 20th-century modernism include the writings of the French and Russian realists of the 19th century, the French Symbolist poets, and Impressionist and Expressionist painters. Spears chooses 1909 as "the beginning of modernism as a specific movement in the arts," as seen in the origins of cubist painting and sculpture; the emergence of Stravinsky's and Schoenberg's music, of Hulme's, Pound's, and Eliot's poetry, and of Woolf's, Stein's, and Joyce's fiction; and the increasing application in the literary arts of Freud's psychology, Frazer's studies of mythology, and Bergson's philosophy of time and memory.

International modernism found its way into the South along many streams. Young southerners who traveled and studied abroad or in the American Northeast returned to spread the gospel of modernism as teachers, writers, or mentors to those only a little younger. William Faulkner's Yale-educated friend Phil Stone is only one of many examples. The prime disciplines that affected and expressed the modernist aesthetic—psychology, anthropology, philosophy, musical composition, painting, sculpture, architecture, and the writing of experimental poetry, fiction, and drama—were discussed and illustrated in such magazines as the *Dial*, *Poetry: A Magazine of Verse*, the *Little Review*, *Vanity Fair*, and the *Smart Set*. With such American figures as Gertrude Stein, Sherwood Anderson, H. D., T. S. Eliot, and Ezra Pound prominently established among the Anglo-American modernists immediately following the First World War, the annus mirabilis 1922 is a focal point, not a pure revelation. In that year were published Joyce's *Ulysses*, Eliot's *The Waste Land*, T. E. Lawrence's *Seven Pillars of Wisdom*, Sinclair Lewis's *Babbitt*, the one-volume abridgement of Frazer's *The Golden Bough*, James Weldon Johnson's *Book of American Negro Poetry*, and the first issue of a modest little magazine entitled the *Fugitive*, which emanated from a group of teachers, students, and associates in Nashville, Tenn. Throughout the United States—and the South was no exception—other limited-circulation "little" magazines began to represent local constituencies. Southern versions appeared in New Orleans, Richmond, and Charleston, and even on provincial college and university campuses, where humor magazines, literary journals, and drama groups took up the modernist aesthetic.

"Modern" implied a break with the experiences and traditions of the past, a break not merely symbolized but actualized by the Great War of 1914 to 1919, with its murderous technology, duration, and results. In the South, the perhaps reluctant or at least slow and somewhat special embrace given to modernism reflects one of the most ironic aspects of the modernist movement. The conservative and largely agrarian South could go modern because modernism is both reactionary and radical, conservative and revolutionary, seeking to recover values and meanings lost in the wake of the rapidly expanding Industrial Revolution and its related phenomenon. The devastation wrought within the South's borders by the region's own great war of 1861–65 resembled what had happened in World War I. The Civil War had many of the same features as the later European war: massive mobilization and movements of personnel, an armory of increasingly lethal industrially produced weapons, and psychological terror through active warfare against civilian populations who did not live anywhere near sites that produced weapons or supplies or were home to rail and shipping facilities.

Louis D. Rubin Jr. has written that the poet-critics of Vanderbilt University who began the *Fugitive* in 1922 and later popularized, with their pupils and allies, the New Criticism, "identified the literature of the Southern Renascence as a culmination of the region's literary and cultural history, rather than some bizarre modernist deviation from it." Yet both their dry ironic poetry and their setting aside issues of history and biography in favor of keen linguistic focus on the autonomous literary text are, while not bizarre, deviations from previous southern and indeed American practice. That they were also "fugitives" from the "high-class brahmins" and sentimentality of the recent southern past also puts the intent of their little magazine on a revolutionary par with similarly metaphorical titles created here and abroad: *Blast*, *Transition*, *Secession*, or the *Double Dealer*. It appears, in fact, that the new ideas and aesthetic fashions of modernism helped weaken the sentimentality and false mythologizing to which the Victorian South had succumbed as it recovered economically from the Civil War. The First World War also potentially helped youngsters who had grown up hearing the cheery and heroic tales of the old veterans comprehend what the Civil War was really like, and war aside, a postwar poem like *The Waste Land* could inspire both the tone and the structure of Fugitive Allen Tate's somber and nonmemorial *Ode to the Confederate Dead*.

The southern writer Walker Percy has argued that the dawn of science some three centuries ago spawned an age that ended with the advent of modernism in the early 20th century, and along with it also ended the lessons science offered for human self-understanding. Those who realized this abyss, and took it seriously, Percy says, suffered the symptoms of alienation, either wordlessly because they did not know the cause of their problem or, like Percy himself, by going in search of new meanings. Percy's writing, like Faulkner's, but also like that of Carson McCullers, Flannery O'Connor, Eudora Welty, or Robert Penn Warren, reflects this suffering.

The Literary Renaissance in the 20th-century South is interpreted variously as an expression of international modernism. Some scholars see it as outside the pale of the modernist movement because, as Richard James Calhoun has written, the region's writers did not fully feel "the historical and metaphysical discontinuities of the most modern writers" and were not "completely modern." But Lewis Simpson argues that the southern movement was "fully joined in the wider literary and artistic opposition to *modernity*," and that qualifies it. Again, the list of events and conditions listed by historian C. Vann Woodward as the "burden of southern history" — losing a war, enduring occupation, failing morally and economically in a country that has thought itself always successful and always morally right — had from the slave era through Reconstruction given the South cultural parity with most of the rest of the Western world where modernism leapt into prominence before and after World War I. Rubin has observed that the writers who emerged in the South in the 1920s represented the first generation of southerners since the slave era to confront directly "the vanguard of the most advanced thought and feeling of their times" and to embrace much of that thought. Regional historical experience had provided the southern writer with paradoxical advantages in exploring the uncertainties and dislocation in which modernism has traditionally taken an interest. The fall of traditional southern society, personified in the decline of families, was an excellent local metaphor for a world condition observed by even more than the three writers Faulkner described as the "best" of his time: Proust, Thomas Mann, and Joyce.

Harry Levin has identified the experience of expatriation as one of the chief preconditions of becoming a modernist. The most acclaimed southern literary figures — Glasgow, Faulkner, Warren, Welty, Wright, for example — traveled widely outside the South, giving them a perspective on changes occurring in the region different from that of writers who stayed home. One might speculate that those writers willing or able to return home with a sharpened vision continued to study the local with greater depth, monitoring locally the subtle evidence for emerging discontinuities, and to portray it with strikingly new techniques.

Modernist expression in the South took other than literary form, chiefly music derived from long-existent folk traditions: blues, gospel, and what is called country. At about the same time that the Vanderbilt group was starting the *Fugitive* and writers in New Orleans were founding the *Double Dealer*, recordings and radio broadcasts of somewhat refined performance versions of this music emerged as popular entertainment and gained a national audience. Jazz, in particular, bears on the issue of modernism, though the rapid fusion of jazz, blues, gospel, and country makes them all cognate, in some respects, as expressions of the modernist aesthetic: uniquely marked by performance styles just as much as poetry and fiction bore the specific signatures of their makers — frank, addressing the contingencies of the human dilemma, improvisational, and playful. Jazz and blues, especially, are southern by origin, and regional expatriates have been their prime practitioners; they are existential, laying stress on the individual psyche and on the present moment. No wonder Louis Armstrong was billed as the "Master of Modernism."

One of the most memorable expressions of modernism is, of course, the painting associated with it, and the idea of a Southern Renaissance should also be applied to 20th-century painting in the region. "For painters in the South," writes art historian Rick Stewart, "the period between the two world wars was marked by the problematical relationship between a romantic sectionalism and a modernist internationalism." To be sure, southern painters generally followed Missourian Thomas Hart Benton's direction in combining modernist forms with the idea that art had a moral obligation to instruct. But Black Mountain College in North Carolina was the institutional center of more experimental modernist painting in the region, especially through the influence of Charles Olson and Josef Albers. One can date the beginnings of modern painting in the region from 1933, when Albers came to Black Mountain. However, the full impact of the movement was not felt until the 1960s. George Bireline's painting *Malcolm's Last Address*, for example, was an influential abstract painting exhibited in 1965. It seriously challenged the dominance of realism in regional work and has led to the increased prominence of abstract forms. By 1976 critic Elizabeth C. Baker could write that contemporary southern art "bespeaks an almost universal acceptance of the modern vernacular."

The failure to relate modernism adequately to 20th-century southern cultural development, and especially to the Southern Literary Renaissance, has fostered the idea that the renaissance is over. This may be just to say that modernism is over, or that modernism has entered another stage. Much post–World War II southern writing can be characterized as postmodern, but that should not imply an end to the flowering of literary expression that followed in the wake of H. L. Mencken's well-known 1920 benediction for southern culture in his essay "The Sahara of the Bozart." And the great and moving work of the southern modernists is still very much there to be read and pondered by subsequent generations. These writers, modernists all, perfectly aware of the discontinuities and strangeness of even everyday life and conversant with the psychological and cultural construction of identity, history, and even place, nonetheless rendered southern place with such skill that their fictional versions have become "real." As modernist production, which is always about itself, these fictional places are in fact more "real" than the everyday realms through which we or our forebears might have walked. What empowered the best artists within southern modernism was precisely what Alan Bullock suggests in an essay in *Modernism 1890–1930*: the breakup of so many old patterns and the arrival of "new forms, new languages, in which to project" the "trends and conflicts—social, moral, intellectual, spiritual" of the new era, "that improbable, disturbing, fragmented world in which we still live."

THOMAS L. MCHANEY
Georgia State University

Alfred Appel Jr., *Jazz Modernism: From Ellington and Armstrong to Matisse and Joyce* (2002); Malcolm Bradbury and James McFarlane, eds., *Modernism 1890–1930* (1976); Richard H. King, *A Southern Renaissance: The Cultural Awakening of the American South, 1930–1955* (1980); Thomas L. McHaney, *The Southern Renaissance* (2001); H. L. Mencken, *Prejudices, Series Two* (1920); Albert Murray, *Stomping the Blues* (1976); Michael O'Brien, *The Idea of the American South, 1920–1941* (1979); Louis D. Rubin et al., *The History of Southern Literature* (1985); Daniel J. Singal, *The War Within: From Victorian to Modern Thought in the South, 1919–1945* (1982); Rick Stewart, in *Painting in the South, 1564–1980* (1984).

Motherhood

Street slang and graffiti that commonly refer to one's mother in northern cities are less frequently found in the South, even in its urban areas. Call a southern boy a "son of a bitch" and he might break both your legs. Not because you have insulted him; you have done far, far worse: you have insulted his mother. And to insult any southern mother is to insult virtue, piety, honor, and the South.

Images and popular stereotypes of "southern mothers" have differed along regional, economic, class, and racial lines, yet two particular stereotypes of southern motherhood abound in popular literature and movies—the black mammy and the upper-class white lady, both portrayed to perfection in *Gone with the Wind*.

Doris Ulmann photograph of a mother and her infant somewhere in the South, c. 1933
(Southern Historical Collection, University of North Carolina, Chapel Hill)

Although a remarkable group of gifted scholars has written on southern white women, at present less is known about the white southern mother than about the African American mother in the South. This is at least partly because reality is confused with an image central to the development of the southern white identity. Although David Potter argued that women have not participated in the formation of the national character of the United States, William R. Taylor claims that the South adopted essentially feminine characteristics because the region failed in the masculine world of the marketplace. Most recent studies demonstrate that the South did not fail in the chase after wealth but simply took a different and perhaps more lucrative path. After the Civil War, however, both adherents of the Old South legend and advocates of the industrial New South acquiesced in a sentimental portrayal of the plantation South, which held the southern lady at center stage to justify the existing social order.

In its worst forms the idealization of the southern mother and, hence, the southern white woman was used to justify the barbarism of lynching black men. Winthrop D. Jordan has shown how sexual fantasies of Europeans, especially the English, were projected onto Africans and combined with slavery to foster an intense racism. After slavery ended, protection of southern womanhood became a battle cry for the repression of southern blacks. Many whites portrayed the African American as a destroyer of social order, and they saw the white family, the basis of social stability, as the most obvious point of defense against imagined or real attacks. According to this myth, white women symbolized the family and needed protection from rape or from intermarriage with black men. Thus, whites' fears expressed both sexual and social concerns.

W. J. Cash called the idolatry of southern white women "downright gyneolatry. . . . Hardly a sermon . . . did not begin and end with tributes in her honor, hardly a brave speech . . . did not open and close with the clashing of shields and the flourishing of swords for her glory. At the last, I verily believe, the ranks of the Confederacy went rolling into battle in the misty conviction that it was wholly for her that they fought."

Despite romantic plantation literature, the aristocratic southern white wife was not the only figure idealized. All successful southern men owed their accomplishments to their mothers; whatever heights they obtained were attributed to their mothers' love, teachings, sacrifices, and examples. Two southern leaders identified with the common man were Andrew Jackson of the antebellum South and Ben Tillman of the late 19th-century period of agrarian unrest. Both men's fathers died before they were born, and both were reared solely by their mothers—women celebrated for teaching correct patriarchal values to their famous sons. President Jackson praised his mother: "She was as gentle as a dove and as brave as a lioness. . . . The memory of my mother and her teach-ings were after all the only capital I had to start life with." U.S. Senator Tillman explained that his mother taught "habits of thrift and industry; to be ambi-tious; to despise shams, hypocrisy, and untruthfulness; to bear trouble and sor-row with resolution." As their nicknames "Old Hickory" and "Pitchfork Ben" imply, both Jackson and Tillman were celebrated for the so-called masculine traits one might expect from leaders in a patriarchal society.

Historically, the southern woman was the guardian of the family. She had children with remarkable frequency, rarely disclosing the pain and suffering that accompanied almost constant childbearing. Usually she celebrated her childbearing role. When she was not confined to bed in pregnancy or child-birth, environmental, social, and economic conditions dictated her day-to-day routines: gardening, canning, preserving, cooking; spinning, weaving, sewing, knitting; washing, ironing, cleaning; nursing and caring for husband, children, friends, and animals.

Despite the differences between the North and the South, the role of the mother in the 19th century was very similar in both sections. She was the pri-mary rearer of children and the inculcator of domestic moral values. According to the prevailing view, the southern woman was the moral superior of her hus-band, so upon her fell the burden of making a decent and moral home, provid-ing a good example for her young children and a refuge for the family patriarch from the turmoil of the workplace or the realm of politics.

Because few public schools were available, the southern white matriarch played a substantial role in educating her children. The early education of most southerners therefore depended upon the knowledge of their mothers and the degree to which they took this role seriously. Some southerners were extremely well taught, but others lacked the most rudimentary book learning. Most moth-ers taught their girls to sew, weave, and care for younger children, while fathers taught their boys to handle responsibility.

As the upholder of key moral values, the woman was also expected to teach the children piety. She did this primarily by example. Although men were active in southern churches, the mother typically was the more constant churchgoer and usually inducted her children into the social order by taking them to church and by reading them the Bible. With religious values so closely allied to family solidarity, the woman's role in introducing the children to religious faith in the South was seen as an effective way for her to strengthen family ties. As keeper of the family's religious flame, the woman made sure her home was a refuge from the meanness of everyday life.

One of the reasons women increasingly took on teaching positions in the

North in the 1840s and later in the South was that the female teacher was widely regarded as a sort of classroom surrogate mother who eased the transition of the young child from the home to the community and furthermore prepared the child to take his or her place in the rapidly emerging industrial society. Women assumed an important role in the classroom in the South even though industrial changes occurred very slowly there. Once public schools took hold in the South, the female teacher rapidly became almost universal in elementary schools, carrying out her maternal function of imparting the right values to the young.

The role of southern mother, nonetheless, sometimes conflicted with the southern ideal of womanhood. Whereas the mother was expected to be a preeminent moral guardian and a tower of strength, as well as efficient, protective, and self-reliant, the ideal woman was often seen as gentle, submissive, flighty, independent, and seemingly unfit to rear children. Certainly, southern women, like northern women, struggled under such contradictions and limitations. If there was a resolution to this dilemma for southern women, it emerged with age, the flighty behavior of the southern belle, desirable in young adulthood, changing suitably with the bearing of the first child.

As novelist Gail Godwin pointed out, the roles of wife and mother have traditionally given identity to the southern woman. Godwin's fictional composite southern lady responds to the question of identity: "Who am I? I am the wife of a wonderful husband and the mother of four adorable children, that's who I am." Modern writers have been much more unkind about the image and its impact on the South. Among others, Flannery O'Connor, Lillian Smith, and William Faulkner have portrayed the damage done to women and to the South as they tried to live with the requirements of perfectionism that symbolized white southern motherhood. Women struggled to reconcile the expectations and realities of the modern world and the legend of southern motherhood. And southern white men have been accused by many pop psychologists of exhibiting a "madonna-whore" attitude toward women; the southern mother was worshipped and put upon a pedestal while other women, those of lower economic status—the daughters of white tenants and textile workers, African American or Indian women—were fair game for the South's youngbloods.

The sentimentality of the Victorian era helped shape the image of southern white motherhood and has been preserved in modern regional popular culture. Early country singer Jimmie Rodgers typically sang "Mother, Queen of My Heart" and Hank Williams later wrote and recorded "Message to My Mother," one of a number of poignant country tunes dedicated to mourned mothers.

Dolly Parton's "Coat of Many Colors" is a tale of the triumph of a mother's love over poverty. Southern popular culture, black and white, conveys images of endlessly toiling, long-suffering mothers. "Mama Tried" is Merle Haggard's tribute to a mother whose good influence was unable to keep her boy from trouble. "I'm the Only Hell My Mama Ever Raised" similarly is Johnny Paycheck's lament of a boy hell-bent for trouble who rejected his mother in favor of questionable friends and fast cars.

The image of the southern black mother has taken a different path altogether. Although most black women worked in the fields and not in the planter's house, the most popular image of the black woman has been the mammy. The black mammy, like the southern lady, was also born in the white mind, a creation of slavery: "the black mammy, that creature of impeccable virtue, administrative skill, power and nurturing ability, who yet inexplicably remained in bondage." Suckling a white baby at one breast and a black child at the other, mammy was simple, religious, strong, practical, and tough enough to knock about male slaves caught with a finger in the pie or scores of home-sacking Yankee "blue-bellies" and poor white trash scalawags. Unlike mythical southern aristocratic mothers, mammies were not ladylike; whereas white women were viewed as unladylike if they worked, black women were considered lazy and impudent if they resisted working long hours at hard labor. The black mammy sweated over boiling cauldrons, toiled with wash, scrubbed the kitchen, and minded the children. The black mother had to take care of herself and she had to teach her children to survive their inferior place in society. Mammy's religious strength was elevated to sainthood by William Faulkner's character Dilsey.

Whereas white mothers were stereotypically submissive to their patriarchal husbands, the strength of the black mother led to the myth of the black matriarchy. The myth that black women were the dominant force within their families and that fathers were often absent originated with well-intentioned reformers and goes back at least to abolitionist literature. Early depictions of slave mothers pointed to the horrors of breaking up the family by selling children and spouses, the arbitrary beatings of slaves by whites, and the sexual exploitation of slave women by white men. Until the 1970s, scholars and the public generally accepted the notion of the "weak," meaning fatherless, black home, and this in turn reinforced and influenced white society's attitudes toward black people in general. The concept of black matriarchy dominated scholarly literature and became a political issue in the wake of the controversial 1965 study by Daniel Moynihan, who held that the contemporary black matriarchal family had its principal origins in slavery.

In the mid-1980s concerns about the black family gained new attention because of the increase in the percentage of black single-parent, female-headed families. For example, in six southern states in 1980 over 60 percent of all the single-parent, female-headed families were black. In 1980 nationally 40 percent of African American families were headed by a female, with no husband present, and that figure rose to 44 percent in 2000. This increase in female-headed households among African Americans has been attributed to such factors as racism, the economic vulnerability of blacks, the shorter life spans of African American men, the increasing rate of out-of-marriage parenthood, and changing gender roles accompanying the growth of female autonomy. The discrepancy in male and female populations among African Americans also works against possibilities of married-couple families: in 2000 there were 86 males to every 100 females in the United States.

Many studies have corrected the grosser misconceptions about black family life, including that of the matriarchy. Herbert Gutman in particular provided clear evidence of the African American commitment to the family as an institution, in both slavery and freedom. He and other historians have confirmed for African Americans what is normally assumed for other groups: the two-parent nuclear family was the normal means for organizing primary experience (sex relations, child rearing, and descent). As a result, scholars increasingly concentrate on other questions, such as illegitimacy, attitudes toward working wives, the influence of religion, and the division of authority in the family. Nevertheless, black leaders are also calling for more attention to the needs of poor, single-parent black families and to means for enhancing the stability of black families.

A certain irony in the study of the black matriarchy suggests, however, a symbiotic relationship between racism and sexism. For over 60 years, scholars, mostly male, pointed to the black family and called it matriarchal and therefore deficient. With the civil rights movement young northern white women who came South began to see heroes in strong black women such as Rosa Parks and Fannie Lou Hamer. When the feminist movement needed heroes, it turned to the scholarly literature on the black matriarchy for role models. *Ms.* magazine devoted an issue to black women as historical heroes for modern women, at the same time that mostly white male scholars have been arguing that there was no black matriarchy.

One of the paradoxes within recent historical scholarship has concerned the place of black and white women within American families. As scholars have "rehabilitated" the male role in the black family, feminist scholars have shown the power of the wife within white middle- and working-class families. Historians are just beginning to understand the images and the roles of black and white mothers in the American South.

ORVILLE VERNON BURTON
University of Illinois

Maxine Alexander, ed., *Speaking for Ourselves: Women of the South* (1984); Irving H. Bartlett and Glenn Cambor, *Women's Studies*, vol. 2 (1974); Orville Vernon Burton, *In My Father's House Are Many Mansions: Family and Community in Edgefield, South Carolina* (1985); Bette D. Dickerson, ed., *African American Single Mothers: Understanding Their Lives and Families* (1995); Walter J. Fraser Jr., R. Frank Saunders Jr., and Jon L. Wakelyn, eds., *The Web of Southern Social Relations: Women, Family, and Education* (1985); Herbert G. Gutman, *The Black Family in Slavery and Freedom, 1750–1925* (1977); Sally G. McMillen, *Motherhood in the Old South: Pregnancy, Childbirth, and Infant Rearing, 1800–1860* (1990); Stephanie J. Shaw, in *Mothers and Motherhood: Readings in American History*, ed. Rima D. Apple and Janet Golden (1997); U.S. Bureau of the Census, Current Population Reports, Series P-20, no. 380 (1983), General Social and Economic Characteristics, 1980 (by state) (1981).

Museums

The South's approximately 1,800 museums represent almost 23 percent of the 6,000-plus institutions recognized by the American Association of Museums (AAM). By the AAM definition a museum is "an organized and permanent nonprofit institution, essentially educational or aesthetic in purpose, with professional staff, which owns and utilizes tangible objects, cares for them, and exhibits them to the public on some regular schedule." The AAM recognizes 13 major categories of museums: art, children's and junior, college and university, company, general, history, science, and specialized museums; exhibit areas; libraries with collections in additions to books; national and state agencies, councils, and commissions; nature centers; and park museums and visitor centers. Within these categories are such diverse settings as archaeological sites, zoos, planetariums, and wildlife refuges. Many museums span several classifications, and certain museum types predominate in the South, as is true in other regions. The tremendous variation in museums is well represented in the South.

The growth of all types of museums in the South accelerated in the 20th century, although more slowly in the Deep South than in states such as Virginia, Maryland, and the Carolinas, all of which stand out in the history of American museums. The Charleston Museum, founded in 1772, was the first permanent museum in the American English colonies and began as a natural history museum containing such objects as an Indian hatchet, human skeletal remains, and minerals. One of the nation's oldest and most renowned historic house museums is Mount Vernon, George Washington's Virginia plantation. Ann Pamela Cunningham of South Carolina spearheaded the campaign to restore Mount Vernon, and she ranks as one of the country's first and most noted historic preservationists. Arlington, home of Robert E. and Mary Ann Custis Lee, became the first federally owned historic home following a 22-year controversy. Federal troops occupied the house in 1861, and the federal government auctioned off and illegally bought Arlington and established a national cemetery on its grounds in 1864. In 1882 George W. C. Lee, Robert and Mary's son, won his case before the U.S. Supreme Court regarding ownership of the estate, but he stuck by an earlier offer to convey the property to Congress in return for a fair monetary settlement.

The South has led the way in other aspects of museum history. Colonial Williamsburg, the beautifully restored capital of 18th-century Virginia, opened in 1926 as the nation's first major outdoor museum and is still considered by many to be second to none. Preservation of historic districts began in the South: Charleston, S.C., and New Orleans, La., both of which were developed in the 1930s, were the first such projects in the United States. In historic districts selected buildings are designated as museums, but the architecture serves as the setting for modern-day activities. Outdoor museums of other sorts also have roots in the South. The zoos in St. Louis, Mo. (1913), and Fort Worth, Tex. (1923), were two of the first major zoos in the United States; and the nation's first safari zoo, Lion Country Safari, opened near West Palm Beach, Fla., in 1966.

Other landmarks in the nation's museum history exist in the South. Two of the country's battle galleries, a museum type uncommon in the United States, are in the South. In Battle Abbey of the Virginia Historical Society, Richmond, Va., stand four large murals of Confederate heroes and battles painted by Charles Hoffbauer; and at Stone Mountain, Ga., loom Gutzon Borglum's gigantic sculptures of the Confederate leaders Lee, Davis, and Jackson. Somewhat similar in concept and popular in the 1800s were panoramas, or cycloramas, which surrounded the viewer with a huge circular painting of a battle or other scene. One of only two panoramas of the 1880s still being shown in the United States is the Battle of Atlanta at the Cyclorama in Atlanta. The battle galleries and panoramas effectively represent the post–Civil War South's penchant for memorializing Confederate heroes and their war efforts.

History museums are the most prevalent museum type in the South and include, among other things, historic structures and sites, preservation projects, and military museums, many of which are overseen by national and state agencies, councils, and commissions. Many of the South's historic museums grew from the burgeoning efforts in the 1890s and early 1900s to establish memorials, museums, and monuments and to preserve historic buildings associated with the Civil War. Economic difficulties of the Reconstruction period severely limited efforts at historic preservation in the South, but in the 1890s countless preservation organizations—primarily women's societies—were created. Monuments were erected in courthouse squares throughout the South, and numerous local museums preserving Civil War relics were established. The preservation societies' efforts drew much popular support, even though funds garnered from the scattered, rural, largely poor populace of the South were often limited. In undertaking large-scale restoration projects southern preservationists usually relied heavily on state or federal monies and fundraising activities rather than on the support of wealthy individuals. Such was true, for instance, of the Ladies' Hermitage Association's efforts to preserve Andrew Jackson's home in Nashville. For many years the preservation of buildings and relics associated with the Civil War far outstripped museum efforts of other types in the South. The South's homage to military sacrifice is further seen not only in the battlefields of the Civil War, such as Shiloh National Military Park and Cemetery, Shiloh, Tenn., but also in battlefields of the American Revolution, such as Cowpens National Battlefield, in South Carolina, and in battleship museums commemorating World War II combat, such as the USS *Alabama* at Mobile, Ala.

The heritage of the South is evident in a wide variety of other historic museums. The struggles and triumphs of the South's African American citizens are commemorated in such institutions as the Old Slave Market Museum and the Avery Institute of Afro-American History and Culture, both in Charleston, S.C. The civil rights story is told at museums in Memphis and Birmingham. Numerous sites and museums preserve the heritage of the South's Native Americans. Examples include the Natchez, Miss., Grand Village of the Natchez Indians, site of the capital village of the Natchez Indians from 1700 to 1730; New Echota, Calhoun, Ga., where the Cherokee Indians constructed a capital in 1825; Marksville State Commemorative Area, Marksville, La., site of a prehistoric Indian ceremonial center from A.D. 1 to 400; and the Native American Museum at Pembroke State University, Pembroke, N.C., an institution preserving relics and images of tribes throughout the South. The ethnic diversity of the region is further celebrated in museums ranging from the Bayou Folk Museum in Cloutierville, La., and the Acadian House Museum in St. Martinville, La., to the Mexican American Cultural Heritage Center in Dallas, Tex.

The South's religious background is evident in numerous historic churches, religious museums, and settlements established by religious groups. Examples include not only the World Methodist Building at Lake Junaluska, N.C., and the Baptist Museum of the Southern Baptist Historical Commission at Nashville, Tenn., but also the Archives Museum, Temple Mickve Israel at Savannah, Ga., and the Immaculate Conception Catholic Church, Natchitoches, La. Other fascinating examples of the South's religious heritage include Old Salem in Winston-Salem, N.C., and Shakertown at Pleasant Hill, Ky. Old Salem, a town founded in 1766 by Moravian settlers from Pennsylvania, has well-restored homes, shops, taverns, and a church plus the Museum of Early Southern Decorative Arts. At Shakertown the restored buildings and exhibits of tools, weaving looms, and other implements reflect the lifestyle of the Shakers, a religious group whose adherents lived communally at the site from 1805 to 1910.

Homes or birthplaces of countless famous individuals have been preserved in the South. Some statesmen whose homes or birthplaces have become museums include John C. Calhoun, Henry Clay, Jefferson Davis, Andrew Jackson, Thomas Jefferson, Abraham Lincoln, James K. Polk, and George Washington. Numerous writers with southern links have been commemorated, including Pearl S. Buck, William Faulkner, Ernest Hemingway, O. Henry, Flannery O'Connor, Edgar Allan Poe, Marjorie Rawlings, Carl Sandburg, Mark Twain, Eudora Welty, Thomas Wolfe, and Richard Wright. In addition to female writers, other famous southern women honored by historic sites include Clara Barton, Helen Keller, Mary Todd Lincoln, Annie Riggs, and Lurleen Wallace. Booker T. Washington and Martin Luther King Jr., two of the nation's most prominent black leaders, have been recognized through southern museums. Commemorated, too, have been scientists such as George Washington Carver and John James Audubon, military leaders such as Francis Marion and Douglas MacArthur, and musicians such as W. C. Handy, Stephen Foster, and Elvis Presley.

Vestiges of the antebellum South are preserved at numerous plantations and historic homes, ranging from Boone Hall Plantation, Mount Pleasant, S.C. (one setting for the movie *Gone with the Wind*) to Madewood in Napoleonville, La., and Melrose in Natchez, Miss. The plantation homes represent many architectural styles, and numerous historic home museums and other historic buildings interest both the general public and preservationists primarily because of their design. For example, the Sarasota, Fla., residence of circus owner John Ringling represents the ornate architecture of the Gilded Age. Palatial Biltmore House in Asheville, N.C., designed for George Vanderbilt, dazzles visitors with its opulent French Renaissance features. The elaborate, eclectic Victorian-style Bishop's Palace, Galveston, Tex., has been cited by the American Institute of Architects as one of the most outstanding buildings in the United States. These are but a few of the historic home museums in the South that represent archi-tectural trends and reflect lifestyles of earlier eras.

An overview of other museum types in the South provides a picture of the region's diverse institutions. Art museums include such long-standing institu-tions as the Telfair Academy in Savannah and the Gibbes in Charleston, plus city-owned art museums in most major southern cities. Newer art museums include the Roger Ogden Museum of Southern Art in New Orleans, the Morris Museum in Augusta, the Walter Anderson Museum in Ocean Springs, Miss., and the George Ohr Museum in Biloxi, Miss. Various museums, libraries, mon-uments, and historic sites are classified as libraries with collections in addition to books. The Historic New Orleans Collection was established in 1966 with a museum and research facilities in a historic French Quarter building. The Harry Ransom Humanities Research Center at the University of Texas at Austin has temporary exhibits as well as such permanent ones as a Guttenberg Bible and the world's first photograph. A historical focus is important in these and many other southern museums, although there is increasing emphasis on experien-tial learning in museum settings. Children explore the collections of such in-stitutions as the Cobb County Youth Museum in Marietta, Ga., the Estelle Car-mack Bandy Children's Museum in Kingsport, Tenn., the Junior Museum of Bay County in Panama City, Fla., and the Youth Cultural Center of Waco, Tex. Many southern college and university museums exhibit outstanding art collec-tions. Other college and university collections take the form of planetariums, arboretums, historical exhibits, herbariums, marine science exhibits, and even zoos. The George Washington Carver Museum at Tuskegee Institute and the Tuskegee Institute National Historic Site are examples of college-based muse-ums honoring renowned southerners, in this case both Carver and Booker T. Washington. Obviously, southern college and university collections are not re-stricted to large institutions. The Berea College Museums at Berea, Ky., are an excellent example of small museums that effectively display the region's cul-ture. Three museums at Berea College focus on the folk culture of the southern Appalachian highlands through exhibits of native arts and crafts, demonstra-tions by craftsmen, photographs, and oral history tapes.

Other examples of museums exhibiting southern folkways are the Blue Ridge Institute, Ferrum, Va.; the Mississippi Crafts Center, Ridgeland, Miss.; the Mu-seum of Appalachia, Norris, Tenn.; the Ozark Folk Life Center, Mountain View, Ark.; and the Rural Life Museum, Baton Rouge, La. On display at these mu-seums are such items as folk artwork, crafts, farm tools, and household fur-nishings and implements. Several notable folk art museums focus on musical and literary contributions, such as the Stephen Foster State Folk Culture Center, White Springs, Fla., and Wren's Nest, the Joel Chandler Harris Memorial, Atlanta, Ga.

The last decade has seen a proliferation of museums devoted to music in the South. The Georgia Music Hall of Fame includes a library, archives, exhibits, and educational programs. The Mississippi Musicians Hall of Fame is in Jackson, and the Alabama Music Hall of Fame is sponsored by the Muscle Shoals Music Association. The Country Music Hall of Fame opened its new facility in Nashville in 2001. Dollywood, Tenn., is home to the Southern Gospel Music Hall of Fame and Museum.

The South has a limited number of company museums, but two related to textiles are located in North Carolina: Biltmore Industries' Biltmore Homespun Shops in Asheville and the Cannon Mills Company's Cannon Visitor Center in Kannapolis. Other company museums include the U.S. Tobacco Company's Museum of Tobacco Art and History in Nashville, Tenn., and the Coca-Cola Company's Schmidt Museum of Coca-Cola Memorabilia in Elizabethtown, Ky. Other museums commemorate particular industries; for example, the Fort Worth, Tex., Western Company Museum, which highlights the history of the petroleum industry, and the McCalla, Ala., Iron and Steel Museum of Alabama at Tannehill Historical State Park.

Exhibit areas vary widely and include such examples as the Branchville Railroad Shrine and Museum, Inc., Branchville, S.C.; the Morehead Planetarium at Chapel Hill, N.C.; and the Barnwell Garden and Art Center at Shreveport, La. At Dry Tortugas Island off of Key West, Fla., visitors to the Fort Jefferson National Monument examine the largest masonry fort in the United States and see brown noddies and frigate birds in their natural habitat. Similar sights exist at such nature centers as the Seashore State Park Natural Area Visitor Center, Virginia Beach, Va.; the Audubon Park and Zoological Garden, New Orleans, La.; and the Big Bend National Park, Big Bend, Tex. Many nature areas are also classified as park museums, a designation that applies as well to many historical sites.

In the category of general museums are institutions such as the Kiah Museum, Savannah, Ga., which exhibits African, folk, 15th-century, and contemporary art, among other things. The Cottonlandia Museum in Greenwood, Miss., and the Daughters of the Republic of Texas Museum in Austin, Tex., are but two of the many other general museums. The former exhibits regional agricultural implements and household furnishings plus artifacts of the Mississippian-period Indians. The latter, housed in an 1857 land-office building, contains Indian artifacts, archives, and objects relating to early Texas history, coins, stamps, and artwork.

Southern science museums encompass varied collections, including the following: the Huntsville, Ala., Alabama Space and Rocket Center; the Salisbury, N.C., Catawba Museum of Anthropology; the Winter Park, Fla., Beal-Maltbie Shell Museum; the Dallas, Tex., Dallas Arboretum and Botanical Garden and the Dallas Zoo; the Birmingham, Ala., Red Mountain Museum; the Murrells Inlet, S.C., Brookgreen Gardens, society for southeastern flora and fauna; the Asheville, N.C., Colburn Memorial Mineral Museum; the Bailey, N.C., Country Doctor Museum; the Charleston, S.C., Macauley Museum of Dental History; and the Memphis, Tenn., Mississippi River Museum at Mud Island. Specialized museums include such sites as the Tifton, Ga., Georgia Agrirama, the State Museum of Agriculture; the Fort Smith, Ark., Patent Model Museum; the Pine Ridge, Ark., Lum and Abner Museum and Jot 'em Down Store; the Front Royal, Va., Warren Rifles Confederate Museum; the Louisville, Ky., Kentucky Derby Museum; and the Murray, Ky., National Museum of the Boy Scouts of America.

Clearly, the South's museums preserve and promote countless national, regional, and local treasures, and the growth of museums in the South parallels a national trend toward heightened appreciation for such institutions.

SHARON A. SHARP
Boone, North Carolina

Edward P. Alexander, *Museums in Motion* (1979); American Association of Museums, *The Official Museum Directory, 1998* (1997); American Heritage Publishing Co., *Historic Houses of America* (1980); Edward D. C. Campbell Jr., *Journal of Regional Cultures* (Fall/Winter 1981); Charles B. Hosmer Jr., *Presence of the Past: A History of the Preservation Movement in the United States before Williamsburg* (1965); Reader's Digest Association, *Treasures of America* (1974).

Mythic South

Has the South always been mainly a region of the mind, as many have said, something that exists because people think it exists? Or has it been mainly a region defined by material characteristics of geography, climate, and resources — together with traits it has acquired in the course of its history?

Most would probably say it has been both. Historian U. B. Phillips, for instance, moved from one to the other in two classic definitions of the South. In "The Central Theme of Southern History" (1928), he described the unifying principle of the South as an idea, "a common resolve indomitably maintained" that the South should be and remain "a white man's country." In *Life and Labor in the Old South* (1929), on the other hand, he wrote: "Let us begin by discussing the weather, for that has been the chief agency in making the South distinctive." Geography and climate led in turn to staple crops, the plantation system, chattel slavery, racial problems, sectional conflict, and ultimately the Confederacy. Any serious effort to know the character of a people must confront its mythology, and Phillips's interpretations both belong in some respects to that realm, however matter of fact both may at first appear.

The term "mythology," of course, conveys variant meanings. While myths are rooted in the religious impulse, they have become in the modern world increasingly secular in character. Some years ago anthropologist Raphael Patai offered a definition: "Myth . . . is a traditional religious charter, which operates by validating laws, customs, rites, institutions and beliefs, or explaining socio-cultural situations and natural phenomena, and taking the form of stories, believed to be true, about divine beings and heroes." Later, in his book *Myth and Modern Man* (1972), Patai reaffirmed the definition but deleted the word "religious." Upon further reflection, he said, he would emphasize more the role of myth in shaping social life: "As I see it, myth not only validates or authorizes customs, rites, institutions, beliefs, and so forth, but frequently is directly responsible for creating them." Thus, the modern world has invented a great variety of myths of both past and future, ranging from Marxist and Nazi myths to myths of planetary escape, with or without theological overtones.

To place the more down-to-earth idea of the South in the realm of social myth is to place it firmly in the region of the mind, where close relatives are such concepts as ideology, symbol, image, and stereotype—the last in the sense that Walter Lippmann gave in his *Public Opinion* (1922), where stereotypes come to mean "pictures in our heads" that have more to do with preconceptions than with reality.

The distinguishing characteristic of social myths is that they develop more or less abstract ideas in concrete and dramatic terms. In the words of Henry Nash Smith, they "fuse concept and emotion into an image." Secular myths, like religious myths, remain true to their origin in a root word meaning "tale."

HISTORICAL MYTHS. The classic myths of the South can be summed up briefly in the oft-quoted statement of Jonathan Daniels: "We Southerners are a mythological people, created half out of dream and half out of slander, who live in a still legendary land." He was referring to the contrary images of the South that grew up in the 19th-century sectional conflict: the plantation idyll versus the abolitionist critique, the "Sunny South" versus the "Benighted South," or to cite the cultural events that have most vividly fixed them in the popular mind, *Uncle Tom's Cabin* versus *Birth of a Nation* and, more recently, *Gone with the Wind* versus *Roots*.

Major myths have given structure to the chronological development of the South. Southern myths have frequently been analyzed as discrete entities, but together their stories tell the story of the South. The myth of a southern garden paradise, a new Eden, provided the initial image of the region for many colonial southerners and northerners. It was a myth rooted in the perception of a bountiful environment. By the late 1700s the democratic, egalitarian South of Thomas Jefferson had become the norm, according to William E. Dodd. Dodd's theme has been reflected in the writing of other historians, largely in depicting a region subjected to economic colonialism by an imperial Northeast. The Jeffersonian image of agrarian democracy has been a favorite recourse of southern liberals.

By the 1830s, though, the myth of the Old South was becoming a dominant literary and cultural construct for northerners and southerners alike, as William R. Taylor has shown. The Old South evokes images of kindly old marster with his mint julep, happy darkies singing in the fields, coquettish belles wooed by slender gallants. It is a romanticized moonlight-and-magnolias world, which yields all too easily to caricature and ridicule. Francis Pendleton Gaines noted that "the plantation romance remains our chief social idyl of the past; of an Arcadian scheme of existence, less material, less hurried, less prosaically equalitarian, less futile, richer in picturesqueness, festivity, in realized pleasure that recked not of hope or fear or unrejoicing labor."

The myth of the Lost Cause focused on the Civil War experience of southerners. It told of noble, virtuous Christian warriors, the highest product of the Old South, defending the southern homeland from rapacious Yankees. Defeat was inevitable because of superior northern resources, but southerners defended their honor and in the process achieved spiritual victories. The Reconstruction era gave birth to a mythic view of southern whites facing the internal and external challenges to their maintenance of an orderly civilization. Exploitive northern carpetbaggers, traitorous southern scalawags, ignorant blacks, and brave but desperate ex-Confederates were the chief characters in this tale of good and evil.

Redemption of the South by the Bourbons brought peace to the region, in the mythic narrative, and promoted the emergence of a New South. Newspaper editors were the prime mythmakers, creating a New South creed that Paul Gaston has discussed at some length. New South advocates of the late 19th century promised to make the South as "rich, triumphant, and morally innocent" as the rest of the nation. They looked forward to a region absorbed into the national abundance of progress and equality.

The late 19th century, though, gave birth to a different myth as well — Populism. Despite talk of a New South, the region's people remained predominantly poor farmers, and the Populist myth made them southern heroes. Populist agrarian leaders were defenders of the poor, out to right the wrongs of industrial-commercial exploitation.

In the clever decade of the 1920s a myth of the Benighted South took shape. An older neoabolitionist myth of the Savage South was reinforced by a variety of images in that decade and after: the Scopes Trial, the Ku Klux Klan, lynchings, chain gangs, the Fundamentalist movement, hookworm and pellagra, the Scottsboro trials, labor violence. The response to the civil rights movement in the 1950s and 1960s gave new life to the Benighted South myth.

The Agrarianism of the Nashville Agrarians spoke, like the message of the Populists, in a mythic rhetoric about the virtues of living on the land, although the Agrarians seemed unclear whether God's chosen people had been southern planters or small farmers. Their manifesto, *I'll Take My Stand*, by Twelve Southerners, appeared by fortuitous circumstance in 1930, when industrial capitalism seemed on the verge of collapse. The ideal of traditional virtues such as, in Donald Davidson's words, "family, bloodkinship, clanship, folkways, custom, community" took on the texture of myth in their image of the agrarian South.

Another image from the Great Depression era was the Problem South, a concept emerging from the writings of sociological regionalists such as Howard W. Odum and Rupert B. Vance at the University of North Carolina. They told of a region with indisputable shortcomings but with potentialities that needed constructive attention and the application of regional social planning.

CONTEMPORARY SOUTHERN MYTHOLOGY. "The myth-making faculty is still active in contemporary America," Max Lerner wrote in *America as a Civilization* (1957). During the 1970s and 1980s a new myth of the South emerged, an ambivalent mixture of extremes, combining elements of the Sunny South and the Benighted South with some ingredients of its own. The new "mythopoets" began to sight on the southern horizons an extended "Sunbelt," stretching from coast to coast, its economy battening on agribusiness, defense, technology, oil, real estate, tourism, and leisure. The geographical definition of the Sunbelt remained uncertain, but it came more and more often to be synonymous with the South.

Something about the Sunbelt image has had a seductive appeal to southerners, so long consigned to the role of underdogs, although the Sunbelt seems to have been, like other myths, less the invention of southerners than of Yankees. The Sunbelt image surfaced first in a book by Kevin P. Phillips, *The Emerging Republican Majority* (1969), but lay dormant until revived by Kirkpatrick Sale in *Power Shift: The Rise of the Southern Rim and Its Challenge to the Eastern Establishment* (1979). Sale's book focused on the Southeast as a likely growth area for investment. The economy of the South since then has become the fastest growing in the nation, and Sunbelt politicians arguably have controlled national politics since the 1980s.

Mythology, which seemed more than four decades ago a new frontier of southern history, has since been penetrated by a number of scholars; but many areas have been little explored, and others are scarcely touched. Myths continue to appear in modern areas of southern cultural achievement. Popular culture increasingly produces America's celebrities and heroes, and those who come from the Sunbelt South take on aspects of earlier southern mythology. Sports produced Paul "Bear" Bryant, one of the nation's most successful college football coaches and a folksy agrarian hero out of an earlier regional tradition. The death of Dale Earnhardt revealed and nurtured a rich symbolic iconography found in stock car racing. Elvis Presley drew on the region's rich heritage of black and white music and himself remains a potent symbol of the modern South. More recently, such television reality shows as *American Idol* have produced a disproportionate number of winners from the South, who reproduce in their performances the classic figures—country musician, blues singer, southern belle, or rebellious rock and roller.

COMPLEXITY AND CONTRADICTIONS. The complexity and contradictions of southern mythology, one can argue, make the mythology of the American West seem fairly simple by comparison. Fred Hobson, in his *Tell about the South: The Southern Rage to Explain* (1983), made up a suggestive list of myths, some overlapping, simply by compiling selected titles of books and articles published since 1945: "*The Emerging South*, *The Changing South*, 'The Disappearing . . . South,' 'The Vanishing South,' *The Enduring South*, 'The Distinctive South,' 'The American South,' 'The World South,' 'The Provincial South,' *The Democratic South*, 'The Embarrassing New South,' 'The South as a Counterculture,' *The Romantic South, The Uncertain South, The Militant South*, 'The Benighted South,' 'The Poetic South,' 'The Backward South,' 'The Progressive South,' The Lazy South, 'The Turbulent South,' 'The Squalid South,' 'The Solid South,' 'The Divided South,' 'The Devilish South,' 'The Visceral South,' 'The Massive, Concrete South.'"

These titles neglected, among other things, the Jeffersonian yeoman, the

Jacksonian frontiersman, chivalrous Southrons, New South boosters, insurgent Populists, the Fighting South, the Liberal South, the Anglo-Saxon (or Scots-Irish?) South, the Vanderbilt Agrarians, the Chapel Hill Regionalists, the Bible Belt, and a gallery of patricians, rednecks, village nabobs, good old boys, and in general the surfeit of southern fried chic cooked up to celebrate the emergence of Jimmy Carter, the only president to date who was born and bred in the brier patch of the Deep South. Bill Clinton, the next recent southern-born president, became known as Bubba to some commentators, popularizing a new stereotype.

There have also been a variety of black and female stereotypes that have either captivated or shocked the American sensibilities. The Old South generated enduring types: the matriarchal mammy, the erotic Mandingo, the suffering Uncle Tom, and the revolutionary Nat Turner, to name a few. The images of the black Union soldier and the black Confederate soldier have recently become more prominent, as well as the Reconstruction politician as a seminal mythic figure in the South. The film *Sounder* portrayed black tenant farmers as noble icons, while *The Color Purple* and *Crossroads* projected appealing images of the blues singer. The television series *Roots* was a powerful and influential popular culture presentation of African tradition bearers in the antebellum and post-bellum South. The African American community long understood the contrasting figures of the entrepreneurial-accommodationist Booker T. Washington and the idealistic-reformist W. E. B. Du Bois, both of whom wrote seminal works that presented a South resonant with mythic overtones. The courageous civil rights worker should also be added to the list of mythic African American figures specifically rooted in southern narratives. Statues, plaques, and museums are among the forms that honor sit-in demonstrators, freedom riders, and voting rights organizers as icons of the recent South. Most recently, the 2005 film *Hustle and Flow* mythologizes a small-time Memphis hustler who aspires to rap music stardom.

Women have always been among the foundational figures of southern mythology, and recent work in women's studies has illuminated many stereotypes and social typologies. The lady and the belle are among the central images of the South, but they should be set beside such other figures as church ladies and maiden aunts, Eudora Welty's teachers and Dorothy Allison's hard-scrabble poor women. Popular culture presentations such as the 1980s television series *Designing Women* updated images of southern women from the past, transforming them as they drew from familiar tropes. The white trash slut has come to the forefront of popular culture, as has country singer Gretchen Wilson's "redneck woman." Mythic images are expressions of regional styles, and the range of female figures has recently broadened to include a more diverse list than ever. Issues of beauty and femininity have been central to women's traditional images in southern culture, although with social class and racial meanings as well.

Southern myths have been fostered in a variety of cultural forms. In the antebellum era, writers such as William Gilmore Simms and John Pendleton Kennedy helped create the plantation legend of the Old South as well as creating the tradition of popular literature fostering mythology. In the late 19th century, northern periodicals printed nostalgic articles and stories by southerners about the prewar era, and northerners seemed as taken with them as southerners were. Since the beginning of the 20th century, American popular music has been a carrier of southern mythology. Tin Pan Alley's tunes, Broadway shows, country music, and even rock music have told of Dixie's virtues. Film and television are the most recent sources to create and spread mythic news of the South, drawing on previous symbolism. Throughout southern history, political speeches and religious sermons have spread regional mythology in the South's oral culture.

GEORGE B. TINDALL
University of North Carolina at Chapel Hill

David Bertelson, *The Lazy South* (1967); Carl Bridenbaugh, *Myths and Realities: Societies of the Colonial South* (1963); Edward D. C. Campbell, *The Celluloid South: Hollywood and the Southern Myth* (1981); W. J. Cash, *The Mind of the South* (1941); F. Garvin Davenport Jr., *The Myth of Southern History: Historical Consciousness in Twentieth-Century Southern Literature* (1970); Michael Davis, *The Image of Lincoln in the South* (1972); Carl N. Degler, *The Other South: Southern Dissenters in the Nineteenth Century* (1974); Clement Eaton, *The Mind of the Old South* (1964); Howard R. Floan, *The South in Northern Eyes, 1831 to 1861* (1958); J. Wayne Flynt, *Dixie's Forgotten People: The South's Poor Whites* (1979); John Hope Franklin, *The Militant South* (1956); George Fredrickson, *The Black Image in the White Mind: The Debate on Afro-American Character and Destiny, 1817–1914* (1971); Francis Pendleton Gaines, *The Southern Plantation: A Study in the Development and Accuracy of a Tradition* (1924); Paul M. Gaston, *The New South Creed: A Study in Southern Mythmaking* (1970); Patrick Gerster and Nicholas Cords, eds., *Myth and Southern History*, 2 vols. (1974); Dewey W. Grantham, *The Democratic South* (1963); Fred Hobson, *Tell about the South: The Southern Rage to Explain* (1983); Winthrop D. Jordan, *White over Black: American Attitudes toward the Negro, 1550–1812* (1968); Alexander Karanikas, *Tillers of a Myth: Southern Agrarians as Social and Literary Critics* (1966); Jack Temple Kirby, *Media-Made Dixie: The South in the American Imagination* (1978); Lawrence W. Levine, *Black Culture and Black Consciousness: Afro-American Folk Thought from Slavery to Freedom* (1977); Bernard Mayo, *Myths and Men: Patrick Henry, George Washington, and Thomas Jefferson* (1963); Forrest McDonald and Grady McWhiney, *History Today* (July 1980); Shields McIlwaine, *The Southern Poor-White: From Lubberland to Tobacco Road* (1939); Gary B. Nash, *William and Mary Quarterly* (April 1972); Michael O'Brien, *The Idea of the American South, 1920–1941* (1979); Rollin G. Osterweis, *Myth of the Lost Cause, 1865–1900* (1973), *Romanticism and Nationalism in the Old South* (1949); Raphael Patai, *Myth and Modern Man* (1972); Merrill Peterson, *The Jefferson Image in the American Mind* (1960); David Potter, *The South and the Sectional Conflict* (1968); John Shelton Reed, *The Enduring South: Subcultural Persistence in Mass Society* (1971), *One South: An Ethnic Approach to Regional Culture* (1982); Louis D. Rubin Jr., *Writers of the Modern South: The Faraway Country* (1963); Anne Firor Scott, *The Southern Lady: From Pedestal to Politics, 1830–1930* (1970); Charles G. Sellers Jr., *The Southerner as American* (1960); Lewis P. Simpson, *The Dispossessed Garden: Pastoral and History in Southern Literature* (1975); David L. Smiley, *South Atlantic Quarterly* (Summer 1972); Kenneth M. Stampp, *Era of Reconstruction, 1865–1877* (1965), *Journal of Southern History* (August 1971); William R. Taylor, *Cavalier and Yankee: The Old South and American National Character* (1957); George B. Tindall, *The Ethnic Southerners* (1976); Frank E. Vandiver, ed., *The Idea of the South: Pursuit of a Central Theme* (1964); John William Ward, *Andrew Jackson: Symbol for an Age* (1962); C. Vann Woodward, *The Strange Career of Jim Crow* (1955; rev. ed., 1966); Charles Reagan Wilson, *Baptized in Blood: The Religion of the Lost Cause, 1865–1920* (1980), *Judgment and Grace in Dixie: Southern Faiths from Faulkner to Elvis* (1995); Howard Zinn, *Southern Mystique* (1964).

New South Myth

Defeated and frustrated, the postbellum South furnished fertile soil for the growth of myth, for grafting the imagined upon the real to produce a hybrid that itself became a force in history. Hardly had Union armies sealed the fate of the Old South in 1865 before some people began to speak of a New South. By the early 1870s, optimists were taking hope from defeat and were envisioning a society that would be less sumptuous but more substantial than the antebellum plantation order to which they paid homage but which, they believed, had been shown wanting in the ordeal of war.

Advocates of a New South believed that economic regeneration was the region's most pressing need. To solicit the northern capital necessary to effect that regeneration, they encouraged reconciliation between the old enemies. They promised to treat black people fairly in their sphere, thereby seeking to soothe any northern consciences troubled by the abandonment of Reconstruction and to promote a harmony between the races that would foster the social stability so highly prized by potential northern investors. Racial accommodation and sectional reconciliation would do much to guarantee the sine qua non of the New South program, the development of an industrial economy that would restore prosperity and prominence to the region.

During the 1880s, largely because of the ceaseless labors of publicists such as Henry W. Grady of the Atlanta *Constitution* and Richard H. Edmonds of the Baltimore *Manufacturers' Record*, the New South idea became increasingly popular. To such molders of opinion, the proponents of the industrial ethos were broad-minded and progressive, its opponents, their numbers ever diminishing, narrow and reactionary. In his celebrated "New South" address before an appreciative audience in New York in 1886, Grady proclaimed that southerners, having been converted to the Yankee way, were rejecting the ideal of leisure, replacing politics with business as their chief endeavor, and sharing the region's mounting prosperity generously with black people. Three years later, Edmonds wrote that the South's vast resources were already insuring the recovery of the position the region had held in 1860 as the richest section of the country. For Edmonds, Grady, and others of like mind, the ideal had been transformed into the actual. By 1890 the myth of the New South as a land that was rich, just, and triumphant was perceived as reality by many southerners.

To a great degree the ascendancy of the myth was the result of wishful thinking. At the end of the century, black southerners existed in circumstances little better than those of slavery, the prosperity vaunted by New South spokesmen was largely illusory, and the industrialization that had occurred — and it was never so great as claimed — was often controlled by northerners. Still the stepchild of the nation, the South was hardly triumphant, rich, or just.

Nevertheless, the New South myth survived not only the challenge of statistics but also the attacks mounted by the desperate agrarians who embraced Populism in the 1890s. With Populism dying, the intellectual temper of the next 30 years, like that of the 1880s, was characterized by a romantic, optimistic faith in progress. By the 1920s the business boosters were excelling their ideological forebears in touting the advance of southern industrialization.

That advance was indeed rapid. As numerous industries underwent significant expansion during the 1920s, the number of manufacturing workers in the South rose by almost 10 percent while the rest of the nation suffered a decline of the same proportion. Yet if the boosterism of the dollar decade had a sounder basis in reality than did the boomerism of the 1880s, there was ballyhoo in generous measure all the way from the Mason-Dixon line to Florida's Gold Coast. The second-generation New South enthusiasts portrayed the region as a land basking in the rays of prosperity, even though the profits of southern industry often wound up outside the region and southern workers labored longer and earned less than did those in the North.

The bone-grinding poverty of the Great Depression, exposed in works by Erskine Caldwell and other southern writers, obscured the myth for a time. By the end of the 1930s, however, the booster spirit was again ascendant, lifted by hopes of recovery and by southern indignation over the region's being labeled the nation's primary economic problem. Moreover, the agrarian myth, which had earlier served as a counterpoise to the New South myth, lost much of its force as many of its adherents either abandoned farming as a commercial enterprise or, succumbing to hard times and New Deal policies, left the land altogether.

World War II ushered in a degree of industrialization long dreamed of by southern promoters. Between 1939 and 1972 the number of factories grew by more than 160 percent and the number of workers in them by more than 200 percent. Prosperity accompanied the expansion of industry as per capita income in the South increased by 500 percent between 1955 and 1975 — a rate 300 percent higher than that of the nation as a whole. The New South myth grew ever more compelling as the region's economic advance became ever more real. Yet just as important to strengthening the myth were the labors of the region's industrial promoters, who rivaled the boomers of the 1880s and the boosters of the 1920s in the quest for material progress. Intent upon maintaining what was called an excellent business climate, chambers of commerce, development boards, and newspapers often urged local and state governments to offer industrialists a variety of inducements such as public financing of plant construction, "start-up" programs for new industries, tax reductions or exemptions, and courses in "union busting" at public universities to keep labor cheap, docile, and unorganized. Some promoters also encouraged the token integration of the races to help create a proper image elsewhere, which was but a minor variation on a major theme of the New South movement of a century before.

So striking was the region's economic advance and so successful was the selling of the South that by the late 1960s pundits began referring to the latest New South as part of the Sunbelt, that region spanning the southern portion of the nation and growing rapidly in population, prosperity, and power. Underdogs for so long, southerners sometimes took what they considered well-deserved delight in the discomfiture of residents of the Frostbelt, who lamented the migration of workers to factories that had been relocated to the South. As had occurred a hundred years earlier, many southerners saw their region as just, triumphant, and rich—just in its treatment of black people, triumphant in its economic struggle with the North, and rich in material goods.

Yet again, the myth failed to reflect reality adequately. Despite changes in the law, blacks found that they were sometimes still the victims of segregation and inequality. Despite the hyperbole accompanying the Sunbelt phenomenon, the belief that the South would soon reduce the North to beggary betrayed an ignorance of the facts. Despite increasing prosperity, the South was hardly rich; as of 1981, average annual per capita income in the region lagged behind that of the rest of the country by almost $2,000. Nearly 20 years later, median hourly wages in the South were almost $1.50 less than those in the rest of the country, and only one state of the old Confederacy—Virginia—could boast annual per capita income that was above the national average.

For all the hope that the New South myth has inspired—no mean achievement in itself—it has countenanced complacency toward social ills, resignation to the abuse of the natural environment, and the rise of a mass culture that diminished the personalism in human relations long cherished in the southern folk culture. Unless the New South myth can be more tightly harnessed in order to serve the general welfare, the idea could remain a negative influence.

WAYNE MIXON
Augusta State University

Edward L. Ayers, *The Promise of the New South: Life after Reconstruction* (1992); Numan V. Bartley, *The New South, 1945–1980* (1995); Jared Bernstein and Lawrence Mishel, *Economic Policy Institute Issue Brief* (February 1999); James C. Cobb, *The Selling of the South: The Southern Crusade for Industrial Development, 1936–1980* (1982); Paul M. Gaston, *The New South Creed: A Study in Southern Mythmaking* (1970); Richard B. McKenzie, *Tax Review* (September 1982); Wayne Mixon, *Southern Writers and the New South Movement, 1865–1913* (1980); George B. Tindall, *The Emergence of the New South, 1913–1945* (1967), *The Ethnic Southerners* (1976), *Houston Review* (Spring 1979); U.S. Census Bureau, *Statistical Abstract of the United States* (2001); C. Vann Woodward, *Origins of the New South, 1877–1913* (1951).

Northern Mythmaking

The southern cultural landscape is surely as diverse as the human, geographical, or economic landscapes that comprise it. Just as surely, southerners remain, as journalist Jonathan Daniels said, "a mythological people . . . who live in a still legendary land." Southern mythology, in turn, is the product of many cultural forces, both interregional and national in character.

The South has had sufficient materials, and certainly the imagination, to shape a fictitious past that its people could regard as true. But regions to the north of the Mason-Dixon line also had an important hand in these legendary creations. Perhaps because of the long-standing desire to discover a central theme for the southern experience, historians have not cultivated enough of a national perspective on the role the Yankee has played in both the original creation and the tenacious upholding of the South's legendary past. Studies of southern myths have too often failed to explore how regional myths attracted a national audience.

As historian Henry Steele Commager has emphasized, "the most familiar of Southern symbols came from the North: Harriet Beecher Stowe of New England gave us Uncle Tom and Little Eva and Topsy and Eliza, while it was Stephen Foster of Pittsburgh who sentimentalized the Old South, and even 'Dixie' had northern origins." Connecticut Yankee Stowe based her impressions of the South on extremely limited firsthand experience and, penning *Uncle Tom's Cabin* (1852) in Brunswick, Me., gave national narrative strength and attention — to say nothing of credibility — to a kaleidoscope of mythical images and stereotypes, which a good many people even today assume are historically accurate portraits of the South and southerners before the war. She devised the faithful darky (Sambo) image of blacks; graphically portrayed a villainous version of the plantation overseer who uniquely symbolized the acquiescence of the North to southern myth by being of Yankee origins, from Vermont; and indirectly gave vitality to the related ideals of Cavalier and southern belle. By extension, the Old South of legend materialized in great measure out of what Robert S. Cotterill has called "the ignorance, or malice of northern abolitionists and . . . southerners suffering from nostalgia."

To the same effect, Stephen Foster composed "Susanna" (1847) and "Old Folks at Home" (1851) prior to a one-month excursion into the South in 1852, after which he published "Massa's in de Cold, Cold Ground" (1852), "My Old Kentucky Home" (1852), and "Old Black Joe" (1860). These songs not only appealed to the emotions, but their lyrics voiced a strong sense of nostalgia for the old plantation. Immensely popular over the years, Foster's songs fed the American romantic imagination with a sentimentalized view of what life in the South allegedly was like before the Civil War, although most of them were composed in Allegheny County, Pa. Undeniably, Foster's plantation songs have had a legend-creating impact on the American popular mind, conveniently offering succeeding generations easily voiced and recyclable visions of an idealized life in the sunny South.

Three years after the appearance of Harriet Beecher Stowe's faithful old Tom, suffering Eliza, and sadistic Simon Legree, and in the midst of Stephen Foster's mythic musical production, another northerner came forward to offer additional weight to the developing myth of southern antebellum luxury. In 1855 David Christy of Ohio published his book *Cotton Is King* and, in the process, touched off a great deal of discussion both in America and Europe about the industrial world's dependence upon the raw cotton of the South. The effect of this book was to obscure the realities of the South's diversified economy and create the impression that Dixie was an empire of plantations and slaveholders.

Even considering the influence of Harriet Beecher Stowe, Stephen Foster, and David Christy, perhaps nothing more emotionally captured the flavor of the southern image than the song "Dixie." Symbolic of the southern way of life, it was written in New York City by an Ohioan, Daniel Emmett, in 1859. Though used as a marching tune by both Union and Confederate forces during the Civil War, it soon became the unofficial national anthem of the South and has remained one of the most important sentimental expressions of southern regionalism ever since. By the time Jefferson Davis and Alexander Hamilton Stephens assumed the leadership of the Confederate States of America, the Emmett-inspired romance had already begun to work its magic. Clement Eaton has described the scene in this fashion: "On February 18, 1861, they were inaugurated in the state capitol at Montgomery, and at the ceremonies a band played the new song 'Dixie,' with its pervading nostalgia. Like the candles, coffins, patent medicines, tall silk hats, plows—indeed, most manufactured articles used in the South—the song that was destined to become the unofficial anthem of the Confederacy was also an import from the Yankee." Even with regard to their regional mythology, apparently, southerners had cause to regard themselves as a colony of the North.

The efforts of northerners to romanticize the South artistically are of course not limited to Stowe, Foster, Christy, and Emmett. Francis Pendleton Gaines has argued that northern drama and northern minstrelsy, to say nothing of northern artistic images of the South such as Eastman Johnson's *My Old Kentucky Home* (1859) and Winslow Homer's *Sunday Morning in Virginia* (c. 1870), gave special consideration to mythical plantation materials. The case can also be made, as William R. Taylor has done, that it was the literary energy of the North as well as the South—the work of James K. Paulding of New York, for example—that seeded the fictional plantation in literature. And in the critical judgment of Ann Rowe, for northern writers the South has often functioned as an "Enchanted Country." Not to be forgotten also are the numerous sentimental lithographs of Nathaniel Currier of Roxbury, Mass., and James Merrit Ives of New York City, who offered a national audience unblemished images of Americana, both North and South. Collectively, northern works of art from Stowe and Foster to Currier and Ives did much to create an image of southern history the verisimilitude of which was seldom examined by its avid consumers—an image at times at odds with fact, but of critical importance nonetheless to the development of a regional mythology.

But the questions remain: Why did the North find myths of the South so very comfortable and comforting? What caused this fusion of southern and northern sentiment? How was it that so many northerners became so distinctly of the southern persuasion? The South and the North became copartners in the creation of a regional pseudopast for a multitude of reasons: a latent "love of feudalism" and "romantic hunger" (democratic pretense to the contrary notwithstanding), "status anxiety" or "hankering after aristocracy" on the part of northerners being displaced in either the social or political power structures of 19th-century America, a pristine nostalgia for agrarianism while in the throes of national industrialization and urbanization, a need to hide and sustain an emergent national consensus regarding the place of race in American life. For some (Herman Melville and Mark Twain, for example), the mannered South served as an imaginative alternative to the frayed culture of America during the crass inelegance and inarticulateness of the Gilded Age.

Southern mythology has a clearly national as well as regional character. Northern writers such as Henry James and F. Scott Fitzgerald accorded the legends literary respect; disseminators of American values in popular school textbooks—such as the staunch New Englander David Saville Muzzey— adopted the southern mythical perspective in gushing sentimentally about the demise of the great plantation while also offering interpretive endorsement of white southerners' views of Reconstruction. It may well have been a northern army officer who first coined the term "New South," as an expression of only slightly hidden regret for a southern civilization now "gone" and a cause now "lost," and the New York Southern Society, organized during the 1880s, carried on the Confederate tradition while promoting New South reconciliation and materialism. As the North experienced rapid urbanization, accelerated industrialization, and the ethnic complexities of immigration, the need for a "usable opposite" in relation to these forces of cultural change proved readily at hand via the special stabilizing attractions of the myth of Dixie. Northern complicity in the crafting of charming representations of southern life added value to the emergent mythology even as it dramatized an important alignment of cultural values between the regions.

The northern regard for the South as "The Enchanted Country," in short, is long-standing. Many of the myths of the South were cultivated by those—

North and South—who never owned a slave or planted an acre of cotton. The nation's genuine fondness for both the South and its mythology remains alive in Philadelphia (whether Mississippi or Pennsylvania), and in both Minneapolis and Montgomery. Southern mythology bears, of course, an indelible southern birthmark, but it also stands as testimony to the durable value of seeing the "southerner as American."

PATRICK GERSTER
San Jose City College

Robert S. Cotterill, *Journal of Southern History* (February 1949); Frances FitzGerald, *America Revised: History Schoolbooks in the Twentieth Century* (1979); Howard R. Floan, *The South in Northern Eyes, 1831–1861* (1958); Francis Pendleton Gaines, *The Southern Plantation: A Study in the Development and Accuracy of a Tradition* (1924); Patrick Gerster and Nicholas Cords, *Journal of Southern History* (November 1977); Patrick Gerster and Nicholas Cords, eds., *Myth and Southern History* (1974); Ann Rowe, *The Enchanted Country: Northern Writers in the South, 1865–1910* (1978); Nina Silber, *The Romance of Reunion: Northerners and the South, 1865–1900* (1993); William R. Taylor, *Cavalier and Yankee: The Old South and American National Character* (1957); George B. Tindall, in *The Idea of the South: Pursuit of a Central Theme,* ed. Frank E. Vandiver (1964).

Plantation Myth

The plantation myth is a body of tales, legends, and folklore defining the antebellum plantation; the myth is frequently extended to explain the social order of the entire South from Jamestown to Fort Sumter. It emphasizes the precapitalistic and essentially feudal characteristics of the plantation, with specific links to an English Cavalier tradition. It makes, for example, the early colonial South a refuge during the Puritan Revolution for royalist and Anglican gentry. In this context the plantation develops primarily as a social or cultural institution rather than an economic one. Money, then, economic self-interest, and capitalistic gain are secondary to a primitive, premodern desire for honor, distinction, and deference. Individuals function less as autonomous figures than as parts of a living social organism extending through time and space.

In the plantation myth, relationships are ordered along hierarchical lines, and the patriarchal family is the central defining device and metaphor. The wellborn father/plantation master and his sons dominate the structure; beneath them are their women, wives and daughters, then children, and finally white dependents and black slaves. The slave order is similarly hierarchical and familial, if with some skewing in the gender roles: house servants rate higher than

Plantation owner's home, Marshallville, Ga. (Dorothea Lange, photographer,
Library of Congress [LC-USF34-018010-E], Washington, D.C.)

fieldworkers, craftsmen higher than unskilled workers, and the fair higher than
the dark.

The actors in this social drama perform prescribed roles. Manners, behavior, and deportment lie at the heart of the system. Performance and appearance
form its supreme good. The gentleman and the lady represent only the most
popular and outstanding of the various roles or forms dictated by the system.

This legendary order centers on the Tidewater of Virginia and South Carolina. These areas constitute the two "mountains of conceit" of the old regional
adage (with North Carolina as the "valley of humility"). The system, however,
possesses notable outposts in various other localities around the region such
as the Mississippi Delta, the Bluegrass counties of Kentucky, central Tennes-

see around Nashville, and the Piedmont of Georgia—the triangle northwest of Macon and Augusta. Insofar as plantation mythology might affect the entire region, most southern communities would have had a local version or model represented by a particular family or families. In this system, lesser slaveholding families of less prestigious origins defer to the greater, all slaveholders dominate whites without slaves, whites and males prevail over blacks and women, the country rules the cities, and aristocratic values overshadow commercial and business interests.

The plantation legend has four major sources. The first is the pre–Civil War southern impulse to differentiate itself ideologically from the North. A comparable northern attitude exaggerated southern peculiarity. The novels of John Pendleton Kennedy, the poetry of William Grayson, and the sociology of William Fitzhugh illustrate the southern impulse; Harriet Beecher Stowe's *Uncle Tom's Cabin* exemplifies the northern attitude.

The second source of the plantation legend lies in the post–Civil War period and in the southern need to romanticize its past as a means of comprehending its defeat and its radically altered situation after Appomattox. The former Confederates explained their defeat by creating a legendary chivalric past. Summarized in a plantation order, prewar society was too noble, good, and bright to survive the onslaughts of industrial, middle-class capitalism from the North. In this way, the war itself developed as the capstone of the plantation legend. It became the ultimate knightly adventure: the Quixotic Quest, the Lost Cause, all the more precious because it was foredoomed to failure. The Old South thereby became a place out of time, its inhabitants as immortal as the Olympians. The plantation South became mythology.

The romances of John Esten Cooke and Thomas Nelson Page mirror the nostalgia of the ideal. Even they, however, fail to measure the full power of the mythology as a regional belief system up through the Southern Literary Renaissance. Indeed, that cultural revival stems in considerable measure from the efforts of a new generation to define its own identity in contrast to the heroes of the mythic past. Thus, the myth might be seen to receive its fullest expression as southerners of the 1920s and 1930s tried to exorcise the plantation ghosts, notably in William Faulkner's *Absalom, Absalom!*, in W. J. Cash's *Mind of the South*, and in realistic and debunking aspects of Margaret Mitchell's *Gone with the Wind*, all of which appeared in a cluster between 1936 and 1941. This defeat-generated mythologizing existed between 1880 and World War II.

Although less chronologically confined, the third source of the plantation myth arose and thrived in the same period. It was a northern phenomenon, and its sources varied. Rooted partially in guilt and ambivalence about the war, especially its racial implications, Yankee celebration of the plantation myth derived a powerful dynamic from a bourgeois impulse to fantasize an alternative to the North's egalitarian, commercial, materialistic social order. By this means, the plantation legend functioned as a domestic version of the historical novels of Sir Walter Scott that were popular on both sides of the Atlantic in the early 19th century. The southerners in Henry Adams's works *Democracy* and *The Education of Henry Adams* and in Owen Wister's *The Virginian* stand for the northern idealization of the old southerner. The enormous northern popularity of Page's work and the still larger national audiences of the mythologized *Birth of a Nation*, of Margaret Mitchell's book *Gone with the Wind*, and of the film made from the latter represent the same, continuing influences.

Historical reality offers the final source of the plantation myth and its vitality: the existence of some essential, material sources or roots of the mythological belief. This remains its most debated and even polemical aspect. In modern society the very concept of mythology is laden with negative values; "a truth that cannot be proven," the traditional definition of myth, stands in low repute in a modern, scientific world. The linking of a distinctive regional culture with mythology, then, has the effect of discrediting the notion of an essentially premodern order represented in the plantation South. Pernicious, self-serving uses of plantation mythology (by southerners and northerners alike) have further discredited the concept. Nevertheless, scholars still argue the basic validity and accuracy of the social system suggested in the popular mythology.

Two general lines of thought have emerged among those committed to material accuracy behind plantation mythology. One group, led by Eugene D. Genovese, advances the material reality of a feudal system in the South that arose out of regional peculiarities of demography and economics, such as settlement patterns, mortality and morbidity rates, religious institutions, slavery, and debt and credit structures. Without dismissing these elements, a second group maintains that a value system came first and shaped the material reality toward the form of a feudal order. Bertram Wyatt-Brown leads this line of thought. By analyzing its material bases, both groups illuminate the sources of the plantation myth's persistence and vitality over time and suggest reasons why even modern southerners perceive their lives and manners in peculiar ways.

DARDEN A. PYRON
Florida International University

W. J. Cash, *The Mind of the South* (1941); Nathalie Dessens, *Myth of the Plantation Society: Slavery in the American South and the West Indies* (2004); Francis Pendleton Gaines, *The Southern Plantation: A Study in the Development and Accuracy of a Tradi-*

tion (1925); Paul M. Gaston, *The New South Creed: A Study in Southern Mythmaking* (1970); Eugene D. Genovese, *Roll, Jordan, Roll: The World the Slaves Made* (1974), *The World the Slaveholder Made: Two Essays in Interpretation* (1969); Raimondo Luraghi, *The Plantation South* (1975); Darden A. Pyron, *Recasting "Gone with the Wind" in American Culture* (1983); Helen Taylor, *Circling Dixie: Contemporary Southern Culture through a Transatlantic Lens* (2000); William R. Taylor, *Cavalier and Yankee: The Old South and American National Character* (1957); Frank E. Vandiver, ed., *The Idea of the South: Pursuit of a Central Theme* (1964); C. Vann Woodward, *The Burden of Southern History* (revised ed., 1982); Bertram Wyatt-Brown, *Southern Honor: Ethics and Behavior in the Old South* (1982).

Postmodernism

It is a characteristically postmodern irony that the student of postmodernism and the South must sort through overlapping definitions of the term "postmodernism" itself. The Marxist critic Fredric Jameson, for instance, sees postmodernism as the contemporary cultural effort to "think" or express the predicament of individuals and groups caught up in the great global networks of multinational or "late" capitalism. Philosopher Jean-François Lyotard describes the postmodern condition in terms of the declining authority and relevance of "master narratives" that once organized the pursuit and production of knowledge and gave meaning and intelligibility to social life in liberal societies. Literary scholar Linda Hutcheon offers a more aesthetically grounded definition of postmodern representation as given to thick historical awareness and radical linguistic self-reflexiveness and play, extremes captured neatly in Hutcheon's concept of "historiographic metafiction" and pursued simultaneously through parody, for Hutcheon the quintessential postmodern technique. There have been other influential definitions as well, but these three offer a useful starting point for an analysis of the contemporary South.

There can be no denying, for instance, that southern existence is, as Jameson would predict, now global in its reach and implication. Through their everyday activities and habits, today's southerners routinely participate in worldwide networks of consumption, production, distribution, and finance. Multinational corporations such as Coca-Cola, IBM, Dell Computers, Delta Airlines, Federal Express, and First Union Bank are headquartered in major southern cities. Atlanta, Ga., has emerged as the South's closest thing to a postmodern metropolis: already hinted at in the 1981 film *Sharkey's Machine* (directed by Burt Reynolds), whose climactic scene was set atop the Peachtree Plaza hotel, the first of the gleaming glass towers that now define the city's thoroughly postmodern skyline, the transformation was arguably complete by the time the 1996 Olympic Games arrived in Atlanta and Tom Wolfe chose the city's corporate culture for the setting and theme of his mammoth 1998 novel *A Man in Full*. Similarly, traditional southern place yields to postmodern space in Richard Linklater's 1991 film *Slacker*, which tracks with seeming randomness the movements of its characters through an Austin, Tex., landscape that is virtually devoid of regional landmarks or signifiers. Nor are the deracinating effects of globalization in the South limited to the region's urban areas: the rural and small-town Kentuckians of Bobbie Ann Mason's fiction face the steady encroachment of Burger King and K-Mart, MTV and HoJo's, on local identities and worlds that prove all too susceptible to such disorienting, homogenizing forces; and the Virginia edge city of Darcey Steinke's 1997 novel *Jesus Saves* plays host to a violence and sickness that can no longer be traced to regional sources: suburban rather than southern gothic.

Moreover, Lyotard's account of the waning credibility of master narratives can be applied to the contemporary South as well, where, especially in the wake of the civil rights movement, the stories that once constituted and sustained (white) regional identity have lost much if not all of their social and cultural power. The historian U. B. Phillips was still able to proclaim white supremacy "the central theme of southern history" in the high modernist year of 1928, but today, against a postmodern awareness of the multiethnic, balkanized interests that inform southern politics and society, that particular narrative no longer shapes consensus in or about the region. Neither, for the most part, do the myths of the Lost Cause, the plantation romance, black Reconstruction, "outside agitation," and "southern honor" that helped give a sense of identity and coherence to white southerners across class and gender lines, keeping the South "solid" throughout the Jim Crow period from 1877 to 1965. Not only have these narratives lost their ability to motivate and explain; other narratives have been slow in emerging to take their place. It could thus be argued that the contemporary southerner is caught betwixt and between master narratives — free from their mystification and coercion, yes, but in an equally real sense adrift without stories to live by, without their promise of self-recognition and membership in a collective project — a liminal predicament explored most fully in the novels of Walker Percy and Richard Ford.

Hutcheon might suggest, however, that such master narratives and the guiding concepts associated with them remain available to today's southerners, only in quotation marks. They persist, in other words, less as a set of lived experiences or living, shared traditions than as manipulable signifiers, gestures, and codes, a semiotic vocabulary to be tapped (or "cited") for purposes of stylization, parody, pastiche, and commodification. Scott Romine, for example, has traced the gradual retreat of the theme of community, long considered a defining element of southernness, toward "community" in contemporary southern writing. Michael Kreyling has analyzed the recycling and reappropriation of the foundational signifier "Faulkner" in the work of numerous southern writers of the past half-century — starting with Faulkner himself! — and Barbara Ching has noted something similar at work in contemporary country music's subversive play with the historical and rhetorical "figure" of George Jones. The North Carolina band Southern Culture on the Skids has, as its name implies, made a career out of poaching wittily and self-reflexively on musical and lyrical signifiers of regional distinctiveness. And Lee Smith closes her 1983 novel *Oral History* with the conversion of a remote Appalachian holler into "Ghostland," a fictional theme park not so unlike the real-life enterprises of Dollywood and Opryland in its reduction of southern hill country "authenticity" to commodity, spectacle, and camp.

Far from simply gratuitous or sterile, this engagement with history and culture as code offers contemporary southerners a means of exploring the limits of historical and linguistic understanding in a region long preoccupied with storytelling and the past. Perhaps this in turn helps explain why southerners have played a leading role in American literary postmodernism: not only John Barth, Donald Barthelme, and William S. Burroughs in the 1950s and 1960s but also, more recently, Frederick Barthelme, Barry Hannah, Randall Kenan, and Ishmael Reed. Indeed, if historiographic metafiction is postmodernism's distinctive aesthetic achievement, as Hutcheon claims, then perhaps Brian McHale is right to cite another southern classic, Faulkner's *Absalom, Absalom!* (1936), as the first postmodernist novel.

So does a postmodern South amount to a postsouthern one — or even, as some critics have recently begun to argue, a postcolonial one? Kreyling credits literary scholar Lewis P. Simpson with coining the term "postsouthern" in a 1980 essay, and there are compelling reasons to grant it descriptive accuracy. The South, after all, emerged during the same historical moment we now associate with the emergence of modernity itself, within an already global network of commerce, capital, and labor that linked the entire Atlantic rim and found its great material and ideological engine in the colonial plantation. Its major period of cultural consolidation and self-definition, reaching from the proslavery apologists of the 1850s to the Nashville Agrarians of the 1930s, coincided not only with the birth and development of the Euro-American artistic and intellectual movements now lumped broadly together under the sign of modernism, but also with the historical high-water mark of Euro-American colonialism. And some of the South's most eloquent 20th-century spokesmen (Allen Tate, John Crowe Ransom, Robert Penn Warren, Cleanth Brooks) were also among the architects of New Criticism, the unofficial aesthetic of high literary modernism in the United States.

With the South's historical, intellectual, and ideological origins thus rooted in the modern and colonial projects, one might expect the eclipse of the modern (and the emergence of the postcolonial) to be accompanied by the eclipse of southernness itself. And this has arguably been the case. Inasmuch as the postmodern South is also a post–civil rights South, the case for an ignominious regional distinctiveness based on institutionalized racism grows ever weaker in the movement's wake. Moreover, in the aftermath of the Vietnam War, the postcolonial conflict also described by Jameson as "the first terrible postmodern war," the United States lost its special exemption from, and the South lost its regional monopoly over, the legacy of defeat, guilt, irony, and shame that historian C. Vann Woodward once labeled the peculiar burden of southern history. The historical legacy of the 1960s, then, was to bring southern and American sensibilities closer than they had been at any point since the early Federal period.

For these reasons alone, a postmodern South might appear considerably less southern, in any fundamental or distinctive sense, than the South of even a few generations before. It might not even appear southern at all.

JAY WATSON
University of Mississippi

Barbara Ching, in *White Trash: Race and Class in America*, ed. Matt Wray and Annalee Newitz (1997); Linda Hutcheon, *A Poetics of Postmodernism: History, Theory, Fiction* (1988); Fredric Jameson, *Postmodernism, or, The Cultural Logic of Late Capitalism* (1991); Michael Kreyling, *Inventing Southern Literature* (1998); Jean-François Lyotard, *The Postmodern Condition: A Report on Knowledge* (1979; 1984); Brian McHale, *Postmodernist Fiction* (1987); U. B. Phillips, *American Historical Review* (1928); Scott Romine, *The Narrative Forms of Southern Community* (1999); Lewis P. Simpson, *The Brazen Face of History: Studies in the Literary Consciousness of America* (1980); C. Vann Woodward, *The Burden of Southern History* (revised ed., 1982).

Racial Attitudes

Although it is impossible to measure racial attitudes directly, they may be gauged from written and oral expressions, gestures, and institutional arrangements. Attitudes may be analyzed as discrete entities. As one authority has suggested, the term attitude "suggests thoughts and feelings (as opposed to actions) directed toward some specific object (as opposed to generalized faiths and beliefs)." The term also "suggests a wide range in consciousness, intensity, and saliency in the response to the object."

Racial attitudes in the South have primarily involved whites and blacks. Attitudes toward American Indians and toward Asians have been less consistent and less pervasive. In general, both whites and blacks have held less pejorative attitudes toward these groups than toward each other. Nonetheless, both large groups have tended to see Indians and Asians as separate groups with distinguishing characteristics of their own. Blacks have had to deal with the fact that whites usually have less pejorative attitudes toward other nonwhite groups. Members of these smaller groups, of course, have their own attitudes toward other people whom they perceive as being racially different.

Among both blacks and whites, racial attitudes have hinged on a bipolar system of racial classification. Whites especially have defined all persons with perceptibly African ancestry as "colored," "Negro," or "black." Gradations of intermixed African and European ancestry, based largely on complexion, have carried some meaning. Both groups, while accepting the bipolar system, have accorded some measure of preference to lighter-skinned members of the "Negro" category. The phenomenon of "passing" testifies to the strength rather than the weakness of the bipolar system.

White attitudes toward blacks in America have never been peculiar to the South. Their expression and institutional implementation have indeed been more salient in areas where slavery persisted after the Revolutionary era, but the underlying attitudes have always been remarkably similar throughout the country. Pejorative attitudes toward blacks were evident from the period of early settlement in all the English colonies. Regional distinctions within the southern colonies were fully as important as differences between the nascent North and South.

The origins of white racial attitudes may be found in the interaction of two powerful forces: certain important attributes of English culture and the need for bound labor in land-rich colonies, which needed to export in order to survive. More generally, these origins lay in powerful urges for domination. The content of the attitudes was powerfully molded by the social and psychological insecurities engendered by the Anglo-European migration across the Atlantic into a land that worked to undermine traditional social controls.

Some scholars have held that these attitudes emerged inevitably as the ideology of an oppressive master class. Others have maintained that they were built into English cultural traditions that themselves formed a part of an ancient

Stereotypical sheet music cover, "Coon, Coon, Coon," 1901 (Kenneth W. Goings personal collection)

Western European heritage. A third group has viewed these two possibilities as simultaneous forces that interacted with each other to produce racial attitudes that have been remarkable in the history of world cultural contacts for their virulence, consistency, pervasiveness, and persistence through time.

Few scholars dispute these characteristics. From their earliest contacts with West Africans, both in Africa and America, the English regarded them as heathen, uncivilized, brutelike, and oversexed. They also placed great emphasis on physiognomic differences, on hair, on facial characteristics, and especially on complexion. In that age, the concept of innateness of human characteristics was itself inchoate, but there was a persistent tendency to ascribe inherency to the black's physiognomy and cultural attributes.

The actual persistence of the "black" color was matched by the persistence on the part of whites in trying to explain it, in hoping that it might be changed by the American environment, and in using it as a social marker of degraded status. The sexual charge in white attitudes also persisted, showing itself in fears of the sexually potent and aggressive male and in ambivalence toward the black female's sexuality. The sexual fears of white males were evident throughout several hundred years of violent retribution against black males and in the yawning gap between expressed ideals and actual practice concerning contact between white men and black women.

Racial stereotypes may be defined as the bundles of belief carried by the energy of attitudes. Common American stereotypes about blacks are at least two or three hundred years old. There is evidence in the 17th and 18th centuries of virtually all the imputations that can be found today. The reason, or energizing component, underlying the stereotypes varies. Expressions of these beliefs have appeared in such disparate media as jokes; informal and formal speech; symbols — human, bestial, and otherwise; locker-room walls; the *Congressional Record*; and somber scientific treatises. Any given stereotype may have little, much, or no basis in fact. Such stereotypes and their primary animating energies include the well-hung male and the hot and easy female (sexual aggression), shiftlessness (imposed social role), dark fingernail moons in light-skinned individuals (inherency, the taint of ancestry or "blood"), affinity with apes (sexuality, historical happenstance, and supposed physiognomic attributes), peculiar musicality (cultural reality). The very common imputation of mental inferiority has been heatedly debated for more than two centuries.

The reaction of blacks to this barrage has shown great variability and ambivalence. For many years blacks could not openly or safely express their attitudes. Undoubtedly many blacks acquiesced to or embraced the value whites placed upon light complexion and straight hair. Some black men welcomed and absorbed the imputation of special sexual potency. While rejecting the charge of mental inferiority as a slur and a fabrication, a great many black children were placed in such positions of inferiority that they could not help but develop a self-negating posture about their own abilities.

Blacks have long displayed and probably actually held a wide and inconsistent range of attitudes toward whites. Black attitudes are especially difficult to assess because American society has discouraged their open expression to whites and even to other blacks, as well as self-acknowledgment. These attitudes are probably more variable and complicated than those of whites toward blacks. In general, black attitudes have not had the shaping and sustaining support that white attitudes have had; they have not been molded into ideologies in defense of existing institutions such as slavery and segregation. As the controlling group, whites have formalized and institutionalized their attitudes through literature, scientific dogma, laws, institutions, the economy, and enforced interracial etiquette. Blacks have in some measure been forced to react to these formulations.

Out of necessity, blacks have been more realistic and more discerning about individual differences among whites, and thus less inclined to think stereotypically. The instinct for sheer survival in American culture has placed a premium on quick and perceptive analysis of white characteristics and behavior. Unable to afford the luxury of misassessment, blacks have been less prone to generalize and ascribe inherency in white people. Sheer rage has animated some blacks, but often this force has been effectively checked by communal values that reject dysfunctional vengefulness. Obviously the imputation of dangerous aggressiveness to whites has a solid basis in fact. Less well known is the black perception of sheer stupidity on the part of whites, a view that for blacks often has a strong moral dimension.

Since 1960 there has been more change in racial attitudes than at any previous time. Some of this change is more apparent than real, for it has involved only the level of formal expression, not underlying attitudes. Thus, it is no longer polite (in the broadest, most potent sense of the term) to institutionalize pejorative attitudes in an obvious way or to express them in more public forums, such as the news media, advertising, political discourse, and directly to members of the other race. How much these changes are affecting actual attitudes is open to question. Certainly there has been some effect, especially among younger people. Yet there is much evidence to show that these attitudes have in some measure merely gone underground. Their presence is still revealed in private conversations, snide allusions, small-group confrontations, and such literary media as hate mail and toilet stall doors.

The South has shared in these attitudes and in recent changes. What has distinguished the South has been the more open expression of broadly shared attitudes, through the institutions of prolonged slavery and segregation, and in the open frankness of literate and oral expression. In recent years many blacks have voiced a preference for this openness, as permitting blacks at least to know where they stand. On the other hand, many southern blacks have hated the institutional and economic results of these attitudes, as well as the implicit and actual violence that they have encouraged. Changing black views on this matter can be partially gauged by the tread of feet northward and now to a lesser extent back "home."

Thus, racial attitudes in the South have been peculiar not for their existence or their content but for their virulence, saliency, pervasiveness, and the predisposition of white people to overt action and of black people to fear, accommodation, resistance, and retaliation. In the South, open expression and implementation of white racial attitudes have been encouraged by the frequent contact between large numbers of blacks and whites over a long period of time. One can still find traces of these racial attitudes in Maine, but they have played a far more important role in the society and culture of Mississippi. And because they have been so long and deeply embedded in southern culture especially, the chances are that they will persist for a very long time. Certainly it is clear that the South has suffered in this respect from tendencies that have long existed in American society as a whole. In this respect, the South seems like the entire nation — only more so.

WINTHROP D. JORDAN
University of Mississippi

Gordon W. Allport, *The Nature of Prejudice* (1958); Angus Campbell, *White Attitudes toward Black People* (1971); John Dollard, *Caste and Class in a Southern Town* (1937); George M. Fredrickson, *The Black Image in the White Mind: The Debate on Afro-American Character and Destiny, 1817–1914* (1971), *White Supremacy: A Comparative Study in American and South African History* (1981); Grace Elizabeth Hale, *Making Whiteness: The Culture of Segregation in the South, 1890–1940* (1998); Reginald Horsman, *Race and Manifest Destiny: The Origins of American Racial Anglo-Saxonism* (1981); Winthrop D. Jordan, *White over Black: American Attitudes toward the Negro, 1550–1812* (1969); Paul M. Kellstedt, *The Mass Media and the Dynamics of American Racial Attitudes* (2003); Robert J. Norrell, *The House I Live In: Race in the American Century* (2005); Hortense Powdermaker, *After Freedom: A Cultural Study in the Deep South* (1939).

Reconstruction Myth

When historians christened the civil rights struggle of the 1960s "the Second Reconstruction," it came as no surprise to anyone. Ever since Rutherford B. Hayes pulled the last federal troops from the southern states in 1877, the specter of renewed national intervention on behalf of racial equality had been the fundamental myth of southern political culture. The events of the Reconstruction period (usually seen as 1865–77), dramatic enough in their own right, took on demonic proportions in the imaginations of southern white conservatives who saw control by the "white supremacy Democrats" as the only road to salvation for their society. It took these "Redeemers" another quarter century to codify and institutionalize segregation and disfranchisement following the defeat of the Populist Party—whose political revolt, according to Democratic campaign rhetoric, threatened to return the South to "the evils of Reconstruction." For yet another seven decades every proposal to alter the southern caste system or one-party rule prompted conservative Democrats to parade the great Reconstruction myth before their constituents or on the floor of Congress.

The Republican effort to reconstruct southern society and politics in the 1860s was, to be sure, a radical innovation in the American political tradition. The abolition of slavery during the Civil War was a revolutionary alteration of the southern economic system. In order to preserve a meaningful freedom for the former slaves, the Republican Party favored a postwar policy of civil equality for blacks coupled with the establishment of a Freedmen's Bureau that would supervise the establishment of a free labor system in the South. In the political realm, Republicans found it necessary to enfranchise the freedmen after the war in order to prevent the former Confederates from dominating the new civil governments through the Democratic Party. The votes of the freedmen, together with the support of a minority of southern whites, gave the Republicans an electoral majority in each state for at least a few years. This brief phase of Republican control in the South, together with the passage of egalitarian federal laws and constitutional amendments, was what conservative whites meant by the term Reconstruction.

Reconstruction's mythic cast of characters included the "carpetbaggers," whom southern whites portrayed as greedy interlopers exploiting the South; the "scalawags," who were traitorous native southern whites collaborating with the Yankees; the freedmen, who were sometimes seen as violent and depraved in the myth but mostly seemed ignorant and lost; and the former Confederates, who were the heroes of the story, all honorable, decent people with the South's best interests in mind.

Southern Democrats were willing to use any means necessary to end Republican control of their states, including political violence. Initially through secret organizations such as the Ku Klux Klan and later more openly, as with Wade Hampton's "Red Shirts" in South Carolina, the Democrats resorted to beatings, assassinations, and armed bands of horsemen at the polls to "redeem" the South from "Negro rule." They justified these extreme methods on the grounds that Reconstruction threatened the fundamental stability of their society: economic control by "the better sort," the social elevation of all whites, and the protection of white women from sexual aggression by blacks were at stake.

During the next two decades violence was occasionally used to discourage black political efforts, but large-scale electoral corruption—against both black and white opponents—was a much more common Democratic tactic. Electoral corruption and violence escalated during the 1890s, when the People's Party bolted the Democratic Party. White conservatives justified both violence and corruption as necessary to prevent a return to black officeholding and Republican rule. By the turn of the century a growing number of northerners (even within the Republican Party) had come to agree with the southern view. Ignoring the Fourteenth and Fifteenth Amendments—the "Reconstruction amendments"—the Supreme Court refused to overturn disfranchisement and accepted segregation as constitutional under the separate-but-equal formula.

During the Progressive era the southern view of Reconstruction became enshrined in the popular culture of the nation. Thomas Dixon's *The Clansman* (1905) was a fictional embodiment of the Reconstruction myth, and William A. Dunning's *Reconstruction, Political and Economic, 1865–1877* (1907) was the best example of a series of historical monographs portraying white suffering in the era. In 1915 Woodrow Wilson held an enthusiastic showing of D. W. Griffith's new film, *Birth of a Nation*, at the White House. The president applauded its cinematic tribute to the great Reconstruction myth, complete with the stereotypical rescue of a white damsel from the hands of a black rapist by the heroic Ku Klux Klan. Two decades later *Gone with the Wind* provided a celluloid update of the myth that survives into the age of the DVD.

Whenever Congress considered a federal anti-lynching bill in the years between the two world wars, southern Democrats warned of a return to Reconstruction. The same refrain greeted certain New Deal programs, Franklin D. Roosevelt's Fair Employment Practices Commission, and Harry Truman's desegregation of the armed forces. As the Supreme Court began to strike down the white primary, segregated institutions of higher education, and restrictive covenants in the late 1940s, southern conservatives grew concerned that the justices might actually decide to interpret the Reconstruction amendments literally. In *Brown v. Board of Education*, which decided the school desegregation cases in 1954, the Court looked seriously at the intent of the framers of the Fourteenth Amendment — ignoring the myth, for once, in favor of serious historical analysis — but concluded that the issue was irrelevant to its unanimous opinion outlawing segregation. In their denunciation of the *Brown* decision, the Citizens' Councils of the Deep South resuscitated the white supremacy views of the 19th century and warned of the perils of a new Reconstruction.

The myth was not just the shibboleth of the far right. When John F. Kennedy published his *Profiles in Courage* in 1956, he pictured the first Reconstruction as a tragic mistake. Even after he gained the presidency, Kennedy held to the southern view and initially resisted federal intervention on the side of civil rights activists because he did not want to ignore what he regarded as the lessons of history concerning federal intervention in the South. Displaying an intellectual curiosity rare among chief executives, however, Kennedy actually invited historian David Donald to the White House to lead an after-dinner discussion of what modern historians were saying about the Reconstruction era. Whether this discussion had any impact on the president's thinking is undocumented, but he proceeded to put the federal government behind the enforcement of civil rights in the South to a degree unprecedented since the 1870s.

For white southerners who had grown up believing in the Reconstruction myth, the prospect was terrifying and infuriating. To refer to federal intervention as a Second Reconstruction was, in their eyes, to condemn such an idea out of hand. They characterized northern whites who came south as Freedom Riders, voter registration workers, or demonstrators on picket lines as latter-day abolitionists or carpetbaggers. Southern whites who criticized segregation, disfranchisement, or the jailing of civil rights workers were scalawags. A rejuvenated Ku Klux Klan engaged in savage beatings, bombings, and assassinations, only to have the perpetrators of these crimes acquitted by all-white juries.

The Second Reconstruction was, however, far more successful than the first. This time federal intervention included systematic enforcement of civil rights legislation by the U.S. Justice Department; the Health, Education, and Welfare Department; and the courts. This time southern blacks engaged in civil disobedience, manipulated the national media, won the support of northern public opinion, obtained effective legal representation through public interest law firms, and created their own heroes of mythic proportions.

By 1970, when a series of political leaders below the Mason-Dixon line were proclaiming a "New South" that turned its back on racial prejudice, a great change had taken place in the region's political culture. Racial prejudice was still alive and well, of course, but for the most part public discussion of the race question was couched in euphemisms and code words of the sort familiar outside of Dixie. No longer could white politicians expect to be taken seriously if they yelled about the evils of Reconstruction. The Second Reconstruction had arrived — and white southerners had learned to live with it. Some, including historians of that first experiment in racial equality, even came to relish being called scalawags.

PEYTON MCCRARY
University of South Alabama

Claude G. Bowers, *The Tragic Era: The Revolution after Lincoln* (1929); Carl M. Brauer, *John F. Kennedy and the Second Reconstruction* (1977); John Hope Franklin, *Reconstruction after the Civil War* (1961); Paul M. Gaston, *The New South Creed: A Study in Southern Mythmaking* (1970); William Gillette, *Retreat from Reconstruction, 1869–1879* (1979); V. O. Key Jr., *Southern Politics in State and Nation* (1949); J. Morgan Kousser, *Colorblind Injustice: Minority Voting Rights and the Undoing of the Second Reconstruction* (1999); Manning Marable, *Race, Reform, and Rebellion: The Second Reconstruction in Black America, 1945–1990* (1991); James M. McPherson, *Ordeal by Fire: The Civil War and Reconstruction* (1982); Robert J. Norrell, *Reaping the Whirlwind: The Civil Rights Movement in Tuskegee* (1985); Kenneth M. Stampp, *Era of Reconstruction, 1865–1877* (1965); C. Vann Woodward, *The Burden of Southern History* (revised ed., 1982).

Regionalism

The word "region" comes from the Latin "regere," to rule, and in early English usage came to mean something governed. This might be a place (size did not matter), but it might also be part of a human body, indeed almost any space subject to will and command. By the early 19th century, in the American South, the word still had this organic usage, as when Thomas Dew in 1841 spoke of "the region of the intellect." But, in the sense of a place, region had drifted from the notion of subjection and come to mean somewhere of some geographical coherence, as when George Frederick Holmes in 1849 wrote of the "tide-water region of Virginia." But the term then was never applied to the South as a whole, and there was no derivative notion of "regionalism." However, Romanticism had begun to transform the possible meaning of region, since Romanticism held that there was an organic relationship between land and people, climate and social custom, which created social groups that, evolving historically, were recognizable by (and manifested themselves in) distinctive and persistent patterns of language, ideology, and polity, from which the individual took his or her identity. Hence, human culture made landscape, too, which made it theoretically possible to expand the scope of region beyond the narrower scope of river valleys, mountain ranges, and so forth, toward the wider South. The political venture and failure of the Confederacy suggested the boundaries of such a South, but it is striking that the late 19th century often deepened the older, more restricted sense of locality. Local color writers, who flourished between the 1870s and 1890s, specialized in capturing through the use of dialect and folk stories the pervading spirit of such places as New Orleans (George W. Cable), the Tennessee mountains (Mary Murfree), the Virginia Tidewater (Thomas Nelson Page), and the Georgia Black Belt (Joel Chandler Harris). But these were making, nonetheless, a significant contribution, for regionalism was to become an apolitical construct and these writers portrayed and invented a depoliticized folk. From them, a national periodical readership learned about the curious and harmless ways of other and different Americans, who no longer threatened secession and war.

Region came into different use in the later 19th century in the management of capitalism. Newly national corporations began to categorize their organizational subdivisions as regional, though these units might bear little relationship to traditional geographical and political divisions. And the United States government got into the business, more systematically, of collecting statistics for the use of the wider powers gathered to it in 1865 and after. These numbers, too, were often conveniently subdivided. The U.S. Geological Survey, for example, divided the country into regions. Indeed, it was in the idea that a rational science might manage the human condition—better than it had been managed by raucous politicians and voters—that the South arrived at one version of the modern conception.

By the 1920s regionalism had become a topic and a word available for sociologists, of whom the most important were Howard W. Odum and Rupert B. Vance, both of the University of North Carolina at Chapel Hill. Odum was much influenced by German social science, but also by British traditions of social planning. It was in the United Kingdom in the 1880s that "regionalism" had first been used, imitated from the French *régionalisme* (1875), though the French had from the first understood this to mean the conservation of traditional societies against the dangers of a centralized and modernizing state, while the British had seen regionalism as a mediation, something that might nurse incoherent premodernity into a tidier and more symmetrical future and preserve the British state from the centrifugal tendencies of Scottish, Irish, and Welsh nationalisms. The southern tradition lay somewhere between those poles, more nostalgic than the British, more modernizing than the French, but also more wary of political power than someone like Lewis Mumford in New York. Odum and Vance attempted to develop a sociology for a southern folk, in which the poverty of its colonial economy might be defined and remedied by voluntary action posing no threat to the stability of the nation, all directed by groups of planning experts. Odum was insistent that regionalism was a healthy recognition of diversity, not in conflict with national interests, whereas sectionalism was egocentric and disruptive: this distinction was challenged as spurious, most notably by the poet and social critic Donald Davidson. Hence the problem of nationality lay (and lies) at the core of the conception, since regionalism came to rest on the presumption that the nation is politically and morally preeminent, but for psychological or administrative reasons needs to use and legitimate smaller units, which have some spatial coherence or cultural resonance. But even Odum, especially in his *Southern Regions* of 1936, found the conflict between administrative rationality and cultural habit intractable. There he parceled out what many thought of as "the South" into several regions: a Southwest that included Texas and Oklahoma; a Southeast that included nine states from the old Confederacy (plus Kentucky); a Northeast that absorbed West Virginia, Maryland, and Delaware; and a Middle States, which was given Missouri.

By the 1940s this tradition had failed, mostly because scientific regionalism required administrative mechanisms to enact its planning, but (save in the instance of the Tennessee Valley Authority and various ad hoc interstate organizations) these intermediate units never emerged to challenge the federal government and state governments, which were the main beneficiaries of the New Deal order. Hence the especial enemy of regionalism was the conservative rigidity of the American constitutional order, which was too traumatized by the experience of civil war to tolerate the experimentalism of what the British call devolution and the European Union refers to as "subsidiarity." With the failure of the Chapel Hill Regionalists, regionalism was released for vaguer usages, usually conservative and sympathetic to the premise that life is more richly lived when controlled from a locality. This usage had, indeed, been in competition with that of Chapel Hill even before 1941 among many cultural experimentalists and folklorists in various parts of United States, such as Ralph Borsodi, B. A. Botkin, and Carey McWilliams.

Currently, "regionalism" has come to be used as a rough and often anachronistic term for the structure of American cultural and geographical diversity, in which the South is one region among many, among them the West, the Midwest, and the Northeast (the most elusive of the regions), each of which is described as having the usual possessions of a cultural nation (a history, a literature, a music, an art, a social structure, a religious sensibility, an encyclopedia). But, if the South is and was a region, this has left the difficulty of how to describe what in 1850 and 1900 were called regions, that is, such smaller divisions as the Mississippi Delta or the South Carolina Upcountry. For this purpose, the word "subregion" has been pressed into service and become habitual in the last 30 years or so. Just to complicate matters, in this same period, the growth of administrative planning by international organizations (the United Nations, the World Bank) has led to aggregates of nations in different parts of the world being described as regions; so there is said to be an East Asian region, and the United States belongs to a North American region. But the implications of this usage have not been digested by southern discourse.

MICHAEL O'BRIEN
Jesus College, Cambridge

American Historical Review (October 1999); Robert L. Dorman, *Revolt of the Provinces: The Regionalist Movement in America, 1920–1945* (1993); Howard W. Odum, *Southern Regions of the United States* (1936); Roy Porter and Mikulá Teich, eds., *Romanticism in National Context* (1988).

Religion and Mythology

Believed reality maintains that religion rests at the heart of southern culture and what it means to be a southerner. Even critics of the region, convinced that the South can be dismissed as the proverbial "buckle on the Bible belt," concede as much. Unleashing diatribes against the South as was his fashion, H. L. Mencken abrasively declared the South of the 1920s to be "a cesspool of Baptists, a miasma of Methodism, snake charmers . . . and syphilitic evangelists." Southerners, as James McBride Dabbs has said in a more positive vein, are those Americans most "haunted by God." The central theme of southern culture, Samuel S. Hill has added, is religion, at least in the sense that to be southern is most often to see oneself as having "a radical dependence upon God." Protestantism is to the South what Islam is to Afghanistan or Judaism to Israel. Currently, evangelical Protestantism accounts for 90 percent of the religious loyalty of the region. Public opinion polls disclose that nine out of every ten southerners openly declare themselves Protestant, with nearly four out of every five of these being Baptist, Methodist, or Presbyterian. Thus, most observers of southern culture come to terms with the region's abiding sense of religiosity.

Recent revisionist research, however, takes issue with the traditional story—the myth—of the South's storied fundamentalism of faith and its resultant cultural conservatism. While not in denial that the regional life of the South is strongly flavored by the fundamentals of faith, Samuel S. Hill has come to see fundamentalism to be rather a recent social phenomenon in the designed fabric of southern life. While the South by cultural impulse long has been "committed to evangelization," to the contrarian notion that "compromise is vice," to the "cultivation of personal piety," to "local autonomy," and to "doctrinal exactitude"—in both a spiritual and a political sense—only within the past quarter century or so has the fundamentalist "reputation" of the South been solidified within American culture. Institutionalized evangelical Protestant religion —historically that active agent of southern-based cultural conservatism—now undergirds national fundamentalist religious movements. By endorsing the Religious Right's moral agenda (which is not always rooted in traditional southern evangelical concerns), Hill concludes, fundamentalist movements "have weakened the internal unity of the traditional denominations, prying them loose from their comfortable line with traditional Southern culture." In this sense, southern fundamentalism has seceded from its traditional alignment with southern ideology by commanding national attention, largely via alliances with the national Religious Right and its political agent, the Republican Party. In so engaging the "culture wars," it has become increasingly diverse, thus loosening its ties to the very localist and homogeneous culture it traditionally sought to cultivate. The traditional myth of southern religiosity, in at least some respects, begs a new, more nuanced, reading.

The relationship of southern religion to southern mythology, although not at first glance obvious, is nonetheless significant. Religion in almost every society stands in service to the process of social integration. The earliest meaning of the word "religion" is "to bind together." In this sense religion is a bonding agent of culture—it shapes community. Religion makes the business of relating to one's fellow cultural travelers somewhat involuntary, by binding all to a common purpose, by forging identity out of a sense of blood and belonging rooted in geographical imperatives. The sociologist Emile Durkheim says as much in his *Elementary Forms of the Religious Life* (1912). Religion, Durkheim argues, is the most basic of human symbolic systems, the key to culture, the "primal act." Religion renders a cosmology, thereby summarizing the deepest collective experiences of the cultural group as it aids and abets cultural kinship. Religion, in this sense, is thick with meaning as it both shapes and expresses cultural ideology. In important respects this is the human norm, as state religions offer a core identity to many imagined cultural communities—whether Anglicanism to England, Catholicism to Spain, or Islam to Iraq.

Myth functions in much the same fashion as religion and is nearly inseparable from it. Myth is at base a narrative, a tale of the tribe, the traditional stories a culture tells itself about itself. In edited, abbreviated form it simultaneously expresses, establishes, and enhances meaning for the cultural group.

Myth conveys a culture's collective consciousness. Its function is to characterize a society's cultural paradigms that codify and structure the group's sense of reality, image of itself, and ultimately its collective behavioral expectations. The collective dimension of myth serves as "bearer of cultural meaning." Myths, psychologically, assure the mind and reaffirm the ancient collective way. In narrative form they act as culturally articulated mechanisms crucial to the dissemination and transmission of tradition and culture. Mythic tales are received and understood with a "religious" seriousness, for they afford an explanation of a culture, especially with regard to its origins and subsequent destiny. Both myth and religion, then, structure community and culture by providing a unified measure of meaning for the group. They both are social facts, not collective fantasies. They offer cultural portraits, which establish group identity by linking past experiences, current circumstances, and future expectations.

Southern culture in its formative stages was structured by a blending of religion and myth. The first Europeans to come to the South explored and settled the region in accordance with the religious and mythological premises of their age. Whether articulated in verse, fiction, or sermons, or borne ultimately at unconscious levels, myth pictured the region as a new Garden of Eden. Georgia, for example, was early declared to be "that promis'd Canaan." And as early as Robert Beverley's *The History and Present State of Virginia*, published in London in 1705, one witnesses, according to Lewis P. Simpson, "the origin of the plantation in the literary imagination as the fruition of the errand into paradise." Settlers planting themselves in the southern colonies filtered their experience through an imagination structured by religiously inspired, mythically designed, and historically conveyed attitudes about the South, and later generations of southerners would see their experience as but an extension of these attitudes. Thus, by the antebellum era a religious substructure to southern culture was established.

Slavery, as the centerpiece of the South's antebellum pastoral world, not surprisingly assumed the character and quality of a religious institution, with its paradigm of cultural assumptions and its associated rituals of social reinforcement. Southern culture and its peculiar institution became situated, ideologically and imaginatively, both within the arenas of social performance and within a sacred and cosmic frame of reference at the hands of writers like William Gilmore Simms. Simms, from his plantation, Woodlands, offered the argument that because blacks were totally unprepared for freedom, it was only appropriate that white southerners, under a holy contract with God, serve as stewards and "moral conservators" of Africans. Early in the southern experience it was believed that European culture was planted in New World soil out of divine purpose, and later southern generations developed racial myths based on the biblical myth of Ham. The "author" of the southern way of life, it was said, was God. Slavery, grounded in the Bible, was an extension of His law. Stories that explained the southern cultural experience were thus ultimately derived from religion and structured and sustained by mythology. Such cultural tales framed white southerners' beliefs, values, and behavior within a sacred history and functioned as myth. It was predictable that southerners would come to see themselves as being a "people" in the classical and biblical sense of the word.

By the time of the Civil War the South interpreted its historical experience in light of a transcendent religious-mythological reality. "We have pulled a temple down," exclaimed convention delegates in Charleston, S.C., as they seceded from the union in December of 1860. The so-called War for Southern Independence carried with it the aura of holy war. A Confederate myth born of the war years stoked the South's social imagination with stories of high purpose, high heroism, high drama, and high redemption. A Crusade of the Planters bent on the region's salvation stirred the soul of the South as only religious energies could.

As the South emerged from the ashes of Shiloh, Vicksburg, and Chattanooga and discovered its cause to be "lost," it nonetheless carried with it the sense, as Charles Reagan Wilson has aptly suggested, that the region had been "baptized in blood." The myth of the Lost Cause, like earlier southern myths, resonated with religious imagery. Rituals celebrating the Lost Cause exploited the southern talent for ceremonial style. Through the introduction of social rituals such as Confederate Memorial Day and Confederate reunions, the southern past of both religion and myth was revalorized and reunited with its tragic present. Southern mythology was institutionalized as a civil religion. Protestant churches and their clergy celebrated the Lost Cause, declaring that while the chosen people had lost their holy war, they had been purified and anointed for a yet greater purpose. Heroes such as Robert E. Lee were compared to Moses.

A new set of prophets arose in the South to voice new southern visions. For some, the Promised Land was destined to be one of racial harmony, economic fulfillment, and political parity with the North — a New South. For others, the Ku Klux Klan, replete with its religious symbolism and religious rituals, offered visions of a recycled South wherein an indomitable commitment to white supremacy would once again prevail. For still others, conservative Democrats — the Redeemers — seemed to represent a higher order of political virtue and to uphold antebellum codes of white rule, pay proper homage to the Lost Cause, and endorse the fiscal policies of the New South. Religion and myth once again coalesced in reciprocal fashion to structure a new cultural order in a reconstructed South.

Aristotle's *Poetics* long ago defined myth in a general sense as an old story, a traditional tale, but offered the further observation that myth, in essence, is not simply the story told but the plot within it. Herein, perhaps, lies the best cultural clue to the convergence of southern myth and southern religion. Both share a common infrastructure, a patterned plot of paradise, paradise lost, and paradise regained. The Christian myth relates the story of a human destiny born to Edenic perfection, lost to an earthly salvation by the fall, yet capable of being born again to a paradise regained. The South, in relation to its historical experience, long has felt itself a participant in just such a pattern of existence, experience, and expectation.

As initially conceived, the South was an Edenic paradise; its plantation paradise was lost via the Civil War; and the South since has entertained visions of a paradise regained. Southern blacks, as southerners too, also have seen their mythic history tied to a religious, Christian paradigm—a paradise symbolized by their ancestral African heritage. The plantation South was their "time on the cross" and paradise lost. Their more recent experience, inspired by Martin Luther King Jr.'s dream of having seen the Promised Land, was a paradise regained. Jonathan Daniels characterized southerners—both white and black—as "a mythological people . . . who live in a still legendary land" and are Bible centered. The Bible, with its tales of paradise and human destiny, is the South's ultimate cultural text in both a religious and mythological sense.

PATRICK GERSTER
San Jose City College

James McBride Dabbs, *Haunted by God: The Cultural and Religious Experience of the South* (1972); Samuel S. Hill, *Journal of Southern Religion* (1998), *Southern Churches in Crisis* (1966); John Shelton Reed, *The Enduring South: Subcultural Persistence in Mass Society* (1972); Lewis P. Simpson, *The Dispossessed Garden: Pastoral and History in Southern Literature* (1975); Charles Reagan Wilson, *Baptized in Blood: The Religion of the Lost Cause, 1865–1920* (1980); Daryl White and O. Kendall White Jr., eds., *Religion in the Contemporary South: Diversity, Community, and Identity* (1996).

Romanticism

"Romanticism" is a term applied to certain artistic and intellectual developments in Europe and America from roughly 1790 to 1830, the period, as it happened, in which the South began to think of itself as a separate culture. Indeed, Michael O'Brien has suggested that romantic modes of thought made possible a burgeoning consciousness of something distinctively southern. Though romanticism has a wide range of meanings and connotations, the focus here is on the importance of romanticism in shaping antebellum conservative social and cultural thought in the region, its usefulness in reference to black and white folk cultures particularly in the 1920s and 1930s, and its applicability to various salient traits of white and black southern writing.

Where New England transcendentalism was a form of romanticism that was concerned with the relationship of the self to nature, southern thought prior to 1865 tended to focus on tradition and society. Specifically, while transcendentalism tended to celebrate the isolated self seeking to reintegrate with nature, southern organic conservatism sought a hierarchically structured community. Southern social thought in the 1840s and 1850s increasingly rejected the contract theory of society and politics, free trade and the free market, and the utilitarian, materialistic, and secular tenor of the newly emerging industrial society in the North—and in Britain. Ideal social relations were to be modelled on the family, while the plantation system cum chattel slavery stood at the center of economic and cultural life. Though largely destroyed by the Civil War, the ideal of an organic community based upon an agrarian way of life reemerged as the animating idea of the Vanderbilt Agrarians in their 1930s manifesto, *I'll Take My Stand*, and has constituted one strand of American conservatism since then.

At the other end of the spectrum, the post–World War I South witnessed the rediscovery of southern folk cultures in the Appalachian Mountains and in the rural and small-town communities of the Black Belt. Some of the Chapel Hill Regionalists rediscovered the folk cultures of the white southern rural and mountain population, while, most famously, Zora Neale Hurston of Florida, who had trained as an anthropologist in the North with Franz Boas and Melville Herskovits, and folklorists such as the Lomax Brothers, collected the music and folktales of the black South threatened with extinction by the modernizing tendencies in the New South and the massive migration northward of black southerners. Though this empirical research was enormously valuable in its own right, much of it, particularly Hurston's, was informed by what Hazel Carby has referred to as a "romantic imagination." What Hurston's ethnology shared with romanticism generally was a concern with rediscovering a premodern folk community "outside of history" (Carby) and devoid of serious social tensions or deep divisions.

Modernist fiction in the South also kept alive several traits of literary romanticism that had emerged as early as in the work of Edgar Allan Poe: the centrality of an alienated, self-conscious protagonist, a proclivity for the gothic and the extravagant, a preoccupation with decline and fall, and the cultivation of a kind of cultural melancholy. William Faulkner, Tennessee Williams, Flannery O'Connor, and Carson McCullers all perpetuated this tradition. In addition, the southern folk tradition was marked by a colorful extravagance that lent itself to a vernacular form of romanticism, traces of which can be detected in the work of Barry Hannah, Harry Crews, and Ishmael Reed. On the other hand, several of the central figures of the Southern Literary Renaissance, such as W. J. Cash and Richard Wright, Faulkner and Lillian Smith, implicitly or explicitly condemned the romantic habit of the southern mind and its tendency to monumentalize the antebellum South and sentimentalize black southern folk life.

Finally, many of the romantic tendencies in southern culture persist in the form of defiant gestures against the federal government, adherence to the cult of the Confederacy, and veneration of the Confederate battle flag. The fact that Margaret Mitchell's *Gone with the Wind* continues to be read (and rewritten from white and black points of view) suggests that there is still life in a tradition that remains suspicious of modern secular society and yearns for the simpler truths of an earlier time. That said, such phenomena have become something of a cultural tic, trotted out on special occasions or in emergencies but rarely interfering for long with the South's effort to become (post)modern.

RICHARD H. KING
University of Nottingham

Hazel Carby, in *"Their Eyes Were Watching God": A Casebook*, ed. Cheryl A. Wall (2000); W. J. Cash, *The Mind of the South* (1941); Zora Neale Hurston, *Dust Tracks in the Road* (1942); Michael O'Brien, in *Rethinking the South: Essays in Southern Intellectual History* (1988); Rollin G. Osterweis, *Romanticism and Nationalism in the Old South* (1949); Scott Romine, *The Narrative Forms of Southern Community* (1999).

Sexuality

The South is often portrayed as a subculture obsessed with sexual repression yet charged with undercurrents of sexual tension. Little concrete social science evidence exists, however, for evaluating the uniqueness of sexual attitudes and behaviors among southerners, despite widespread attention to the study of human sexuality in the 20th century. Many social science researchers either do not control for or do not consider regional differences in analyzing their data. In addition to the limited data from social science, however, many insights about southerners and sexuality can be found in the region's history, literature, music, and oral folklore.

Richard Godbeer's *Sexual Revolution in Early America* (2004) details regional differences between southern and northern colonists and how those changed over time. Catherine Clinton and Michele Gillespie argue that "sex and race must be situated at the heart of southern colonial history," and recent work has shown how Anglo-American laws prohibiting interracial sex were important in reinforcing slavery and racism. From early on in southern history, sexuality was intertwined with issues of not only race but also gender and social class within an emerging hierarchical, patriarchal society. Violence was an everyday part of life in the early South and proved a powerful weapon enforcing racial and gender dichotomies. Scholars document incidences of rape, castration, murder, infanticide, and physical brutality.

Probably the best-known images of southern sexual relations are the portrayals of steamy antebellum era trysts in the vein of Kyle Onstott's *Mandingo*, emphasizing miscegenation and brutal control and use of sexuality. Historians generally agree that certain codes of behavior dominated the antebellum South: white men had the greatest latitude in fulfilling their sexual desires; black women were expected to be sexually accessible and more sexually expressive than white women; black men's sexuality was viewed as threatening and was tightly controlled; and white women were expected not to have sexual desires and to stand as asexual paragons of virtue. These cultural assumptions reflected the reality of power and dominance in a hierarchal society. Sociological studies such as John Dollard's *Caste and Class in a Southern Town* (1937) confirmed the persistence of some of these attitudinal and behavioral patterns during the early 20th century.

The household was a defining institution in the antebellum South, tying together whites across social class and providing an ideological justification for the presence of blacks in southern society. The transformation of the household in the postemancipation years led to legal and political debates about governance of sexuality in the new society. Peter Bardaglio sees "a new paternalistic ideal of government regulating the treatment of dependents," replacing an older model of the patriarchal head of the household governing it with undisputed authority. White anxiety about black male sexuality in this era led to increased violence against black men. Observers have long written of the "southern rape complex," which represented an unyielding white racial solidarity in the face of any black male challenges to white male sexual dominance. Diane Miller Sommerville has recently questioned this complex, arguing that white elites were often able to protect black men accused of rape. In addition, poor white women and black women were viciously stereotyped as sexually depraved, leading to a misogyny that prevented successful prosecution in rape cases brought by poor white and black women.

Aspects of striking gender- and race-based double standards were not endemic to the South but represented national trends as well. Nineteenth-century physicians, moralists, and social commentators were obsessed with appropriate channeling of men's sexual urges and with suppression of women's sexuality. Physicians writing in the *New Orleans Medical and Surgical Journal* in the mid-1850s, for example, recognized men's strong sex drives but warned against masturbation because it drained men of the will for self-sufficiency. Women were exhorted to be virtuous, chaste, and pious — to keep their minds above sexuality. Married women, though, were also duty-bound to be available sexually to their husbands. Historian Barbara Welter refers to this view as "the cult of true womanhood," which flourished nationwide between 1820 and 1860. Although historian Carl N. Degler and others question the extent of actual acceptance of such exhortations, a strong double standard prevailed and was probably intensified by the chivalric code in the South.

At times, sexuality was brutally repressed in the South. The 18th- and 19th-century trend was toward disapproval of the use of castration as a legal punishment. However, notes Eugene D. Genovese, "scattered evidence suggests that some masters continued to apply it [castration] especially to slaves who had become their rivals for coveted black women." Female castration became common throughout the country after 1872, when Georgia physician Robert Battey developed the surgical techniques for "normal ovariotomy," a procedure he enthusiastically endorsed for "problems" ranging from "erotic tendencies" to "troublesomeness." As G. J. Barker-Benfield notes, this technique remained popular until about 1921, and numerous female circumcisions and clitoridectomies were also performed.

Scientific studies of sexual behaviors and attitudes began in the late 1800s. Unfortunately, no regionally specific data are available from such early studies as those of Dr. Clelia Mosher and Katherine Davis. Even Alfred Kinsey and associates employed no regional identifiers in analysis of the data from their landmark 1948 study, *Sexual Behavior in the Human Male*. Other demographic variables such as religion, education, and urban-rural residence that are confounded with region of residence were the primary bases for analyses. According to Kinsey and associates' *Sexual Behavior in the Human Female* (1953), approximately 3,600 of their total male and female samples of 16,392 cases were southerners. Nevertheless, the researchers commented in the 1953 volume that despite widespread assumptions about regional differences in sexual behavior, "we have an impression, as yet unsubstantiated by specific calculations, that there are actually few differences in sex patterns between similar communities in different portions of the United States." This impression seems to have guided much subsequent research.

As the so-called sexual revolution gained momentum, interest grew in the changing rates of premarital intercourse, and regional comparisons became more common. One important early investigation was Winston Ehrmann's 1959 study of premarital sexuality among students at the University of Florida. Sixty-five percent of the 576 males and 13 percent of the 265 females in the sample reported having had premarital intercourse. In a major 1964 study, Ira Reiss concluded that there was a nationwide trend toward acceptance of premarital intercourse on the basis of affection but not necessarily commitment to marriage, though in behavior the double standard still prevailed. Sixteen percent of the high school and college students in Reiss's Virginia sample accepted the "permissiveness with affection" standard compared to 72 percent of the respondents in New York.

Attention to regional differences heightened with publication in 1968 of Vance Packard's *The Sexual Wilderness*. Packard reported results of a study of college juniors and seniors nationwide, with a total of 185 respondents from 3 southern institutions represented. Among the southern respondents about 69 percent of the males and 32 percent of the females reported having had premarital intercourse. This rate for males was the highest in the country; the rate for southern females was next to the lowest. Furthermore, southern males were the most likely to have taken part in a one-night affair with someone they never dated again. "The South has the nation's strongest reputation for a double standard in regard to sexual behavior," said Packard. "That reputation receives support in the survey results." Regarding attitudes, Packard found the strongest support of the double standard among females from the South and the Midwest. Commented Packard, "A major surprise (to us) was that next to the Easterners the males most untroubled by the idea of courting a non-virginal girl were the Southerners (36 percent responding 'no')." More recent investigations have shown that southerners are now following the trend toward "permissiveness with affection." For example, researchers who compared data from 1965, 1970, and 1975 samples of students at one major state university in the South found trends congruent with national ones, particularly in the "dramatic liberalization in both premarital sexual behavior and attitudes for college females."

Beyond the information on premarital sexual standards, especially among the college-educated, however, little reliable information exists about regional variations in sexual behavior and attitude, whether normative (e.g., sexual relations among married couples) or nonnormative (e.g., extramarital sexual relations, homosexual relations). Most recent large-scale studies of sexuality have not dealt with regional patterns. Laws in the South regarding sexual activities, however, provide valuable insights about the mixture of attitudes regarding sexuality.

For a brief period during the Civil War, Nashville registered and periodically inspected prostitutes, the first such system in the nation. As of 1885 Louisiana, Arkansas, and New Mexico were the only states in which "red light" districts for prostitution were legal. New Orleans's notorious district, Storyville, was such an accepted institution in the late 1800s that guidebooks for it were distributed at restaurants, taverns, and tourist attractions. As of 1975 Mississippi was the only state that allowed conjugal visits for married prisoners and provided cottages for such meetings. As of 2005 the state is one out of only five in the nation that permits the practice and one of two that distributes condoms to participating married inmates. When the streaking craze hit the country and many locales prosecuted the participants for indecent exposure, the Louisiana legislature "excluded from prosecution streakers who did not attempt to arouse the sexual desires of their viewers." Also, southern states legalized use of birth control by married couples and interracial marriage before some other states.

On the other hand, although many states in the 1960s and 1970s revised their penal codes to allow adults to engage in any sexual acts in private, Georgia doubled its penalties for consensual sodomy. Georgia, Kentucky, South Carolina, and Wisconsin stood out for years as the few states specifically penalizing both female and male homosexual practices (most states overlooked lesbian activities). In 1986 national attention focused on the Georgia sodomy statutes when the U.S. Supreme Court upheld the state's right to define sodomy (oral or anal sex) as a felony punishable by 20 years in prison. As of 1986, 12 of the 24 states that had criminal penalties for sodomy were southern, with maximum penalties in the South ranging from a $200 fine in Texas to Georgia's 20-year term. Southern laws gained further attention in 1986 when a federal appeals court panel upheld Virginia's laws against fornication and cohabitation, enacted in 1829 and 1860 respectively. But in 2003, in *Lawrence v. Texas*, the Supreme Court overturned state sodomy laws and expanded the right to privacy.

Impressionistic information about southern sexuality abounds in anecdotal accounts, literary images, and representations in television, movies, and popular music. According to historian Thomas L. Connelly, southern folklore contains a variety of sexual stereotypes, such as "the high school bad girl," who dresses provocatively and undulates rather than walks, and the "good old boy tribal shouter," who hangs out of his pickup truck to "deliver ancient Celtic tribal shouts such as 'who-oo-wee'" when an attractive girl passes by. Southerners have not been reticent about examining sexuality's role in their lives. Writers such as Florence King, author of *Southern Ladies and Gentlemen* (1976), and Rayna Green, a contributor to *Speaking for Ourselves: Women of the South* (1984), provide lively personal observations on southern morals, sex roles, and sexual behaviors. For decades southern poets and novelists have grappled with "sin, sex, and segregation," according to Richard H. King, and examples of southern writers' struggles with the theme of sexuality are innumerable.

Anne Goodwyn Jones and Susan V. Donaldson use the body as a defining concept in exploring how cultural texts can reveal continuing intersections of sexuality with other central themes of southern culture. "From the body of the white southern lady, praised for the absence of desire, to the body of the black lynching victim, accused of excessive desire," they write, "southern sexuality has long been haunted by stories designating hierarchical relationships among race, class, and gender." Southern newspaper columnists write openly about sex and social relationships in the region; country music and blues lyricists have long incorporated many frank sexual themes and hip-hop contests feature sex as a key part of "The Dirty South"; "common folk" readily swap sexual tales and advice; and such celebrities as Jessica Simpson, Britney Spears, and Billy Bob Thornton cast images of southern sexuality. Suzi Parker's *Sex in the South: Unbuckling the Bible Belt* (2003) is a state-by-state chronicle of sexual sites, institutions, and experiences. "The region is a full-to-capacity carnal playground," Parker writes, "where the den mother buys dildos, the principal is a swinger, and the preacher is a porn fiend."

Finally, the increasingly public presence of lesbian, gay, bisexual, and transgender (LGBT) people and the growth of the Religious Right movement opposing that public role have contributed to a new frankness about discussion of sexuality in the contemporary South. The nationwide lesbian/gay rights movement has distinctive southern dimensions. Queer studies scholars examine the historical and cultural role of LGBT people who have lived within a regional context dominated by evangelical religion, racial obsessions, and gender dichotomies. A considerable body of scholarship and memoirs demonstrates the long role of LGBT people in the region and their distinctive place within the national LGBT community. Leaders of the Religious Right, on the other hand, make sexual issues the core of their efforts to use political successes to change southern life. Opposition to pornography, premarital sex, the Equal Rights Amendment, and gay marriage comprise central elements of the Religious Right's agenda. Passage of constitutional amendments prohibiting gay marriage in many southern states in 2004 reflects a new militancy by conser-

vative religious groups in attempting to restore traditional moral strictures in
southern public life.

SHARON A. SHARP
Boone, North Carolina

Edward G. Armstrong, *Journal of Sex Research* (August 1986); Peter W. Bardaglio,
Reconstructing the Household: Families, Sex, and the Law in the 19th-Century South
(1995); G. J. Barker-Benfield, in *The American Family in Social-Historical Perspective*,
ed. Michael Gordon (2d ed., 1978); Catherine Clinton and Michelle Gillespie, *The
Devil's Lane: Sex and Race in the Early South* (1997); Thomas L. Connelly, *Columbia
Record* (30 August 1985); Carl N. Degler, in *The American Family in Socio-Historical
Perspective*, ed. Michael Gordon (2d ed., 1978); John R. Earle and Philip J. Perricone,
Journal of Sex Research (August 1986); Winston Ehrmann, *Premarital Dating Behav-
ior* (1959); Paul H. Gebhard, *Sexual Behavior in the Human Female* (1953); Eugene D.
Genovese, *Roll, Jordan, Roll: The World the Slaves Made* (1972); Rayna Green, in
Speaking for Ourselves: Women of the South, ed. Maxine Alexander (1984); Martha
Hodes, *White Women, Black Men: Illicit Sex in the 19th-Century South* (1997); John
Howard, *Carryin' On in the Lesbian and Gay South* (1997), *Men Like That: A South-
ern Queer History* (2001); Anne Goodwyn Jones and Susan V. Donaldson, *Haunted
Bodies: Gender and Southern Texts* (1997); Herant A. Katchadourian and Donald T.
Lunde, *Fundamentals of Human Sexuality* (2d ed., 1975); Karl King, Jack O. Balswick,
and Ira E. Robinson, *Journal of Marriage and the Family* (August 1977); Richard H.
King, *A Southern Renaissance: The Cultural Awakening of the American South, 1930–
1955* (1980); Alfred C. Kinsey, Wardell B. Pomeroy, and Clyde E. Martin, *Sexual
Behavior in the Human Male* (1948); Tara McPherson, *Reconstructing Dixie: Race,
Gender, and Nostalgia in the Imagined South* (2003); *Newsweek* (14 July 1986); Vance
Packard, *The Sexual Wilderness* (1968); Suzi Parker, *Sex in the South: Unbuckling the
Bible Belt* (2003); Ira L. Reiss, *Journal of Marriage and the Family* (May 1964), *The
Social Context of Premarital Sexual Permissiveness* (1967); Bradley Smith, *The Ameri-
can Way of Sex* (1978); Diane Miller Sommerville, *Rape and Race in the 19th-Century
South* (2004); Barbara Welter, in *The American Family in Socio-Historical Perspec-
tive*, ed. Michael Gordon (2d ed., 1978); John Wheeler and Peter Kilman, *Archives of
Sexual Behavior* (June 1983).

Stereotypes

Stereotypes, in the end, offer a conceptual composite of accurate generalization
and dubious belief. The term "stereotype" — introduced to the social sciences
by Walter Lippmann's book *Public Opinion* (1922) — refers to those "pictures in
our heads" drawn from the proverbial "kernel of truth." Stereotypes are men-

tal overstatements of difference, preconceived beliefs about classes of people, images that are sustained precisely because they contain an image, but never the essence, of truth. Stereotypes are, in this sense, mental portraits drawn from a modicum of fact, exaggerated and simplified—yet in the end, mental clichés.

Findings regarding the so-called Contact Hypothesis—alleging that the greater the frequency of interaction between groups the lower the level of prejudice and stereotype—suggest the difficulty of abolishing southern or other stereotypes. Although findings appear mixed, increased exposure or contact can actually work, in some cases, to increase stereotyping. Those with an intermediate degree of interregional experience seem most likely to generalize about regional differences. In short, moderate amounts of both direct exposure and education have the potential to solidify rather than weaken the impulse to stereotype. Regional stereotypes are thus likely to continue, along with the quest to understand the exact nature of the regional differences—North and South—that pattern these thoughts.

The South is often viewed as a land populated by a succession of emotionally and conceptually available social types—colorfully contrived, and therefore predictable, stock characters—formerly a land of happy darkies with watermelon or banjo, sadistic "Lords of the Lash" overseers, coquettish belles, socially sophisticated southern ladies, chivalrous Cavaliers, vengeful Klansmen, and more recently a land of rambunctious good old boys, demagogic politicians, corrupt sheriffs, country and western good old girls, country bumpkin "Bubba" boys brandishing beer or *Southern Comfort*, nubile cheerleaders, "Steel Magnolia" women of fragrant manners but mettled resolve, football All-Americans with three names, neurotic vixens with affinities for demon rum, Bible-thumping preachers haunted by God, sugary Miss America candidates of unwavering patriotism, toothless grizzled "po' white trash," and military "lifers" of considerable spit but little polish.

This stereotyped South is a region on the mental map of the national imagination, its citizenry a distillation and amalgam of both fact and fiction. To many students of southern culture, the South has sustained its measure of regional distinctiveness because of an abiding set of cultural values that southerners believe clearly separate them from American culture at large. The South, in this sense, has done much to create and perpetuate its regional stereotypes owing to their usefulness in helping to shape a self-image and a regional consciousness and identity. For northerners the South is seen largely through a kaleidoscope of regional stereotypes and images, borne both of interregional ignorance and provincial prejudices. To them the South simultaneously serves as both America at its extreme and as "Uncle Sam's other province." As an addi-

Grocery store window, Mebane, N.C., 1939
(Southern Historical Collection, University of North Carolina, Chapel Hill)

tive, the cultural cuisine of the South — fried chicken, catfish, greens, grits, bis-cuits, red-eye gravy, barbecue, Creole, Cajun, and soul food recipes — itself is stereotyped, adding its unique aromatic flavor to how the South is mentally di-gested irrespective of region.

George B. Tindall suggests that the temptation is to deal with the South men-tally in accordance with the generally held categories of a serene Sunny South versus a Benighted South. Mentally and emotionally edited cartoons of social reality portray on the one hand an ornamental, utopian, mythic South of gal-lant Cavaliers and beauteous belles (or more recently, a Sunbelt South of the nouveau riche) and on the other a semisavage South of abject poverty feed-ing moral degeneracy. America's and the world's views of the South seldom transcend these hardened stereotypes. One's mental vision of the South seems either given to the romantic glow of late antebellum palatial plantation splen-dor (or modernized versions thereof) or the counterimage of what W. J. Cash once saw fit to call the "romantics of the appalling." One must mentally arbitrate between and among the list of supposed southern traits that flow from such stereotyped belief. Southerners, as the story is told, are conservative, radical, tradition loving, courteous, loyal to family ties, conventional, generous, lazy, faithful, gifted at storytelling, very religious, ignorant, stubborn, regionally righteous, excessively nationalistic, jovial, honest, witty, kind, superstitious, naive, revengeful, stolid, and flamboyant — all at once. Indeed, the South and southerners have been many things to many people.

The notion of the Sunny South dates from earliest eras of southern history and southern consciousness. The "pre-South," or if one prefers, the South of the colonial era, tried to fashion a Sunny South stereotype for public consumption. The discovery and exploration of the New World climaxed a European tradition of grand historical visions of a golden age, of paradise, and of a pure and sacred Eden, and such a view held particularly for the South. For Europeans, America was a mythical land from the beginning, but the South especially was thought destined to be paradise regained. The fresh, green landscape of the region seemed a confirmation of utopian promises. Early settlers on Roanoke Island in present-day North Carolina claimed to find "the soil richer, the trees taller, the ground firmer and the topsoil deeper." In 1716 Lieutenant Governor Alexander Spotswood of Virginia argued that the Blue Ridge Mountains shone with the sun's perpetual splendor. The Sunny South inspired the imagination with what Sir Robert Montgomery in 1717 called "natural Sweetness and Beauties." For later generations the South of course became, as W. J. Cash phrased it, "a sort of stage piece out of the eighteenth century, wherein gesturing gentlemen moved soft-spokenly against a background of rose gardens and dueling grounds, through always gallant deeds, and lovely ladies, in farthingales, never for a moment lost that exquisite remoteness which has been the dream of all men and the possession of none." The plantation South of the proverbial moonlight-and-magnolias myth — as well as it obverse image — enjoyed, and still enjoys, a career in song and story and has been celebrated in various media — from novel, to theater, to musical ballad, to motion picture.

The sectional stereotype of most recent vintage, yet very much in the Sunny South tradition, is the congenial view of the Southland as the Sunbelt. Building upon established mental and narrative conventions, the vision of the region is now said to be one of corporate profits, retirement havens, and a salubrious climate. The new, bright image of the Sunbelt South, as with most social stereotypes, is partly based on fact. Although the image of the Sunbelt is a mental caricature of the southern situation, the features it exaggerates are indeed real ones. The South is, as many have reported, closing the economic gap between itself and other regions of the country. Yet, as A. J. Cooper, the black mayor of Pritchard, Ala., aptly put the matter in 1978: "There is a lot of shade in the Sunbelt." The South still has a higher proportion of poor than the rest of the nation. The Sunbelt image is at best a case of "sloppy regionalizing" (its patterns of supposed affluence better fit the West than the South). At worst, it is yet another case of mental shorthand at work—stereotyping on a grand scale, albeit with considerable impact on public policy and provincial perception.

Scenarios of "another South," populated by rednecks, hillbillies, prototypical itinerant suspenders-snapping Bible-toting preachers, political demagogues, crackers, Klansmen, and degenerate aristocrats, have also been part of the nation's mental image of Dixie—midnight in the garden of good and evil, so to speak. Long ago William Byrd II wrote of the region's "indolent wretches" in his *History of the Dividing Line*, while Augustus Baldwin Longstreet offered a fictional composite of the "bad southerner" in Ransy Sniffle, as did Johnson Hooper with Simon Suggs. The literary portrait of the mindless, moonshine-drinking, pickup truck–driving, NASCAR-addicted, inarticulate, degenerate southern "yahoo," with chewing tobacco stains on his beard stubble, contributed to the view of the Sunny South as a region cursed by the ravages of pellagra and hookworm, a land of Baptist barbarians and vigilantes, which South-baiter H. L. Mencken dismissed as a grotesque, a country populated by the peculiar American species *Homo Boobiens*. This contrived South, of so-called hog-wallow politics and abnormal neuroticism, found additional portrayals in the southern gothic drama of Tennessee Williams (*The Glass Menagerie*, 1945), media advertising (Mountain Dew ads), cartoons (think *Li'l Abner*), and television shows and movies (*Dukes of Hazzard, Easy Rider*, and *Deliverance*). The dysfunctional, clueless, loose and lascivious "white trash" redneck woman, addicted to the gothic strains of country and western music, is yet another modern rendition of the Benighted Southerner, as is the *Dallas*-style scheming temptress of recent memory and media. The media South continues to be portrayed in such demon images—via Jeff Foxworthy's "You Might Be a Redneck If" routines and via films such as *The Apostle* (1997) and *Sweet Home Alabama* (2002). Northerners, of course, have usually been quick to affirm their belief in such images, which prompted William Faulkner to observe that they have an "almost helpless capacity and eagerness to believe anything about the South not even provided it be derogatory but merely bizarre enough and strange enough."

Southern stereotypes—ranging from images of a proslavery South, the prosecession South, the agrarian South, the states' rights South, and the Confederate South, to the conservative South, the one-party South, the fighting South, the lazy South, the Klanish South, and the civil rights South—all offer, after their fashion, a vision of a monolithic South that is out of keeping with the region's intricate complexity. As a result, southerners seldom have been understood much beyond these sharply etched categories. Perhaps, ultimately, a region so replete with symbols is especially susceptible to stereotypes, since symbols and stereotypes both are representational renditions of the real—not reality itself.

PATRICK GERSTER
San Jose City College

Walter Lippmann, *Public Opinion* (1922); Tara McPherson, *Reconstructing Dixie: Race, Gender, and Nostalgia in the Imagined South* (2003); John Shelton Reed, *The Enduring South: Subcultural Persistence in Mass Society* (1974), *My Tears Spoiled My Aim and Other Reflections on Southern Culture* (1994), *One South: An Ethnic Approach to Regional Culture* (1982), *Southern Folk, Plain and Fancy: Native White Social Types* (1986); Harry Triandis and Vasso Vasiliou, *Journal of Personality and Social Psychology* (November 1967); Frank E. Vandiver, ed., *The Idea of the South: Pursuit of a Central Theme* (1964); Robin M. Williams, *Strangers Next Door: Ethnic Relations in American Communities* (1964).

Stoicism

Stoicism entered the South through the influence of the Enlightenment, when there was renewed appreciation of the classical tradition. Cosmopolitan southerners of the Revolutionary era were familiar with Greek and Roman writings. One of the most influential of southerners, Thomas Jefferson, read avidly at an early age the classical moral philosophers, although no comprehensive philosophy emerged from his study and he was never a true disciple of them. Jefferson was attracted to both stoicism, with its emotional restraint, and Epicureanism, with its hedonistic ethics. He saw moral advantages in each position and tried to hold them in balance. Stoicism seemed especially strong in his youth. In one of Jefferson's earliest letters he wrote that human beings must "consider that whatever does happen, must happen," and they must "bear up with a tolerable degree of patience under this burden of life." Jefferson surely admired the discipline of the will he saw in stoicism. Like many Enlightenment thinkers, Jefferson saw both stoicism and Epicureanism as systems of practical morality, separate from any church or governmental connection. He used the classical Stoics to prove that an adequate moral philosophy could exist without any supernatural justification. In general, for Jefferson and early southern students of classical thought, Epicureanism provided the goal of a good life, and stoicism, with its control of the will, offered the means of attaining it.

A few intellectuals like Jefferson had been attracted to stoicism in the 18th century, but the philosophy took on a broader social significance in the antebellum period of the 19th century. The southern cult of honor became deeply rooted in the region under the influence of Enlightenment rationalism. The southern model of honorable behavior conformed to the classical heritage. One had to face public examination for a moral failure rather than experience private alienation from God. James McBride Dabbs once wrote that the "basic flaw at the heart of the South" was "the unresolved conflict between Christianity and Stoicism." Walker Percy, another analyst of regional stoicism, has agreed, arguing that the South was always more stoic than Christian. When a southerner named a city Corinth, Percy wrote, "he did not mean Paul's community." Whatever degree of nobility and graciousness has existed in the South, according to Percy, "was the nobility and graciousness of the Old Stoa."

Stoicism took root in the Old South partly because of its stress on individualism, which seemed to suit the planter elite. Human freedom was all important to the early Stoics, and living surrounded by slaves apparently made the same concern a central one of southern planters. But freedom was not unrestrained. In its social role stoicism in the South was based on paternalism, reflecting a hierarchical social structure, as had the earlier Greek version. It taught the southern elite to behave with noblesse oblige. Not to behave honorably would be, again in Percy's words, "to defile the inner fortress which was oneself."

From another direction, a pronounced moralistic tendency among some southerners also provided fertile ground for stoic thought. Religious moralism set forth clear guidelines for life, and southern Protestants could use stoic moralism to reinforce their views. The religion of the Old South was predominantly evangelical, concerned primarily with individual sin, guilt, and private redemption. Evangelical Protestantism, with Calvinistic theology one of its sources, promoted a fatalistic view of the world, an outlook that fit comfortably with practical stoicism. Dabbs claimed that stoicism enabled southerners to be both Cavaliers and Puritans, nurturing both a romantic outlook toward the social world and a moralistic outlook toward individual religious experience, combining outward grace and inner sternness.

The Civil War provided a crucial stage in the development of stoicism in the South. Rather than destroying the philosophy of the prewar elite, the conflict and its aftermath confirmed a fatalistic, even tragic outlook on life. The collapse of the outer world confirmed the southern stoic's original decision to invest everything in the sanctity of the inner self. Just as evangelical Christianity took stronger hold of the South as a result of defeat, so did stoicism. Stoicism has generally been most influential in societies undergoing social decay and collapse, and this seems true of the postbellum South. Robert E. Lee exemplifies this postwar stoicism. An admirer of Marcus Aurelius, a fanatic in his dedication to such stoic virtues as duty, honor, patriotism, loyalty, and humility, Lee combined with these qualities the moralism and Christian piety that in the South could rub off even on an Episcopalian. Lee was notably ambivalent — confident in the material world, yet brooding and guilt ridden in in his religious outlook. Lee embodied the southern tendency toward stoic reserve. Honor, which in many times and places has been related to pride, in Lee was tied in with humility. He was the supreme example of the South's attempt to balance Stoic and Christian virtues. Dabbs saw two religions in the late 19th-century South — "the social religion of this world and the individualistic religion of another." The result of the first, which was a reflection of stoic influences, was to equate God with the southern way of life and to provide a philosophical basis for what would emerge after the war as a southern civil religion.

Stoicism in the late 19th century became tied in with, and hard to separate from, Victorianism. James Branch Cabell, Ellen Glasgow, and other transitional writers of the turn-of-the-century South were skeptics. They saw decline in the region and tried to face it with the dignity and courage that Victorians valued. Sometimes, to be sure, they seemed detached from their society and from pondering humanity's fate, but at other times they preached of enduring the tragedies of life with fortitude. Glasgow, who came from a Presbyterian background, wrote of the "vein of iron" that was necessary for survival in her era. She came to believe that the universe was governed by blind chance and her society was coming apart. Renewed moral fiber was the only hope. Her novel *Barren Ground*, with its good stoic title, came out of her inner turmoil. The central character, Dorinda Oakley, learns to live a joyless existence and to suppress her natural instincts. As Daniel Singal argues, *Barren Ground* illustrates "nineteenth-century theology got up in stoic dress." However, southern stoicism was not complete in Glasgow; Dorinda cannot stop longing for something more than the "agnostic realism" that seemed to be Glasgow's position. Her stoicism was different in origins, then, from that of earlier southerners. Hers was an attempt to reconcile her Calvinistic legacy with the realities of late 19th-century naturalistic science, with its belief in the evolution of an unstable universe. The result was what can be called her "stoic realism," a position that saw little meaning in human events.

The Agrarian writers of the 1920s and 1930s also reflected stoic influences.

John Crowe Ransom, for example, struck a pose of stoic detachment in dealing with conflicts in his own mind between the modern demands of balancing rationality and spontaneity. He hid his inner conflicts behind a front of stoic reserve—self-control, mannerly behavior, and ironic humor. Ransom believed that artists should tap and express their emotions, but his stoicism made this difficult for him to do in practice. William Alexander Percy shared many of the literary concerns of the Agrarians, and he achieved perhaps the South's greatest literary expression of the stoic philosophy. *Lanterns on the Levee* (1940) reflected a profound debt to the *Meditations* of Marcus Aurelius in both the form of the work and its content. Percy, the descendant of a distinguished family and himself both a planter and a poet, believed that the good do not triumph, and he chronicled the decline of the southern elite, as seen in his own history and that of his family. The Agrarians believed the old order could be restored, but Percy did not. He strove in his personal life and his writing to embody the stoic virtue of graceful acceptance of defeat. As Richard King says, "he was the melancholy Roman to the end" and found only temporary relief from his prophecies of southern decline. He did affirm the ability of the individual to effect at least limited change through individual actions in a limited area. Percy was a respected leader of his local community (Greenville, Miss.), and he believed that in such a place a person could do good. In any event, the important point was individual integrity and courage in making the effort. No one better exemplified what Walker Percy calls the spirit of "a poetic pessimism" at the heart of modern southern stoicism.

William Faulkner portrayed southern stoicism through numerous characters. Quentin Compson's father speaks of "fate, destiny, retribution, irony" and of the "stage manager" behind it all. Rosa Coldfield calls her region a "land primed for fatality" and "cursed with it." But stoicism by Faulkner's time was difficult to separate from a generalized Calvinism, a predestinarian, mechanistic philosophy that was also a 20th-century southern legacy. Faulkner did not draw directly on the ancient or modern stoic philosophers. Cleanth Brooks suggests that Faulkner's stoicism cannot be understood apart from its close connection with Christianity, in both of which the essence of human living is freedom. The Christian concept that God grants freedom through grace, though, is weak in Faulkner, who seems closer to Epictitus's belief that man achieves freedom through self-discipline.

Faulkner, then, saw the human problem in Christian terms—the world is a fallen world—yet he did not advocate the Christian solution of redemption through God's grace. He was willing to rely on individual virtue, as embodied by a Sartoris during the Civil War, to gain a modicum of dignity, if not redemption. Man must rescue himself through stoic virtues such as courage, honor, justice, duty, endurance, and reason. Stoicism was transmuted in Faulkner into the generalized trait of endurance. Dilsey in *The Sound and the Fury* and other black literary characters in the modern South embody the ancient wisdom best of all. Theirs is no grim stoicism, but a cheerful one of overcoming. As Isaac McCaslin says of blacks in "The Bear," "they will endure. They will outlast us." Poor whites also are blessed with endurance, for example in *The Mansion*, where Mink Snopes waits 40 years to carry out an act of vengeance. Faulkner's appreciation of endurance reflects the stoic attitude toward time. The Stoics believed one could transcend time through detachment and patience. Characters such as Quentin Compson and Gail Hightower in *Light in August* seem almost primitive in their belief in re-creating the past, so that the normal historical boundaries are overcome.

Writing in the 1950s in the midst of the conflicts over racial desegregation, Walker Percy argued that the South could no longer afford stoicism alongside Christianity. In a democratic society, he said, stoicism cannot exist as the social philosophy of any social class. "What the Stoic sees as the insolence of his former charge—and this is what he can't tolerate, the Negro's demanding his rights instead of being thankful for the squire's generosity—is in the Christian scheme the sacred right which must be accorded the individual, whether deemed insolent or not."

Stoicism, then, since the early 19th century has been a philosophy of the educated southern elite, held alongside of and sometimes in contradiction to evangelical Protestantism. The philosophy was less influential on society as a whole in the 20th century than earlier, but is probably still held by some southerners as a guide to individual behavior.

CHARLES REAGAN WILSON
University of Mississippi

Cleanth Brooks, *William Faulkner: The Yoknapatawpha Country* (1963); James McBride Dabbs, *Who Speaks for the South?* (1964); Richard H. King, *A Southern Renaissance: The Cultural Awakening of the American South, 1930–1955* (1980); Adrienne Koch, *The Philosophy of Thomas Jefferson* (1943); Walker Percy, *Commonweal* (6 July 1956); Daniel J. Singal, *The War Within: From Victorian to Modernist Thought in the South, 1919–1945* (1982); Bertram Wyatt-Brown, *Southern Honor: Ethics and Behavior in the Old South* (1982).

Tobacco

Tobacco was the most important herb among the American Indians and later became closely associated with the South. The Indians used it as snuff, chewed it, smoked it as cigars, smoked it as cigarettes wrapped in corn husks, and used its leaves to wrap poultices of snake fat. They sometimes also swallowed tobacco pellets as a tranquilizer. But pipe smoking was the near-universal method of use in North America. Tobacco in the sacred calumet was the ritual way to seal peace. American Indians smoked "ancient tobacco" (*Nicotiana rustica*), which dated to pre-Columbian times. They used it in medicine and religion, realms that were believed to be connected. Sickness was believed to stem from spiritual imbalance, and Native Americans used tobacco to nurture their spirituality before sacred rituals.

European colonists in the South thought of tobacco mainly in medical terms and discounted its religious significance. It was seen as a panacea that would cure cancer, asthma, headaches, coughs, cramps, gout, worms, female troubles, and any other ailment. Physicians supported this belief, disagreeing only on the best way to use the weed. The medieval theory of the humors—which taught that sickness came from an imbalance in the body's four humors (blood, yellow bile, black bile, and phlegm)—still had its adherents, who saw tobacco consumption as a way to keep balance in the body and thus maintain good health. In early America, including the South, tobacco was used to cure respiratory, head, internal, and skin diseases.

Tobacco growing and its use became the bases for early Virginia's prosperity. North American Indians had long smoked *Nicotiana rustica*, but it proved too bitter for many European colonists. John Rolfe in 1612 introduced into Virginia a sweet-scented tobacco developed by the Spanish in the West Indies. Sir Walter Raleigh is credited with making tobacco use a fad among the elite in London. The tobacco market expanded, and soon the people of Jamestown were growing it in the streets. By 1624 the Jamestown colony was exporting 60,000 pounds of tobacco a year, and in the colonial era it also became the major crop in Maryland and North Carolina. The English Navigation Acts of the 1660s made tobacco one of the "enumerated goods" that were regulated by shipment from the colonies through English ports.

The dominant form of tobacco consumption in the colonial era was pipe smoking. Snuffing became popular, though, among the colonial elite by the mid-1700s. They used the snuffbox and its required gestures, a ritual that came from France, through London, to the colonies. In the second third of the 19th century the way of using snuff changed: instead of sniffing it through the nose, people began dipping it, placing a pinch in the mouth.

In the first half of the 19th century chewing became the main method of consumption. It was popular after the American Revolution and was seen as an American way to use tobacco, a variation from the European styles. Appropriately, the use of chewing tobacco seems to have peaked in the Jacksonian era, the age of the common man. The frontier now seemed to be setting the tone for society. English traveler Charles Mackay thought the national symbol for the United States should not be the eagle but the spittoon.

From the Civil War to World War I the annual consumption of tobacco in the United States rose dramatically. The cigar became something of a fad in the South after the Mexican War and was certainly popular among, and associated with, the upper classes in the Gilded Age. In fact, the cigar was an accessory of power for important southern politicos throughout the 20th century as well.

A sudden shift to smoking tobacco occurred during and after the Civil War. This was the era of cigarettes, both hand rolled and machine made. Brightleaf tobacco was developed beginning in the 1850s in North Carolina, and by 1880 it was grown from Virginia south to Georgia. In this age of the New South the tobacco industry grew and expanded. Durham and Winston-Salem, N.C., Louisville, Ky., and Richmond, Va., became the centers of the cigarette industry, bringing economic prosperity to North Carolina, Virginia, and Kentucky, in particular, and promoting the use and consumption of the weed by southerners. A southerner, James A. Bonsack of Virginia, invented the cigarette-rolling machine in 1880, and this led to a steady increase in demand. Annual national per capita consumption rose from 1.5 pounds in 1860 to 5.5 pounds in 1900, a 267 percent rise. The Duke and Reynolds families became new power brokers in the South and symbols of success. The southern landscape reflected the new importance of tobacco. Tobacco barns became pervasive, and by the 1880s the towering, stolid tobacco factories producing cigarettes were new symbols on the landscape. In 1929 the South produced 60 percent of all tobacco in the United States and 84 percent of the cigarettes.

This success story has a dark side, though. Opposition to tobacco use goes back to the colonial era. By the late 1600s debunkers of tobacco smoking were dismissing it as a nasty, ungodly, dangerous habit. King James I opposed smoking tobacco, calling it a "stinking weed." It was, he said, "a custome Lothsome to the eye, hatefull to the Nose, harmfull to the braine, dangerous to the Lungs, and in the blacke stinking fume thereof, nearest resembling the horrible Stigian smoke of the pit that is bottomeless." Others charged that smoking actually upset the balance of the body instead of maintaining it. The American Anti-Tobacco League led opposition to tobacco in the 19th century. The antitobacco crusade of 1830–60 was led by northerners, but Virginian John Hartwell Cocke was one southerner actively involved in the movement. Cole Blease of South Carolina and Dr. Alton Ochsner of New Orleans later were prominent southern opponents of "Demon Nicotine." Religious groups, even in North Carolina, have periodically been vocal in opposition to the sinfulness of tobacco use.

Tobacco advertising long enlivened the southern countryside and provided some of the region's most notable material artifacts. James B. Duke used promotion of his tobacco products as one way to consolidate his dominance of the tobacco industry. Tobacco vendors used wooden Indians in front of shops selling cigars and tobacco goods. A landmark of advertising was when John Ruffin Green adopted the symbol of the bull after the revival of the tobacco business in Durham at the end of the Civil War. He saw a bull's head on a jar of Colman's mustard, which came from Durham, England. A neighbor had a breeding bull, which became the model for the trademark Durham Bull. It caught the imagination of rural southerners and others as well. His company later fought hard in courts and elsewhere for control of the bull as a trademark and won. The company blanketed the southern rural countryside with testimonials from prominent people, including ministers. The greatest sign painter of the bull symbol was J. Gilmer Koerner, who was known as Reuben Rink.

By the 1890s the industry was more sophisticated in marketing, and more artifacts began to appear. Chewing plugs now had tin or paper tags with the name of the maker and the brand name of the product. Colorful lithographs were pasted on wooden boxes of chewing tobacco. This was a regionally produced and identified pop art that used a variety of images: flowers, historical events and people, animals; nude girls sometimes appeared. The sides of barns became the canvas for painters such as Koerner. Whereas cigar salesmen and advertising, with strong ethnic overtones, had become identified with the North's urban areas by the early 20th century, advertising for smoking and chewing tobacco stressed rural themes appropriate to the South.

In the 20th century several tobacco products were especially identified with the South. Snuff is one. Margaret J. Hagood reported in 1939 that half of the North Carolina Piedmont tenant women she studied used snuff. In Erskine Caldwell's *Tobacco Road* the Lester family's landlord, Captain John, stops giving rations and snuff at the store, and the grandmother in the story is desperate for restoration of her snuff. "There were times when she would have been willing to die, if she could only have for once all the snuff she wanted." Even after World War II sales of snuff in the region did not drastically decline. Black women, farm women, and mountain women all had reputations as snuff dippers.

The South is also still identified as the home of tobacco chewing. In 1947, 100 million pounds of chewing tobacco were still produced, most being consumed in the rural South, and cuspidors were common until the 1950s. Texas author John Graves has written of the virtues of chewing tobacco, which he calls "a great solacer." Unlike the "fury of a tense cigarette smoker's puffing," chewing is a laid-back method of use that calms and offers perspective.

Chewing tobacco made a comeback in the 1970s and 1980s, appealing to the young and the middle class, as well as to blue-collar and farm workers, who had never abandoned it. Chewing tobacco takes three forms. The first is the plug, which is a compressed brick of tobacco wrapped in a light brown leaf. A variation of the plug is the "twist," which has become rare except in rural parts of the South. A second form of chewing tobacco used to be called "scrape." It is coarse, sweet shreds, packed in foil pouches. Legendary brand names include Beech Nut, Red Man, and Mail Pouch. The third form of chewing tobacco in the modern South is "smokeless tobacco," or "snoose" as it is known in the Midwest (that name probably comes from *snus*, the Swedish-Danish name for snuff). Smokeless tobacco is a wet, grainy tobacco, flavored with mint, wintergreen, and the unlikely raspberry, packed in cylindrical boxes with tin lids. It has brand names such as Skoal, Copenhagen, and Levi Garrett. A communal symbol of the regional importance of chewing tobacco is the tobacco spitting contest, which has become a staple of several southern communities.

Tobacco's pervasive role in southern culture rested on distinctive tobacco cultures in the Upper South, but these tobacco cultures underwent profound transformation from World War II to the end of the 20th century. Technological advancement and federal government legislation worked to concentrate power in the hands of large landowners. Changes in the allotment system of tobacco-growing acreage in the 1960s promoted farm consolidation. Between 1964 and 1974 the average size of a North Carolina tobacco farm increased from 5.2 acres to 9.5 acres, and leasing increased substantially. As with other southern crop production, tobacco growing is part of a global system, with multinational companies now controlling the process.

The smoking of tobacco has changed meaning in the last two decades, as earlier fears of its health threats have been validated. The United States Surgeon General stated in 1990 that "smoking represents the most extensively documented cause of disease ever investigated in the history of biomedical research." Awareness of the dangers of passive smoking has also increased, leading cities and towns throughout the South, as well as the nation, to ban smoking in public places.

CHARLES REAGAN WILSON
University of Mississippi

Iain Gately, *Tobacco: A Cultural History of How an Exotic Plant Seduced Civilization* (2003); Jordan Goodman, ed., *Tobacco in History and Culture: An Encyclopedia* (2004); John Graves, *Texas Monthly* (November 1978); Charles Hudson, *The Southeastern Indians* (1976); Katherine T. Kell, *Journal of American Folklore* (April–June 1965); David B. Moyer, *The Tobacco Book: A Reference Guide of Facts, Figures, and Quotations about Tobacco* (2005); Joseph C. Robert, *The Story of Tobacco in America* (1949); Robert Sobel, *They Satisfy: The Cigarette in American Life* (1978).

Victorianism

When, in 1953, the Armstrong Browning Library at Baylor University acquired a first edition of Robert Browning's *Pauline*, its collection of the poet's first editions was complete. Housed in a magnificent building of Texas stone, Italian marble, bronze doors, and stained-glass windows, this library today is a surprising conglomeration of memorabilia, first editions, manuscripts, and scholarly works dealing with the Brownings and their Victorian world. In Browning's day scholars and critics of the poet would not have imagined traveling to Waco, in the central plains of Texas, to pursue their research. This splendid collection of Victoriana in a seemingly unlikely place is partly the result of Texas wealth, regional pride, and especially the indefatigable work of A. Joseph Armstrong at Baylor. But the Browning Library is also a reflection of the profound and persisting influence of Victorian ideas, ideals, and personalities on the culture of the South, even as it extends itself westward into Texas.

In the imagination of the southerner, Browning epitomizes many of the Victorian qualities particularly appealing to a people whose lives and history bristled with losses, spiritual and material. In his robust optimism, Browning represents the profound belief that, despite the disillusionment of lost causes, the law of history is one of development and progress. One who "marched breast forward," and "never doubted clouds would break," he incarnated in his person and his work an optimism that refused in a benighted world of crass materialism to give up the notion that human beings are more than biological organisms or economic animals devoid of a higher destiny and significance. His influence in the South was assured by hundreds of Browning Societies that developed in communities throughout the region in the 20th century. And Pippa Passes, Ky., was named for one of his more sentimental poems.

In good Victorian fashion the South has always been given to heroes and hero worship. "You can know a man by his heroes" has the force of a southern proverb. For southerners, as for Matthew Arnold, the ancient heroes were Hellenic and Hebraic, captured in the personalities of Socrates and Jesus and in the ideas and myths associated with these seminal figures. In a narrower vein, the South idealized with great imaginative power the Founding Fathers, particularly Jefferson and Washington. After the tragedy of the Civil War, southern healing was promoted by the nostalgic romanticization of Robert E. Lee, who became an incarnation of the Victorian ideal of the complete gentleman: patriot and statesman, military genius, scholar, educator, philanthropist, and Christian family man. Only slowly, through several decades, did Lincoln take his place in the pantheon of southern heroes. Even Texas's own particular frontier heroes—Houston, Travis, and Crockett—became Victorian heroes.

To such heroic status southern imagination also elevated the eminent Victorian literary geniuses: Arnold, Carlyle, Tennyson, Sir Walter Scott, and Browning. But the typically Victorian anti-Catholic feeling in the South made John Henry Newman suspect despite his literary and religious genius. Southerners, like their English counterparts, could never fully forgive a man of Newman's brilliance and stature for having given up his Oxford heritage to join forces with that most un-English of traditions, the church of Rome. On the other hand, despite his secular humanist assumptions, John Stuart Mill has enjoyed heroic status among that intellectual elite in the South who are jealous of individual liberty. In declaring "eternal freedom from the dual tyranny of priest and sword," early Texas heroes, for example, sought to establish constitutionally the personal freedoms that later found classic formulation in Mill's *On Liberty*.

But among the eminent Victorians, Browning seems most to have epitomized the southern ideal of the heroic. Himself a commoner, he nevertheless enjoyed status and favor with the nobility, including Queen Victoria herself. Not personally identified with the ancient centers of learning and authority at Oxford and Cambridge, he yet was acclaimed a poet of the intellect. Many southern intellectuals could admire that. Without allegiance to any particular dogma or institutional tradition, Browning was still deeply religious—a classic example of that muscular Christianity fully at home in the world, a temporal existence ennobled and idealized by the confident assumption that "God's in his heaven, all's right with the world." Like Matthew Arnold, Browning represented and espoused the sweetness and light that combined the humane intelligence of Socrates with the reverence for life and passion for social justice of Jesus.

The higher criticism of the Bible emanating from German universities touched Christianity in the South even less than it affected the Christianity of Victorian England. Southerners were, like their English ancestors, a people of the book—and that book was the Bible. Despite isolated struggles over the implications of Darwin and the new geology—and some momentary debates dealing with Strauss and the historical Jesus—popular biblicism in the South went fundamentally unchallenged well into the middle of the 20th century.

As in Victorian England, in the South a cultural hallmark has been a profound commitment to Protestant Christianity. Puritan influences, also at work in Victorian England, have left their indelible mark, not only on the role of the Bible in popular culture but also on the most basic human institutions and daily activities: the understanding of family life and sexuality, attitudes toward work and leisure, the significance of education and learning, and ultimately the very meaning of human life.

Southern life has been dominated by the Victorian notion of the primacy of the patriarchal family, centered around a deference to the father and an idealization of the mother, extended in concern and caring to children, cousins, and other kin. This family ideal captures that most basic of southern convictions, biblical in origin, that human beings are, above all, relational creatures. Rooted in an unacknowledged sexism, the cultural ideal of the family elevated women to a special status and role. Women represented the altruistic virtues of nurturing, compassion, morality, and religious piety. Their place was in running the home, in educating the young, and in caring for the sick. They were far removed from the areas of finance and commerce, the manufacture and distribution of goods, military service, the law, or politics and public policy. Men were, therefore, in the ideal, thrust into positions and roles of power and responsibility for the common good. Such roles demanded knowledge, a high level of intelligence and rationality, emotional toughness, and a sense of justice. Not surprisingly, higher education in the South, as in Victorian England, was therefore dominated by classic Christian models designed for a male intellectual elite.

Southern sexual attitudes and mores reflected the deep ambivalence also found in English Victorian responses to sexuality. Tenaciously holding to the biblical and Christian view that all God's creation is essentially good, southern culture managed to affirm sexuality as a part of God's good intention. Hence celibacy was strongly suspect, both as a religious ideal and as a personal way of life. Unmarried males were peculiarly problematical, smacking of the unnatural. Although, like the "other Victorians" among their English counterparts, southerners allowed a certain unspoken sexual license in private, the cultural norm has always been an idealized version of erotic love, buttressed by the Christian notions of monogamy and lifelong fidelity. This made it possible to glorify the virtue and purity of wives and mothers while allowing certain concessions to the animal nature of males. Sexual expression before and outside of marriage for males, although never fully accepted as a norm, was nonetheless tacitly tolerated.

It is impossible to understand the sexual values of the South without recognizing their deep, indeed symbiotic, relationship to the region's racial values. Here again, English Victorian notions gave southerners categories of thought that explained existing social arrangements and sensibilities. Victorian England often justified to its Christian conscience its expansive colonialism and imperialism as a way of bringing civilization to the heathen. "Darkest Africa" symbolized the aboriginal savages' life before the impact of the humanizing influences of Christianity and culture. Much of this Victorian attitude is found in southern conceptions of blacks after emancipation: blacks at best were children, to be tolerated and patronized; at worst they were savages, to be controlled and kept in their place. Never fully citizens nor quite finally seen as human, blacks evoked a complex set of symbols in the white southern imagination. It is no surprise that such elemental racist symbols should form a symbiosis with elemental sexist symbols to produce cultural mores and sensibilities defying rational explanation or rational redress. In this sense, southern racism has been and is deeply sexual in nature and origin.

In its grand outlines southern culture has been formed and informed by staple Victorian certainties: an idealized anthropology, a confidence that history reveals an inevitable progress in human affairs, the conviction that the universe is ordered and its laws are discoverable by human reason. Such confident views of epistemology and morality were grounded in a nondogmatic, personalistic biblical Christianity. Darwin, Freud, and Marx were long ignored or resisted by southerners, who viewed humankind as rational, free, and responsible. The nether regions of the psyche, the animalistic dimensions of the self, fundamental economic instincts and interests—all these were covered up or ignored by an emphasis on the freedom and dignity of man. History, in its inevitable progress, reflects the rationality of humankind and the order of the cosmos, energized and directed ultimately by the providential intentionality of God.

Hence the moral certainty. Hence the anxiety before change, and the emphasis upon personal, social, and political peace and equanimity. Hence the genteel insistence upon courtesy and propriety of conduct, and the disfavor toward critical temperaments and unconventional ideas and behaviors. Above all, uncertainty, open conflict, and overt criticism are to be kept in check and resisted. Victorian cultural traits represented a restraint on contrary, paradoxical southern tendencies toward extreme individualism and brutal violence. When

Victorian restraints dropped, the result was what W. J. Cash called the "savage ideal." Only in the 20th century was a fusion of ideological elements forced to yield to modern circumstances and intellectual categories. And even in the latest New South the forces of Victorianism have not yet been fully spent.

W. D. WHITE
St. Andrews Presbyterian College

William L. Burn, *The Age of Equipoise: A Study of the Mid-Victorian Generation* (1964); Gertrude Himmelfarb, *Ideas and Beliefs of the Victorians: An Historic Revaluation of the Victorian Age* (1966); Walter E. Houghton, *The Victorian Frame of Mind* (1957); Richard H. King, *A Southern Renaissance: The Cultural Awakening of the American South, 1930–1955* (1980); Richard A. Levine, ed., *Backgrounds to Victorian Literature* (1967); Daniel J. Singal, *The War Within: From Victorian to Modernist Thought in the South, 1919–1945* (1982); Kevin White, *Sexual Liberation or Sexual License?: The American Revolt Against Victorianism* (2000).

Visiting

Human beings have probably "visited" ever since they developed enough language and leisure to communicate about something other than access to food, safety, and a mate, but southern Americans have tended to make visiting especially central to their lives. Joe Grey Taylor (1982) quotes an Alabamian who, in the 1920s, described visiting as a "happy recreation," which was, nevertheless, taken "very seriously." Southern newspapers still include reports about people visiting from out of town, whether in a society column focused on the local elite or in reports from small-town church congregations. Certain common expressions of hospitality have long reflected the belief that southerners should always give the appearance of being willing to set aside whatever they are doing to visit with someone: "Y'all come to see us sometime," "Come again real soon," and "Come set a spell." Southerners who announce that they have "had a good visit" with someone usually mean their conversation made them feel closer and that they are looking forward to seeing each other again.

The primary purposes of any visit have usually been to have fun and escape daily worries, to help solve problems, and/or to establish and reinforce personal ties. There has not been enough research to determine what visiting traditions, if any, have been exclusively southern, but many practices have been affected by their cultural and historical contexts. Until the 20th century, most southerners lived in relatively isolated rural settings, making them especially appreciative of any opportunity to talk with anyone, whether neighbors or strangers. Until the

Visiting on a Saturday afternoon in Franklin, Heard County, Ga., 1941
(Jack Delano, photographer, Library of Congress [LC-USF33-020841-M2], Washington, D.C.)

spread of air-conditioning, people wishing to escape both the summer heat and the isolation of their houses would sit on front porches, where they could invite passersby to join them for a chat. The Sunday highlight for many churchgoers has been the chance to visit after the service either outside or in a "fellowship hall." At weddings, funerals, revivals, and other special gatherings, southerners have talked around tables groaning with massive platters of food (or, before football games, by the tailgates of each other's cars and trucks). Small sets of people wishing to be alone, particularly courting couples, have, throughout southern history, "gone for a ride," whether on horseback, in a carriage, or in an automobile.

The enduring social hierarchies in the South inspired complex regulations about who can see whom under what circumstances and how each individual should behave. Men have staked out special contexts for stag visits, including fishing, hunting, militia musters, political meetings, business luncheons, private clubs, locker rooms, bars, brothels, gambling, and various sports venues. Small-town men have gathered to chat and play cards or checkers in front of courthouses, in barbershops and country stores (sometimes open late to serve as a male community center), and, in recent decades, at a common table in "meat and three" restaurants. Melton McLaurin (1987) noticed that men in his grandfather's store kept rehashing the same subjects rather than approaching topics that might stimulate tensions, but many male conversations have ended in fights, especially when they were fueled by alcohol.

Women have been most apt to visit in each other's kitchens or parlors, in beauty shops (significantly called "beauty parlors" by many southern women), or while shopping together. Urban ladies of the 18th century followed the English pattern of holding "tea-tables" at which they discussed fashions and people who were not present. Gossip has often been the special purview of females, allowing them to share opinions on who needed to be helped, reined in, or shunned. The primary "work" for the wives and daughters of wealthy planters, besides making sure that their servants did as they were bid, was to nurture relationships with other elites through frequent visits. One young antebellum wife complained about having to give up her quiet days at home "to pay morning calls" but acknowledged that it was "a duty we all owe society, and the sacrifice must be made occasionally."

Visits involving members of the opposite sex have occurred most often at parties, whether casual and spur of the moment or formal and planned. Each generation of southerners in each social class has set standards for what kind of visiting was suitable for young men and women with romance on their minds. Until ready to court one special female seriously, young males in the 19th century tended to gather in small groups and then visit a series of young women. Young people of the New South spent entire evenings riding a streetcar, much as their great-grandchildren would "hang out" at a mall. For most of the 20th century, however, couples went on formal "dates" during which the young women were expected to feign interest in whatever fascinated their male companions.

Although visiting has never been an exclusive class privilege, access to particular gatherings has often been restricted. The wealthy have always had more leisure time as well as more money to spend on food, drink, servants, and congenial private and public spaces in which to entertain, but this may have made opportunities to visit more precious to people who had to spend most of the day working. Zora Neale Hurston, in *Their Eyes Were Watching God* (1937), describes members of an all-black community who "had been tongueless, earless, eyeless conveniences all day long" enjoying "the time for sitting on porches" when they might "hear things and talk." Members of the lower classes have faced restrictions on their ability to unify through visiting since the earliest slave traders prevented Africans with the same language from being chained next to each other. Mills and other workplaces have been decorated with "no talking" signs. In spite of this, workers have met clandestinely in the woods and swamps of plantations, during stolen moments when overseers were out of sight, in workplace and school bathrooms, and during coffee and smoking breaks. Such visits have often included making jokes about the authorities being crossed.

The most significant visiting taboo in southern history has been that against people of different races interacting as if they were peers. White men could have sex with both willing and unwilling black women, but they were never to be caught eating at the same table with African Americans. White women and their enslaved or free black servants might gossip together and help each other in childbirth, but they were never to let their "friendships" develop to a point that might challenge their social differences. Byron Bunch, in Faulkner's *Light in August* (1932), criticized Lena Grove, the daughter of humanitarian carpet-baggers, for visiting sick black people "like they was white."

In the 20th century, historical developments such as the civil rights movement and the migration of northerners to the South eroded some of the restrictions concerning who can interact with whom. Visiting practices among 21st-century southerners are probably less distinctive than in earlier times, but visiting, for whatever reasons and in whatever form, remains a favorite pastime across the South.

CITA COOK
State University of West Georgia

John W. Blassingame, *The Slave Community* (1979); Joyce Donlon, *Swinging in Place: Porch Life in Southern Culture* (2001); Elizabeth Fox-Genovese, *Within the Plantation Household: Black and White Women of the Old South* (1988); Jacquelyn Dowd Hall et al., *Like a Family: The Making of a Southern Cotton Mill World* (1987); Crandall A. Shifflett, *Coal Towns* (1991); Joe Gray Taylor, *Eating, Drinking, and Visiting in the South* (1982).

Agrarians, Vanderbilt

The Vanderbilt (or Nashville) Agrarians were in a sense an extension of the literary circle that came to be known as the Fugitives in the early 1920s. By mid-decade the *Fugitive* magazine of poetry and criticism (1922–25) had ceased publication, and the Fugitives began to disperse. Two of its principal participants, John Crowe Ransom and Donald Davidson, remained on the Vanderbilt faculty and stayed in close touch with other members of the Fugitives, especially Allen Tate and Robert Penn Warren. These four were in large part responsible for planning and seeing into print the "southern book" they and others on the Vanderbilt campus talked about sporadically in the late 1920s.

The book was *I'll Take My Stand: The South and the Agrarian Tradition* (1930), by Twelve Southerners, the basic statement of the social, economic, political, and cultural position of the Agrarians, often referred to as a "Southern Manifesto." Just as the name *Fugitive* was applied to the magazine that launched a major literary movement, so the designation "agrarian" labeled participants in what many perceived to be a translation of the Fugitive spirit into a related social movement.

The Fugitives had largely ignored politics in their concern with literature, and, according to Donald Davidson, they shifted their focus to social problems because of the Scopes Trial in Dayton, Tenn., in July 1925. The trial involved a contrived violation of a Tennessee statute prohibiting the teaching of evolution in public schools. It was conducted in a circus atmosphere under a powerful spotlight of national publicity designed, in the view of the incipient Agrarians, to ridicule the local culture and humiliate the plain folk of Tennessee. Not until the late 1920s did the conversations and exchanges of letters that followed result in the development of an eclectic manuscript containing contributions by such people as historian Frank Owsley, psychologist Lyle Lanier, political scientist H. C. Nixon, biographer John Donald Wade, and novelists Robert Penn Warren, Stark Young, and Andrew Lytle. Ransom drafted, and the others subscribed to, a short introductory "Statement of Principles," in which the authors declared themselves southerners, "well acquainted with one another and of similar tastes . . . and perhaps only at this moment aware of themselves as a single group of men."

I'll Take My Stand is a defense of a traditional culture with an agricultural economic base threatened by a modern urban-industrial society. Allen Tate was later to refer to a more universal dimension of the book—a defense of religious humanism. The Agrarians eventually admitted that they were stronger on the critical side than they were in articulating positive values and developing practical ways of realizing their goals. The continuing appeal of the Agrarian manifesto is its critique of the centralized state and the modern mass society produced by an expanding industrial order that reduces man to a functional cog in a production machine, ruthlessly exploits nature, and makes a cash agreement the only binding one. The Agrarians are increasingly recognized as far-sighted, even prophetic, observers rather than the reactionary, impractical supporters of the southern romantic moonlight-and-magnolias myth that many early critics accused them of being. Their failure to question racial segregation, nonetheless, complicates their embrace by some critics.

As a movement Agrarianism made little or no headway, although some effort was made to expand the public's awareness of its main doctrines. In the early 1930s Ransom in particular debated prominent critics of the Agrarians before surprisingly large audiences in several cities. He also devoted himself to the pursuit of economic study with a view to producing a treatise on agrarian economics, but the project never went beyond a draft stage. For several years various members of the group were actively engaged in social and political criticism, much of which appeared in the *American Review*. Their last major group publication was *Who Owns America?* (1936), jointly edited by Herbert Agar and Allen Tate. In this book, essays by a substantial majority of the Agrarians were published with contributions from various English Distributists, whose leading advocates were Hilaire Belloc and G. K. Chesterton—Catholic traditionalists and prominent literary figures in England. Shortly thereafter, Ransom left Vanderbilt, and he and the other Agrarians turned entirely to their literary and academic preoccupations, although a number of them continued to engage in social commentary and political activism on an individual basis. Davidson never ceased to hope for further collective efforts to implement an Agrarian program.

WILLIAM C. HAVARD
Vanderbilt University

William C. Havard and Walter Sullivan, eds., *A Band of Prophets: The Nashville Agrarians after Fifty Years* (1982); Bethany L. Johnson, *The Southern Agrarian and the New Deal: Essays after "I'll Take My Stand"* (2001); Paul V. Murphy, *The Rebuke of History: The Southern Agrarians and American Conservative Thought* (2001); Thomas Daniel Young, *Waking Their Neighbors Up: The Nashville Agrarians Rediscovered* (1982).

Anglo-Saxon South

The term "Anglo-Saxon" has been more a self-congratulatory and exhortatory banner than a precise definition. It enjoyed its greatest vogue after the Mexican War and in the period from the 1890s through the 1920s. Nationally, it was associated with territorial expansion and ethnic comparison, buttressed by Darwinian racial theorizing and hostility toward Southern and Eastern European immigration. In the South it came to represent white supremacy and the solidarity of Northern European stocks. Although the term was initially used to distinguish the English from Celts or Latins, the Huguenots were easily embraced as Southern Anglo-Saxons, as were the Scots and the Scots-Irish countrymen of Andrew Jackson and John C. Calhoun. In her epic of southern suffering and pride, Margaret Mitchell derived her quintessential heroine, Scarlett O'Hara, from well-assimilated Irish seed, without raising purist complaint.

While the pre–Civil War manifest Anglo-Saxon destiny was to absorb other lands and peoples, by the end of the century it had become an exclusionist philosophy. European and American theorists gave it a racial base. Teutonist professors such as Herbert Baxter Adams traced American democracy back to early Germany. Georgia's Methodist bishop Warren A. Candler lauded Anglo-Saxon expansion as God's chosen religious instrument. The Anglophile North Carolina–born editor and diplomat Walter Hines Page believed that the Anglo-American race held the key to world progress.

The pessimistic side of Anglo-Saxon theorizing was represented by the patrician New England exclusionist Henry Cabot Lodge, who feared that the high birthrate of America's new immigrants held the danger of old stock decay and submergence. Southern senators such as Alabama's Tom Heflin picked up the exclusionist refrain.

Although racial theorizing was the particular province of the Northeast, it was easy for southerners to clothe white supremacy in the popular Anglo-Saxon metaphor. Tribunes of white racialism led by South Carolina senator Ben Tillman called upon Anglo-Saxon yeomen to enforce black subordination. As new immigrants poured into the rest of the nation, it was popular to picture the South as the remaining bastion of Anglo-Saxon purity.

Post–World War I restrictionism diminished the immigrant flow. The vogue of Anglo-Saxonism declined, leaving only the promise of the reborn Ku Klux Klan to protect "Anglo-Saxon civilization" from submergence by "alien peoples," while textile mills were lured South by promises of "pure Anglo Saxon labor" that would not join unions or strike.

After 250 years of slavery and another hundred of segregation and subordination, migration into the cities of the North and West and the civil rights revolution of the 1960s finally made African Americans players in national life, culture, and politics. By the beginning of the 21st century, heavy non-European immigration, legal and illegal, and the high birthrate among these immigrants meant that Euro-Americans would likely become a minority before the century was out. Radical white supremacist organizations such as the Aryan Nation joined the Ku Klux Klan in angry protest. While conservatives denounced multiculturalism and diversity, the "neo-Confederate" Council of Conservative Citizens and the academic-led League of the South emerged in the 1990s to rally around the Confederate battle flag, praise the "Old South," and claim, with thinly described racism, that the South was home to a distinct and superior culture.

DAVID CHALMERS
University of Florida

Peter Applebome, *Dixie Rising: How the South Is Shaping American Values, Politics, and Culture* (1997); Thomas F. Gosset, *Race: The History of an Idea in America* (1963); Tony Horwitz, *Confederates in the Attic* (1998); Martin E. Marty, *Righteous Empire: The Protestant Experience in America* (1970).

Appalachian Myth

For the local writers and home missionaries who "discovered" Appalachia during the 1870s, the "otherness" of the region was axiomatic, and it gave shape to their activities. It yielded travel sketches and short stories that identified Appalachia as an exotic "little corner" of the nation, cut off from the more pleasing aspects of modern American life. It yielded home missionary work designed to integrate the mountaineers into the mainstream of American (Protestant) civilization.

Largely as a result of the literary exploitation of Appalachia by local color writers and the publicity generated to support home missionary work in the region, by the mid-1880s the image of Appalachia as a strange land inhabited by a peculiar people had become so well established in the American consciousness as to require both elaboration and explanation. Of what exactly did the otherness of Appalachia consist? Why was a region close to the centers of American population a strange land and its white, native-born, Protestant population of Anglo-Saxon descent a peculiar people? The answers to these questions, framed in a variety of ways and with a variety of possible implications to be drawn from them, comprised the myth of Appalachia, which contained the following assumptions: (1) the mountainous portions of six or more southern states formed a coherent topographic region; (2) the mountain people formed a homogeneous population; (3) social and economic conditions were the same throughout the mountain region; (4) the culture of

the mountaineers—both their beliefs and their behaviors—was consistent throughout the region. Which of these was the cause of the others was much debated from the mid-1880s, as were the supposedly real characteristics of the region's topography, population, society, economy, and culture. Also of concern, of course, was the matter of how Americans should feel about the existence of this strange land and peculiar people, and what they should do about it. Should they idealize the speech and music and folk traditions of supposedly isolated, supposedly pure Anglo-Saxon people that Berea College founder John Frost described as "Our Contemporary Ancestors?" Or should they pity their separation from economic and technological change? The myth of Appalachia functioned to normalize and make acceptable Appalachian otherness, even if it did not convince everyone of the wisdom of the situation.

Those who saw Appalachian otherness as a threat to the achievement of national unity, or who identified one or another of the characteristics of mountain life and landscape as undesirable, viewed Appalachian otherness as a problem in need of explanation and the characteristics of mountain life as a fact needing modification. The identification of Appalachia as a distinct region of the nation and the mountaineers as a discrete population during the 1880s and 1890s occurred at the same time that social theory generally was beginning to view culture less as a stage in a universal process of development than as a particular set of beliefs or behaviors. Many people interested in the region argued that Appalachian otherness was legitimate in a nation characterized by regionalism and pluralism, but they wished nonetheless to understand the origin of this otherness. Many of these were also skeptical about one or another aspect of mountain life.

Although the myth of Appalachia has made Appalachian otherness seem normal for Americans, it has not impeded efforts by outsiders to the region to modify some aspects of mountain life. Indeed, since the 1880s it has focused continuing attention on the area and has facilitated the planning (and legitimation) of a variety of schemes for "improving" conditions in the mountains. Ironically, from the 1890s onward, reformers claiming to love Appalachia but wanting to improve it made efforts to teach the mountain people their "own" folklore and their "own" folk dance, including the Sword and Morris dances, which they had supposedly forgotten long before their emigration from England and Scotland but which were considered their native tradition nonetheless. As David E. Whisnant has shown, reformers systematically suppressed a variety of indigenous patterns of culture, like banjo playing and the celebration of "old" Christmas, as being inappropriate to a modern folk culture in Appalachia.

The myth of Appalachia emerged as a way of explaining the image of Appalachia as a strange land inhabited by a peculiar people, but the myth itself generated additional images. The most prominent of these have been (in approximate historical sequence): (1) Appalachia is the opposite of America; (2) the mountain economy is primitive; (3) the mountaineers are a survival of America's pioneer population; (4) the mountaineers cannot leave the mountains without becoming deracinated; (5) the mountaineers are a hyper-rural population; (6) the mountaineers are a folk and their culture a folk culture; (7) the mountain economy is based on self-sufficiency in agriculture and manufacturing; (8) Appalachia serves as a model against which American civilization may be evaluated (in a wide variety of ways); (9) Appalachia is a pocket of poverty; (10) Appalachia has been victimized by outside (American) interests; (11) Appalachia has been (is) a colony of America; (12) the mountaineers when leaving the region retain their culture and thus become aliens in a strange land and among a peculiar people. The last three are currently dominant, although most of the others persist in one way or another in contemporary thought and action. Perhaps the clearest recent example of the continuing popularity of the notion of Appalachian folk wisdom lies in the popularity of the *Foxfire* books, a series of volumes published from the 1960s through 2004 that describe, with illustrations and great admiration, ways older Appalachian people did just fine without modern technology. Complex issues of envy, romance, and pity continue in tourism, with some mountain towns offering a range of old-time music and handmade goods amid a larger array of waterslides, luxury hotels, and theme parks, and in movies and television programs that use Appalachia as a setting for admirable traditions but also for the danger and backwardness dramatized in *Deliverance*.

HENRY D. SHAPIRO
University of Cincinnati

Allen W. Batteau, *The Invention of Appalachia* (1990); Harry M. Caudill, *Night Comes to the Cumberlands: A Biography of a Depressed Area* (1962); Rodger Cunningham, *Apples on the Flood: The Southern Mountain Experience* (1987); Ronald D. Eller, *Appalachian Journal* (Autumn–Winter 1983–84), *Miners, Millhands, and Mountaineers: The Modernization of the Appalachian South, 1880–1930* (1981); John Gaventa, *Power and Powerlessness: Quiescence and Rebellion in an Appalachian Valley* (1980); Helen M. Lewis et al., *Colonialism in Modern America* (1978); W. K. McNeil, ed., *Appalachian Images in Folk and Popular Culture* (1989); Henry D. Shapiro, *Appalachia on Our Mind: The Southern Mountains and Mountaineers in the American Consciousness, 1870–1920* (1978), *Appalachian Journal* (Winter 1983); David E. Whisnant, *All That Is Native and Fine: The Politics of Culture in an American Region* (1981), *Modernizing the Mountaineer: People, Power, and Planning in Appalachia* (1981); J. W. Williamson, *Hillbillyland: What the Movies Did to the Mountains and What the Mountains Did to the Movies* (1995).

Babylon, South's (New Orleans)

In the antebellum period numerous travelers commented on New Orleans's reputation as the South's Babylon. Many of them, like James Davidson and Rachel Jackson, referred to the city's well-known culture of sensual excess in biblical terms. The first lines Davidson wrote after arriving in the city in 1836 were "I am now in this Great Southern Babylon—the mighty receptacle of wealth, depravity and misery." Fifteen years earlier Jackson had expressed strikingly similar sentiments while on a visit to the city with her husband, Andrew. She wrote, "Great Babylon is come up before me . . . oh the wickedness, the idolatry of the place! Unspeakable the riches and splendor." Many other writers captured the contradictory nature of the city's appalling appeal as well, pointing out the city's sins and scandals while simultaneously being charmed by its aura of disorder and its culture of sexual permissiveness and sensual excess.

For most antebellum visitors, New Orleans's reputation as the South's Babylon sprang from its reputation as a center of tolerated prostitution and its position as the region's largest slave market. And, as many antislavery writers were anxious to point out, those two functions sometimes overlapped in the city's notorious fancy girl auctions, which featured the sale of light-skinned female slaves for implicitly sexual purposes. The city's reputation as a bastion of commercial sexuality and sex across the color line survived the Civil War and emancipation and, in the years that followed, generated enormous economic dividends and considerable controversy.

The city's reputation combined with its location in an otherwise overwhelmingly rural and Protestant region set it apart from the rest of the South, as did numerous attempts by local authorities to regulate prostitution while still profiting from it. Between 1857 and 1897 the city acted at least eight times to establish vice district boundaries. Ironically, the last and smallest of these districts, which came to be known as Storyville in mock-homage to city alderman Sidney Story who drafted the ordinance that created it, became the most notorious and well known. Storyville, which existed from 1897 to 1917, became an economic powerhouse that generated graft, enhanced the city's erotic reputation, and helped it to become one of the South's most popular tourist destinations.

Even as debates about the necessity of racial segregation raged, whites from all over the region and the rest of the nation descended on New Orleans in droves. Storyville provided a space where almost anyone might indulge in activities that were taboo outside the vice district's boundaries, including crossing the color line sexually and socially. The district was one of the few places in the turn-of-the-century South where people from all social classes, ethnicities, and races mingled so intimately, casually, and freely in the pursuit of sex and leisure activities. In fact, the existence of a ribald, racially mixed place like Storyville allowed white visitors to take a vacation from the so-called requirements of Jim Crow yet maintain the pretension that white supremacy and racial segregation were absolute necessities in their own communities. In many ways, Storyville was a geographical expression of the 19th-century belief that naturally virulent male sexuality required an outlet in order to protect respectable white women. In keeping with the city's repu-

tation as the South's Babylon, Storyville has remained an icon of New Orleans's sybaritic appeal and a sexually alluring beacon to tourists from the Bible Belt and beyond.

ALECIA P. LONG
Louisiana State Museum

Alecia P. Long, *The Great Southern Babylon: Sex, Race, and Respectability in New Orleans, 1865–1920* (2003).

Black Collectibles

Black collectibles/memorabilia are objects of material culture made in or with a derogatory image of a black person. These objects originated in the time period immediately following Reconstruction, when the nation was trying to come to grips with African Americans who were now free and technically equal. What was to be their "place" in this American society? The historian Rayford Logan has termed this period beginning in the 1880s "the nadir," the worst time period for African Americans in this nation's history outside of slavery.

One of the reasons that this period was so disastrous for African Americans was that the North became tired of the divisiveness left over from the Civil War and not only decided to let the South deal with its own race relations but indeed adopted the South's view of black people. Hence, in the North and South a fairly uniform popular image of African Americans began to emerge. From the 1880s to the 1930s, the darkest days of the nadir, humorous caricatures of happy-go-lucky old-time "darkies" were generated. These images

Mammy cookie jar (Kenneth W. Goings personal collection)

played off a new mythology of the Old South in which slavery was pictured as beneficent and black people were said to have been happy working for their masters. These myths were physically reinforced by the production of advertising and consumer items such as food products, figurines, and trading cards that portrayed African Americans as very dark, bug-eyed, nappy-headed, childlike, stupid, lazy, and deferential—but happy. And in the segregated world of the United States the infrequency of contacts between the races (except in employer/employee relationships) meant that these stereotypes were rarely, if ever, challenged.

From the late 1930s to the late 1950s the hardened edge of racism began to soften. One of the greatest motivations for a less racially charged image of African Americans was the impact of World War II. African American participation in the war helped to bring black people into the American mainstream, and the overall colors on the collectibles became more subdued. The wide white grin grew more restrained, and skin tones softened to browns and tans rather than the earlier dark black. But African Americans were still pictured as servants: young and old, male and female, all doing something, thus reinforcing the stereotype that the proper role of black people was still the servant, working for the master and still "happy."

After the mid-1950s, with the start of the increased activism of the modern phase of the civil rights movement, it became ever more problematic to continue to produce the collectibles. Through the media, if not daily experience, Americans saw that black people were not "happy" with their place in modern America. The production of the collectibles almost ceased. However, by the mid-1970s a market for the reproduction of these items began emerging. The civil rights movement had helped suppress the more stereotypical images of black people, but as the nation became weary of the effort to create a racially just society, more and more stereotypical images (the reproductions) were being remanufactured. Today collectibles are once again in peoples' homes (African American and white) and can be bought at flea markets, in souvenir stores, and on the Internet.

KENNETH W. GOINGS
Ohio State University

Kenneth W. Goings, *Mammy and Uncle Mose: Black Collectibles and American Stereotyping* (1994); Grace Elizabeth Hale, *Making Whiteness* (1998); M. M. Manring, *Slave in a Box: The Strange Career of Aunt Jemima* (1998).

Black Confederates, Myth of

In the 1990s the role of African Americans in the Confederacy emerged as an important topic of considerable contention. Several books, newspaper articles, and Web sites sought to document the important role of African Americans in the Confederate army and their alleged overwhelming allegiance to the Confederacy. For example, despite the fact that until February 1865 the official policy of the Confederate government was to restrict African Americans to support and labor details, some revisionists have asserted that thousands of African Americans bore arms and fought as soldiers. According to these revisionist accounts, the number of African Americans serving as soldiers for the Confederacy ranged anywhere from 15,000 to 93,000.

Historical scholarship documents that some African Americans bore arms as pickets and saw actual combat in Confederate regiments. In cities such as Charleston, S.C., and New Orleans, where African Americans were an indispensable part of the labor force and where those who were free had achieved a level of economic success, many chose to support the Confederacy and to volunteer their services to the Confederate cause. The most notable example of this phenomenon is the Louisiana Native Guards, a regiment of 1,800 "free men

of color" who offered their services to defend the city of New Orleans against Union forces in 1862. After the surrender of the city, however, many of its members changed their allegiance and formed one of the first all-black Union army regiments under the command of Benjamin Butler.

There is no evidence that any other regiment like the Louisiana Native Guard served in the Confederacy. Except for the extant documentation that thousands of African American slaves served as body servants, cooks, and laborers for the Confederate army, there is no evidence that there was an organized effort to recruit African Americans as soldiers. Nor is there sufficient documentation to support the myth that thousands bore arms and expressed a willing allegiance to the Confederate cause. Instead, there is ample evidence that many African Americans, who were caught in a no-win situation and in a situation that they did not control, acted in their own best interests by choosing to accompany their masters, who took them to the war or to labor for the Confederacy. Thousands of other African Americans voted with their feet by running away or by becoming part of the 90,000 or more documented ex-slaves who joined the Union army.

The myth of "Black Confederates" emerged in the 1990s in defense of the Lost Cause ideology. Lost Cause supporters maintained that the Civil War was fought to defend states' rights and the rights of southerners against northern aggression. Most important, the war was not fought, in their view, to defend the institution of slavery. As Lost Cause supporters defended their southern heritage, and more specifically the flying of the Confederate battle flag on the statehouses in several southern states, they used the allegedly volunteer service of thousands of African Americans as soldiers and supporters of the Confederacy to challenge and deny the contention that the Confederacy and its symbols represented racism.

W. MARVIN DULANEY
College of Charleston

Charles Kelly Barrow, J. H. Segars, and R. B. Rosenburg, eds., *Forgotten Confederates: An Anthology about Black Southerners* (1995); James H. Brewer, *The Confederate Negro: Virginia's Craftsmen and Military Laborers, 1861–1865* (1969); Alexia J. Helsey, *South Carolina Historical Magazine* (1973); James G. Hollandsworth Jr., *The Louisiana Native Guards: The Black Military Experience during the Civil War* (1995); Ervin L. Jordan Jr., *Black Confederates and Afro-Yankees in Civil War Virginia* (1995); W. Scott Poole, *Never Surrender: Confederate Memory and Conservatism in the South Carolina Upcountry* (2004); Richard Rollins, ed., *Black Southerners in Gray: Essays on Afro-Americans in Confederate Armies* (1994).

Burma Shave Signs

In 1930, travelers on southern roads joined in a rapidly spreading national pastime—reading Burma Shave signs. Set 100 paces apart along the roadside, a series of six signs containing a catchy jingle promoted Burma Shave, a new brushless shaving cream. A typical gem was "Water Heater / Out of Kilter / Try the Brushless / Whisker / Wilter / Burma Shave." The humorous,

often public-spirited advertising tickled the nation's fancy for almost 40 years, providing a focal point for travelers throughout the country.

Clinton Odell and his sons, Allan and Leonard, introduced Burma Shave, the key product of their Burma-Vita Company, in Minneapolis in 1925. A year later Allan proposed using sets of roadside signs with witty jingles to plug the new product. The signs' soaring popularity was matched by impressive sales records throughout the Midwest in 1926 and 1927, on the Pacific and Atlantic Coasts in 1929, and in the South and New England in 1930.

Though lacking the population density—and therefore the potential market—of more urbanized regions, the South offered many locations suitable for the Burma Shave signs. After finding a good spot, a company agent would contact the landowner and offer him a jar of Burma Shave and a small fee for a year's lease of the site. Many of the farmers purportedly became very attached to the signs, monitored their defacement or disappearance, repaired damaged ones, and willingly renewed the leases.

The 600 jingles used between 1926 and 1963 did not have specifically regional themes, but one jingle referred to a southern locale: "From Saskatoon / To Alabam' / You Hear Men Praise / The Shave / What Am / Burma Shave." Regional marketing campaigns and contests were used to come up with new jingles, and the contests sparked a tremendous response. One Alabama woman, for example, contributed the safe-driving jingle, "A Girl / Should

Hold On / To Her Youth / But Not / When He's Driving." Another example was the 1952 series used in the South, "Missin' / Kissin'? / Perhaps Your Thrush / Can't Get Thru / The Underbrush — Try / Burma Shave."

By the mid-1950s the Burma-Vita Company and its most famous product were in decline, and in 1963 Philip Morris, Inc., bought the company and abandoned the Burma Shave signs, which had become a less effective marketing tool among faster-moving commuters. The demise of the signs caught the public's attention, however, and one set was eventually placed in the Smithsonian Institution. With their special place in the nation's store of folk humor, Burma Shave signs have reappeared occasionally, as when the 1970s television show *Hee Haw* used them in evoking its image of a largely rural South, unhurried and jocular.

SHARON A. SHARP
Boone, North Carolina

Frank Rowsome Jr., *The Verse by the Side of the Road* (1965); Bill Vossler, *Burma-Shave: The Rhymes, the Signs, the Times* (1998); Martin Waterman, *Backwoods Home Magazine* (1998).

Carter Era

The 1976 presidential campaign and subsequent election of Jimmy Carter signaled a major change in the South's image. The negative 1960s image of the South as the place of civil rights conflict gave way to the more favorable image of a land of charming eccentricities, a pleasant lifestyle, traditional small-town American values, and a booming Sunbelt economy.

When the 1976 campaign began, Carter was a hopeless long shot, but after he put together a string of primary victories, including capture of the black vote, the national media began to take notice. Carter's southern background became the key element in the national attention focused on the Georgian. Carter was soon being portrayed as a southern version of a Frank Capra film hero, talking about a government "as good and decent as the American people themselves." In the aftermath of Vietnam and Watergate, the nation seemed naturally to choose its presidential candidate from a region that knew the moral complexities of life and yet asserted simple Baptist moralisms and religiosity as a way of dealing with them. Carter played up his southern ties, telling cheering southern audiences, "Come January we are going to have a President in the White House who doesn't speak with an accent."

The Democratic Party convention, held in New York City's Madison Square Garden in August of 1976, was a symbolic triumph not only for Carter but for the South as well. In the bicentennial year of the nation's independence, 111 years after the end of the Civil War, another stage of sectional reconciliation occurred, with a national political institution turning over its leadership to a son of the Deep South. The emotional high point came on the last day of the meeting, when Martin Luther "Daddy" King led the convention in the singing of "We Shall Overcome."

After the convention, the national media devoted even more attention to understanding this new South that had produced Carter. *Saturday Review* published a symposium on the "South as the New America" in its 4 September 1976 issue; *U.S. News and World Report* did a feature on the "New South" on 2 August 1976; and *Time* magazine provided an in-depth look at the region through the "South Today" special section of its 27 September 1976 issue, which had articles not only on politics but on "The Good Life," "Those Good Old Boys," "Segregation Remembered," "Home-Grown Elegance" (food), football, stock car racing, and honky-tonk music, as well as an essay, "The South Tomorrow," by historian C. Vann Woodward.

Southern writers, particularly humorists, were kept busy chronicling and interpreting the Carter family and the South to the nation. Larry L. King wrote "We Ain't Trash No More" for *Esquire* (November 1976). Roy Blount Jr. emerged as one of the preeminent southern interpreters of the Carters. Watching Carter's nomination in New York City, Blount had said he felt "like a man who goes from being half eat up with hookworms to catching nice speckled trout with them." Labeling himself a "Crackro-American" writer, he published a series of magazine articles, later collected as *Crackers* (1982), which dealt with country music, opossums, southern women, good old boys, and other topics essential to understanding the region.

The mythology of the Carter era combined various existing images of the South. Interest in the Carter family as a collection of southern eccentrics

was particularly pronounced. Wife Rosalyn seemed to be the "iron magnolia," sweet and gentle on the surface but tough underneath; Miss Lillian, the candidate's mother, was a feisty grand dame; sister Ruth Carter Stapleton was a faith-healing evangelist. And, finally, brother Billy was the beer-guzzling good old boy. Writers struggled to determine how "southern" Jimmy himself was. A peanut farmer, a nuclear engineer in the navy, a born-again Baptist, a businessman—Carter embodied paradoxical images of the Old and New South.

Carter's hometown, Plains, Ga., emerged as a new symbolic center of the southern experience. It appeared in news stories as a typically southern, yet also American, community. Its train depot, café, service stations, pool halls, and barber shops and beauty parlors could have been midwestern, yet the presence of a seemingly high percentage of stereotypical southerners, as well as the ever-present racial and evangelical religious aspects, set Plains off as a clearly southern landscape. The peaceful quality of life in the rural and small-town South was much praised by observers, many of whom also lauded the bustling cities of the region.

Carter's inauguration day, 20 January 1977, evoked images of Jeffersonian simplicity, as the new president walked to the ceremonies. His inaugural address was a sermon, notable for its explicit use of civil religious "God language," seeing the nation under divine judgment. There were southern touches, such as the presence of James Dickey, the unofficial poet laureate of the administration, who wrote a poem entitled "The Strength of Fields," which he read at the preinaugural gala. "Everybody wants to be a southerner now," he was quoted as saying. In addition to the seven inaugural balls, the world's largest square dance was staged. Peanut souvenirs were everywhere in the nation's capital. *Newsweek* magazine described "the dawning of a Dixiefied new era." Soon southern writers were being fêted in the White House, and musicians such as the Allman Brothers, Charlie Daniels, and Willie Nelson performed there. *Carter Country*, a network television situation comedy featuring an inept white sheriff, a hip black deputy, and assorted small-town Deep South characters (it was set in Georgia), premiered in 1977.

As time passed, though, Carter and his administration were less frequently portrayed by the national media simply in southern terms. On a trip to the South in the summer of 1977, Carter noted that he was pleased to see fewer stories in the national media about his being a southerner. "Now I, like you, am an American," he said. In the 1980 campaign, the South, like the rest of the nation, deserted Carter. Nonetheless, the earlier Carter campaign and presidency helped to focus national attention on the South and led to changes in perception about the region and its people.

CHARLES REAGAN WILSON
University of Mississippi

Robert M. Pierce, *Perspectives on the American South*, vol. 2, ed. Merle Black and John Shelton Reed (1984); Stephen A. Smith, *Media, Myth, and the Southern Mind* (1985).

Cash, W. J.

(1900–1941) JOURNALIST.

Wilbur Joseph Cash was a Piedmont southerner, born in Gaffney, S.C., in 1900, a graduate of Wake Forest College, and a journalist for the Charlotte *News*, who died by his own hand in Mexico City in 1941. His influence rests upon a single work, *The Mind of the South*, published by Alfred A. Knopf in 1941, which was an attempt to analyze the relationship between social consciousness and culture in the region. As a prose stylist, Cash was a talented rhetorician, much influenced by H. L. Mencken's slashing, witty, and barbed journalism, but developing his own version, narrower in range of reference and accomplishment, conversational, sentimental, humorous, candid, emotional, and possessed of great impetus; it is a style, like that of Thomas Wolfe, best relished in youth and, indeed, once usually read then. For the book was noticed upon its publication, but sold only a few thousand copies in its first 19 years of life. When it was put into paperback by Knopf in 1960, however, it quickly became mandatory reading, especially on northern campuses, as it seemed to offer an explanation for the puzzling society that the crisis of the civil rights movement was obliged to reform.

Cash was the leading proponent of the thesis of southern cultural unity and continuity, which he argued were fashioned by climate, physical conditions, frontier violence, clannishness, and Calvinist Protestantism, all of which conspired to create a romantic hedonism, a zeitgeist of anti-intellectualism and prejudice most brutally expressed in racism, the sum of which Cash called the "savage ideal." Having evolved before the Civil War, this unity connects the Old and New South. For Cash, the South's industrial transformation had failed to create the class consciousness and intellectual flexibility appropriate to such a society, thus the sensibility of the savage ideal had remained the master of southern history, which remained essentially immobile. Cash himself was a liberal in racial matters by the standards of his time, that is, he had adjusted his views to deprecate the enemies of blacks but not yet altered his own opinions to sympathize with black culture and personality. Cash's interpretation has proved most appealing to southern liberals who feel pessimistic about and trapped in southern provincial culture (especially its repressive religion) and find an explanation for their fetters in his embittered but vivid portrait. Southern women find little in him of value, and African Americans tend to be dismissive, but he retains a loyal following.

MICHAEL O'BRIEN
Jesus College, Cambridge

Bruce Clayton, *W. J. Cash: A Life* (1991); Charles W. Eagles, ed., *The Mind of the South: Fifty Years Later* (1992); Paul D. Escott, ed., *W. J. Cash and the Minds of the South* (1992).

Cavalier Myth

The Cavalier myth generally functioned as a prominent aspect of the larger mythic worlds of the plantation and the Lost Cause. According to the myth, the southern Cavalier began his career as a planter or the son of a planter and reached his maturity as a Confederate soldier, generally, but not necessarily, an officer. The Cavalier myth evoked elements of English squirarchy, feudalism, and aristocracy. The Cavalier was courtly, wealthy yet nonmaterialistic, brave, honorable, and gentle. His martial aspects dominated during the Civil War, when his conduct was most frequently described as knightly — meaning courageous, devoted to the cause, pure, and still tender. General Robert E. Lee stood as the primary example of the Confederate Cavalier.

The Cavalier began to emerge as a mythic character in plantation novels such as William Alexander Carruthers's *The Cavaliers of Virginia* (1834); he became stock in the plantation domestic novels and polemic writing of the immediate prewar decades; and this ideal reached a stereotypical apex in reminiscences and novels in the first half century after the Civil War, including such works as Thomas Nelson Page's "Marse Chan" (1887) and Thomas Dixon Jr.'s *The Clansman* (1905). By the 1930s the Cavalier myth was becoming fragmented, as indicated by the Rhett Butler–Ashley Wilkes split in Margaret Mitchell's *Gone with the Wind* (1936).

The Cavalier supplied the glamour of wealth, caste, and lineage that Americans envied. He also stood as an antipode to the restless, materialistic society of the North. After the Civil War, he continued to function in these ways as a national ideal, but in the South he had special meaning as the standard bearer of chivalry's last stand and as the apotheosis of manly virtue. The Cavalier myth served both as an inspiration for those who wanted to push on into the New South and as a consolation for those who embraced the Old South as an unattainable Golden Age. With the coming of the civil rights movement, industrialism, and literary realism to the South, the romantic Cavalier ideal as part of the southern plantation setting no longer seemed a usable ideal, although elements of the cluster of Cavalier traits lingered. The Cavalier type, however, is still a major ideal in modern romances.

SUSAN S. DURANT
University of Kentucky

Nicholas Cords and Patrick Gerster, *Myth America: A Historical Anthology* (1997); Francis Pendleton Gaines, *The Southern Plantation: A Study in the Development and the Accuracy of a Tradition* (1925); Jack Temple Kirby, *Media-Made Dixie: The South in the American Imagination* (1978); William R. Taylor, *Cavalier and Yankee: The Old South and American National Character* (1957).

Celtic South

The notion of a Celtic South is very much associated with historians Grady McWhiney and Forrest McDonald, who contend that the pervasive culture of the southern states, up until the Civil War at least, was formed by immigrants from the recognized Celtic regions of the British Isles: Ireland, Scotland, Wales, and much of the north and west of England. They base their controversial thesis principally on an analysis of surnames in the censuses between 1790 and 1860, which suggest that well over half of the white southern population came from those regions, thus placing southerners from the non-Celtic parts of the British Isles distinctly in the minority. They also find many cultural similarities between British Isles Celts and southerners: open-range herding, eating and drinking habits, a preference for play over work, a love of honor and its attendant violence, and, more positively, a general disposition toward hospitality. In this scenario, the Civil War was a cultural clash between a Celtic South that was hospitable, impractical, and reckless and an Anglo-Saxon Northeast that was shrewd, disciplined, and pragmatic; the issue of chattel slavery recedes into the background.

While McWhiney and McDonald's Celtic thesis is certainly new in its comprehensive sweep, many of its individual elements are not especially original or even controversial, and there has long been a general recognition of the tangled and uncertain origins of large portions of the South's inhabitants. Even Thomas Nelson Page, a stalwart defender of the South's Anglo-Saxon legacy, acknowledged a significant Celtic heritage, and the word "Celt" was often applied to prominent 19th-century southern writers such as John Pendleton Kennedy and William Gilmore Simms, while the most famous fictitious southerner in the 20th century, Scarlett O'Hara, was undoubtedly of the tribe.

Although often conveniently ignored, the Celtic South thesis has received cautious but surprisingly respectful acceptance from many professional historians, African Americans among them. Still, scholars from Northern Ireland claim that all of the American work in this area is insufficiently aware of the historical complexity of the British Isles. McWhiney and McDonald have been criticized also for relying far too heavily on middle-class travelers' accounts of similarities between customs in the Celtic parts of the British Isles and customs in the South, since these accounts were frequently designed to meet audience preconceptions. Finally, the Celtic South thesis has taken on a rather ugly form in its adoption by groups anxious to assert the heritage of the white South in the face of what they see as a corrosive multiculturalism, though it has positively engaged many southerners who would not identify with such xenophobia.

In the wider world of academic research, a lively debate currently rages among scholars of ancient history as to whether there were ever any Celts at all in the British Isles. Simon James, of the British Museum, has argued provocatively that the very idea of the "Celt" is a post-1700 invention. More conciliatorily, but in opposition to James, Oxford University's Barry Cunliffe has acknowledged the appeal of seeing oneself as a Celt, concluding that "perhaps the only real definition of a Celt, now as in the past, is that a Celt is a person who believes him or herself to be Celtic." Southerners anxious about their Celtic roots should draw some

consolation from Cunliffe's generous concession.

KIERAN QUINLAN
University of Alabama at Birmingham

Rowland Berthoff, *Journal of Southern History* (November 1986); Barry Cunliffe, *The Ancient Celts* (1997); Forest McDonald and Grady McWhiney, *American Historical Review* (December 1980), *Journal of Southern History* (May 1985); Grady McWhiney, *Cracker Culture: Celtic Ways in the Old South* (1988); Kieran Quinlan, *Strange Kin: Ireland and the American South* (2004); Celeste Ray, *Highland Heritage: Scottish Americans in the American South* (2001); Helen Taylor, in *South to a New Place*, ed. Suzanne W. Jones and Sharon Monteith (2002).

Chosen People Myth

Biblical imagery has deeply informed the self-understanding of the evangelical South. One of the region's most enduring symbols has been the biblical theme of "the Chosen People." In the Hebrew Bible, God particularly chooses the Jewish people to be his "peculiar possession." The Christian scriptures borrowed this imagery in their description of the Church, the people chosen and called out from the world. Southerners, in large part because the biblical idiom intertwined even with everyday speech, readily used this Chosen People myth to express their own self-understanding.

The Chosen People myth has played an important role, not only in the South, but also in the larger cultural life of the American people. The Puritan settlers of the Massachusetts Bay colony believed they had embarked on "an errand into the wilderness" and had been specially chosen to build "a city on a hill." Although this idea either disappeared or became thoroughly secularized in much of the nation, it continued to hold much cultural power in the American South. The Chosen People myth came to be applied to the South's historical circumstances, becoming a way to invest historical events with theological significance.

White southerners have deployed the Chosen People myth to defend both slavery and the right of secession. God, white southern apologists argued in the 19th century, had ordained slavery. The use of Old Testament imagery in the defense of slavery (particularly references to the practice of slavery in the "Abrahamic Households" of the Old Testament) did much to strengthen southern attachment to the Chosen People ideal. Ministers proclaimed secession as an effort by God's chosen to separate themselves from the ungodly.

Defeat in the Civil War did not diminish the white South's devotion to the Chosen People myth. In fact, through the celebration of the Lost Cause, white southerners were able to view themselves as the suffering people of God. They readily borrowed biblical imagery of God's people as a suffering servant whose historical trials would play an important role in the world's redemption. The Southern Baptist Church became especially attached to this imagery in the postbellum period, believing it gave legitimacy to their own efforts at worldwide missionary activity.

Black southerners have also utilized the Chosen People myth to endure the oppression of slavery and to embolden their work for liberation. The image of the Exodus for slave preachers, leaders of slave revolts, and African Americans fleeing slavery both before and during the Civil War proved especially powerful. African Americans in the South have easily been able to identify with God's people suffering in bondage, as well as to rejoice in the promise of deliverance.

In modern times, the power of the Chosen People myth remains strong in the American South, as evidenced by the disparate movements and personalities who have employed it. South Carolina civil rights activist James McBride Dabbs made fascinating use of the idea in his insistence that the white and black South, in its sins and its sufferings, had a special role to play in the modern world. God, he believed, had made the American South His "special project," and suggested that from its tragic history might come the wisdom to build a true biracial community. Television evangelists, most of them located in the South or with strong southern roots, also make frequent use of Chosen People mythology, though frequently using it in reference to the American nation rather than the South alone. They generally employ the imagery for very conservative causes, such as strengthening the American military or giving unqualified support to the state of Israel. Meanwhile, the image of the Exodus remains a powerful symbol in African American religion, symbolizing the continued goal of liberation.

The strength of the Chosen People myth suggests both the elasticity of religious imagery and the enduring importance of religion in the American South.

W. SCOTT POOLE
College of Charleston

Bill Leonard, *God's Last and Only Hope: The Fragmentation of the Southern Baptist Convention* (1990); Albert J. Raboteau, *Slave Religion: The Invisible Institution in the Antebellum South* (2004); Mitchell Snay, *Gospel of Disunion: Religion and Separatism in the Antebellum South* (1993); Charles Reagan Wilson, *Judgment and Grace in Dixie: Southern Faiths from Faulkner to Elvis* (1995).

Christmas

The first celebration of Christmas in North America was likely by the Spanish in the 1500s, and it certainly took place in the South, although whether in Florida or the Southwest is unknown. The first recorded commemoration of Christmas in the British colonies on the mainland was in Jamestown, Va., in 1607. About 40 of the original 100 colonists, unsure of their survival, gathered in a primitive wooden chapel for a somber day. Until well into the 19th century, the Protestants of New England looked with suspicion upon Christmas as a "popish" day, but southerners generally encouraged a joyous celebration.

Gentleman farmers, in particular, regarded the day more as a time of relaxation and social activity than as a religious holiday. They preserved such European customs as caroling, burning the Yule log, and decorating with greenery. But the environment worked to make a distinctive festival. Native seafood and turkey replaced the traditional European dishes of beef and goose. Southerners added regional touches such as eating fried oysters, drinking eggnog with rum, and going on a Christmas morning hunt for foxes or other small game. Pines replaced European firs and cedars for the Christmas tree, and Spanish moss was used as a primitive "angel hair" for decorating in the Deep South. The poinsettia became a custom in 1825, when Charlestonian Joel Poinsett brought a red flower back from Mexico as a gift, and others were soon decorating with poinsettias.

The French in Louisiana introduced the tradition of Christmas fireworks, setting off firecrackers and firing rifles. Until the World War I era southerners rarely used fireworks on the Fourth of July but did punctuate the Christmas holiday with them. A long-standing Cajun custom is Christmas Eve bonfires, known as *feux de joie* (fires of joy), burning all night along the Mississippi River from Baton Rouge to New Orleans.

Three southern states were the first in the nation to make Christmas a legal holiday—Louisiana and Arkansas in 1831 and Alabama in 1836. The plantation was the center for the most elaborate and distinctive antebellum southern celebration of Christmas. In backcountry rural areas plantation houses became the scene of sometimes extravagant Christmas partying, eating, and playing, including the morning hunt. For slaves, Christmas had special meaning. December was a slow work month on the typical plantation, and it became the social season for them. The slaves' holiday lasted until the Yule log burned, which sometimes took over a week. The setting off of fireworks became a noted custom among slaves as well as whites.

Christmas as currently celebrated, in broad outline, was an invention of the 19th-century Victorians, who sentimentalized the day and made it the focus for new traditions. By the 1930s the celebration of Christmas had become even more secular than before, with the exchange of gifts for adults and Santa Claus for children. The religious aspects of Christmas were played down by the Victorians, but by the mid-20th century this dimension had become stronger. Some Protestant churches now imitate, in modified manner, the Catholic midnight Eucharist. In Jewish communities the festival of Hanukkah has expanded and absorbed many of the characteristics of Christmas. Kwanzaa celebrates African American culture between Christmas and New Year.

Christmas has become the holiday par excellence in the South as elsewhere in the United States. Merchants begin to prepare for it and to advertise their offerings long before Halloween. The Santa Claus parades come early in December, if not sooner, and parties are given throughout the month. Fireworks, the antebellum custom, are still seen. Christmas trees adorn the streets, and one southern state, North Carolina, ranks second nationally in the number of trees harvested and first in terms of dollars made per tree. Christmas programs and music are the fare on television and radio. Cards and presents flood the post office. Charities set up stalls on street corners and, with ringing of bells, summon passersby to make contributions. Churches, of course, have special services. A few southern families make some effort to celebrate the 12 days culminating on 6 January, a day sometimes called "Old Christmas" (which is perhaps a faint recollection of when Britain adopted the Gregorian calendar in 1752, changing the celebration of Christmas from the 6 January date on the Julian calendar). In New Orleans the season of Carnival officially begins with Twelfth Night parties on the eve of Old Christmas. Many communities now sponsor candlelight tours of historic places at Christmas, reinforcing the holiday's ties to the idea of tradition itself.

ALLEN CABANISS
University of Mississippi

William M. Auld, *Christmas Traditions* (1968); John E. Baur, *Christmas on the American Frontier* (1961); Emyl Jenkins, *Southern Christmas* (1995); Harnett T. Kane, *The Southern Christmas Book: The Full Story from the Earliest Times to the Present: People, Customs, Conviviality, Carols, Cooking* (1958); Joanne B. Young, *Christmas in Williamsburg* (1970).

"City Too Busy to Hate" (Atlanta)

Atlanta's reputation for moderation in racial issues was built on the context of its region and time. By 1959 Atlanta had reached a metropolitan population of 1 million and was pulling away from its old rivals Birmingham, Memphis, and New Orleans. Touting the milestone, longtime mayor William B. Hartsfield repeated his usual mantra to a reporter for *Newsweek*, "We say we're too busy to hate—it's the pattern of modern Atlanta set by Henry Grady." On another occasion, in a televised speech, he bragged, "Other southern cities falter in growth on account of their bad race relations. . . . Trade, industry, and business is not coming their way. On the other hand, it is coming to Atlanta, a city that calmly says to the world, 'We are too busy to hate anybody.'"

The slogan stuck, and since the early 1960s virtually every journalistic and academic account of Atlanta has used the moniker as a reference point to mark the city's accomplishments and to measure its shortcomings. Blacks understood that profit and pragmatism rather than reconciliation and repentance were business leaders' motives, but they still saw significant truth in the slogan. For example, NAACP leader Lonnie King recalled, "Birmingham ducked its head in the sand on issues—and Atlanta was willing to say that 'we were the city too busy to hate.' It was a code word for saying that it was progressive." Seldom, if ever, has a single phrase so pervasively dominated analysis of a city. The slogan became the construct for both hyperbole and hypothesis.

Bill Hartsfield began his political career in the 1930s as a staunch segregationist, and even when he left office in 1962 after nearly a quarter century as mayor, he was, in the memory of his police chief, "just as liberal as necessary to get the black vote." But under his political leadership the "too busy" city had avoided civil rights violence and

had made limited steps toward integration. The key to this accomplishment was the firm political alliance forged between the city's white business elite and the leaders of the black community. After the U.S. Supreme Court struck down the white primary in 1946, African American voting strength grew rapidly in Atlanta and stood at 25–30 percent throughout the 1950s.

Hartsfield responded to the black vote with gradual concessions and symbolic gestures—the appointment of a few black policemen, the desegregation of golf courses, and the welcoming of black and interracial conventions, including that of the NAACP in 1951. In the waning years of the Hartsfield administration, careful negotiations between the business community and established black leaders led to desegregation of major department stores, many restaurants, and, most important, the public schools. Younger civil rights organizers chaffed at the go-slow approach of old guard black leaders such as John Wesley Dobbs and A. T. Walden, but the gradual approach held. The national press lauded Atlanta for accomplishing the transition ahead of other southern cities and without the violence that had broken out in such places as Little Rock.

With the strong support of business leaders, office supply executive Ivan Allen Jr. succeeded Hartsfield as mayor. As it had been for Hartsfield, the black vote was the key to Allen's success. Rabid segregationist Lester Maddox, who would later serve as Georgia's governor, opposed Hartsfield in 1957 and Allen in 1961. Victory over such an opponent made both mayors appear liberal by comparison. Allen further solidified his and the city's reputation for moderation when he was the only prominent white southern politician to testify before Congress in favor of the Civil Rights Act of 1964. Being the home of Martin Luther King Jr. added luster to Atlanta's civil rights credentials. Although many white businessmen were critical of King, Robert Woodruff of Coca-Cola insured that Atlanta would honor King properly for his Nobel Peace Prize. Allen's hospitality, with Woodruff's behind-the-scenes support, helped keep the city calm for King's funeral procession in 1968. Such moderation in contrast with the rest of the South played extremely well with the national media. This positive image had already paved the way for Allen and the business community to lure the Milwaukee Braves south, making Atlanta the region's first "major league city." Upon Allen's death in 2003, U.S. senator and former governor Zell Miller eulogized him, saying that Allen had done "more to make the saying, 'Atlanta: A City Too Busy to Hate' a reality . . . than any other."

Allen was followed in city hall by another white progressive, Sam Massell, but the biracial coalition was fraying, and he would be the city's last white mayor. By the 1970s demographic changes resulting from white flight to the suburbs and Atlanta's failure to make any significant annexations after 1952 shifted the balance of political power to the black community. Many old-line black politicos were willing to support Massell for a second term, but

the young black vice mayor Maynard Jackson believed that the time was ripe for change. He was right, and in 1973, in a racially polarized vote, the "city too busy to hate" elected Jackson. Andrew Young had been elected to Congress the previous year, and more and more city council and state legislative seats were being won by blacks. From that point forward liberal and moderate white voters would serve mainly as the swing group that could determine which black won.

Jackson's administrative appointments, his revamping of the police department, and his insistence on an extensive affirmative action program, especially in airport construction, led to strains with the white business community. Congressman Young followed Jackson as mayor, and he worked to mend fences with the white power structure. After Young's two terms, Jackson returned in 1989 for a second round as mayor. His successor, Bill Campbell, proved often to be racially divisive, but he was followed by Shirley Franklin, a close Jackson ally more prone to collaboration between city hall and business interests.

Throughout the era of black mayors, the "too busy to hate" appellation continued to be the standard by which commentators judged Atlanta. The chamber of commerce proudly pointed to booming growth that often led the nation, and by the time of the 2000 census, metropolitan population had surpassed 4 million. Boosters emphasized that the increase included a large influx of affluent, educated blacks who wanted to make the vibrant, modern capital of the South their home. Although population growth in the central city stagnated, commercial construction remained strong within the city limits except during a brief cyclical downturn. The urban core remained the metropolitan area's cultural focus, with the Woodruff Arts Center and gleaming new facilities for the city's NFL, NBA, and MLB teams.

The national business press often touted Atlanta as having one of the best business climates in the country. Without its reputation for diversity and moderation, Atlanta could never have been chosen as the site of the 1996 Olympics. Andrew Young proudly spoke of how a group of local preschoolers impressed visiting IOC members by telling them that Atlanta should get to host the 1996 Olympics "because we're a city too busy to hate." In a speech praising affirmative action, President Clinton singled out Atlanta, saying, "I am confident that Atlanta's success—it is now home to more foreign corporations than any other American city, and one year from today it will begin to host the Olympics—all began when people got too busy to hate."

But the phrase also made an easy rhetorical foil. Liberal skeptics said that the city was really "too busy to love" or "too busy to care." One anthropologist wrote that Atlanta was a "city of hype" with an "official mythology" that was more "imagineering" than reality. A report on locally based CNN conceded that Atlanta was "not too busy to quarrel." Other critics said that the city was "too busy to plan" and "to busy to fix its aging sewers." Such naysayers correctly cited undeniable statistics of continuing discrimination and poverty, especially in the central city. They rightly complained of the problems of urban sprawl and traffic congestion, but they were at a loss to offer a convincing counterhypothesis that would explain how Atlanta changed from sleepy southern city to booming Sunbelt metropolis.

In 1999 city council president Marvin Arrington wrote, "The mantle of Atlanta as a city too busy to hate served us well during that critical period of race relations. Now, however, it is not enough to be too busy to hate." Arrington never achieved his goal of becoming mayor, but the city of Atlanta's official Web site now optimistically reflects similar sentiments, declaring, "In the turbulent '60s, Atlanta was 'the city too busy to hate.' And today, in the 21st century, Atlanta is the 'city not too busy to care.'"

In mid-2003, three key figures from Atlanta's history, one who flamed hatred and two who tried to suppress it, died within a few weeks of each other. Hardly anyone in the city cared to memorialize the hopelessly anachronistic Lester Maddox. Allen was widely eulogized, and the city will erect a statue to the mayor who defined the 1960s. Most notably, a movement quickly sprang up to rename Atlanta's Hartsfield International Airport in memory of Maynard Jackson, who oversaw its great expansion. A split along racial lines soon developed between those who wanted to memorialize Jackson and those who wanted to continue to honor the mayor who coined the city's unofficial motto. *USA Today* told the nation that "it doesn't look good for a place nicknamed 'The City Too Busy to Hate' to be embroiled in such a fracas." Bad national press was anathema to Atlanta, and Mayor Franklin set about to defuse the crisis by appointing a biracial commission of distinguished Atlantans including the elderly George Goodwin, an old ally of Hartsfield. She also scheduled public meetings to allow citizens to express their opinions. Then, in the best tradition of the "too busy to hate" style, she engineered a compromise designed to satisfy both business leaders and the black community. The nation's busiest airport, in the "city too busy to hate," is now aptly named William B. Hartsfield–Maynard H. Jackson International.

BRADLEY R. RICE
Clayton College and State University

Ronald H. Bayor, *Race and the Shaping of Twentieth-Century Atlanta* (1996); Virginia Hein, *Phylon* (Fall 1972); Alton Hornsby Jr., in *Southern Businessmen and Desegregation*, ed. Elizabeth Jacoway and David R. Colburn (1982); Tamar Jacoby, *Someone Else's House: America's Unfinished Struggle for Integration* (1998); Harold H. Martin, *William Berry Hartsfield: Mayor of Atlanta* (1978); Gary M. Pomerantz, *Where Peachtree Meets Sweet Auburn: The Saga of Two Families and the Making of Atlanta* (1996); Bradley R. Rice, in *Sunbelt Cities: Politics and Growth since World War II*, ed. Richard M. Bernard and Bradley R. Rice (1983); Southern Regional Council, "The City Too Busy to Hate," script of show 24 of "Will the Circle Be Unbroken," an audio history of the civil rights movement (1997); Stephen G. N. Tuck, *Beyond Atlanta: The Struggle for Racial Equality in Georgia, 1940–1980* (2001).

Civil War Reenactments

Each spring and summer thousands of white southerners don Confederate-style uniforms and civilian wear more or less appropriate to the mid-19th century and drive considerable distances to spend weekends reenacting the bloodiest conflict in American history. The phenomenon is not new, but it has grown considerably in terms of spectators and participants since the early 1990s. Major reenactments such as the one at Gettysburg are hot tickets requiring advance purchase if one wants to catch a glimpse of hundreds of reenactors banging away at each other with Italian-made Springfields and Enfields. Such events exhibit continuity and change in aspects of southern culture.

Reenactments emphasize the Lost Cause interpretation of the Old South and the Civil War. One Lost Cause image reinforced at reenactments is that of ill-clad but brave and chivalrous Confederates fighting bravely against overwhelming odds. Many Rebels have patches all over their uniforms and carry Federal gear (haversack, canteen, cartridge and cap boxes) almost exclusively, demonstrating that the Confederate government could not supply its poor troops. There is little evidence to sustain such ideas and impressions, but like the Lost Cause interpretation itself, they are romantic oversimplifications. The issue of slavery rarely, if ever, comes up because it would put a damper on the celebration.

Not surprisingly, with so many people interested in reenactments, vendors (booksellers, artists, sculptors, general souvenir dealers) are in abundance. Many tents display Confederate iconography. Artwork, offered for sale, depicts Confederate officers or celebrates particularly famous Rebel units but gives few renderings of northern officers or units. The Rebel flag is on sale everywhere, and baseball caps, T-shirts, key chains, and license plates emblazoned with the Army of Northern Virginia's battle flag are also readily available. The businesspeople selling these items understand very well that there is plenty of money to be made supplying white southerners with all sorts of goods celebrating the Confederacy.

Reenactments may suggest that white southerners remain trapped in ahistorical traditional beliefs about the Old South and the Confederacy, but subtle yet important changes from past ways are at work as well. For one thing, the Lost Cause generation romanticized the institution of slavery, which is not part of reenactments. In fact, Confederate units are generally very scrupulous about informing new members that their use of the battle flag is for historical purposes only and is in no way meant as a racial statement. Another significant change from the past is that earlier generations of white southerners sometimes harbored serious ill will toward northerners. Today there is a considerable amount of good-natured kidding among reenactor Yanks and Rebs but very little, if any, simmering bad blood over the war among southerners. In fact, many southern reenactors routinely "galvanize," i.e., spend some weekends portraying Yankee soldiers—an act that would surely have sent a collective shudder through the Lost Cause generation of the late 19th century.

Without a doubt, there is still an element in the South that enjoys indulging in romantic notions about the Confederacy and the Civil War, but it would be a hasty judgment to conclude that interest in the war and its mythology illustrates that southerners are "still fighting the war." Too many breaks with past generations can be found at reenactments to allow such a pat conclusion. Few romanticize slavery or lament the war's ultimate conclusion and fewer still are openly hostile toward northerners. So while modern white southerners may buy mountains of Confederate memorabilia at Civil War reenactments as a tangible expression of regional pride, their display means little more than that.

JAY GILLISPIE
Sampson Community College

Tony Horwitz, *Confederates in the Attic* (1998).

Confederate Memorial Day

Honoring the graves of warriors is an ancient custom, and southern whites after the Civil War made the custom a central ritual of southern life. Vicksburg, Miss.; Petersburg, Va.; Columbus, Miss.; Charleston, S.C.; and Columbus, Ga., have all claimed the first observance honoring the Confederate dead after the war. The early observances were spontaneous efforts by individuals or small groups.

Southern states could not agree among themselves which day would serve as the official Memorial Day, but by 1916, 10 states had designated 3 June, Jefferson Davis's birthdate. Other dates set aside have included the fourth Monday in April (Alabama and Mississippi); 10 May, the date of the capture by Union troops of Jefferson Davis in 1865 (North Carolina and South Carolina); and 26 April, the anniversary of the final surrender in 1865 of Confederate general Joseph E. Johnston near Durham, N.C. (Florida and Georgia). The choice of a date has sometimes been tied to an event of local importance, such as the death of a Confederate leader or the anniversary of a nearby battle.

Whenever celebrated, Confederate Memorial Day was a time of solemn ritual, with speeches, sermons, prayers, the decoration of graves with flowers and Confederate flags, the singing of religious and wartime anthems like "Dixie," and the playing of Taps. A military honor guard usually fired a salute to end the ceremonies. The day's rhetoric reminded white southerners of a regional identity based in the Confederate experience. Women played a key role in this ritual, with the United Daughters of the Confederacy particularly prominent in organizing activities. Groups like the United Confederate Veterans, the Sons of Confederate Veterans, and the Children of the Confederacy also assisted. Various states—

Georgia, Florida, Arkansas, Alabama, and Mississippi—soon adopted state flags based partially or fully on the design of Confederate banners. They also proclaimed state holidays commemorating Robert E. Lee's birthday (19 January), Jefferson Davis's birthday, or a separate Confederate Memorial Day. Ministers were actively involved in this holy day. As one would expect, black southerners were not prominently involved in the day's events, although former slaves regarded as "loyal" occasionally were encouraged to speak. After World War II, Confederate Memorial Day declined as a vital holiday in the South. In states where it still exists, Confederate Memorial Day is observed on Mondays to give state employees long weekends. Many small towns continue to have popular ceremonies, but even in these places the Fourth of July has emerged as a more notable community event.

CHARLES REAGAN WILSON
University of Mississippi

William Blair, *Cities of the Dead: Contesting the Memory of the Civil War in the South, 1865–1914* (2004); David W. Blight, *Beyond the Battlefield: Race, Memory, and the American Civil War* (2002), *Race and Reunion: The Civil War in American Memory* (2000); Wallace Evan Davies, *Patriotism on Parade: The Story of Veterans' and Hereditary Organizations in America, 1783–1900* (1955); Lucille C. Lowry, *Origin of Memorial Day in Dixie* (1937); Charles Reagan Wilson, *Baptized in Blood: The Religion of the Lost Cause, 1865–1920* (1980).

"Crackers"

Americans have long stereotyped poor white southerners with a variety of contemptuous terms including "honky," "redneck," "peckerwood," "linthead," "hoosier," "shit kicker," and "cracker." The word "crackers" is among the oldest epithets used to describe white southerners, especially those from south Georgia and north Florida. The term extends back at least to the mid-1700s, when it was used in Scotland as a colloquialism for boaster. In Samuel Johnson's famous dictionary of 1755, a cracker was defined as a "noisy, boasting fellow."

By the 1760s the word was commonly used by coastal residents as an ethnic pejorative to designate Scotch-Irish frontiersmen in the South. These backcountry folk tended to be herdsmen who depended on an abundance of land for grazing livestock. With diminishing open rangeland in the early 19th century, some of these plain folk moved westward across the Appalachians to the frontier, but others headed into the piney woods of Georgia and Florida, an area that became the cracker "homeland."

Travelers in this area in the 19th century wrote of the crackers as poor white farmers, often dismissing them for "cracking," or pounding, corn for food. On the other hand, local histories and other accounts show the existence of a prosperous middle class, whose members typically owned a slave or two, grew corn and other commodities, and grazed cattle and hogs. From this perspective, most of these piney woods folk were not poor "corn crackers" but respectable "whip crackers," who used a long whip with a tip called a "cracker."

After the Civil War, the debt-ridden states of Georgia and Florida sold off much of the public land that crackers had used for grazing livestock. Their economic lot worsened in the late 19th century, and landless crackers went to mill towns for work or became sharecroppers or marginal farmers. By the turn of the 20th century the term "cracker" was a pejorative for a poor millworker or rural sharecropper. Some plain folk in south Georgia and north Florida managed, however, to continue a cattle-herding economy until after World War II.

"Cracker" is also a racial epithet used by black Americans as a contemptuous term for a southern white. In the early 1800s southern slaves and free blacks used the word "buckras," which is from an African word, to refer to whites. By the 1850s, though, "cracker" was becoming the preferred term. After the Civil War, racial tension rose in the piney woods, as whites blamed freed slaves for their deteriorating economic situation. Mob violence against blacks occasionally occurred there, and the black population declined. Migrant southern blacks took their contempt for "crackers" with them to northern cities in the 20th century, and today the term is often used in ghettoes in referring to all prejudiced whites.

In the 1970s "crackers" became a term of ethnic pride for some southern whites. The election of a south Georgian, Jimmy Carter, to the presidency in 1976 led to media stories about Cracker

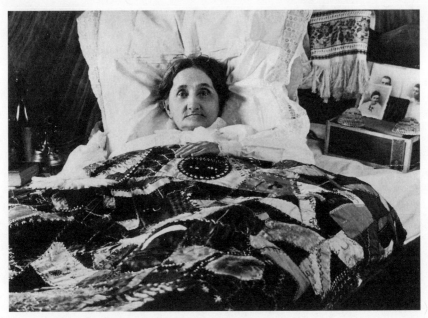

Cabinet card of an elderly woman lying in her bed, Newnan, Coweta County, Ga., c. 1900
(Georgia Department of Archives and History, Atlanta)

Chic, and humorist Roy Blount Jr. used *Crackers* as the title of his book about southerners and the Carter era.

CHARLES REAGAN WILSON
University of Mississippi

Raven I. McDavid Jr. and Virginia McDavid, *Names* (1973); John S. Otto, in *Perspectives on the American South*, vol. 4, ed. James C. Cobb and Charles Reagan Wilson (1987).

Elderly

In recent years the South has become a haven for elderly Americans. According to the U.S. census, by 1970 the region led the nation in the number of residents over age 65, and more than 6 million aged individuals lived below the Mason-Dixon Line. As of 1980 the median age of Floridians, 34.7

years, was the highest in the nation; and Florida's proportion of residents aged 65 or older, 34.7 percent, was higher than any other state's.

The growing elderly population in the South is a modern development. Traditionally, both the Northeast and North Central states have had far larger concentrations of elderly persons. In the 19th century, in fact, the South was noted for its young population. Two factors explained this historic condition. First, in contrast to other regions, the South experienced extremely high mortality rates, even among its adult members. One was far more likely to grow old in the North than in the South. Second, many of the southern states were relatively "new" and rural. They attracted the young and mobile, leaving the old to die in the cities of the East Coast.

The South of the 19th century, therefore, provided little in the way of special services for its aged population. Unlike in the North, there were relatively few old-age homes or other provisions for those over 65. The status of the old in southern society remained tied — as it traditionally had been in America — to the ownership of property and control of kin.

In the last four decades much of this has changed. Nationwide, demographic trends associated with birthrates, infant mortality, and longevity have led to a higher proportion than ever before of persons aged 65 and over in the population — approximately 11 percent in 1980 and 12.4 percent in 2000. Migration of the elderly to the Sunbelt has transformed both the nature of southern old age and the communities in which the elderly live. Although an overwhelming proportion of all migrants head for Florida, every southern state has been affected by their numbers. According to census data, the southern states with the highest proportion of elderly residents in 1980 were Florida (17.3 percent), Arkansas (13.6 percent), and West Virginia (12.2 percent). The states with the lowest proportion included Georgia (9.4 percent), South Carolina (9.2 percent), and Virginia (7.5 percent). By 2000 the following states had the highest proportion of elderly residents: Florida (17.6 percent), Arkansas (14.0 percent), and Alabama (13.0 percent); the lowest proportion was seen in Virginia (11.2 percent), Texas (9.9 percent), and Georgia (9.6 percent). In most

southern states only a slightly higher percentage were urban rather than rural residents; and in Mississippi, West Virginia, and North Carolina, the majority of the elderly live in rural areas.

On the whole, elderly newcomers are better educated and wealthier than natives; yet they come to the region without the traditional status granted by land, occupation, and family. As a result, for the first time the region is developing social services to meet the needs of elderly persons. In places like the peninsula of Florida, the Ozark Mountains, and the Texas hill country the effect is undeniable. In new communities, older cities, and even rural areas, southern culture is being transformed by the politics, recreational demands, and medical and housing needs of older citizens. Clearly, the growth in attention to the elderly's needs will continue. The future of the South will be one in which the elderly will play an ever larger and more significant role.

CAROLE HABER
University of Delaware

Forrest J. Berghorn, Donna E. Shafer, et al., *Dynamics of Aging: Original Essays on the Process and Experience of Growing Old* (1980); Carole Haber, in *Handbook on Women and Aging*, ed. Jean M. Coyle (1997); Charles F. Longino and Jeanne C. Biggar, *The Gerontologist* (June 1981); Daniel Scott Smith, Mark Friedberger, and Michel Dahlin, *Sociology and Social Research* (April 1979); U.S. Senate Special Committee on Aging, *America in Transition: An Aging Society*, 1984–85 ed. (1985).

Evangeline Myth

Evangeline, the protagonist of Henry Wadsworth Longfellow's 1847 romantic poem of the same name, is at once a symbol of ethnic identity and a case study in the evolution of cultural memory in southern Louisiana. *Evangeline* is the story of a betrothed couple that is separated during the expulsion of ethnic French citizens from British-controlled Nova Scotia in 1755. In the poem, Evangeline searches tirelessly for her lost love, Gabriel—including a brief stop in St. Martinville, La.—until, after many years, she finds him on his deathbed in Philadelphia, Pa.

Statue of Evangeline at St. Martin de Tours Church, St. Martinville, La. (Alice Berges, photographer)

Beginning in the late 19th century, as the once isolated French Louisianans began to assimilate into mainstream American culture, many felt compelled to cultivate the rapidly disappearing remnants of their Acadian roots. Recognizing in *Evangeline* familiar themes from Cajun oral tradition, Louisiana raconteurs and amateur historians embraced the essence of Longfellow's tale. According to one popular version, Evangeline catches up with her intended in St. Martinville only to find that, having given up hope of ever seeing her again, he has married someone else. The lovelorn maiden dies of a broken heart.

In the 1890s, in a combined attempt at cultural edification and economic boosterism, the town of St. Martinville began proudly boasting of its "famous Evangeline tree," a giant oak under which their heroine was said to have discovered Gabriel's betrayal, and of her purported grave beside the St. Martin de Tours Catholic Church. In the 1920s the town became home to an expansive public park named in honor of Longfellow and Evangeline. The park included the "Acadian House" museum, a 19th-century Creole cottage that was erroneously hailed as an example of 18th-century Acadian architecture and that its proprietors imaginatively endorsed as having been the home of Evangeline's faithless beau. The Acadian House played an important role in the myth, representing the successful rebuilding of Acadian culture in Louisiana while providing a domestic setting in which the rustic image of the Cajun female could be molded into one befitting the American notion of ideal womanhood. By 1930, when Governor Huey Long, before an audience of 15,000 people, dedicated a monument to Evangeline near her so-called burial site, Longfellow's heroine had evolved from a fictional character into a full-fledged cultural icon.

Ancestral myths, especially those like the story of Evangeline that involve legacies of oppression, can be powerful cultural unifiers. Proponents of Cajun cultural conservation have eagerly adopted Evangeline as a rallying point for ethnic pride. Commercial interests have also used Evangeline as a magnet for heritage tourism. Most important, she has served as a bridge between preindustrial Cajun culture and its 20th-century counterpart. Evangeline's bucolic image helps to remind modern Cajuns of their rural past at a time when their livelihoods increasingly depend on the oil industry and other decidedly nonpastoral pursuits. She helps to connect a region and its people to a lost homeland, while at the same time linking them to a quintessentially American literary tradition.

SUSAN DITTO
University of Mississippi

Carl A. Brasseaux, *In Search of Evangeline: Birth and Evolution of the Evangeline Myth* (1988); Susan Ditto, "Maison Olivier: The Public and Private Life of a Creole Raised Cottage in the Longfellow-Evangeline Park, St. Martinville, Louisiana," M.A. thesis, University of Southwestern Louisiana (1990); Henry Wadsworth Longfellow, *Evangeline: A Tale of Acadie* (1847); Felix Voorhies, *Acadian Reminiscences: The True Story of Evangeline* (1907).

Family Reunions

"Next week be the fourth of July and us plan a big family reunion outdoors here at my house," says Celie, the main character in Alice Walker's *The Color Purple*. On the day of the reunion family members analyze the custom this way: "'Why us always have family reunion on July 4th,' say Henrietta, mouth poke out, full of complaint. 'It so hot.' . . . 'White people busy celebrating they independence from England July 4th,' say Harpo, 'so most black folks don't have to work. Us can spend the day celebrating each other.'" Among the other attendees are two women who sip lemonade and make potato salad, noting that barbecue was a favorite food for them even while they were in Africa. The reunion day is especially joyful for the two women, who had been thought lost until their appearance at the reunion, where they are joyfully reunited with Celie and the other family members.

Southern family reunions are characteristic of extended and elaborated families, who plan the occasions around celebration, abundant good food, shared reunion responsibilities, simple recreational activities, and, above all, talk.

Although summer is the most popular season and the Fourth of July a frequent date for family reunions for both black and white southern families, family reunions can happen at any time. Some families have them annually; others have them on a schedule best described as "every so often"; and still others have them only once or twice in a generation's lifetime, depending on some member's initiative in getting the reunion organized.

Just as the date for family reunions is indefinite, there is an inexactness as to who constitutes "family" for each gathering. Some families invite only the descendants of a given couple and those descendants' spouses and children. Others invite the eldest couple's brothers and sisters and their children, plus in-laws and some of the in-laws' relatives. Some gather households that have only a vague bond of kinship — those who are "like family" because of strong friendships. There is inevitably a logic of kinship and affection to each family reunion, and such a party is hard indeed to crash.

The impetus for a family reunion, if it is not an annually scheduled event, may be a late-decade birthday party for one family member, a holiday, a wedding anniversary, or the celebration of an achievement such as paying off a home mortgage. Sometimes a family holds a reunion for a homecoming of one of its members, as happens in Eudora Welty's novel *Losing Battles*, which is a family reunion story focused around the day a son and husband return from a stay at Parchman, the Mississippi state prison.

Families often gather in someone's home, though summer picnic versions are commonly held in state or city parks. Motels, hotels, or restaurants host them, as do clubhouses or community centers, but by far the most popular settings after homes are churches. "Dinner on the grounds" in the churchyard, with an abundance of food on tablecloth-covered makeshift tables set on sawhorses, is a happy memory of family reunions for many southerners.

The occasion for catching up on relatives' news and gossip, perhaps for transacting a little family business, for settling or even stirring up family disputes, for generally getting in touch again, a family reunion in the South usually has no program. There might be an occasional game or swim or boat ride, but the main activities are conversation and eating. The time span may be overnight or even several days, but it is most frequently only over one meal.

The food might be barbecue with baked beans and coleslaw or fried fish with hush puppies, fried potatoes, and a salad. A restaurant meal might be ordered, but in a great many cases family reunion food is a large and generous potluck dinner where each participating household brings versions of its best offerings of food and drink — fried chicken, ham, meat casseroles, rice dishes, cooked garden vegetables, fresh raw vegetables, potato salad, gelatin salad, seafood salad, homemade rolls and breads, cakes, pies, cookies, jams, preserves, pickles, watermelons, iced tea, and lemonade. A time for eating, conversing, and coming together, a southern family reunion is a special occasion for reaffirming family ties.

GAYLE GRAHAM YATES
University of Minnesota

Alice Walker, *The Color Purple* (1982); Eudora Welty, *Losing Battles* (1970).

Farm Security Administration Photography

Originally known as the Resettlement Administration, the Farm Security Administration (FSA) was created by executive order in 1935. It was the brainchild of Columbia University economist

FSA photograph of Alonzo Bankston, a furnace operator in a TVA plant producing carbide for use in manufacturing synthetic rubber, Alabama, 1942 (Alfred T. Palmer, photographer, Library of Congress [LC-USE6-D-010105], Washington, D.C.)

Rexford Tugwell, who had come to Washington, D.C., in 1933 as one of Franklin Roosevelt's most influential New Deal advisers. Tugwell was appointed undersecretary of agriculture in 1934.

The FSA's mission was to alleviate rural poverty, especially that of the most destitute portion of the farm population—people displaced by mechanization, drought, and the unintended consequences of the Agricultural Adjustment Act of 1933, which had benefited large landowners but forced many small farmers, renters, and sharecroppers off the land. In the South, where a large percentage of the farm population was tenants, rural poverty was especially acute. Among the FSA's proposed solutions were rural resettlement programs, the establishment of

farm cooperatives, the construction of model suburban communities (known as greenbelt towns), and a program of modest grants and loans for the poorest of farm families.

Many viewed these programs as overly socialistic. In order to help justify the agency's agenda to Congress, Tugwell invited Roy Stryker, his former student and protégé at Columbia, to join the FSA as head of the Historical Section of the agency's Information Division. In that position, Stryker took on the task of creating a photographic file that would both give witness to the harsh realities of rural poverty in the United States and record the agency's efforts to improve the lives of the rural poor.

Forty-four individuals made more than 168,000 photographic negatives for the FSA's Photographic Unit between 1935 and 1943, when the agency was first merged into, then subsumed under, the Office of War Information. During that time, Stryker, who remained with the FSA throughout its existence, selected about 77,000 of the negatives to be made into prints for the agency's permanent file. Most of the images were the work of a core group of about 15 accomplished photographers employed by the agency for varying amounts of time. Among these were Walker Evans, Dorothea Lange, Russell Lee, Gordon Parks, Arthur Rothstein, and Marion Post Wolcott. Once printed and in the file, the photographs were available, free of charge, to any magazine, newspaper, publisher, or organization that had a use for them.

Conditions in the South, one of the

FSA photograph of Mr. Watkins planting peanuts, Coffee County, Ala., 1939 (Marion Post Wolcott, photographer, Library of Congress, [(LC-USF34-051480-D], Washington, D.C.)

nation's poorest and most rural regions, were the subject of much of the FSA's photographic work. Some of the better known examples include Marion Post Wolcott's extended series on the cotton culture of the Mississippi Delta; Arthur Rothstein's treatment of rural African American life in Gee's Bend, Ala.; Russell Lee's portrait of small-town life in east Texas; and Walker Evans's photographs of white sharecropping families in Hale County, Ala., which were later published, in collaboration with writer James Agee, as *Let Us Now Praise Famous Men* (1941).

DAVID WHARTON
University of Mississippi

Carl Fleischhauer and Beverly W. Brannan, eds., *Documenting America, 1935–1943* (1988); F. Jack Hurley, *Portrait of a De-*cade: Roy Stryker and the Development of Documentary Photography in the Thirties* (1972); Michael Lesy, *Long Time Coming: A Photographic Portrait of America, 1935–1943* (2002); Hank O'Neal, *A Vision Shared: A Classic Portrait of America and Its People, 1935–1943* (1976); Maren Stange, *Symbols of Ideal Life: Social Documentary Photography in America, 1890–1950* (1989); William Stott, *Documentary Expression and Thirties America* (1973).

Feuds and Feuding

Southern feuding shares many characteristics with feuding found elsewhere in the world. Feuding can be defined as blood revenge following an aggravated assault or homicide. The killings or attempted killings occur as revenge for perceived injustice. The terms "duty" and "honor" and the adjectives "righteous" and "legitimate" often appear in discussions of the motivation for the attacks.

A feud takes place within a political entity, which can be as large as a nation-state; it involves kin of the wounded or deceased victim; and the retaliatory attack usually leads to counterattacks. The attacks can alternate back and forth for decades, perhaps even centuries. This definition is meant to include feuds in which an unsuccessful attempt at a counterkilling leads to the killing of one or more of the revenge-seekers, as occurred on several occasions in 19th-century eastern Kentucky in the Turner-Howard feud. Mortality in this feud was one-sided, as 13 Turners died while no Howards were killed.

Southern feuding lies on a continuum between violence and dueling. Generalized feuds have been most common from southern West Virginia, across western Virginia, Kentucky, Tennessee, and Arkansas, into eastern Texas. Feuds also occurred in Arizona and Colorado. In extremely isolated areas in the 19th century, where courts and kinship groups were absent, violence—from drunken brawling to banditry to cattle rustling—occurred with extremely high frequencies. The development of revolvers and repeating rifles in the last half of the century facilitated an escalation in homicides. At the other end of the continuum lies dueling, a highly structured and rule-based activity. Duels, which were fought by gentlemen to preserve their honor, were found in the Lowland South from Virginia through the Caro-

linas, to New Orleans. Feuding and dueling are usually not found in the same region. If a duel were to occur in an area where feuding kinship groups existed, the resulting injury or possible death would start a feud.

Several different approaches or theories have been used to explain feuding in general and southern feuding in particular. Since kinship groups are involved in feuds, anthropologists have often focused on the nature of these groups. Anthropologist Keith Otterbein has argued that the presence of fraternal interest groups—localized groups of related males—produces feuds when the interests of group members and the groups themselves are threatened. Another anthropologist, Christopher Boehm, has argued that feuding prevents all-out warfare—but it has to be feuding that can be stopped by payment of compensation. Since southern feuding rarely involves compensation, some feuds from this region led to such wholesale killing that they were called "wars" (e.g., the so-called wars of Clay County, Ky.).

Historians have come to prefer the world-systems theory, an approach that argues that social change brought on by commercial expansion in the 19th century created the feuds. The Hatfield-McCoy feud is explained in this manner by Altina Waller, but not by Otis Rice or by Joe Ed Pearce. Historians with a folklore bent, such as David Hackett Fischer, look to the border region of Scotland and England for the origin of southern feuding. A culture of violence was brought from the border region to Appalachia by early settlers in the 18th century. Conditions were the same in both regions, and hence feuds persisted in both into the 20th century. Anthropologists and folklorists have also viewed feuding as "self-help," "folk justice," or "quasi-law." In regions where courts are weak, folk justice may arise from an individual exercising what he believes is his right to get even. If fraternal interest groups are present, feuds occur. If fraternal interest groups are absent, retaliatory killings occur but the scattered kinsmen of the disputants do not become involved, as described by William Montell for an area along the Tennessee-Kentucky state line.

A comparative study of Kentucky feuds by Keith Otterbein is based upon Joe Ed Pearce's detailed study of five Kentucky feuds. Similarities among the feuds include the structure of the feuding groups. The groups were large in membership, with descent traced through both sons and daughters (such a kinship group is termed an "ambi-lineage" by anthropologists). They were economically well off, they had members who held local political and judicial offices, and they had access to state governors' offices. The kinship groups were under the leadership of "clan" heads, typically vicious individuals who sought wealth and power through illegal activities such as distilling whiskey. Groups often violated the honor of members of rival kinship groups. Homicidal retaliation would occur. Homicidal encounters included ambushes (the most common type of armed combat employed), gun fights (next in frequency), house attacks, and encounter and arranged battles. Al-

though there was no set sequence of homicidal encounters, ambushes and gunfights were likely to occur early in the feud sequence, while battles and house attacks were likely to occur late in the sequence. Otterbein concludes that since Kentucky feuds took place in a market economy, the pursuit of economic and political power was often more important than the defense of honor. "Market-based" feuding seems less concerned with righting a wrong than with eliminating a rival kinship group. Otterbein views feuding as a form of violent crime.

KEITH F. OTTERBEIN
University at Buffalo

Dwight B. Billings, Kathleen M. Blee, Pam Goldman, Sharon Hardesty, and Lee Hardesty, in *The Road to Poverty: The Making of Hardship in Appalachia*, ed. Dwight B. Billings and Kathleen M. Blee (2000); Christopher Boehm, *Blood Revenge: The Anthropology of Feuding in Montegegro and Other Tribal Societies* (1984); David Hackett Fischer, *Albion's Seed: Four British Folkways in America* (1989); William L. Montell, *Killings: Folk Justice in the Upper South* (1986); Keith F. Otterbein, *American Anthropologist* (June, 2000), in *The Encyclopedia of the Martial Arts*, ed. Thomas A. Green (2001); Keith F. Otterbein, ed. *Feuding and Warfare: Selected Works of Keith F. Otterbein* (1994); John Ed Pearce, *Days of Darkness: The Feuds of Eastern Kentucky* (1994); Charles Leland Sonnichsen, *I'll Die before I'll Run: The Story of the Great Feuds of Texas* (1962); Altina Waller, *Feud: Hatfields, McCoys, and Social Change in Appalachia, 1860–1900* (1988).

Flag, Confederate

The red flag with the star-studded blue St. Andrew's cross has become in effect *the* Confederate flag. Although modern Americans often mistakenly call it the "Stars and Bars," it represents the rejection of the flag that properly bears that name.

In 1861 the Confederate States of America adopted a national flag (the Stars and Bars) that intentionally resembled the Stars and Stripes. Used also as a battle flag by Confederate military units, the Stars and Bars created confusion on battlefields throughout the South, prompting generals to design distinctive battle flags. The main army in Virginia, subsequently Robert E. Lee's Army of Northern Virginia, adopted the St. Andrew's cross pattern in the autumn of 1861. "Consecrated" by its association with the Confederate dead and with the South's most successful army, the St. Andrew's cross became the most common of the Confederacy's many battle flag patterns.

By 1862 many southerners viewed the St. Andrew's cross pattern as the proper symbol of the Confederacy's mature nationalism and wanted it to replace what critics denounced as "the detested parody of the stars and stripes." In May 1863 the Confederate Congress adopted a new national flag—called the "Stainless Banner"—that was simply the St. Andrew's cross battle flag emblazoned on a rectangular field of white. Although it never was officially the Confederacy's national flag, the St. Andrew's cross flag was the most visible and powerful symbol of the wartime South.

The Confederate generation further elevated the pattern's importance after the war, revering and using it more than the national flag patterns. In 1904 the United Confederate Veterans issued a report declaring the St. Andrew's cross to be *the* Confederate battle flag—something that it never was during the war. Confederate veterans considered the battle flag to be the flag of the soldier, not a "political flag," and believed it should be spared any lingering hostility toward the Confederacy itself. During the era between 1865 and World War II, the battle flag was used rarely outside of veterans' reunions and memorial activities, and white Americans, North and South, came to see it as a symbol of soldierly valor. Ironically, the flag's symbolic importance made it the most prominent icon of the Confederate cause for both supporters and critics.

Since World War II the Confederate battle flag has been a highly visible popular culture symbol and the source of frequent public controversies. The flag apparently entered pop culture in the hands of southern-born American servicemen and southern college students. In widely publicized incidents, servicemen in World War II and the Korean War carried the battle flag as a symbol of home and of the Confederate martial tradition. College students used it in the 1940s as southern schools competed with northern schools in intercollegiate sports. A "flag fad" that swept the nation in 1950–51 and a flood of flag trinkets during the Civil War centennial confirmed the flag's place as a pop culture symbol.

The Confederate flag—an icon of the trucking culture (William Ferris Collection, Southern Folklife Collection, Wilson Library, University of North Carolina at Chapel Hill)

Simultaneously, the battle flag became associated closely with southern political resistance to federally enforced racial integration. Some local Ku Klux Klan organizations and other white supremacists began using the battle flag in their rituals in the mid-1940s (there is no evidence that the KKK used the flag in the 1860s or in the 1910s and 1920s). Supporters of the Southern States Rights "Dixiecrat" Party—many of them college students—made the flag an informal party symbol during the 1948 presidential election. In the wake of the 1954 Brown decision, segregationists throughout the South made the battle flag a prominent symbol of their cause.

By the 1970s the St. Andrew's cross was known simply as "the Confederate flag" and had acquired diverse meanings. It was an instantly recognizable shorthand for "the South." Flying on car antennas, suspended in the back windows of pickup trucks, emblazoned on motorcycles, and decorating the front grilles of freight-hauling trucks, the flag became a totem for fiercely independent "rebels" of all types and for "rednecks" and "good old boys" as depicted in the popular 1979–84 television show The Dukes of Hazzard. Hate groups continued to use the flag as an explicit symbol of white supremacy, while Confederate heritage organizations insisted that the flag was rightfully theirs and stood only for the honor of their ancestors.

Different perceptions of the flag's meaning have provoked hundreds of controversies over government and school symbols featuring the Confederate flag and over the rights of individuals, especially students, to wear clothing bearing the flag. As the preeminent symbol of the Confederate South—so closely associated with issues of race and Constitutional principle— the St. Andrew's cross flag is likely to remain a source of controversy.

JOHN M. COSKI
*The Museum of the Confederacy
Richmond, Virginia*

Robert Bonner, *Colors and Blood: Flag Passions in the Confederate South* (2002); John M. Coski, in *Confederate Symbols in the Contemporary South*, ed. J. Michael Martinez et al. (1999), *North & South* (September 2001), *Southern Cultures* (Winter 1996); Chris Springer, *History Today* (June 1993).

Gardner, Dave

(1926–1983) ENTERTAINER.
Gardner, stand-up entertainer, comedy recording star, and shrewd observer of southern manners in the 1950s and 1960s, was born in Jackson, Tenn., on 11 June 1926. Christened David Milburn Gardner, he grew up in and near Jackson, where he attended junior high school—the last he would see of school until his brief enrollment in a Baptist college. His brother, Kent, recalls that "Dave was always a quiet kid, rather puny, and never much of an outgoing person. His comedy did not show up until he was in his twenties, and then it evolved as an off-the-top-of-his-head thing. He never had writers."

In fact, Gardner, who was playing the drums professionally when he was 13, began his career in the late 1940s as a drummer and singer. Then he struck out on his own as a comedian. It was 1957 before opportunity knocked, and he made the first of a number of appearances on NBC's *Tonight Show*, then hosted by Jack Paar. Almost overnight "Brother Dave," as he liked to be called, found himself with a national following; but nowhere was he more warmly received than on the college campuses of the South, where, cigarette in one hand, microphone in the other, he ad-libbed his way through performances.

Brother Dave's routines were a crazy mixture of one-liners, stories that enabled him to make use of his amazing ear for regional speech, jive talk, and sly profundity. He picked no particular target but poked fun at them all: black civil rights leaders, bikers, good old boys, preachers, presidents. "Dear hearts," he would say in the midst of the protests of the 1960s, "I'm for the minorities—the Armed Forces and the Po-leece." Though he was accused by some of racism, he may have been closer to the truth when he told one interviewer toward the end of his life, "I was left when the world was right."

At the peak of his success he made several comedy albums for RCA and later for Capitol. His popularity faded in the social and political turmoil of the Vietnam years, but after a writer for the Atlanta *Constitution* found him living in obscurity in Dallas in 1981 and wrote a Sunday magazine article about him, Gardner made a comeback in Atlanta. While doing a film in 1983, he suffered a heart attack and died in Myrtle Beach, S.C.

CHARLES EAST
Baton Rouge, Louisiana

Larry L. King, *Harper's* (September 1970); Robert Lamb, *Atlanta Weekly* (22 November 1981).

Good Old Boys and Girls

The terms "good old boy" and "good old girl" are of southern origin and describe social types, that is, persons with particular social characteristics that make them identifiable to others. Although similar social types can be found in other regions of the United States, the southern label may make them more obvious in the South.

The good old boy and girl have been pictured most frequently in popular literature. Perhaps the first reference to the social type appears in William Byrd's *Histories of the Dividing Line*

Betwixt Virginia and North Carolina (1728). W. J. Cash discussed the type in *The Mind of the South* (1941), but the first writer to use the term itself was Tom Wolfe, in an essay on stock car racing hero Junior Johnson (*Esquire*, October 1967). William Price Fox, in *Southern Fried* (1962), presented several portraits of the type, including the legendary Georgia politician Eugene Talmadge. Willie Morris's *Good Old Boy: A Delta Boyhood* (1971) was autobiographical, and Paul Hemphill in *The Good Old Boys* (1974) wrote lovingly of them, mainly because his father was one. Florence King's *Southern Ladies and Gentlemen* (1975) saw the good old boy as mean and nasty. Sharon McKern's *Redneck Mothers, Good Old Girls, and Other Southern Belles* (1979) was one of the first literary applications of the concept to women. In *Crackers* (1980), Roy Blount Jr. suggests that "'Good old boy' means pretty much the same as 'mensch.'"

The good old boy frequently appears in such country music songs as "Bar Room Buddies," "If You've Got the Money, I've Got the Time," and "Dang Me," and the term itself was used in Ansley Fleetwood's "Just Good Ol' Boys" (1979). Sometimes the term is used synonymously with "cowboy" in country music. Burt Reynolds embodied the good old boy in a series of movies in the 1970s.

The good old boy is described as blue collar, an outdoorsman, a patriot, something of a populist, basically conservative—a "man's man." He is also somewhat self-centered and scheming, particularly toward out-groups. Yet to his in-group he is an affable comrade and a man of integrity. Billy Carter, the brother of President Jimmy Carter and himself the essence of the type, defined the good old boy as someone who rides around in a pickup truck, drinking beer and putting his empties in a sack. A redneck, by contrast, rides around in a pickup, drinking and tossing his empties out the window. The "redneck" as a concept describes a more menacing figure.

The good old girl has not been studied as systematically as the good old boy. She has traits of bluffness, camaraderie, and loyalty, which make her more comfortable with men than with other women. She is usually not seen as a sex object and, in fact, is somewhat asexual in social interaction. She is likely to possess the same affability and integrity as the good old boy and the same ability to manipulate people.

INGRAM PARMLEY
Francis Marion College

Gail Gilchrist, *Bubbas and Beaus: From Good Old Boys to Southern Gentlemen, a Close Look at the Customs, Cuisine, and Culture of Southern Men* (1995); Ingram Parmley, in *Perspectives on the American South*, vol. 1, ed. Merle Black and John Shelton Reed (1981); John Shelton Reed, *Southern Folk, Plain and Fancy: Native White Social Types* (1986); Edgar T. Thompson, *South Atlantic Quarterly* (Autumn 1984).

Graceland

Graceland, formerly the estate of an aristocratic Memphis, Tenn., family, became the home of the rock and country music icon Elvis Presley from 1957 until his death in 1977. Graceland has since ceased to be a private residence and now enshrines the memory and meaning of Elvis. Located off Highway 51, about eight miles from downtown Memphis, Elvis's former home has become a favored destination for thousands of tourists every year. The largest single gathering takes place on 18 August, the anniversary of Elvis's death. Thousands of the curious, the contemptuous, and the utterly worshipful make a pilgrimage that involves tours of the home, candlelight vigils, and a slow procession by the grave of "the King" of rock and roll.

Elvis purchased the estate for himself and his parents, Vernon and Gladys Presley. Frequent renovations completely transformed the colonial-style estate: the first was an enlarged bedroom and living area for his mother and the second a soda fountain, "a real soda fountain with cokes and an ice cream thing," added to the kitchen.

Ironically, Elvis purchased Graceland to find relief from the constant attention of his persistent fans. The mansion sits on grounds of a little more than 13 acres, with a lush, forested park stretching from the front door down to the iron gates and stone wall that surrounds the property. Graceland, however, became closely identified with its owner in large part because fans, and Elvis himself, worked to prevent the home from being a truly "private" residence. The large stone wall offered devoted fans the opportunity to mark, stencil, and chalk their love for Graceland's owner. Presley himself seemed to invite such attention, at one point

stringing bright blue Christmas lights from Highway 51 all the way up to the mansion's front steps. He also made it a practice to leap the wall dramatically and sign autographs at least once a day. During Elvis's frequent absences, the gates opened between 8:00 A.M. and 5:00 P.M., and fans were allowed to walk the grounds and even look in the windows.

Elvis, and his heirs, emphasized the rural past of Graceland, hoping to play on both Presley's southern roots and the "cowboy" imagery he dearly loved. Elvis himself attempted to build on this mythic image in 1967 when he purchased over 160 acres south of Memphis off Highway 51. Purchasing innumerable pickup trucks, horses, and cattle, as well a trailer for himself and his wife, Priscilla, he named the spread the Flying G Ranch (the "G" maintaining the connection to Graceland).

Following Elvis's death, Graceland underwent extensive renovations in 1980–81 under the guidance of Priscilla Presley. A restaurant and hotel complex now sits across the highway from the mansion, boasting an enormous gift shop containing Elvis memorabilia of every description. Today, a bus carries visitors from the hotel/restaurant complex through the front gates and up to the very steps of the mansion, much as lucky fans that crowded outside the gates in the 1950s and 1960s would occasionally be taken in a large hot-pink jeep to the house to have dinner with Elvis and his family and friends.

W. SCOTT POOLE
College of Charleston

Peter Guralnick, *Careless Love: The Unmaking of Elvis Presley* (1998), *Last Train to Memphis: The Rise of Elvis Presley* (1994); Karal Anne Marling, *Graceland: Going Home with Elvis* (1996).

Holidays

Sunday has been the most frequently commemorated holiday in the South. Originally kept with some solemnity, it has now become largely a celebration of the cessation of work, although it is still a *dies non* in law. Once there was also a weekly half holiday, usually on Wednesday or Thursday, but a tendency to slacken work on Saturday has recently appeared. Banks have generally transferred most of their holidays to a Monday.

The only total holiday is Christmas and perhaps the day following. New Year's Day shares in some of the Christmas festivities, but it has become mainly an occasion for viewing football bowl games. The popular meaning of Memorial Day is that it is the beginning of summer and vacation season. Early in the 20th century the South observed it as a memorial to veterans of the Spanish-American War. In many southern states 26 April is the special Confederate Memorial Day; in others it is 3 June; still others combine it with the national Memorial Day. For a long time, the Fourth of July Independence Day was observed by southern blacks, but whites mainly viewed it as a nonworking day or picnic day. The 1976 bicentennial commemoration revived its significance, and it has grown in popularity. Labor Day used to be marked by a parade and baseball game, but now it generally marks the end of summer and vacation time. Thanksgiving in the South never had quite the importance it held outside the region. It is a time of hunting and feasting, and also the date for special football games.

The preceding holidays are of primary regional importance, but southerners, like other Americans, celebrate a variety of additional special occasions as well. St. Valentine's Day (14 February) is an occasion promoted by gift and stationery shops. The George Washington observance, also in February, is a bank and post office holiday. Mardi Gras (Shrove Tuesday) is a major festival in New Orleans, Mobile, and Pensacola, the culmination of a season of Carnival preceding Lent. St. Patrick's Day (17 March) has grown from an ethnic Irish commemoration to a more extensive observance, once again promoted by gift and stationery shops. Easter Sunday is a high religious festival but, being a Sunday, is somewhat less commercialized than the season-long Christmas. The Jewish holidays of Rosh Hashanah, Yom Kippur, and Hanukkah are quietly recognized by the news media and stationery shops. Halloween (31 October), especially the night, is a party festival and a time of pranks by children and some adults.

A third group of holidays includes those that are, as yet, only minor days to be noted. The birthdays of Robert E. Lee (21 January), "Stonewall" Jackson (22 January), and Matthew Fontaine Maury (24 January) are observed by organizations of descendants of Confederate veterans. Groundhog Day (2 February) is noted by news media and schools. St. Joseph Day (19 March) attracts major attention in New Orleans and some other Roman Catholic communities, and Good Friday is a legal holiday in Louisiana. May Day evokes some school attention. Flag Day (14 June) is a legal holiday. The days of St. John (the baptizer, 24 June, and the evangelist, 27 December) are occasions for observance by Masonic lodges (picnics in summer, banquets in winter). There is a sentimental Francophile notice of Bastille Day (14 July) and a school recognition of Columbus Day. All Saints' Day (1 November) is a legal holiday in Louisiana. In nearby states it is an occasion for decorating cemeteries, although the latter practice belongs more aptly to the following day, All Souls' Day. Armistice Day (11 November) used to be a widespread observance, but under the designation of Veterans' Day it has become a day noted by veterans' organizations of all wars from World War II onward.

Four holidays—Christmas, New Year's, the Fourth of July, and Thanksgiving—are times when most institutions of a community are closed. Memorial Day and Labor Day are also nonworkdays for many; they serve to signal the opening and closing respectively of resort areas and vacation spots. Other holidays attract less attention (except for Easter), but they are nonetheless generally commemorated. The Jewish high holy days have gradually become more significant, especially because of the prominence of Jewish merchants and Jewish academics, many of whom celebrate Rosh Hashanah and Yom Kippur.

Among African Americans there used to be extensive, if informal, commemoration of Emancipation Day (variously 8 May, 19 June, and perhaps others); businesses did not close, but blacks frequently did not report for work. African Americans in Texas celebrated the distinctive Juneteenth holiday. More recently Emancipation Day has been pushed into the background by the civil rights movement of the 1960s and, for some people, disillusionment with the progress blacks have been able to achieve even in the wake of that movement. Begun in 1966, Kwanzaa (26 December–1 January) gained tremendous popularity in the 1990s as a time for celebrating African American people, their ancestors, and their culture. In 1983 the late Martin Luther King Jr.'s birthday (15 January) won approval as a federal holiday.

ALLEN CABANISS
University of Mississippi

Hennig Cohen and Tristram P. Coffin, eds., *The Folklore of American Holidays* (1987); Jane M. Hatch, *The American Book of Days* (3d ed., 1978); Robert Lee, *National Forum* (Summer 1982); Robert J. Myers, *Celebrations: The Complete Book of American Holidays* (1972); William E. Woodward, *The Way Our People Lived: An Intimate American History* (1944).

Hospitality

In the popular imagination, "southern hospitality" signifies both graciousness and excess: the barbecue at Twelve Oaks, mouth-wateringly depicted in *Gone with the Wind*, the kindness of strangers at Mardi Gras, the second and third helpings of pound cake and iced tea pressed on a guest, the quick and apparently easy intimacy with visitors. The South of benign myth is a sort of Eden, where people are as warm as the weather and good manners paper over poverty, ignorance, and racism.

Of course, hospitality in the South is also genuine; indeed, it can be a social imperative. In the 17th and 18th centuries, as Bertram Wyatt-Brown points out, planters were "obliged to share good fortune with less well-fixed kinfolk or be severely criticized for Yankeefied tightfistedness." Poor widows would sometimes "visit" better-off relatives for a year or more. Outsiders—if they had the right connections—could be treated with great munificence. The English writer Harriet Martineau was impressed with planter hospitality, even though she was an abolitionist. The elite represented themselves as unfailingly generous. In Caroline Gilinan's 1838 novel *Recollections of a Southern Matron*, Cornelia Wilton, the lady of the Big House, says, "I was early taught to lay fresh roses on the pillows of strangers."

The proslavery novels published in response to *Uncle Tom's Cabin* stress the Christian largesse of planters who would give food and shelter to anyone, high or low, and treated their "servants" like their own children. To some extent, the South's self-generated legend of hospitality was developed to counter the negative images of mistreated slaves, lynchings, and later Bull Connor's thugs beating civil rights demonstrators with truncheons.

Historical accounts reveal an ambiguous story. While the tiny number of very rich planters, with their double parlors and Limoges china, entertained handsomely—since hospitality and honor were intertwined—they reserved the right to withhold graciousness. Frederick Law Olmstead in *The Cotton Kingdom* (1861) reports that he usually had to pay 75 cents or a dollar for a night's "southern hospitality." In *The Adventures of Huckleberry Finn*, the extent of aristocratic hospitality depends on the conduct of a feud. When Huck opens the door of the Graingerford house, "three big men" point guns at him. When they find that he is not a member of the hated Shepherdson clan, he's smothered with attention: "Get him something to eat, quick as you can, poor thing; and one of you girls go wake up Buck and tell him— Oh here he is himself. Buck take this little stranger and get the wet clothes off from him and dress him up in some of yours that's dry." Politicians were an exception. Thomas Jefferson felt honor-bound to host every considerable person who came near Monticello. In 1864, when most Confederate soldiers were going hungry, Mrs. Jefferson Davis felt it her duty to keep up appearances, holding a luncheon at which, according to Mary Chesnut, she served "Gumbo, ducks and olives, *supreme de volaille*, chickens in jelly, oysters, lettuce salad, chocolate jelly cake, claret soup, champagne, etc. etc." Candidates for political office still hold fish fries and pig roasts to court voters.

Hospitality among working-class whites and blacks of necessity took a different form. Much "entertaining" was done via the church, with dinners on the grounds and socials. Hospitality was also less formal and more direct, a way to connect with kinfolk or underline other kinds of connections. In Ralph Ellison's *Invisible Man*, a cold and lonely Alabama boy in Harlem is glad to be fed soup by Mary, a fellow southern diasporist. Hospitality could also be a subset of *caritas*. In *Light in August*, Mr. and Mrs. Armstid are torn between the moral imperatives of upholding the tough strictures of backwoods Protestantism and helping a creature in need, as they discuss taking in the obviously pregnant, obviously unmarried Lena Grove. Armstid says, "What do you want me to do about it? Turn her out? Let her sleep in the barn maybe?" And his wife answers, "You durn men."

Hospitality remains a point of pride among southerners, black, white, and (increasingly) Latino, all convinced the South dispenses more of it than any other region of the country. Statistically, this is probably unprovable. And what southerners see as the special charm and generosity of the land below Mr. Mason's and Mr. Dixon's magical line may in fact be more a characteristic of a not-quite-post-rural society. The same friendliness, the same high-fat-and-sugar-content foods, the same desire to find a connection (geographical, familial, denominational) with a stranger are arguably present in much of the Midwest and the nonurban West as well.

However, hospitality developed a better-articulated vocabulary in the South than in other regions. The success of *Southern Living* magazine, which was selling "lifestyle" years before Martha Stewart waxed her first camellia, testifies to the near obsession with "proper" entertaining shared by the middle classes across the color line in the South. *Southern Living* started life as a "home column" in *Progressive Farmer*. In 1966 it became a magazine—indeed, by 1980, the most profitable magazine in the United States. It provides menus for a Kentucky Derby brunch, an Alabama versus Tennessee game tailgate party, a bridesmaids' luncheon, or a Twelfth Night dinner. It teaches how to make your own crystallized violets, a kumquat centerpiece (for Christmas), or a Lowcountry boil from an old South Carolina plantation cookbook. Hospitality as redefined by the magisterial *Southern Living* is simultaneously heritage-based and aspirational (even the descendants of slaves can participate). The once class-specific high-end "southern hospitality" has been democratized, its snobbery inverted. It's now okay to buy old silver plate and use it for parties tarnished—as if it has been in your family forever but you just don't have time to polish it and make the shrimp remoulade for your guests, too.

Hospitality in the South remains a genuine feature of regional friendliness; it is also a function of the desire to present the South—where the populace is accustomed to being represented as stupid, backward, poor, prejudiced, and degenerate—as a place full of tremendously nice people who'd gladly give you their last piece of Jimmy Dean sausage. In John Berendt's *Midnight in the Garden of Good and Evil*, Jim Williams insists on throwing the annual Christmas fête in his mansion. He has it catered by Lucille Wright, Savannah's most fashionable chef, who lays out a spread of ham, turkey, beef, shrimp, oysters, cakes, brownies, and pies. The fact that Williams has been charged with murder and will soon go on trial is irrelevant to the guests. A good party is a good party.

DIANE ROBERTS
University of Alabama

Diane Roberts, in *Dixie Debates: Perspectives on Southern Cultures* (1996); Joe Gray Taylor, *Eating, Drinking, and Visiting in the South* (1982); Bertram Wyatt-Brown, *Southern Honor: Ethics and Behavior in the Old South* (1982).

Jim Crow

As a term used to describe African Americans, "Jim Crow" probably originated in 19th-century minstrelsy. It has also been suggested that the term referred to a slave trader or an escaped slave, but the most generally accepted explanation credits a white minstrel entertainer, Thomas "Daddy" Rice, with popularizing the term. He performed a song-and-dance routine called "Jump Jim Crow" beginning in 1828. With face blackened from burnt cork and dressed in the rags of a beggar, Rice skipped on stage, doing a shuffling dance, comically singing "I jump jis' so / An' ev'y time I turn about I jump Jim Crow." He cited an old Louisville slave belonging to a Mr. Crow as the inspiration for the act, having observed him entertain other workers in a livery stable. By the late 1830s Rice had made "Jim Crow" a part of his promotional

name. He helped to put the blackface character into American entertainment and introduced a term to the language.

The story of the term "Jim Crow" is apparently more complicated than this traditional explanation of its origins. "Jim Crow" was probably first used outside of minstrelsy to describe segregated facilities in the North. Mitford M. Mathews in *A Dictionary of Americanisms* (1951) cites a reference to a separate railroad car for blacks in Massachusetts in 1841 and also notes an 1842 item from *The Liberator* referring to the "negro pew" and the "Jim Crow car." Leon Litwack in *North of Slavery* (1961) used the term to describe segregated facilities in the pre–Civil War North.

In the late 19th century the term "Jim Crow" took on a new meaning, symbolizing the southern system of legal segregation that emerged after the Civil War. "Jim Crow law" first appeared in the *Dictionary of American English* in 1904, but laws requiring racial segregation had appeared briefly in the South during Reconstruction. They had generally disappeared by 1868, although the persistent custom of segregation did not disappear. Tennessee passed a Jim Crow statute in 1875, and increasingly in the following years blacks and whites were segregated throughout the South on trains, streetcars, and steamboats, and in port facilities. In the mid-1880s African Americans were barred from white hotels, restaurants, barber and beauty shops, and theaters. By 1885 most states in the South legally mandated segregated schools. The state constitutional

Drinking fountain on the county courthouse lawn, Halifax, N.C., 1938
(John Vachon, photographer, Library of Congress [LC-USZ62-100414 DLC], Washington, D.C.)

reforms in Mississippi in 1890 and South Carolina in 1895 codified segregation laws, and reforms in other southern states soon followed. In 1896 the U.S. Supreme Court upheld the Jim Crow "separate but equal" principle in *Plessy v. Ferguson.*

These Jim Crow segregation laws were, according to historian C. Vann Woodward, "the public symbols and constant reminders" of the African American's inferior position in the South. "That code lent the sanction of law to a racial ostracism that extended to churches and schools, to housing and jobs, to eating and drinking," concluded Woodward. It separated the races in sport and recreational activities, on all forms of public transportation, and in prisons, asylums, orphanages, hospitals, and even funeral homes and cemeteries. The term "Jim Crow" came to stand for racial segregation and was physically embodied in separate water fountains, eating places, bathrooms, Bibles in courtrooms, and pervasive signs stating "Colored" and "White" that gave the term a concrete meaning for southerners.

CHARLES REAGAN WILSON
University of Mississippi

Elizabeth Grace Hale, *Making Whiteness: The Culture of Segregation in the South, 1890–1940* (1998); Robert C. Toll, *Blacking Up: The Minstrel Show In Nineteenth-Century America* (1974); William L. Van

DeBurg, *Slavery and Race in Popular Culture* (1984); C. Vann Woodward, *The Strange Career of Jim Crow* (1955; 3d rev. ed., 1974).

Juneteenth

Juneteenth is the popular name among black people in Texas for their emancipation day, which they celebrate on 19 June. On that day in 1865 Major General Gordon Granger officially announced the freedom of slaves when he arrived at Galveston to command the District of Texas following the Civil War.

Three black folktales provide other explanations of the date. In one version Texas landowners refused to announce emancipation until the 1865 harvest had been gathered by the slaves. According to a second story, a black man journeyed by mule from Washington to Texas and arrived in June 1865 with word of the abolition of slavery. The other legend has the end of slavery declared as late as June because an earlier messenger was killed on the way to Texas.

The celebration of 19 June as emancipation day spread to the neighboring states of Louisiana, Arkansas, and Oklahoma, and later to California as black Texans migrated west. It has appeared occasionally in Alabama and Florida, also as a result of migration. It became an official state holiday in Texas in 1980, and the holiday's popularity spread nationwide after a 1991 Smithsonian Institution exhibition featured the day's significance.

Large celebrations began in 1866 and continued to be held regularly into the early 20th century, although blacks in some Texas towns honored emancipation on 1 January or 4 July—days favored in some other states. Observations of Juneteenth declined during World War II but revived with 70,000 black people on the Texas State Fair grounds at Dallas in 1950. As school desegregation and the civil rights movement focused attention on the expansion of freedom in the late 1950s and early 1960s, Juneteenth celebrations declined again, although small towns still observed Texas's emancipation day. In the 1970s Juneteenth was revived in some communities, especially after two black members convinced the Texas legislature to declare Juneteenth an unofficial "holiday of significance . . . particularly to the blacks of Texas."

Typical celebrations over the years included parades, picnics, baseball games or other competitive contests, speeches on freedom and future goals, and dances. Leaders in the black community normally organized the events, although occasionally in the 20th century a business or a black fraternal group assumed that role. Today, 15 states, from Alaska to Florida, officially recognize Juneteenth. In Georgiana, Ala., for example, the Alabama New South coalition sponsors Juneteenth, which includes step teams, drill teams, gospel music, and a question-and-answer session on African American history. Events celebrating Juneteenth often are localized into community events, as in the North Memphis neighborhood of Douglas, which has honored the day every year since 1993.

The community has used the day to recognize the black church, the Underground Railroad, African American farmers, and black educators.

ALWYN BARR
Texas Tech University

Ebony (June 1951); Wendy Watriss, *Southern Exposure* (No. 1, 1977); William H. Wiggins Jr., "'Free at Last!': A Study of Afro-American Emancipation Day Celebrations," (Ph.D. dissertation, Indiana University, 1974); www.juneteenth.com.

Lost Cause Myth

"The Lost Cause" commonly refers to white southerners' memory of the Civil War and the rituals that they created to perpetuate that memory. Memorialization began shortly after Appomattox. Many local communities established Confederate cemeteries and celebrated an annual Confederate Memorial Day; a few erected statues, most often in graveyards. The spirit of mourning gave way to one of celebration in the 1880s and 1890s. In 1889 a regionwide association of veterans, the United Confederate Veterans, was formed and, between 1890 and 1932, it held annual reunions that drew huge crowds. In 1894 the United Daughters of the Confederacy (UDC) was founded, initially bringing together women who had lived through the war with relatives and descendants of Confederate soldiers; two years later the Sons of Confederate Veterans (SCV) was organized. As the veterans themselves aged, leadership of the Lost Cause passed to the women of the UDC. They sponsored the Children of the Confederacy, lobbied for pro-Confederate textbooks in the schools, and erected Confederate monuments. Between 1890 and 1912 the UDC and other groups put up Confederate monuments in many southern towns. Placed on a courthouse lawn or a busy city street, most featured a common soldier atop a column, but some honored specific Confederate leaders.

At the heart of this turn-of-the-century celebration of the Confederacy and of the Lost Cause lay an interpretation of the white South's role in the Civil War. That interpretation championed the legality of secession and the centrality of constitutional issues, not slavery, to the coming of the war. It attributed the South's defeat not to failings by its soldiers or disunity within the Confederacy, but to the overwhelming numbers and resources of the North. Defeat therefore became the inevitable result of northern power, not a judgment on the South. God allowed it, white southerners believed, only to prepare the South for an eventual triumph through a vindication of its principles. In addition, the Lost Cause celebrated the heroism of the Confederate soldier and his deference to leaders and loyalty to society. It praised, too, the unquestioning wartime support of white women and blacks. Some white females countered that Confederate women offered a model of female activism, and African Americans contested the myth of the Lost Cause with their own historical tradition, one that celebrated the contributions of blacks to Union victory and the emancipationist

Confederate battle flags draping the Mississippi capitol, 1930s
(Eudora Welty, photographer, Mississippi Department of Archives and History, Jackson)

legacy of the war. But the myth of the Lost Cause became the dominant public presentation of the past in the New South.

Historians have disagreed on its social functions. A few have found in it a critique of modern society, others a sacralization of the South that resulted in a distinctive southern perspective on life, and still others a means to perpetuate the dominance of a white male elite and a culture of white supremacy. Historians also disagree on how long the Lost Cause remained influential. Some emphasize that it served to heal the wounds of the war and ease the tensions of late 19th-century change and claim its influence waned dramatically after World War I. Others argue it remained important throughout the 20th century. They point to, among other things, the use of Lost Cause symbolism by segregationists in the 1950s and 1960s. At the beginning of the 21st century, though, Lost Cause rituals certainly do not play an important role in southern society. But the UDC and SCV, though small, remain active, and some white southerners still cling to the myth of the Lost Cause.

GAINES M. FOSTER
Louisiana State University

David W. Blight, *Race and Reunion: The Civil War in American Memory* (2001); Karen L. Cox, *Dixie's Daughters: The United Daughters of the Confederacy and the Preservation of Confederate Culture* (2003); Gaines M. Foster, *Ghosts of the Confederacy: Defeat, the Lost Cause, and the Emergence of the New South, 1865–1913* (1987); Gary W. Gallagher and Alan T. Nolan, *The Myth of the Lost Cause and Civil War History* (2000); Grace Elizabeth Hale, *Making Whiteness: The Culture of Segregation in the South, 1890–1940* (1998); Rebecca Montgomery, in *Negotiating Boundaries of Southern Womanhood: Dealing with the Powers That Be*, ed. Janet L. Coryell et al. (2000); Richard M. Weaver, *The Southern Tradition at Bay: A History of Postbellum Thought* (1968); Charles Reagan Wilson, *Baptized in Blood: The Religion of the Lost Cause, 1865–1920* (1980).

L. Q. C. Lamar Society

Founded in 1969 outside Durham, N.C., the Lamar Society brought together middle- and upper-middle-class professionals to share information and ideas about the future of the South. The group named itself after L. Q. C. Lamar, an ardent Mississippi secessionist in the 1860s who became a champion of conciliation after the Civil War.

From the states of the old Confederacy plus Kentucky the Lamar Society accepted members who shared the vision of a South that preserves its regional distinctiveness while overcoming its perennial problems of racism and poverty. The members were particularly concerned with how the South and its way of life would fare in a rapidly growing technological and industrial society. They hoped to point the way for the South to avoid some of the problems that plagued the North after rapid urbanization, such as decay of the cities, destruction of the land, and a government removed from the people.

While the Lamar Society has been compared with the Nashville Agrarians of the 1930s because of the similar structure of the two groups and because each offered a vision of a future South, the agendas of the two are very different. H. Brandt Ayers, one of the Lamar Society's founders, wrote that although this comparison would inevitably be made, the Lamar Society would provide "a new definition of the South, by a new generation of southerners, just as deeply devoted to their region as the Agrarians but more democratic and realistic." The Agrarians felt that the traditional southern culture they applauded was threatened by a modernizing, urbanizing society and called for a return to the values of the agrarian, preindustrial South. The Lamar Society, on the other hand, sought to stress the advantage of a modernizing South in alleviating poverty and overcoming backwardness. Rather than attempting to retard urbanization, the members of the group called for new ideas to help southern leaders create a "humane urban civilization." This concept involved retaining what the members saw as the best of traditional small-town southern life and incorporating these characteristics (such as responsive, direct-participation government) into new cities.

In 1972 the Lamar Society published a volume of essays called *You Can't Eat Magnolias*, which presented their vision of the South in much the same way as did the Agrarians' *I'll Take My Stand* (1930). During the 1970s the society issued the *Southern Journal*, which served as a forum for the ideas of its members. Inspired by the activities of the Lamar Society, the Southern Growth Policies Board was formed in late 1971 to coordinate regional growth strategies, and the Lamar Society eventually merged into that institution. Society members gathered for reunions in the mid-1990s in North Carolina and in 2004 at the University of Mississippi, whose Endowment for the Future of the South works to extend the Lamar Society's progressive legacy.

KAREN M. MCDEARMAN
University of Mississippi

H. Brandt Ayers and Thomas H. Naylor, eds., *You Can't Eat Magnolias* (1972); Stephen A. Smith, *Myth, Media, and the Southern Mind* (1985).

"Mammy"

The "mammy" character is a stereotype derived from history and popular culture. She is a black, middle-aged woman who has a strong, loud voice and wears an apron and a kerchief on her head. Her ample body and open, honest expression reveal that she is maternal and reliable. She is the southern archetype of the earth mother.

Mrs. Wilson's Nurse and Fat Baby, photographer unknown, late 19th century (Everhard Collection, Amon Carter Museum, Fort Worth, Tex.)

Donald Bogle, who has classified the dominant images of blacks in film, said that the mammy figure is a "de-sexed, overweight, dowdy, dark black woman." Mammy is Aunt Jemima, an icon that recurs often enough to be easily recognized.

The mammy character recurs in fiction. She is William Faulkner's Dilsey in *The Sound and the Fury*, Carson McCullers's Berenice in *The Member of the Wedding*, Fanny Hurst's Delilah in *Imitation of Life*, and Margaret Mitchell's Mammy in *Gone with the Wind*. Actresses who played her in films have become icons of the mammy figure. Ethel Waters, Louise Beavers, and Hattie McDaniel are familiar "mammies" who have even become folk heroines.

Mammy as a character is the quintessence of strength, constancy, and integrity. She is not only capable, generous, and kind but also very religious, long-suffering, and sometimes scolding. A Christian oracle of wisdom, she passes her knowledge on to white characters whose lives are thereby enriched. She is the all-loving, loyal mainstay to a white family, giving all of herself to the family in this life and asking for nothing in return but heavenly reward.

Mammy is a dominant antebellum black image, personifying the spirit of endurance during the hard times of slavery. Under slavery, white families relied on black slaves to raise their children, nurse their sick, and cook and clean for them. The mammy character is historically derived from the house slave who was the personal servant of the white plantation owners. It was not unusual for the personal slaves of the master and mistress to sleep in the same bedroom with them to be on call should their service be needed during the night. Although they were better fed and dressed than the field slaves, the house slaves were treated as nonpersons. After emancipation, black women were still treated as mammy figures. The mammy image passed from southern plantation slaves to day workers and domestic maids, and thus from the South to the North.

VICTORIA O'DONNELL
North Texas State University

Donald Bogle, *Toms, Coons, Mulattoes, Mammies, and Bucks: An Interpretive History of Blacks in American Films* (1973); Kenneth W. Goings, *Mammy and Uncle Mose: Black Collectibles and American*

Stereotyping (1994); Carol Hymowitz and Michaele Weissman, *A History of Women in America* (1978); M. M. Manring, *Slave in a Box: The Strange Career of Aunt Jemima* (1998); Victoria O'Donnell, in *The South and Film*, ed. Warren French (1981).

Mencken's South

H. L. Mencken of Baltimore was known in the 1920s as the archenemy of the American South, but in fact Mencken's view of the South was more complex than most of his detractors realized. He was best known for his diatribes against Dixie in such essays as "The Sahara of the Bozart" (1920), in which he claimed that the South was a cultural and intellectual desert, a land run by poor whites, a colossal paradise of the fourth-rate. But if H. L. Mencken was the graphic realist in cataloging the numerous flaws of southern life in the early 20th century, he was also the most romantic of writers when he envisioned an earlier South. In many of the same essays in which he damned those states below the Potomac and Ohio, he also contended that, up until the Civil War, the South had been the American seat of civilization, a cultivated land "with men of delicate fancy, urbane instinct and aristocratic manner—in brief, superior men." In the antebellum South "some attention was given to the art of living. . . . A certain noble spaciousness was in the ancient southern scheme of things."

What Mencken had in mind when he spoke of an earlier cultivated South was, largely, Virginia of the 18th and early 19th centuries—and even in Virginia the spirit of free inquiry that

Mencken prized had begun to decline long before the beginning of the Civil War. But, by his reasoning, the war itself was responsible for the complete "drying up" of southern civilization. After Appomattox, he contended, the aristocrats vanished—died, fled North, or lived out their days in obscurity—and the worthless, depraved poor whites seized control and dominated every aspect of southern life. Fanatical preachers, corrupt politicians, and nostalgic poetasters made the South the laughingstock of the nation. Such was H. L. Mencken's view of southern history, a view which, although not quite historically accurate, was widely circulated in the 1920s and 1930s. The antebellum South, in truth, was never so civilized—nor the postbellum South so barbaric—as the South of H. L. Mencken's imagination.

FRED HOBSON
University of North Carolina at Chapel Hill

Fred Hobson, *Serpent in Eden: H. L. Mencken and the South* (1974); H. L. Mencken, *Prejudices, Second Series* (1920), *Virginia Quarterly Review* (January 1935); Terry Teachout, *The Skeptic: A Life of H. L. Mencken* (2002).

Mitchell, Margaret

(1900–1949) WRITER.
Born 8 November 1900 in Atlanta, Margaret Mitchell was as proud of her long-established Atlanta family as she was of *Gone with the Wind*. She wrote in 1941: "I know of few other Atlanta people who can claim that their families have been associated as long and intimately, and sometimes prominently, with the birth and growth and history of this city."

Mitchell was educated in Atlanta schools and at Smith College. After her mother died in the flu epidemic of 1919, Mitchell returned from Smith to Atlanta to keep house for her father and her brother. She made her debut in 1920 and in 1922 married Berrien Kinnard Upshaw. The marriage lasted barely three months.

In December 1922 Mitchell found a job on the staff of the Atlanta *Journal Sunday Magazine*. On the *Journal* she worked with such writers as Erskine Caldwell and Frances Newman. On 4 July 1925 she married John Robert Marsh, public relations officer of the Georgia Power Company, and in 1926 resigned her job because of ill health. She tried writing short stories but found no market for them, and they were eventually destroyed. Discouraged, she turned to the composition of a long novel for her own amusement during an extended recuperation.

Most of *Gone with the Wind* was completed by 1929. It was still incomplete, however, when in April of 1935 she somewhat quixotically allowed Harold Latham (on a scouting trip for the Macmillan Company) to see the manuscript. Macmillan's almost immediate acceptance was followed by months of checking for historical accuracy, filling gaps in the story, and rewriting. The book was a best-seller the day it was published, 30 June 1936, and dominated its author's life thereafter.

For the next 13 years Mitchell nursed an aging father and later an invalid husband, enthusiastically did war work, and maintained a massive amount of correspondence relating to *Gone with the Wind*. She wrote no more fiction and emerged from private life only occasionally, most notably for the premiere of the film *Gone with the Wind* in Atlanta on 15 December 1939.

Accident-prone throughout her life, she met her death in an accident on 11 August 1949. Crossing Peachtree Street with her husband, she was struck by a speeding taxicab. She died five days later and was buried in Atlanta's Oakland Cemetery.

RICHARD HARWELL
Athens, Georgia

Anne Edwards, *The Road to Tara: The Life of Margaret Mitchell* (1983); Finis Farr, *Margaret Mitchell of Atlanta: The Author of "Gone with the Wind"* (1965); Richard Harwell, ed., *Margaret Mitchell's "Gone with the Wind" Letters, 1936–1949* (1976); Darden Asbury Pyron, *Southern Daughter: The Life of Margaret Mitchell* (1991); a collection of over 50,000 items of Miss Mitchell's correspondence, reviews of *Gone with the Wind*, magazine and newspaper articles, pictures, and other memorabilia is in the Manuscript Department of the University of Georgia Libraries, Athens.

"Moonlight-and-Magnolias" Myth

As a phrase, "moonlight and magnolias" has two distinct but related meanings. It is most commonly used as a derogatory epithet for the more excessive manifestations of sentimental Cavalier-belle-plantation fiction. In this sense, it is a term of derision, as shown in Margaret Mitchell's defense of *Gone with the Wind*: "I've always been slightly amused by the New York critics who referred to GWTW as a 'moonlight and magnolia romance.' My God, they never read the gentle Confederate novel of the Nineties, or they would know better." Mitchell's statement also implicitly indicates the other less pejorative meaning of the phrase — the myth of an antebellum Golden Age, a myth created in the postbellum world of the 1880s and 1890s and a part of the larger myths of the plantation and the Lost Cause.

The conscious and recognized leader in creating this myth was Thomas Nelson Page, but he had a host of colleagues and imitators who can be found in the 17-volume *Library of Southern Literature* (1907), edited by Edwin Anderson Alderman and Joel Chandler Harris. Page's *In Ole Virginia* (1887) and *Red Rock* (1898) exhibit all the myth's elements. He fixed the past in time and held on to it. The antebellum South became the romantic "before the war," an Eden, a dream of chivalry; the Civil War became that period of heroism when the cause was lost but the South was not beaten on the battlefield; and Reconstruction was the vengeful rape by the vulgar North of the beautiful South. Though this idealized view was simplistic, its popularity with late 19th-century southerners was understandable, for in their economic and political privation they could at least remember, in Page's words, the time when "even the moonlight was richer and mellower." In both its glamour and pathos the myth also appealed to nonsoutherners and spread a nostalgic image of antebellum southern life across the nation. The anecdote of Union general Higginson's

Postcard of a romantic southern moonlight scene (Charles Reagan Wilson Collection, Center for the Study of Southern Culture, University of Mississippi)

weeping over Page's "Marse Chan," a story apostrophizing the Cavalier and belle through the words of an ex-slave, has often been noted, and rightly so, for it is a symbol of the myth's effect.

The myth has become in the contemporary era an object of parody and an advertising gimmick. By keeping all the plantation paraphernalia, but adding three new elements, it has been transformed in novels and films into a new antebellum myth of sex, sadism, and miscegenation. The present pejorative meaning derives as much from this transformation as from weaknesses inherent in the original myth and says much about changes in the way both southerners and nonsoutherners have looked at the antebellum South for the past 100 years.

EARL F. BARGAINNIER
Wesleyan College

Earl F. Bargainnier, in *Icons of America*, ed. Ray B. Browne and Marshall Fishwick (1978), *Louisiana Studies* (Spring 1976), *Southern Quarterly* (Winter 1984); Stephen Smith, *Myth, Media, and the Southern Mind* (1986).

Nationalism, Southern

Like the American nationalism of which it was an offshoot, southern nationalism attempted to define clearly the circumstances in which 19th-century southerners found themselves. The coming of peace in 1815 allowed all Americans to turn inward and examine those characteristics and institutions that set them apart from other nations. Like Americans in general, southerners were intimately involved in all phases of this quest for nationality: campaigns for economic development, encouragement of a native literature, calls for improved education, state constitutional revisions to broaden the franchise, religious revivals, and territorial expansion.

Giving each of these movements a peculiarly southern twist was a growing sense that in some fundamental way the southern states possessed shared interests that conflicted with those of the nation at large. As this perception grew and spread, increasing numbers of southerners began to agitate for a separate southern nation, which would possess all the cultural and political attributes they as Americans had long desired, but which also would protect that most vital of all southern interests, slavery. By 1860, though only a minority of southerners favored secession, the efforts of southern nationalists had won such an influential following that a southern nation took form.

The unsuccessful career of the short-lived Confederacy has persuaded many historians that southern nationalism never existed. Evidence to support that argument appears abundant. The Constitution of the Confederate States and that of the United States were virtual duplicates. The rival presidents and their governments moved along strikingly similar paths to strikingly similar policies on conscription, finance, and even battlefield strategy. After a brief and moderate Reconstruction, the South resumed full partnership in the Union. Confederate history does indeed show what southern nationalism was not. But it also convincingly shows what it was: an effort to be more fully and more purely American than other Americans, to subscribe more honorably, as southerners saw it, to the meaning of the Constitution.

By 1860 enough southerners perceived that the only way to live up to the definition of America they had been so instrumental in providing was to rebel, as their grandfathers had rebelled. "There is a habit of speaking derisively of going to war for an idea— an abstraction—something which you cannot see," wrote a southern editor in 1861. "This is precisely the point on which we would go to war. An idea is exactly the thing that we would fight for." Southern nationalism was—and is—above all else a state of mind.

JOHN MCCARDELL
Middlebury College

Avery O. Craven, *The Growth of Southern Nationalism, 1848–1861* (1953); William C. Davis, *A Government of Our Own* (1994); John McCardell, *The Idea of a Southern Nation: Southern Nationalists and Southern Nationalism, 1830–1860* (1979); David Potter, *The South and the Sectional Conflict* (1968); Eric Walther, *The Fire-Eaters* (1992).

Patriotic Societies

Southern reporter Pat Watters once wrote about "all the complex stratifications (clubs and circles and hierarchies of elitism) of high society that the South continued to take more seriously than the rest of the country." He had in mind that web of clubs of all kinds— town, country, yacht, debutante, literary, garden, bridge, luncheon and service, junior leagues and auxiliaries, ball societies, fraternities and sororities, and, not least, hereditary patriotic societies, all of them with their own pecking orders. Patriotic societies, based upon descent from an ancestor's services to colony or nation, received their greatest impetus in the Northeast during the wave of late 19th-century immigration. Nonetheless, they also had southern roots and particularly southern flavors.

The first society in the 13 colonies, named for Scotland's patron saint, was the St. Andrew's Society of Charleston, S.C., founded in 1729 and followed there in 1733 by the St. George's Society. The Society of the Cincinnati, composed of Continental army officers and their eldest male descendants, was founded 10 May 1783, with Virginian George Washington as its first president general. The Society of the War of 1812 was founded in 1814 by the defenders of Fort McHenry after the British withdrawal, and its first commander was Maryland's Revolutionary War hero Major General Samuel Smith of Baltimore, who had led the defense. In Mexico City on 13 October 1847 United States military officers organized the Aztec Club on primogenitive lines, and its first president was John A. Quitman of Mississippi, who had led the successful attack upon "the Halls of Montezuma." However, the greatest impetus to the organization of patriotic societies in the South came after the Civil War and during Reconstruction, with southern women in the lead.

One year to the day after General Joseph E. Johnston surrendered the last large Confederate field army, southern women began organizing to care for Confederate soldiers' graves, and 26 April, "the South's All Souls'

Day," became the popular Confederate Memorial Day. Ladies' Memorial Associations appeared across Dixie, with Columbus, Ga., and Columbus and Jackson, Miss., each claiming the "first." Later, as the South revived in its fortunes and as urbanization increased, came formation of the United Confederate Veterans in New Orleans in June 1889, the United Daughters of the Confederacy (UDC) in Nashville in September 1894, the Sons of Confederate Veterans in Richmond on 1 July 1896, and the Children of the Confederacy under UDC auspices in Alexandria, Va., also in 1896. Much later came the Military Order of the Stars and Bars for the male descendants of Confederate officers, in July 1938 in Columbia, S.C. Robert E. Lee's and Jefferson Davis's birthdays, 19 January and 3 June respectively, also became southern holidays.

Meanwhile, spurred by the centennial celebration of the American Revolution and in reaction to emigration from outside northern Europe, hereditary societies arose to memorialize the Revolutionary War: the Sons of the Revolution in 1883, the rival Sons of the American Revolution in 1889 (both organized in New York City), and the Daughters of the American Revolution in 1890 in Washington, D.C. Two of the three founders of the latter group were southern women. Others reached farther back in time to found the rival Societies of Colonial Dames in 1890 and 1891 and their male counterpart, the Society of Colonial Wars, in 1893. As a rule of thumb, except for the sui generis Cincinnati, the more remote the ancestor, the greater is the society's exclusiveness and prestige and the higher its members' social status. As one Alabama matron put it, "Heaven on earth in the Black Belt is to be a Kappa Delta, a Colonial Dame, and an Episcopalian." By the time of the Spanish-American War, these colonial and Revolutionary hereditary organizations were established in the Deep South.

Also concerned with remembrance of the past, but not organized on hereditary lines, were the societies founded to save historic houses. First came the Mount Vernon Ladies' Association, which Charlestonian Ann Pamela Cunningham organized in 1853 to rescue George Washington's home. Others of note were the Ladies' Hermitage Association, founded in Nashville in 1889 to preserve Andrew Jackson's mansion, the Confederate Memorial Literary Society in Richmond in 1890 to maintain the Second White House of the Confederacy there, and the White House Association of Alabama in Montgomery in 1900 to enshrine the First White House of the Confederacy.

More recent arrivals on the southern scene are such state- or family-oriented organizations as the Daughters (1891) and Sons (1893) of the Republic of Texas, Maryland's Society of the Ark and Dove (1910), the Louisiana Colonials (1917), the Jamestowne Society (1936), the National Huguenot Society (1951), the Southern Dames of America (1962), the Order of First Families of Mississippi (1967), the Society of the Lees of Virginia (1921), the Washington Family Descendants (1954), and the Davis Family Association (1973).

Standing at the head of these is that apotheosis of the FFV, the Order of First Families of Virginia (1912).

Each of these organizations has its place in the social scheme of things for certain southerners. The gentlemen's hereditary societies seem to be important status indicators in the more mobile societies of the New South, in newer industrial cities such as Birmingham, rather than in Old South cities such as Montgomery, where primacy goes to the local Society of Pioneers of Montgomery (1955), the membership of which is limited to 100 gentlemen with ancestors living there before 1855. Historian Francis Butler Simkins once admitted that "in the aristocratic aspiration of Southerners are elements of snobbery," but he added that "ancestor hunting is an important activity" because a "consciousness of illustrious forebears gives satisfactions not unlike those of religion to old people without material assets."

JOHN HAWKINS NAPIER III
Montgomery, Alabama

Cleveland Amory, *Who Killed Society?* (1960); Jerome Francis Beattie, ed., *The Hereditary Register of the United States of America* (1978); Bethany Bultman, *Town and Country* (November 1977); Sophy Burnham, *The Landed Gentry* (1978); Robert Davenport, ed., *The Hereditary Society Blue Book* (1992); Wallace Evan Davies, *Patriotism on Parade: The Story of Veterans' and Hereditary Organizations in America, 1783–1900* (1955); Lucy Kavaler, *The Private World of High Society* (1960); Marie Bankhead Owen, *The Blue Book, Montgomery, Alabama 1909–1910* (1909).

Pickup Truck

The pickup truck in the South has a variety of uses, most of which do not involve hauling cargo. In fact, the pickup is next to worthless for anything but light hauling on paved roads. Being front-end heavy, it bogs down on wet grass, spins out in its own shadow, and can even flip on a straight, dry stretch of roadway. The cab offers little storage space, and anything carried in the bed is open to theft.

Beginning in the second decade of the 20th century, the pickup (essentially a car with the back seat and trunk removed and replaced with a wooden or metal platform) proliferated on farms. Since the 1950s, despite its limited hauling potential, the pickup's popularity has steadily grown. Often constituting a second family vehicle, the pickup has also become a status symbol for many. In a historical and literary context, a "good old boy" without a pickup is like a cowboy without a horse. "Work" (or "rat" or "bad") trucks, battered and rimmed with rust from long-standing farm or construction work, carry lock boxes full of tools and materials of their owners' trades.

In a modern vein, the rising number of fancy pickups, the "showboats," in suburban driveways represents a curious phenomenon in America's love affair with motorized vehicles. New models, unburdened with dents and scratches, offer the means of escape for the suburban family. Various attachments (from simple bed covers to fancy camper tops) allow the entire family to go "camping" on the weekends. Whether for work or for pleasure, the pickup truck represents ties to the bygone rural aspects of American life. And, because of its rural ties, the pickup is associated with the South.

More particularly, the pickup is associated with the male southerner. Usually, the second vehicle in a family, the pickup most often is the man's to drive and to care for, and full-size pickups are by far the best-selling American-made motor vehicles. Sales increased from 1 million in the early 1990s to 2.3 million in 2003. Men drive pickups to work, whether that work occurs in a factory, medical center, or courtroom. For the younger man not tied to a family, the pickup is his chariot, in which he cruises around looking for women. Apparently, the higher riding the pickup (jacked up with large frame-extending shock absorbers and buoyant on oversized mud tires), the more likely the southern boy will land a date with a cheerleader. Of course, the ever-present gun rack (with rifle or shotgun prominently displayed, or, in more urban settings, simply an umbrella) reflects ties to the rural mystique of southern culture.

Ford Motor Company introduced the first mass-produced pickup, the half-ton Model T Runabout with Pickup Body, in 1925, selling 30,000 of that first production. Chevy and Dodge followed suit, producing their own models in the late 1920s. The Depression hit sales hard, and pickups were generally unavailable to consumers during the Second World War, with production facilities geared to wartime needs. The Dodge Power Wagon was a four-wheel drive vehicle created specifically for the military during the war, and a version of it became a popular model in rural America after the war.

Underscoring both its lack of utility and its importance as a status symbol, the pickup has changed drastically in the last half century. In 1950 Ford introduced a handsome pickup with styling of its own, the F-100. Ford still uses the F-series designation on trucks, but the company turned pickup sales around with the slogan "Where men are men, trucks are Ford V8s." Ford dominated pickup sales for several decades until Chevy countered with its "built tough" trucks with cowboy names. The Scottsdale, Silverado, Bonanza, and GMC confirmed Chevy's position, as did the Sierra Classic. Styling and male imagery are key appeals; Power Wagon brought Dodge trucks out of the doldrums, and Ram Chargers and the Little Red Express kept them out. For the upscale consumer, the Hummer H2 SUT converts from a five-passenger sports utility vehicle to a two-passenger pickup with a six-foot cargo box.

Trucks imported from Europe never caught on in America. The Volkswagen suffered from having the truck bed preloaded with its own engine and transmission. The British Morris Minor was good, but faded over 25 years ago. There was country-boy resistance to the first small trucks from Japan. Chevy called its Luv, and Ford's was the Courier, avoiding Asian-sounding names. But as American pickups grew larger and more expensive, Toyota, Datsun-Nissan, Mazda, and Isuzu earned respect with their pickups, as they had with their cars. To counter this market invasion,

Ford introduced the smaller Ranger, Dodge a smaller Ram, and Chevy the S-10, all of were are slightly larger than Japanese trucks and have become popular.

From the basic platform wagon on four wheels, the pickup now embraces a multitude of styles and options. In 2000 Ford introduced the F-150 Super-Crew, the first four-door, half-ton pickup, and it redefined the idea of the family sedan. Dodge and Chevy made their own versions within three years. That pickup now represents a third of all American pickup truck sales. Deluxe pickups (with more chrome trim than found on 1950s automobiles) include passenger seats in the rear of an extended cab, long wheel bases, dual rear wheels, four-wheel drive, magnesium wheels, long-range fuel tanks, and lights similar to those found on 18-wheelers, not to mention quadraphonic stereos and elegant CB radios. Such extraneous options, again, reflect southern values, especially that of individuality. An owner reveals his character with his choice of options.

If the pickup reflects southern culture, its very popularity may tend to whittle away at the "southernness" of its heritage. As with the trucking culture in general, the pickup truck is becoming subsumed in a more general American culture, becoming a common sight in urban areas far removed from the South.

GORDON BAXTER
Car and Driver

Don Bunn and Paul McLaughlin, "The Pickup Truck Chronicles: A History of

the American Pickup Truck," hhtp://www
.pickuptruck.com/html/history/history
.html; Floyd Clymer, *Henry's Wonderful
Model T* (1955); Patricia Busa McConnico,
Texas Monthly (August 2004).

Pilgrimage

In the spring of 1931 the Mississippi
State Federation of Garden Clubs held
its annual meeting in Natchez. For a
combination of reasons, including a
blighting freeze in late spring and the
depressing state of the economy, the
ordinarily ornate gardens of Natchez
were not in peak condition. As an alternative to garden tours, the Garden Club
of Natchez prevailed upon the owners
of the city's antebellum mansions to
open their homes for two daily tours
during the two-day convention. The
response to the mansion tours was so
enthusiastic that Mrs. J. Balfour Miller
organized another tour of Natchez
antebellum homes the next year. She
publicized the week-long pilgrimage
throughout the South and in other
parts of the country where she had
friends or connections with the media.

The response to the first Natchez
Pilgrimage in 1932 exceeded all Miller's
expectations, and, following her slide
presentation explaining the pilgrimage to the National Convention of
Garden Clubs in 1933, the movement
spread quickly throughout the South.
In many southern towns these annual
pilgrimages now provide a significant
boost to the community's economy.
Most southern pilgrimages are accompanied by Confederate pageants or
balls commemorating life in the Old
South, and southern belles who show

the visitors through the mansions are
dressed in Old South styles, which include long, swaying hoopskirts, layers
of petticoats, and bonnets. In recent
years some southern communities have
deemphasized the Confederate connection and have restyled such a tour,
calling it a "Parade of Homes." The new
designation allows other homes in the
community that are not antebellum to
be included on the tours.

DAVID SANSING
University of Mississippi

James T. Black, *Southern Living* (March
1983); Les Thomas, *Southern Living* (March
1978).

Place, Sense of

"One place comprehended can make us
understand other places better," wrote
Eudora Welty in "Place in Fiction." The
term "sense of place" as used in the
South implies an organic society. Until
recently, southern whites frequently
used "place" to indicate the status of
blacks. James McBride Dabbs noted in
1957 that southern whites spent much
time "keeping the Negro in his place"
and foolishly considered themselves
"happy because the Negro had a place."
But racial "place" was only one aspect
of a traditional southern attachment
to the region: one had a place in a
local community, among a broad kin
network, and in history.

Attachment to a place gives an abiding identity because places associated
with family, community, and history
have depth. Philosopher Yi-Fu Tuan
points out that a sense of place in any
human society comes from the inter-

section of space and time. Southerners developed an acute sense of place as a result of their dramatic and traumatic history and their rural isolation on the land for generations. As Welty noted, "*feelings* are bound up with place," and the film title *Places in the Heart* captured the emotional quality that places evoke. "Home" is a potent word for many southerners, and the "homeplace" evokes reverence.

The evidence for a deep-seated southern sense of place is extensive. The first inhabitants of the region, Native Americans, saw the lands of the Southeast as sacred ground, with all happenings in their specific places related to the rest of the cosmos. Native Americans named prominent physical landmarks and plants and animals in their local areas; their place names survive as evocative descriptions of the landscape.

From Mark Twain's Mississippi River to William Faulkner's Yoknapatawpha County, southern writers have created memorable literary landscapes of place. The lyrics of blues singers starkly evoke the Mississippi Delta, and country musicians sing a lyrical version of states' rights with titles such as "My Home's in Alabama," "Mississippi, You're on My Mind," "Tennessee Mountain Home," and "Can't Wash the Sands of Texas from My Shoes." Folk artists draw from the long memory of people living in isolated rural areas for generations. They learn from older generations and convey the texture of life in a particular southern place through painting, carving, sewing, and other crafts.

Sociologists use the term "localism" to describe the sense of place in the South. The analysis of public opinion poll results shows that contemporary southern blacks and whites value their states more than nonsouthern Americans, and they more often emulate local family and neighbors. John Shelton Reed has concluded that "southerners seem more likely than other Americans to think of their region, their states, and their local communities possessively as *theirs*, and as distinct from and preferable to other regions, states, and localities."

Literary critic Patricia Yaeger has recently questioned the traditional grounding of a sense of place in the South. Looking for a "phrenology of place," she does not find it in a special rootedness in the region, but rather in the images that suggest a fragmentation, decay, and melancholy. She finds that southern women writers often portray landscapes that swallow up white women, children, and African Americans. Yaeger concludes that though place was indeed central to southern writers, their landscapes were always haunted by the specter of racial segregation.

Yaeger's perspective is theoretical, but popular opinion continues to see a distinctive regional perspective on place. Contemporary public policymakers have become aware of the threat economic development poses to preservation of the traditional southern sense of place. In the 1974 Commission on the Future of the South, a group of prominent regional leaders suggested to the Southern Growth Policies Board that an important goal of the modern

South should be "to preserve and enhance, in meeting the issues of growth and change, the human sense of place and community that is a vital element of the unique quality of Southern life."

CHARLES REAGAN WILSON
University of Mississippi

William Ferris, *Local Color: A Sense of Place in Folk Art* (1982); Lucinda H. MacKethan, *The Dream of Arcady: Place and Time in Southern Literature* (1980); John Shelton Reed, *The Enduring South: Subcultural Persistence in Mass Society* (1972); Stephen A. Smith, *Myth, Media, and the Southern Mind* (1985); Yi-Fu Tuan, *Space and Place: The Perspective of Experience* (1977); Eudora Welty, *The Eye of the Story: Selected Essays and Reviews* (1978); Patricia Yaeger, *Dirt and Desire: Reconstructing Southern Women's Writing, 1930–1990* (2000).

Wife and child of a sharecropper in cutover bottoms of Mississippi River, 1938 (Russell Lee, photographer, Library of Congress [LC-USF33-011564-M1], Washington, D.C.)

Poor Whites

Both outsiders and native southerners helped create and perpetuate myths about the South's poor whites, some of which had a strong basis in fact. Antebellum English and northern travelers described a white South consisting of plantation grandees at the top and wretchedly deprived poor farmers at the bottom. Both groups, although in fact large, were outnumbered by small yeoman farmers. The school of antebellum writers known as southwestern humorists were themselves from the upper classes, but the people they described were shrewd, somewhat bizarre clay eaters who practiced emotional religion and engaged in violent eye gougings. The notion of the two-tiered society later served well the needs of abolitionists, who blamed slavery for southern poverty; the comic stereotype of the southwestern humorists, although accurate in many respects, furnished the basis for one of the most enduring myths within American popular culture.

In the late 19th century new layers were added. A region struggling to maintain the values of its agrarian past while at the same time striving for material progress found the poor white useful. New South polemicists noted the breakup of the plantation and the rise of small farms, and they applauded the advent of small-farmer independence and democracy; actually, tens of thousands of whites were descending into tenancy. New South promoters also celebrated the textile mill, which in reality replaced one kind of deprivation with another. When other regions criticized the South for its racial violence or its inclination to elect demagogic politicians, southern apologists absolved themselves and generally blamed poor whites, who unfortunately were often prone to vote for racist demagogues.

In Appalachia a strange and peculiar people challenged America's Gilded Age notions of progress and homogeneity, and missionaries both secular and religious tried to convert the hillbilly primitives from their moonshine, religion, feuds, and culture. Later generations of Americans characterized them as backward hillbillies who were inclined toward incest, fundamentalist religion, laziness, and irresponsibility.

Those who sympathized with poor whites created their own set of myths. In James Agee's classic book, *Let Us Now Praise Famous Men*, the author eulogized poor whites caught in a cosmic dead end. In the novels of Erskine Caldwell the myth of "poor white trash" found its most popular expression. An idealistic generation in the 1960s and 1970s glorified Appalachian poor whites as the finest surviving example of primitive American innocence (a poor but self-contained life lived close to the land in relative isolation, with clean water and air and wonderfully imaginative folk crafts, lore, and music). Each of these descriptions of poor whites contained factual information upon which broad and sometimes unfair or inaccurate generalizations could be built.

Many Americans blame the South's problems on the Lester Jeeters (of *Tobacco Road*), degenerates and racists, shiftless wanderers, wife-beaters, drunks, and ne'er-do-wells. They believe that such people also furnish the Ernest Angleys, Jerry Falwells, and Marjoe Gortners of American religion. According to the conflicting images of American popular culture, the southern poor white can be the shrewdly innocent Jed Clampett of *The Beverly Hillbillies* or a Pentecostal haunted by incestuous lust, the sodomite of James Dickey's *Deliverance*, or the tough poor-boy-made-good Paul "Bear" Bryant, who wrestled bears in Fordyce, Ark., because he could make more money by fighting the beasts than by chopping cotton. Poor white music furnished many additional themes— the religious, fatalistic poor white or the "second-hand satin ladies" and "honky-tonk angels." So far as myth is concerned, the poor white has been a man or woman for all seasons.

J. WAYNE FLYNT
Auburn University

Charles C. Bolton, *Poor Whites of the Antebellum South: Tenants and Laborers in Central North Carolina and Northeast Mississippi* (1994); Sylvia J. Cook, *From Tobacco Road to Route 66: The Southern Poor White in Fiction* (1976); Glenn Feldman, *The Disfranchisement Myth: Poor Whites and Suffrage Restriction in Alabama* (2004); J. Wayne Flynt, *Dixie's Forgotten People: The South's Poor Whites* (1979), *Poor but Proud: Alabama's Poor Whites* (1989); Shields McIlwaine, *The Southern Poor-White: From Lubberland to Tobacco Road* (1939); Henry D. Shapiro, *Appalachia on Our Mind: The Southern Mountains and Mountaineers in the American Consciousness, 1870–1920* (1978); Merrill M. Skaggs, *The Folk of Southern Fiction* (1972).

Reb, Johnny

The Confederate soldier's image in regional culture is his cumulative representation in southern novels, poetry, art, and statuary, as well as in photography and historiography. Because the manner of this representation suggests popular beliefs about the Civil War and the Confederate experience, Johnny Reb's image is an important factor in southern history and the myths surrounding it.

This image has been eulogistic, reflecting southerners' sentimental attachment to the Confederate soldier. During the war years, patriotic speeches, editorials, and sermons idealized Johnny Reb as the defender of morality and American liberty. Poetry by William Gilmore Simms, Paul Hayne, Henry Timrod, and others added romantic elements such as knightly valor to the image. The trials of war and defeat dimmed this early idealism, but developments after Appomattox contributed new elements of eulogy to the soldier's reputation. The elaborate rituals of Confederate Memorial Day, begun in 1866 to venerate the war dead, continued to sanctify the common soldier. Starting in the 1880s, veterans' reminiscences extended the warm glow of nostalgia to the war, and in these writings, as well as in the grandiloquent oratory of veterans' reunions, Johnny Reb was exalted for his bravery, endurance, and devotion to duty. Furthermore, southerners' historical writings, begun soon after the war to chronicle — and justify — the Confederate struggle, depicted the fight as a valiant but doomed effort

against overwhelming northern resources. This historiography of the Lost Cause ennobled Johnny Reb, particularly when it recounted his victories under Robert E. Lee against numerically superior enemies. "Overpowered by numbers" became a popular means of explaining defeat while maintaining the Confederate soldier's battlefield prowess.

Pictorial representation was an important element of the image. Two notable contributors were William L. Sheppard and Allen C. Redwood, talented illustrators whose drawings of Confederates appeared abundantly after the war in *Scribner's, Century*, and other northern periodicals. Their work for *Century* magazine's *Battles and Leaders of the Civil War* (1887) was widely circulated. Memorial statuary provided further visual imagery. Monuments to the Confederate dead were erected on courthouse squares throughout the South, especially from 1880 to 1910, and featured sculpted likenesses of Johnny Reb that endowed him with perpetual youth. Effusive monument inscriptions underscored his constancy and courage.

One of the surest signs of sectional reconciliation after the 1880s was the increasing similarity of Johnny Reb's image to Billy Yank's, as eulogists hailed both soldiers for their American idealism and pluck. In the 20th century, though, the viewpoints of some southerners tended to undercut Johnny Reb's nationalism and shaped his image as the opponent of progress in modern America. In the 1920s and 1930s the Fugitive poets of Vanderbilt — notably

Portrait of a Confederate soldier (Civil War Photograph Collection, Library of Congress [LC-B8184-10692], Washington, D.C.)

Allen Tate and Donald Davidson — used the Confederate fighting man as a symbol of their protest against contemporary culture, with its cities, cars, and consumer goods that threatened the traditional southern lifestyle. A generation later, segregationists expropriated the Confederate battle flag as their symbol of adherence to "traditional" southern ways. Still more recently Confederate iconography has been attacked for representing whites-only symbolism of southern culture. To an extent, each of these developments influenced Johnny Reb's image by characterizing him as a diehard defender of outdated values.

The Confederate soldier's image has

consequently aged, as his relevance to modern southerners has waned.

STEPHEN DAVIS
Atlanta, Georgia

Stephen Davis, "Johnny Reb in Perspective: The Confederate Soldier's Image in the Southern Arts" (Ph.D. dissertation, Emory University, 1979); Susan S. Durant, "The Gently Furled Banner: The Development of the Myth of the Lost Cause, 1865–1900" (Ph.D. dissertation, University of North Carolina at Chapel Hill, 1972); Rollin G. Osterweis, *The Myth of the Lost Cause, 1865–1900* (1973); Charles Reagan Wilson, *Baptized in Blood: The Religion of the Lost Cause, 1865–1920* (1980).

Rednecks

In the 1930s the term "rednecks" meant poor, benighted white southerners, and now it often includes most of Dixie's lower- and working-class whites. The word is often used carelessly, even recklessly; indeed, "redneck" is about the only slur on a group of people that is still acceptable in polite society, so critics attack with a vengeance.

The nasty redneck is undereducated and speaks in colloquial, almost unintelligible tongues. Outlandish names abound: men are called Bubba, Ace, Leroy, and T. J., and women answer to Loretta, Mavis, Sue Ellen, and Flo, while the Johnnies, Billies, and Jodies might be either male or female. The redneck is too physical and violent and overemphasizes athletics. He may even scratch when he itches, wherever he or it may be. He wolfs down coarse, greasy food like cornbread and fried chicken and overcooks his vegetables with his beloved pork. He drinks too much and talks long and loud. He does not ski and has never seen a psychiatrist. His presence depresses the local real estate market. He sometimes smells bad, especially after manual labor. He swings back and forth between liberal and conservative and is thus politically unreliable (and incorrect). His women (not ladies) chew gum and wear plastic hair curlers in public, and his children are just as unsavory, and all rednecks share the delusion that they are just as good as anyone else. Above all, they are incorrigible racists.

This critique is wildly distorted, putting style above substance, but it is often swallowed whole by educated people. However, it does have some limited validity. The redneck is plain and direct. He certainly will fight, especially when pushed, and he makes a fine soldier. The redneck is often a racist, but no more than most, including many of his detractors. He is just more candid. Over the centuries, despite friction and even mayhem, rednecks have blended and bonded with blacks more than most other Americans.

Rednecks were the average white folk in the South from the colonial beginning. They surged westward, cultivating cheap land in the blazing sun. A reddened and wrinkled back of the neck marked these agrarians who owned their own land and sometimes a few slaves. They read and wrote functionally, bore arms, voted and held office, worshipped their own God, and generally enjoyed their rights as Americans in a fluid, middle-class white society.

During the Civil War, rednecks were

the backbone of the Rebel armies that almost shattered the Union. They lost the war, retained their pride, and returned to the land. Over the years, hard times drove many into sharecropping and more into booming industries and sprawling cities. Today most southerners no longer farm, but the term "redneck" persists as a put-down and also as a broader designation of blue-collar southern whites. The latter remain a sturdy, enduring folk, still willing to fight and die for a nation that shows them scant respect.

F. N. BONEY
University of Georgia

F. N. Boney, *Georgia Review* (Fall 1971), *Rebel Georgia* (1997), *Southerners All* (1991); John Shelton Reed, *Southern Folk, Plain and Fancy: Native White Social Types* (1986).

Sambo

Sambo was a stereotyped character created by whites to denigrate blacks. The stereotype attacked black men by making them the objects of laughter. The Sambo character was probably the most tenacious stereotype of black people in both southern and American culture until the late 20th century.

The name "Sambo" is Hispanic in origin, deriving from a 16th-century word, *zambo*, which meant a bowlegged person resembling a monkey. By the 19th century the name had come to refer to a person of mixed ancestry, and the word had derogatory connotations. Descended from court jesters of medieval Europe, the Sambo figure was found in the British colonies of North America from the early 1600s. By the

end of the 19th century, according to Joseph Boskin, Sambo's "humorous innocence, reflected in a never-failing grin, was projected everywhere, his natural buffoonery celebrated in every conceivable way."

The Sambo image included such specific types as the Uncle Tom, Coon, Mulatto, Mammy, and Buck. It appeared in oral lore through jokes and stories. It was in newspapers, magazines, travel brochures, diaries and journals, novels (dime novels and belles lettres alike), short stories, and children's bedtime stories. Joel Chandler Harris's Uncle Remus stories reinforced the stereotype. Graphic expressions of Sambo were, if anything, even more prevalent. Prominent illustrators made Sambo drawings to accompany the text of novels. The figure showed up in sheet music cartoons, calendars, postcards, postage stamps, stereoscopic slides, playing cards, and comic strips; it appeared on billboards and posters and was often featured in popular Currier and Ives prints found in late 19th-century middle-class American homes. Businessmen used Sambo to sell household goods such as soaps, polishes, coffee, jellies, and colas. A national restaurant chain picked Sambo for its name and after World War II used the image for its logo. Sambo appeared in performance routines at minstrel shows, circuses, and theatrical shows, and on radio shows, nickelodeon reels, and television programs. Stepin' Fetchit made Sambo the perpetual chauffeur in the movies. Sambo was concretely embodied in material culture in items such as salt and pepper shakers, place mats, shoehorns, pillows, children's banks, dolls, and whiskey pourers. The ceramic Sambo was found on tables inside homes, and an iron version appeared as a jockey on front lawns.

Scholars even used the Sambo image in textbooks and classrooms as an accurate image of the black personality. Historians in the mid-20th century explored the Sambo stereotype more critically, focusing on its relationship to the slave period. Stanley Elkins's *Slavery: A Problem in American Institutional and Intellectual Life* (1959) concluded that slavery was a total institution, like a concentration camp, which created a childish, dependent black personality, but John Blassingame's *The Slave Community: Plantation Life in the Antebellum South* (1972) better reflects current consensus, insisting that Sambo was an assumed identity—one of several slave personality types—taken on and used to manipulate whites for survival. Through Sambo's protective foil, blacks were "laughing to keep from crying."

The Sambo stereotype has been severely attacked since the 1950s. James Baldwin declared Sambo dead in *Notes of a Native Son* (1955). Civil rights protests and the threat of violence behind demands for black power made the Sambo image unbelievable. By the 1970s the nation's electronic and print media projected new cultural images of blacks that challenged the older stereotype. The end of Sambo represented the death of a white attempt to define black personality and culture.

CHARLES REAGAN WILSON
University of Mississippi

Joseph Boskin, *Sambo: The Rise and Demise of an American Jester* (1986); Kenneth Goings, *Mammy and Uncle Mose: Black Collectibles and American Stereotyping* (1994); Daniel J. Leab, *From Sambo to Superspade: The Black Experience in Motion Pictures* (1975).

"See Rock City"

The imperative "See Rock City" became an icon of roadside advertising beginning in the late 1930s. Hand-painted "See Rock City" signs, along with folksy and extravagant claims about Rock City Gardens, a small tourist park near Chattanooga, Tenn., graced some 900 structures, mostly barns, along rural roads and highways in 19 states. Many of the barn signs survive and have been repainted in recent years, but they are less visible to tourists who now use the interstate highway system.

The "See Rock City" ad campaign transcended the tourist attraction it was designed to support. A Chattanooga developer and promotional whiz, Garnet Carter, opened Rock City Gardens in 1932 on Lookout Mountain. The park features walkways through unusual and impressive limestone formations, plus a clifftop viewing area where visitors are said to be able to see parts of seven states. Carter collaborated with Fred Maxwell, of the Southern Advertising Company of Chattanooga, on an idea to paint signs on barns and other structures with good exposure to motorists. The technique had been used before. Beginning in 1897, the Bloch Brothers Tobacco Company paid farmers for the right to paint Mail Pouch chewing tobacco ads on barn sides, and eventually

"See Rock City" barn, Gravel Switch, Ky. (WMTH Corporation, Bowling Green, Ky.)

thousands of them dotted the landscape from New York to Kentucky.

Clark Byers, a painter for the Southern Advertising Company, was the man most responsible for executing the "See Rock City" campaign. Between 1937 and 1968 Byers painted Rock City ads in big, white, blocky letters set against a black background on the plank sides and tin tops of barns. He and his helpers also painted ads on other structures with good roadside visibility: silos, country stores, garages, even post offices. To persuade farmers to turn their barns into billboards, Byers offered free paint jobs, nailed down loose tin, and handed out Rock City thermometers. Later, after imitators got into barn signs, many farmers received rent, usually $3 a year to start. Byers searched for suitable structures along the main routes of the day such as U.S. 41, the old Michigan-

to-Miami Dixie Highway. He made up ad slogans on the spot, fitting words to barn space using a yardstick, chalk, and some string. The ads touted Rock City Gardens as a wondrous place no tourist should miss. Among his slogans:

"When you see Rock City, you see the best."

"Bring your camera to Rock City, photographer's paradise."

"See beautiful Rock City, world's 8th wonder."

The barn signs, while quaint today, were part of a trend some derided. Historian Thomas D. Clark, in his 1961 book *The Emerging South*, observed that "the Southern landscape has been sacrificed in many places to this mad campaign to snatch the tourist dollar. Scarcely a roadside post, tree, fence, or barn has escaped the signmaker." Ads beckoned tourists to Civil War battlefields, Ruby Falls, Silver Springs,

Dogpatch, various caverns, and other attractions. The Highway Beautification Act of 1965, championed by Lady Bird Johnson, changed the landscape by restricting the placement of outdoor ads, particularly billboards, along U.S. highways and interstates. Signs along these routes had to meet new zoning, spacing, lighting, and size requirements. Many Rock City barn signs had to be blacked out, but some were allowed as special "landmark" signs. Other Rock City barns persist along sleepy back roads.

Whether icon or eyesore, the Rock City barn has earned affection. Rock City Gardens annually sells tens of thousands of birdhouses modeled after the old barns. "We beautified the highways with these signs," Clark Byers said in a 1996 interview. He even painted "See Rock City" on the roof of his own house. Byers, who lived near Rising Fawn in northwest Georgia, died in February 2004 at age 89.

WESLEY LOY
Anchorage, Alaska

The Associated Press, "Clark Byers, Painter of 'See Rock City'" (21 February 2004); Thomas D. Clark, *The Emerging South* (1961); Wesley Loy, "Rock City's Roadside Genius," *Reckon* magazine (winter 1996).

Selma March

Throughout the first nine weeks of 1965 Martin Luther King Jr. and the Southern Christian Leadership Conference (SCLC) helped local civil rights activists in and around Selma, Ala., organize demonstrations to protest discriminatory voter registration practices that had long blocked black citizens from casting ballots. In late February, following the fatal shooting of one protester, Jimmie Lee Jackson, by an Alabama state trooper, civil rights workers proposed a march from Selma to the Alabama state capitol in Montgomery, 54 miles away.

On Sunday, 7 March, some 600 civil rights marchers headed east out of Selma on U.S. 80. State and local lawmen blocked the route and attacked the peaceful column with tear gas and billy clubs. News photographers and television cameras filmed the violent scene as the club-swinging lawmen chased the terrified demonstrators back into Selma. National outrage ensued when the film footage and dramatic photographs were featured on television stations and newspaper front pages all across America.

King announced a second march attempt, and civil rights sympathizers from around the nation flocked to Selma to join the effort. Lawmen peacefully turned back that second procession, and SCLC went into federal court seeking government protection for a third, full-scale march to Montgomery. Court hearings delayed a resolution of the question for a week, but on Sunday, 21 March, with King and other dignitaries in the lead, 3,200 marchers set out for Montgomery as federal troops and officials furnished careful protection.

Walking some 12 miles a day and camping in fields at night, the marchers' ranks swelled to more than 25,000 when their procession entered Montgomery on Thursday, 25 March. The march climaxed with a mass rally at

Participants, some carrying American flags, in the civil rights march from Selma to Montgomery, Ala., 1965
(Peter Pettus, photographer, Library of Congress, [LC-USZ62-133090], Washington, D.C.)

the Alabama state capitol, culminating a three-week set of events that represented the emotional and political peak of the 1960s civil rights era. In the weeks following the march President Lyndon B. Johnson and bipartisan congressional supporters speeded passage of the Voting Rights Act of 1965, a comprehensive statute that remedied most of the injustices the Selma demonstrations had been designed to highlight.

DAVID J. GARROW
Emory University

Amelia Platts Boynton, *Bridge across Jordan: The Story of the Struggle for Civil Rights in Selma, Alabama* (1979); David J. Garrow, *Protest at Selma: Martin Luther King, Jr., and the Voting Rights Act of 1965*
(1978); J. Mills Thornton III, *Dividing Lines: Municipal Politics and the Struggle for Civil Rights in Montgomery, Birmingham, and Selma* (2002); Wally G. Vaughn and Mattie Campbell Davis, *The Selma Campaign, 1963–1965: The Decisive Battle of the Civil Rights Movement* (2005).

Stone Mountain

Stone Mountain is a natural landmark, a historic site, and a recreational area located 16 miles east of Atlanta, Ga. The world's largest mass of exposed granite, the 825-foot dome rises 1,683 feet above sea level on a path once used by Creek Indians. The mountain is 285 to 294 million years old. Carved on its side is the world's largest piece of sculpture, a memorial to the Confederacy composed of the mounted figures of Robert E. Lee, Jefferson Davis, and Thomas J. "Stonewall" Jackson. The United Daughters of the Confederacy (UDC) leased the land in 1915 and commissioned Gutzon Borglum, an Idaho sculptor who would later carve Mount Rushmore, to design and execute a carving of Lee. Borglum conceived a grandiose plan—a gigantic model of Confederate leaders riding around the mountain. Little progress on the memorial occurred before the end of World War I. In November of 1915 Colonel William Simmons, a former Methodist circuit rider and salesman, used Stone Mountain as the location for a fiery ritual resurrecting the Ku Klux Klan. The locale thereafter was periodically the scene of Klan rallies.

In May of 1916, with a huge Confederate flag, 30 by 50 feet, draped across the face of the cliff, southerners dedicated the unfinished Stone Mountain as a memorial to the Lost Cause. Still in need of financing, though, Borglum traveled throughout the South promoting the project. In 1923 Atlanta businessmen took charge of the project, forming the Stone Mountain Monumental Association. Borglum began work on the carving in June of 1923 and unveiled the partially carved head of Lee on 19 January 1924, the general's birthday, before an estimated crowd of 20,000. After a rift developed between Borglum and the UDC, Augustus Lukeman began work on the project but was unable to finish the carving before the UDC lease ran out in 1928.

For more than 30 years the memorial remained unfinished, with the property owned by the Venable family.

In 1958 the state of Georgia decided to develop Stone Mountain as a tourist attraction. The state commissioned Walter Hancock to complete the memorial and to develop the park around it. George Weiblin was hired to direct completion of the carving, with Roy Faulkner as chief carver. Using a thermo-jet torch and working at times in the face of 70-mile-per-hour winds on the side of the mountain, the crew finished the project between 1964 and 1970, when the memorial was dedicated.

The carving, which is 90 feet high by 190 feet wide, in a frame 360 feet square, depicts Lee, Davis, and Jackson—the Lost Cause trinity—on horseback; Lee's horse, Traveller, stretches across 145 feet. Stone Mountain became a major tourist attraction at the heart of a 3,200-acre park. More than 5 million people a year come to the park, which is geared, according to promoters, to family recreation. It has two hotels and several golf courses, a riverboat and water theme park, a Civil War museum, a plantation, and an antique car show. Visitors can ride a passenger railroad and a skyride, hit a baseball in batting cages, play putt-putt golf, watch a film at the Tall Tales of the South 4D Theater, or stroll through the gardens, which contain flowers such as the now-rare Confederate daisy (*Viguiera porteri*).

In the summer, tourists now come to see "Laser Spectacular," which is said to be the world's largest outdoor laser show. Laser beams flash onto the carving such images as spiders, spaceships, and animals, accompanied by fireworks. In the finale, the Confederate heroes gallop off the mountain, courtesy of the laser lighting, all to the familiar tune of "Dixie." The park is adjacent to the town of Stone Mountain, whose population is more than 70 percent African American.

CHARLES REAGAN WILSON
University of Mississippi

Robert J. Casey and Mary Borglum, *Give the Man Room: The Story of Gutzon Borglum* (1952); David B. Freeman, *Carved in Stone: The History of Stone Mountain* (1997); Grace Elizabeth Hale, *Making Whiteness: The Culture of Segregation in the South, 1890–1940* (1998); Gerald W. Johnson, *The Undefeated* (1927); Harkness Kenimer, *The History of Stone Mountain: The 8th Wonder of the World* (1993); Bari R. Love, *Southern Living* (June 1984).

Trucking

Trucking culture materialized as the business of trucking transformed the way that goods were transported in the United States. Trucking as a business began in the 1920s, after World War I had proven the commercial value of the new motorized wagons. Veterans of the European conflict and farm boys familiar with steam machinery entered the new business. Lured by travel to exotic places such as New York City, enticed by the money to be made, and drawn by the opportunity to escape the routine of farm life, many midwestern and southern young men became truckers. Although trucking as a business appeared first in the Midwest and East, trucking as a culture quickly took on southern elements, particularly in language, food, music, and religion.

The essential loneliness of trucking—one man, one truck; driving many hours at night—kept the culture out of view of mainstream America until the popularization of the Citizens Band (CB) radio during the oil embargo of 1974. National news personalities featured the cowboy loneliness and the rich, unique language of the truckers on strike. Whether from Montana or Maine, Oregon or Ohio, truckers talked to one another with southern inflections and syntax. Accurately described as a cross between an Arkansas and a west Texas dialect, this "good old boy" style captured the faddish fancy of the American public. Millions of nontruckers purchased a CB and joined in the southern subculture that promoted evasion of highway patrol radar, as well as simple camaraderie during long and lonely drives along the nation's highways. Truckers and automobile drivers alike became "good buddies," many of them attempting to copy the southern dialects. Thus, in the 1970s the American public discovered a distinctly southern subculture that had been in the making since the 1920s.

Trucking culture reflected not only southern language but also other attributes that tended to rest on a peculiarly southern base. Southern fried food appeared in truck stops across the nation. Country songs climbed the popular music charts, and Hollywood movies drew in customers as the mass media exploited the emerging southern image of trucking. New lyrics (set to old cowboy and blues melodies) extolled the virtues of truckers, while detailing the evils and stupidity of governmental regulations and the state and local police who enforced them. Movies featured good old boys breaking speed laws and easily evading potbellied, cigar-chomping southern sheriffs.

Meanwhile, another aspect of southern culture, religion, influenced trucking. Evangelical ministers, such as the Reverend Jimmy Snow, son of country and western singer Hank Snow, used the CB to reach lonely drivers on the road. Other ministers established mobile churches and traveled from truck stop to truck stop looking for converts.

The very media that exposed the southern influence in the trucking culture have also led to a dilution of that regional influence. Certainly truckers continue to wear traditional western clothes (jeans, cowboy boots and hats, and western shirts) and many continue to operate their rigs just the other side of the law (much as southern moonshiners have done). Yet organization of trucking associations, more efficient trucks, and massive truck stops catering to the entire traveling public have muted the rebellious and unique spirit of trucking and, by extension, the southern culture supporting it.

JAMES H. THOMAS
Wichita State University

Frederick E. Danker, *Journal of Country Music* (January 1978); Lawrence J. Ouellet, *Pedal to the Metal: The Work Life of Truckers* (1994); Jane and Michael Stern, *Trucker: Portrait of the Last American Cowboy* (1975); James H. Thomas, *The Long Haul: Truckers, Truck Stops, and Trucking* (1979); D. Daryl Wyckoff, *Truck Drivers in America* (1979).

Uncle Tom's Cabin

Harriet Beecher Stowe set out to portray slavery as an institution, rather than the South as either a geographical or a cultural entity, in *Uncle Tom's Cabin*. The novel was begun in response to the Fugitive Slave Law of 1850. It was addressed to a national, not a regional, audience to whom Stowe made the argument that it was the educated, well-to-do, Christian gentlemen of the country, the hypocritical reader, in fact, who, through an indifference or cynicism that inhibited active opposition to slavery, was actually responsible for its continuation in American society and for the moral offense inherent in it.

The picture of the South that emerges in the novel is developed through three households, presented as types: the Shelbys of Kentucky, middle-class, kind, but subject to the pressures of a capitalist economy of which slavery is a part; the St. Clares of New Orleans, aristocratic, loving, but ineffectual as guardians of their enslaved servants because of a debilitating skepticism that undermines both Christian belief and political action; and the Legree plantation, low-class, brutal, an example of how bad slavery can become. The Shelbys get very little space after the opening of the novel, in which Mr. Shelby's sale of Uncle Tom and of Eliza's son, Harry, to pay some large debts initiates the two main plots. Shelby's predicament, being forced to sell against his own wishes and the strong feelings of his wife, shows the southern slaveholder caught in the grip of economic circumstance that is in no way unique to the South; in-

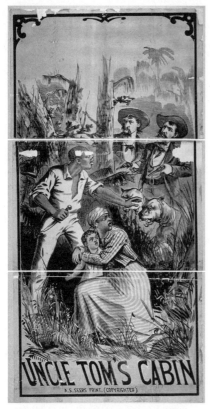

Woodcut print from a theatrical interpretation of Uncle Tom's Cabin, 1882 (Created by A. S. Seers Print., Library of Congress, [LC-USZC2-1461], Washington, D.C.)

deed, Stowe frequently likens American exploitation of slaves to European exploitation of industrial workers. The Legree sequences at the end of the novel, although sensational and meant to provoke outrage at the institution of slavery, are not presented as typical either of it or of southern life. Not only is Legree himself a Yankee, but he also lives virtually beyond the pale of southern society, a day's journey up the Red River in a place described as wild and debauched. The suggestion is that Legree's wild domain is to the west of civilization, a horrible outpost on the Arkansas frontier.

Stowe sets her principle drama of southern life in the St. Clare household. Here, for example, is the kitchen, a place of playful leisure for the servants, where the mystery of the cook's ways fosters an easy tolerance and affectionate community not to be found in the scrubbed and strictly managed kitchen of New England. The emotional atmosphere of the kitchen echoes the unruly abundance of southern land. Similarly, the decor of the bedroom belonging to little Eva, the novel's proselytizing child heroine, enhances her deathbed sermon on the gospel of love by suggesting a place of almost heavenly perfection: "The windows were hung with curtains of rose-colored and white muslin. The floor was spread with matting which had been ordered in Paris . . . having round it a border of rosebuds and leaves. . . . Over the head of the bed was an alabaster bracket, on which a beautiful sculptured angel stood, with drooping wings, holding out a crown of myrtle-leaves." A mosquito net made of "light curtains of rose-colored gauze" hung over the bed. The gardens around this summer "villa" by Lake Pontchartrain are also idealized by the fond, and perhaps envious, gardener/novelist from New England. (One must not forget that Stowe invested in a southern plantation after the Civil War and made her winter home in Mandarin, Fla., for many years. Her letters to northern relatives dwell on the floral paradise at her back door.)

The South as portrayed in the St.

Clare household, and often contrasted to the northern society of the hero's cousin from Vermont, is a humane culture—disorderly, tender-hearted, distressed about slavery. To be sure, the family does include two destructive types: St. Clare's arrogant and despotic brother, who raises a son like himself, and Marie St. Clare, the self-indulgent hypochondriac whose pampered childhood led to unmitigated hard-heartedness. Despite the presence of these hateful characters in its midst, the St. Clare family is a loving home for slaves and owners alike. Its greatest weakness, and by implication that of the southern culture it represents, is its vulnerability to abrupt transformations—from the rosy bower of the angelic child Eva and the kind paternalism of her father to the debauchery of the Legree establishment, a transformation brought about by the sudden accidental death of St. Clare. In sum, Stowe sees the South of 1850 as beautiful, elegant, and weak, unable to sustain its gentlemanly ideal, which she values and praises, against the unscrupulous practices of the slave trade or the barbarity represented by the maddened and desperate Legree. In *Uncle Tom's Cabin*, the South is a garden of innocence and delight threatened by the snake of human cruelty; it is a lovely dream hovering on the verge of a nightmare.

ALICE C. CROZIER
Rutgers University

Alice C. Crozier, *The Novels of Harriet Beecher Stowe* (1969); Thomas F. Gossett, *Uncle Tom's Cabin and American Culture* (1985); Moira D. Reynolds, *Uncle Tom's Cabin and Mid-Nineteenth Century United States: Pen and Conscience* (1985); Eric J. Sundquist, ed., *New Essays on Uncle Tom's Cabin* (1986).

Yerby, Frank

(1916–1991) WRITER.

Frank Garvin Yerby, one of the most popular novelists to set tales in the Old South, was born in Augusta, Ga., on 5 September 1916. He completed degrees at Paine College (A.B., 1937) and Fisk University (M.A., 1938) and did graduate work at the University of Chicago. Yerby, who was black, published several excellent short stories from 1944 to 1946 dealing with racial themes. Although he won a major award for his short fiction, Yerby's fame and fortune rest on his widely popular romance novels, the first of which was published in 1946 and sold over 2 million copies. Like many of his novels to follow, *The Foxes of Harrow* was set in the antebellum South and tapped public interest in the Old South that had been fostered by the phenomenal success of Margaret Mitchell's *Gone with the Wind* (1936).

Yerby's southern romances, including such titles as *A Woman Called Fancy* (1951), *Benton's Row* (1954), and *Griffin's Way* (1962), dominated popular fiction set in the Old South for nearly two decades. His works were meticulously researched and included a wealth of elaborate and surprisingly accurate period detail in such areas as costuming, architecture, southern society, and even slave life. One critic termed *Fair Oaks* (1957) a "primer in black history."

The novels were primarily romantic glimpses of the planter elite and were aimed at a predominantly white, female audience. This led many critics to condemn his work as potboiler fiction, and others have often charged that he ignored racial issues. Yerby once countered the latter charge by saying that the novelist does not have the right to "inflict on the public his private ideas on politics, religion or race." In most respects the charges were unfair, for Yerby managed to influence the ideas and values of far more readers through historical romance than could possibly have been reached by other forms of fiction. This point is demonstrated by Yerby's own career, for he did attempt a few novels with racial themes. These included *The Old Gods Laugh* (1964) and *The Dahomian* (1971), both of which sold poorly in comparison to his plantation novels.

Yet Frank Yerby's impact was not in the area of popular and accurate history. His importance rests on his fostering of public interest in the antebellum South and his fiction's impact on extending the romantic ideal of the South as one great plantation. Besides Mitchell's *Gone with the Wind* and Kyle Onstott's *Mandingo* (1957), the novels of Frank Yerby did more to standardize the plantation fiction genre than did the works of any other author. Apart from his careful attention to historic detail, Yerby's major contribution to the fictional portrayal of the Old South was an entrance into the bedrooms of the planters. His incredibly successful fiction helped to solidify the popular impression of the antebellum South as a land of "moonlight and magnolias," of aristocratic lifestyles, of beautiful belles,

and of dashing and handsome young gentlemen.

CHRISTOPHER D. GEIST
Bowling Green State University

James L. Hill, in *Perspectives of Black Popular Culture*, ed., Harry B. Shaw (1990); Jack Temple Kirby, *Media-Made Dixie: The South in the American Imagination* (1978); Jack B. Moore, *Journal of Popular Culture* (Spring 1975); Frank Yerby, *Harper's* (October 1959).

Yoknapatawpha County

"William Faulkner, Sole Owner & Proprietor," states the legend on the map, and no claim to title is any more indisputable, though we may wander within the realm identified there by the proprietor for as long as we are inclined—and without fear of trespass, for, through one of its paradoxes, Yoknapatawpha County belongs to us as well. It is the setting of all of Faulkner's major fiction, and is itself a fictional creation.

Faulkner named his county after the Yoknapatawpha River, which is the old name of the Yocona River, an actual river that runs south of Oxford, Mississippi. Initially Faulkner used the current name, and it appears as such in *Flags in the Dust*, the first novel in which he referred to it. The *Flags* manuscript was not published until 1973, however, having first been rejected, then edited and published as *Sartoris* (1929). Thus *Sartoris* was the first published novel in the Yoknapatawpha series, followed in the same year by *The Sound and the Fury*, though Faulkner did not employ the old name "Yoknapatawpha" until *As I Lay Dying* (1930), by which time he had a good start on the chronicle that would ultimately include over a dozen novels and numerous short stories spanning the period from the late 1700s to the middle of the 20th century.

Faulkner's county is situated in northern Mississippi and consists of 2,400 square miles. It was settled by whites, some with slaves, in the early 1800s, following the Chickasaw Indian cessions. The county seat, Jefferson, originally a Chickasaw Agency trading post dating from the late 1700s, was founded in 1833 with the hasty erection of a log courthouse and named not after the former U.S. president but for a mail rider serving the area. Faulkner's comic rendering of this founding appears in *Requiem for a Nun* (1951), a dramatic work not otherwise known for levity. The families of some of the founders and early settlers figure throughout the entire Yoknapatawpha saga; others die out or disappear. Their genealogies are often elaborate and sometimes confusing. The trajectories of fortune in their lives—and the lives of characters who appear in Yoknapatawpha later—are as varied as those in our own, though more often than not in Faulkner's world the tracings follow a wildly erratic course. They are families at all levels of southern society, with names such as Beauchamp, Bundren, Compson, Sartoris, Snopes, and Varner; individuals named Luster, Dilsey, or Ikkemotubbe, the chief of the Chickasaws, whose river gave Faulkner a name for his world.

The two Chickasaw Indian words of which the word Yoknapatawpha is constituted mean "split land," though Faulkner said that the two words together mean "water flowing slow through the flatland." And because on one side of the paradox he is the sole owner, "Yoknapatawpha" means what he said.

In addition to the matter of proprietorship, there are other paradoxes, some specific to all literary creations: Jefferson, the geographic center and county seat of Yoknapatawpha County, Miss., is and is not Oxford, the center and county seat of Lafayette County, Miss., where Faulkner grew up and lived most of his life. He drew on the town and region as a primary source, as many writers draw on a particular place, and there are countless identifiable parallels, geographic and cultural; but in the accounting required with art, Yoknapatawpha exists unto itself.

Similarly, Yoknapatawpha exists both in and out of time. It is timeless in the way that the landscape and human motion arrested on Keats's Grecian urn are timeless, and in the way that Keats's ode itself—which Faulkner refers to in "The Bear," summoning the same idea—exists out of time.

Where temporality does obtain, in the recorded history of Yoknapatawpha, there are discrepancies. Its sole historian had lapses of memory and changes of heart in the 37 or so years of its progress as a chronicle and admitted as much in his short preface to *The Mansion*. Yet—the paradox—there is no chronicle any more accurate or rich in information, if one regards the history of Yoknapatawpha as emblematic of the history of the South.

A fanciful way of accounting for all

of these paradoxes would be to observe that Yoknapatawpha County is bordered both to the north and the south by water and is thus mystical (that is, if one accepts Walker Percy's notion that water is the mystical element). Further, these parallel borders—the Tallahatchie River to the north and the Yoknapatawpha River to the south—run east and west, and Faulkner's map (the one drawn for *Absalom, Absalom!* [1936]) shows that in those directions he left Yoknapatawpha County seemingly borderless. His Yoknapatawpha extends irresistibly toward horizons we associate with beginnings and endings, the old and the new, the origins of the world's religions, the myths and archetypes that inform much of the drama of Yoknapatawpha. For the county does indeed exist in a borderless confluence of the mystical and the mythical, the synchronic, the spiritual, and the dramatic.

JAMES SEAY
*University of North Carolina
at Chapel Hill*

Don H. Doyle, *Faulkner's County: The Historical Roots of Yoknapatawpha* (2001); Elizabeth M. Kerr, *Yoknapatawpha: Faulkner's "Little Postage Stamp of Native Soil"* (1969).

INDEX OF CONTRIBUTORS

INDEX

Page numbers in boldface refer to articles.

American Mercury, 28
American Review, 194
American Revolution, 44
Ames, Jessie Daniel, 92
Amory, Cleveland, 49
Ancestor worship, 58
Anderson, Sherwood, 108
Angley, Ernest, 256
Anglo-Saxons, 130, **194–95**
Animals, 9
Ansley Park (Atlanta, Ga.), 42
Apostle, The (film), 174
Appalachia, 38, 256; folk culture of, 163, 197; myth of, **196–98**; images of, 197; otherness of, 197; feuds in, 226, 227
Appalachian Mountains, 9
Architecture, 30, 120, 122
Arkansas, 15, 23, 25
Arlington (estate), 120
Arlington National Cemetery, 45
Armstrong, A. Joseph, 184
Armstrong, Louis, 76, 111
Armstrong Browning Library (Baylor University), 184
Arnold, Matthew, 184, 185
Arrington, Marvin, 214
Art, 30, 137; feminine, 22; folk, 41, 254; modern, 111; painting, 111; museums, 122
Ash, Mary Kay, 22
Ashe, Arthur, 6, 48, 85
Asheville, N.C., 28
Ashmore, Harry, 106
As I Lay Dying (Faulkner), 28, 270
Athelstan Club (Mobile, Ala.), 50
Atlanta, Ga., 3, 11, 13, 50, 81, 83, 107, 143, **211–15**, 245, 264; Olympics in, 144, 214; racial issues in, 211; population of, 211, 213, 214; blacks in, 212, 213; mayors of, 213; suburbs of, 213; business in, 214
Atlanta Braves, 213
Atlanta Constitution, 133, 230
Atlanta International Cotton Exposition, 22
Atlanta Journal Sunday Magazine, 245

Attitudes, racial, **146–51**; origins of, 147; of blacks, 149; changes in, 149
Augusta, Ga., 47
Aunt, maiden, **93–96**
Aunt Phillis's Cabin (Eastman), 87
Aurelius, Marcus, 177, 178
Austin, Tex., 50, 144
Automobiles, **11–17**; accidents caused by, 13; dealerships for, 13; impact on society of, 13; salesmen of, 13; images in popular music of, 13, 14; assembly plants for, 13, 16; and deaths, 13, 16; used for recreation, 14, 15; effect on poor of, 15; impact on urban landscape of, 16; maintenance of, 16; numbers of, 16; production of, 16
Ayers, H. Brandt, 242

Babbitt (Lewis), 108
Babylon, South's (New Orleans, La.), **198–99**
Baker, Elizabeth, 111
Bakker, Tammy Faye, 22
Baldwin, James, 261
Baltimore, Md., 50, 244
Baltimore Manufactures' Record, 133
Banjos, 9
Bankhead, Tallulah, 4
Banner, Lois, 21
Baptism, 3, 40
Barbecue, 85
Bardaglio, Peter, 165
Barker-Benfield, G. J., 166
Barnum, P. T., 21
Barren Ground (Glasgow), 177
Bars, 80, 81
Barth, John, 145
Barthelme, Donald, 145
Barthelme, Frederick, 145
Basketry, 10
Basso, Hamilton, 103
Battey, Robert, 166
Battle Abbey (Richmond, Va.), 120
Battle galleries, 120
Battles and Leaders of the Civil War, 257

Chesterton, G. K., 194

Chevrolets, 13

Chicago, Ill., 11, 45

Children, 23, 54, 56, 58, 94; custody of, 64; and labor laws, 64; names of, 65; and relationships with fathers, 65, 66; and roles for boys and girls, 66; and relationships with mothers, 115; black, 149; redneck, 259

Children of Bondage: The Personality of Negro Youth in the Urban South (Davis and Dollard), 37

Children of the Confederacy, 217, 240, 249

Chinese, 6

Chivalry, 97, 166, 207

Choctaw County, Miss., 24

Chosen People, myth of, **208–10**

Christian, Sara, 15

Christmas, **210–11**, 233

Christy, David, 137

Churches, 40, 122; black, 3, 75; Pentecostal Holiness, 22; clocks and bells in, 34; buildings, 40; as communities, 40; neighborhoods around, 40; women in, 40, 115; gays in, 81

Cities, 16, 29; black and white communities within, 37; social classes within, 37; neighborhoods within, 37, 42

Citizens' Council, 60, 154

"City Too Busy to Hate" (Atlanta, Ga.), **211–15**

Civilities and Civil Rights: Greensboro, North Carolina, and the Black Struggle for Freedom (Chafe), 42

Civil Rights Act, 213

Civil rights movement, 4, 5, 29, 41, 82, 83, 107, 128, 144, 200, 205; and black beauty, 21; demonstrators during, 32; opponents of, 59; sites of, 83; workers of, 130, 154, 263; violence during, 263

Civil War, 1, 3, 5, 83; narratives of, 6; legacy of, 30; soldiers of, 43, 44; monuments of, 43–48; reenactments of, 48, **215–16**; remembrance of, 104; as a holy war, 161

Civil War, The (documentary film), 5

Clansman, The (Dixon), 153, 206

Clarion-Ledger, 25

Clark, Thomas D., 11, 13, 15, 261

Classes, 20, 28, 86; social, 1, 3, 31, 32, 61; upper, 1, 28; elite, 5; middle, 6, 12, 22; upper-middle, 7; relationships between, 11; and automobiles, 14; working, 14, 42; and beauty, 17, 22; aristocratic, 28; identities of, 31; literacy of, 32; in cities, 37; within mill towns, 37; and fathers, 67; manners of, 96, 100; hospitality among, 235

Clay, Virginia, 87

Clay County, Ky., 226

Climate, 1, 15

Clinton, Bill, 7, 82, 85, 130, 214

Clinton, Catherine, 165

Clocks and time, **34–36**; and church bells, 34; dependency on, 34; during slavery, 34; in factories, 34; and natural time, 34; northern conceptions of, 34; mechanical, 35; punctuality, 35; and business schedules, 35; telling time, 35; obedience to, 36; acceptability of, 36; and Daylight Saving Time, 36; "sound of," 36

CNN, 214

Coal camps, 33

Coca-Cola, 83, 85, 143, 213

Cocke, John Hartwell, 182

Collectibles, black, **199–200**

College of Charleston (S.C.), 106

Colonel Sanders, 3

Colonial period, 1, 146; time perceptions during, 34; families of, 56

Color Purple, The (film), 130

Color Purple, The (Walker), 222

Columbia, S.C., 45, 47, 249

Columbia University (New York, N.Y.), 27, 223

Columbus, Ga., 249

Columns, 6

Commager, Henry Steele, 136

Commission on the Future of the South, 254

Ford, Richard, 144
Ford Motor Company, 251
Fordyce, Ark., 256
Forge, The (Stribling), 28
Fort Worth, Tex., 120
Foster, Stephen, 136, 137
Fourteenth Amendment, 154
Fourth of July, 217
Fox, William Price, 231
Foxes of Harrow, The (Yerby), 269
Foxfire (book series), 197
Foxworthy, Jeff, 174
France, William Henry Getty ("Big Bill"), 15
Franklin, Benjamin, 35
Franklin, Shirley, 213, 214
Fraternal groups, **70–77**; black, 70, **74–77**; colonial, 70; immigrant, 70; female, 76
Fraternities, 7, 19, 22, 87, 248
Freedmen's Bureau, 152
Freedom Riders, 154
Freemen, 36, 75
French Quarter, the (New Orleans, La.), 6
Frizzel, Lefty, 14
Frontier, 30; manners on, 97; settlers of, 130
Frost, John, 196
Fugitive, 108, 109, 111, 193
Fugitive Poetry, 108
Fundamentalists, 29, 128, 158, 159

Gaffney, S.C., 205
Gaines, Ernest, 79
Gaines, Frances Pendleton, 127, 137
Gambling, 58, 84
Gangs, railroad, 9
Garden of Eden, 3; South as, 1, 27, **77–79**, 127, 160, 235; plantation as, 78
Gardner, "Brother" Dave, **230**
Gardner, Burleigh and Mary, 37
Garrison, William Lloyd, 27
Gaston, Paul, 127
Gastonia, N.C., 27, 29
Gays, **79–83**, 168; crimes against, 79; friendly environments for, 80; hos-

tility toward, 80; roles of, 80; rural, 80; discrimination against, 81; weddings, 82
Gee's Bend, Ala., 225
Gender studies, 17, 31
Genovese, Eugene D., 65, 142, 166
Gentlemen. *See* Ladies and gentlemen
Georgia, 3, 11, 28, 79, 82, 84, 156, 160; lynching in, 90
Georgiana, Ala., 239
Georgia Power Company, 245
Gettysburg, Pa.: battle of, 214
Gilinan, Caroline, 235
Gillespie, Michele, 165
Gillin, John, 37
Glasgow, Ellen, 95, 110, 177
Glass Menagerie, The (Williams), 174
Glidden tour, 11
Globalization, 144
Godbeer, Richard, 164
God's Little Acre (Caldwell), 28
Goffman, Erving, 30
Golden Bough, The (Frazer), 108
Goldfield, David R., 54
Gone with the Wind (film), 48, 153, 245
Gone with the Wind (Mitchell), 3, 83, 88, 95, 112, 127, 141, 142, 164, 206, 234, 243, 245, 269
Good Old Boy: A Delta Boyhood (Morris), 231
Good old boys, 7, 14, 98, 130, 204, **230–31**, 251
Good Old Boys, The (Hemphill), 231
Good old girls, **230–31**
Goodwin, George, 214
Gortner, Marjoe, 256
Gospel Girls, 82
Gospel music, 24, 111
Gothic South, 1, 144, 163
Government: federal, 13; state, 13; county, 40
Graceland (Memphis, Tenn.), 83, **231–33**
Grady, Henry W., 133
Granger, Gordon, 239
Graves, John, 183
Graveyards: decoration of, 10

IBM, 143
Icons, 3, **83–85**
Identity, 1, 31; white male, 31; regional, 43
I'll Take My Stand, 3, 96, 102, 128, 193, 243
Imagery: cultural, 1; religious, 3; rural, 3
Images, 83; of South as blighted, 27, 28, 29
Imitation of Life (Hurst), 243
Immigrants, 7, 194, 195; Hispanic, 7; from British Isles, 207
Incidents in the Life of a Slave Girl (Jacobs), 57, 87
Indianola, Miss., 20, 37
Industrialists, northern, 35
Industrialization, 20, 133, 134
Industrial Revolution, 109
Industry, 29, 134
Inman Park (Atlanta, Ga.), 42
In My House Are Many Mansions: Family and Community in Edgefield, South Carolina (Burton), 38
In Ole Virginia (Page), 246
Institute for Research in Social Science (Chapel Hill, N.C.), 37
Instruments, musical, 9
Integration, 33, 36, 41, 59, 154, 212; sexual, 59
Intellectuals, 30
Internet, 4
Intruder in the Dust (Faulkner), 39
Invisible Man (Ellison), 100, 236
Iowa, 25
Israel, 209
Italians, 6
Ives, James Merritt, 137, 260

Jackson, Andrew, 97, 114, 115, 121, 194
Jackson, Jimmie Lee, 263
Jackson, John Brinckerhoff, 16
Jackson, Maynard, 213, 214
Jackson, Miss., 25, 47, 50, 249
Jackson, Rachel, 198
Jackson, Tenn., 230
Jackson, Thomas "Stonewall," 43, 83, 233, 265
Jacksonville, Fla., 50

Jacobs, Harriet, 57, 87
Jails, 32
James, Henry, 137
James, Simon, 208
Jameson, Fredric, 143
Jamestown, Va., 1, 180, 210
Jaworski, Gary D., 51
Jaycees, 25
Jazz, 7, 111
Jefferson, Thomas, 3, 78, 127, 184, 235; concept of beauty of, 17, 18; stoicism of, 175, 176
Jesus Saves (Steinke), 144
Jews, 6, 208; holidays of, 233, 234
Jim Crow, 5, 6, 144, 199, **237–39**; etiquette during, 51–55
Jobs, 65
Johnson, Charles S., 52
Johnson, Claudia Alta Taylor ("Lady Bird"), 263
Johnson, Eastman, 137
Johnson, Gerald W., 28, 29
Johnson, James Weldon, 108
Johnson, Junior, 14, 231
Johnson, Lyndon, 85, 264
Johnson, Samuel, 218
Johnston, Albert Sidney, 73
Johnston, Joseph E., 217, 249
Jones, Anne Goodwyn, 19, 31, 169
Jones, George, 145
Jordan, Winthrop D., 17, 114
Juneteenth, 234, **239–40**
Junior League, 88

Kappa Alpha Order, 85
Kenan, Randall, 145
Kennedy, John F., 154
Kennedy, John Pendleton, 78, 87, 131, 141, 207
Kentucky, 43, 84; feuds of, 226, 227
Kentucky Derby, 236
Kimball, Solon T., 38
King, Coretta Scott, 81, 85
King, Florence, 86, 98, 169, 231
King, Larry L., 204

Mothers, 54, 96, **112–19**; slave, 56, 57, 117; Victorian, 58; lesbian, 79; images of, 112, 116; stereotypes of, 112; idolatry of, 114; white, 114; daily routine of, 115; as educator of children, 115; African American, 115, 117; struggles of, 116; working, 118

Motor, 11, 12

Mountain Dew, 174

Mount Vernon, 120, 250

Movies, 131; drive-in, 15

Moynihan, Daniel Patrick, 59, 117

Moynihan Report, 60

Ms., 118

Mulattoes, 32, 75

Mumford, Lewis, 156

Murder, 28, 91, 225; of civil rights workers, 29; rates of, 68; of gays, 79; interracial, 89

Murfree, Mary, 156

Museums, **119–25**; types of, 119, 120, 121, 122; African American, 121; ethic, 121; Native American, 121; religious, 121; art, 122; for children, 122; folkways, 122; university, 122; company, 124; halls of fame, 124; state, 124; science, 125

Music, 6, 7, 13, 137, 145; old-time sacred, 3; blues, 6, 7, 14; jazz, 7; bluegrass, 9; influence of blacks on, 9; country, 13; automobile images in, 14; rock and roll, 14; black, 41; modern, 111; images of mothers in, 116; halls of fame, 124; rap, 130; myth in, 131; sex in, 169; in Appalachia, 197

Muzzey, David Saville, 138

My Old Kentucky Home (Johnson), 137

Myth and Modern Man (Patai), 126

Mythic South, **125–32**

Mythmaking, northern, **135–39**

Myth of the Negro Past, The (Herskovits), 100

Myths: garden, 77–79, 126; Benighted South, 27–30, 128; historical, 126–28; Lost Cause, 127, 240–42; New South, 127, 132–135; contemporary, 128–29;

plantation, 131, 139–43; religious, 158–62; Appalachian, 196–98; of black confederates, 201–2; Cavalier, 206–7; Evangeline, 221–22

NAACP, 212

NASCAR, 15, 174

Nashville, Tenn., 13, 108, 249

Natchez, Miss., 105, 253

Nation, 27

National Association of Automobile Manufactures, 11

National Association of Stock Car Auto Racing (NASCAR), 15

National Convention of Garden Clubs, 253

Nationalism, 1, **247–48**

National Pro-Family Coalition, 60

Native Americans, 56, 254; tobacco use of, 180

The Negro Family: A Case for National Action (Moynihan), 59

Neighborhoods, 37; black, 10; Appalachian, 38; around churches, 40; of kin, 40; rural, 40; ethnic, 42; historical preservation of, 42, 120; urban, 42

Nelson, Willie, 205

Neshoba County, Miss., 92

New American Family, The (Falwell), 60

New Deal, 134, 153, 157, 224

New England, 6

New Orleans, La., 6, 84, 105, 111, 201, 249; free blacks in, 10, 75; traffic in, 13; debutante balls in, 50; Mardi Gras, 50, 211; parades in, 81; magazines in, 108; preservation of, 120; writers in, 156; prostitution in, 168, 198; slave market, 198; race in, 199

New Republic, 9, 27

New South, myth of, 127, **132–35**, 161, 188, 255

Newman, Frances, 245

Newman, John Henry, 185

Newnan, Ga., 91

Newspapers, 12, 92, 188; as mythmakers, 127; New South, 134

Pickup trucks, **251–53**; names of, 251
Piedmont, 9; Carolina, 37
Pike, Albert, 73
Pilgrimages, 6, 105, **253**
Pippa Passes, Ky., 184
A Place in Time: Middlesex County, Virginia, 1650–1750 (Rutman), 38
Places in the Heart (film), 254
Plains, Ga., 204
Plantation County (Rubin), 37
Plantations, 1, 9, 30, 41, 78, 83, 87, 246; women on, 20; institution of, 30; myth of, 131, **139–43**
Planters, 35, 36, 176
Plants, 9
Plants, automobile assembly, 12
Plessy v. Ferguson, 238
Poe, Edgar Allan, 163
Poetics (Aristotle), 162
Poetry, 32, 108
Poetry: A Magazine of Verse, 108
Poinsett, Joel, 210
Politicians, 1, 7; African American, 59
Politics, 5, 7, 85; changes in, 5, 6; blue-state, 7; red-state, 7; black, 106; mythic, 131, 152, 174
Pollution, 16
Poor, 15; whites, 244, **255–57**
Popular culture, 3
Population, 11, 214, 219, 220
Populism, 128, 133, 152, 153
Porches, front, 6, 189
Port Gibson, Miss., 92
Postcards, 4
Postmodernism, **143–46**; in film and literature, 144
Post offices, 35
Pottery, 10
Pound, Ezra, 108
Poverty, 11, 16, 28, 29, 58, 66, 224, 255; African American, 59; of the Depression, 134; Appalachian, 197
Powdermaker, Hortense, 37, 52, 76
Power Shift: The Rise of the Southern

Rim and Its Challenge to the Eastern Establishment (Sale), 129
Pratt, Minnie Bruce, 103
Preachers, 3, 24; black, 31
Preservation, regional, 44
Presidents, U.S., 7, 85
Presley, Elvis, 83, 85, 129, 231, 232
Prewitt, Cheryl, 24
Price, Reynolds, 103
Pride, 3
Pritchard, Ala., 174
Profiles in Courage (Kennedy), 154
Progressive Farmer, 236
Prohibition, 58
Promiseland: A Century of Life in a Negro Community (Bethel), 38
Prostitution, 168, 198
Prout, Mary, 76
PTL Club, 22
Public Opinion (Lippmann), 126, 170
Puckett, Newbell Niles, 100
Pulitzer Prize, 28
Purity and Danger (Douglas), 52

Quilting, 10
Quitman, John A., 249

Race, 5; and etiquette, 5, 41, 51–53; and beauty, 17, 19, 20, 21; injustice based on, 27; identities based on, 31, 147; mulatto, 32; within towns, 37; and sex, 82, 149, 165; riots over, 89; in New South, 133; attitudes toward, 146–51
Racing, road, 11; dirt-track, 14; stock-car, 14, 129
Racism, 27, 28, 52, 206, 259
Railroads, 3; gangs on, 9
Raleigh, N.C., 45, 50
Raleigh, Sir Walter, 180
Ransom, John Crowe, 78, 146, 178, 193, 194
Rap, 130
Rape, 28, 90, 165
Real estate, 29

Smart Set, 108

Smith, Al, 27

Smith, Don, 25

Smith, Henry Nash, 126

Smith, John, 76

Smith, Lee, 145

Smith, Lillian, 31, 58, 80, 116, 164

Smith, Louise, 15

Smith, Samuel, 248

Smith College (Atlanta, Ga.), 245

Smithsonian Institution, 203, 239

Smokey and the Bandit (film), 14

Snopes family (Faulkner), 29

Social Directory of Montgomery, Alabama, 49

Societies, patriotic, **248–50**; listed, 249

Sommerville, Diane Miller, 165

Songs, 3, 136, 137

Sons and Daughters of the American Revolution, 70

Sons of Confederate Veterans, 58, 217, 240, 249

Sororities, 7, 26, 87, 248

Sound and the Fury, The (Faulkner), 28, 48, 86, 179, 243, 270

Sounder (film), 130

South Carolina, 1, 25, 76

Southern Baptist Convention, 209

Southern Belle Primer, A, 102

Southern Christian Leadership Conference, 263

A Southern Community in Crisis: Harrison County, Texas, 1850–1880 (Campbell), 38

Southern Culture on the Skids, 145

Southern Fried (Price), 231

Southern Growth Policies Board, 243, 254

Southern Heritage, The (Dabbs), 96

Southern Journal, 243

Southern Ladies and Gentlemen (King), 86, 98, 169, 231

Southern Lady, The (Scott), 98

Southern Literary Renaissance, 38, 45, 67, 108, 110, 111, 141, 164

Southern Living, 7, 42, 236

Southern Planter, The, 35

Southern Regions (Davidson), 157

Southern Society, 138

Southern States Rights Dixiecrats, 229

Spanish moss, 84, 210

Speaking for Ourselves: Women of the South (Green), 169

Spears, Britney, 169

Spears, Monroe, 108

Speech, 9, 31

Sports, 15, 81

Spottswood, Alexander, 173

Squares, town, 5

Stanley Steamer, 11

Stapleton, Ruth Carter, 204

Stars Fell on Alabama (Carmer), 19, 86

Steel magnolia, 31

Stein, Gertrude, 108

Steinke, Darcey, 144

Stephens, Alexander Hamilton, 137

Stepto, Robert B., 41

Stereotypes, 7, 31, 130, **170–75**, 217; black, 149, 200, 243, 260, 261; sexual, 168, 169; endurance of, 171, 172, 173; Sunny South, 173; Sunbelt, 173–74; in advertising, 174; in films and television, 174; in literature, 174; Cavalier, 206; white, 218

Stewart, Kathleen, 33

Stewart, Martha, 236

Stewart, Rick, 111

Stock cars, 14, 85

Stoicism, **175–79**; of Thomas Jefferson, 175, 176; antebellum popularity of, 176; and civil religion, 177; and Victorianism, 177

Stone, Phil, 108

Stone Mountain, Ga., 43, 83, 120, **264–66**

Store, The (Stribling), 28

Story, Sidney, 199

Storyville (New Orleans, La.), 168, 198

Stowe, Harriet Beecher, 27, 136, 137, 141, 267

Streetcar Named Desire, A (Williams), 95

Stribling, T. S., 28, 29

Stryker, Roy, 224

Stuart, J. E. B., 43, 86

Uncle Remus (Harris), 260
Uncle Tom's Cabin (Stowe), 127, 136, 141, 235, **267–69**
Underground Railroad, 240
Unfinished Cathedral, The (Stribling), 28
United Confederate Veterans, 217, 228
United Daughters of the Confederacy, 47, 58, 105, 217, 240, 249, 265
Universal/Southern Charm pageant, 23
University of Alabama (Tuscaloosa), 19, 84
University of Chicago, 51
University of Florida (Gainesville), 167
University of Mississippi (Oxford), 84, 243
University of North Carolina (Chapel Hill), 37, 128, 156
University of Southern Mississippi (Hattiesburg), 25
Upcountry, South Carolina, 158
Upshaw, Berrien Kinnard, 245
Urbanization, 242
Urban renewal, 41
Urban sprawl, 214
USA Today, 214

Vacations, 12
Values, 38; family, 1, 7, 60; of church communities, 40
Vance, Rupert B., 128, 156, 157
Vanderbilt Cup, 11
Vanderbilt University (Nashville, Tenn.), 108, 109
Vanity Fair, 108
Vermont, 25
Vicksburg, Miss., 39, 161
Victorianism, 98, **184–88**
Vidalia onions, 84
Vigilantes, 90, 91
Villard, Oswald Garrison, 27
Violence, 14, 27, 33, 54, 55, 86, 101, 128, 226, 235, 255; in Faulkner, 28; and honor, 30, 86, 99; proclivity toward, 68; during Reconstruction, 153; against black males, 165; sexual, 165; redneck, 259

Virginia, 1, 78, 99, 173, 180
Virginian, The (Wister), 142
Visiting, **188–91**
Voting Rights Act, 264
Voting, 203, 264

Wade, John Donald, 193
Wake Forest College (Wake Forest, N.C.), 205
Walden, A. T., 212
Walker, Alice, 41, 222
Walker, Madame C. J., 22
Walker, Maggie Lena, 76
Wallace, George, 84
Waller, Altina, 226
Walton, Sam, 3
Ward, Sela, 85
Warren, Robert Penn, 16, 45, 58, 67, 78, 106, 110, 146, 193
Washington, Booker T., 130
Washington, D.C., 50, 224
Washington, George, 120, 184, 233, 249
Waste Land, The (Eliot), 108, 109
Waters, Ethel, 243
Watson, Jay, 30
Watters, Pat, 248
Weiblin, George, 265
Wells-Barnett, Ida, 92
Welter, Barbara, 166
Welty, Eudora, 5, 22, 39, 78, 103, 110, 130, 223, 253, 254
West Indies, 9
West Palm Beach, Fla., 120
West Virginia, 33, 43
Where Do We Go from Here? Chaos or Community? (King), 41
Whisnant, David E., 197
White flight, 213
Whites, 1; Civil War narratives of, 6; concepts of beauty of, 20, 21; poor, 28, 32, **255–56**; in Faulkner, 28, 29; rural, 35; communities of, 37; control over blacks by, 54, 147; children of, 54; notions of family of, 57; mothers, 114; insecurities of, 147; and urge for domination, 147